M000199780

AN

EXPOSITION AND DEFENCE

OF

ALL THE POINTS OF FAITH

DISCUSSED AND DEFINED

BY THE SACRED COUNCIL OF TRENT;

ALONG WITH A REFUTATION OF THE ERRORS

OF

THE PRETENDED REFORMERS,

AND OF THE OBJECTIONS OF FRA PAOLO SARPI.

BY ST. ALPHONSUS M. LIGUORI,

BISHOP OF ST. AGATHA, AND FOUNDER OF THE CONGREGATION OF THE MOST
HOLY REDEEMER.

TRANSLATED FROM THE ITALIAN,

BY A CATHOLIC CLERGYMAN.

DUBLIN:

PUBLISHED BY JAMES DUFFY,
10, WELLINGTON QUAY.
1846.

W. LOWE, PRINTER. 6, LOWER ABBEY-STREET.

ISBN: 978-0-9819901-8-7

This type in this book is the property of
St Athanasius Press and except for brief
excerpts, may not be reproduced in whole
or in part without premission in writing
from the publisher.

Published by:
St Athanasius Press
133 Slazing Rd
Potosi, WI 53820
melwaller@gmail.com
www.stathanasiuspress.com

Specializing in reprinting Catholic Classics

Check out our available Titles at the
end of this book!

CONTENTS.

	Pages
Dedication	xiii.
Advertisement	xv.

FOURTH SESSION.—ON SCRIPTURE AND
TRADITION.

SECTION I.—On the Approbation of the Inspired Books, and Apostolic Tradition . . .	19
SECTION II.—On the Edition and Use of the Sacred Scriptures	26
SECTION III.—Various Observations on the Canonical Books of Scripture, which the Reader will find Useful	32
SECTION IV.—Objections of the Adversaries to the Deuterocanonical Books . . .	34
SECTION V.—Were the Sacred Scriptures Inspired not only as to the Matter, but also as to the Words	38
SECTION VI.—On the Sense of the Sacred Scriptures	41
SECTION VII.—On the different Version of the Scriptures	43
SECTION VIII.—Important Observations on Tradition	46

FIFTH SESSION.

On Original Sin	55

SIXTH SESSION.

On justification, Prœmium	75

SEVENTH SESSION.

Decree Regarding the Sacraments—on the Sacraments in General	125

THIRTEENTH SESSION.

On the Sacrament of the Eucharist . . .	158

FOURTEENTH SESSION.

On the Sacrament of Penance . . .	184

CHAPTER II.—On the difference between Penance and
    Baptism   190
CHAPTER III.—On the Parts of Penance   .   .   191
CHAPTER V.—On Confession   .   .   ·   211
CHAPTER VI.—On the Minister of the Sacrament
    and Absolution   227
CHAPTER VII.—On Jurisdiction, and the Reservation
    of Sins   230
CHAPTER VIII.—On Satisfaction   .   .   231
CHAPTER IX.—On Satisfactory Works   .   234

CONTINUATION OF THE FOURTEENTH SESSION.

On the Sacrament of Extreme Unction   .   242
CHAPTER I.—On the Institution of the Sacrament of
    Extreme Unction   .   .   .   242
CHAPTER II.—On the effect of this Sacrament   .   248
CHAPTER III.—On the Minister of Extreme Uunction,
    and on the time it should be given   .   250

TWENTY-FIRST SESSION.

On Communion under Both Species, and on giving
    Communion to Infants   .   .   259

TWENTY-SECOND SESSION.

On the Sacrifice of the Mass   277

TWENTY-THIRD SESSION.

On the Sacrament of Order   311

TWENTY-FOURTH SESSION.

On the Sacrament of Matrimony   .   .   346
Decree on Purgatory   380
De Invocatione, Veneratione, et Reliquiis Sanctorum,
    et Sacris Imaginibus   .   .   .   397

SIXTEENTH AND LAST TREATISE.

APPENDIX.—On the Obedience due to the Definitions
    of the Council, and consequently of the Roman
    Catholic Church, out of which there is no salva-
    tion.   411

TO HIS

HOLINESS CLEMENT XIV.

Most Holy Father,

The exaltation of your Holiness to the throne of St. Peter has been a source of extraordinary and general joy to the whole Catholic world; but I know not whether any individual has felt greater consolation than I have, in the contemplation of the excellent qualities of your Holiness; of your learning, prudence, detachment from the things of the world, and, above all, of your piety and zeal for our holy religion. These qualities have induced me to seek the honor of laying at the feet of your Holiness the following work, which I have resolved in these the last years of my life (for I have now reached my seventy-third year), to publish, in order to give to all a better knowledge of the dogmas of the Catholic Church, which the sacred Council of Trent, a council deserving of all praise, has defined against the errors of the pretended reformers, who have revived the ancient heresies, and have sought, by sophisms and false doctrines, to destroy the faith of Jesus Christ, and, if possible, to bring with themselves all souls to everlasting perdition.

I hope that in your benignity your Holiness will accept this miserable gift, which I present to you, begging your Holiness to bless the work, the author, and all his companions, that we may be able to co-operate with greater fruit to the salvation of souls by making missions according to the rules of our little congregation, among the people of the rural districts, who are most in need of spiritual helps: and we, your humble children, shall not cease continually to entreat the Lord to preserve your Holiness for a long series of years for the benefit of all the faithful, and the diffusion of the holy faith. In conclusion, I humbly kiss the sacred foot of your Holiness.

> Your most Humble, most obedient, and most devoted Servant and Child,
>
> ALPHONSUS M.,
> Bishop of St. Agatha of the Goths.

ADVERTISEMENT.

In this work all the points of faith discussed and defined by the Council are expounded, the errors of the innovators are refuted, and their objections, along with those of PETER SOAVE, (Fra-Paolo Sarpi,) who has assailed the Council, are answered. The work also contains two treatises, or appendices, one on the manner in which grace operates in the justification of sinners, and the other on the obedience due to the definitions of the Church, which are the rules of the true faith.

OBJECT OF THE WORK.

HAVING considered on the one hand the excellent doctrines which the Council of Trent has taught with

so much accuracy and so much care, against the
errors of the heretics who infested the northern
countries, and seeing on the other, that many
things which were discussed in that ever memorable
Council, though carefully collected by Cardinal
PALLAVICINI into his History of the Council, were
notwithstanding frequently scattered and confused,
in that celebrated work, I several years since undertook the task of bringing them together, that the
reader might have the pleasure of seeing all of them
in the order of the subjects treated, and that thus he
might be able to discover with greater facility the
sophisms of the innovators, and might be still more
firmly convinced of the truth of our holy faith.

I have frequently resumed this work, but more
pressing duties have obliged me to interrupt it.
Being latterly confined to my bed by a severe attack of
rheumatism, which rendered me unable to go about
my diocess as I was formerly accustomed to do, I
have endeavoured to finish the work which I had
commenced, and, with the assistance of the Lord, I
have succeeded in bringing it to a close, after treating
each point at full length, and answering many
objections of the heterodox, which PALLAVICINI
left unnoticed.   Hence I thought it advisable to

treat many scholastic and dogmatic questions appertaining to the doctrines defined by the Council. I hope that my labour will be acceptable to those young students who are desirous of having a fundamental knowledge of the truths of our holy faith, and particularly of the dogmas which have been most violently assailed by heretics.

the decree was passed in 1441. In answer, it was said that the Council of Florence was not terminated in 1439; that it was only the Latin interpretation of Bartholomew Abraham of Candia that terminated in that year; that the Greeks remained only to that period, that is, till the seventh session, and this interpreter registered only the acts which preceded that time. But the Council sat three years longer in Florence, and was thence transferred to Rome: for Eugene the Fourth, seeing that after the departure of the Greeks the illegitimate Council of Basil persisted in holding its sittings, he continued the Council of Florence, in which (as Baronius relates, anno 535,) with the consent of the Fathers, he received the Armenian heretics and Jacobites, and in the instruction on Faith which was given to them, is contained the approbation of the traditions and of the Sacred Scriptures, along with the catalogue of the inspired books. That the Council continued after the year 1439, appears from the two constitutions given by Augustine Patrizio, in his Compendium of the Council of Basil, one published in 1440, annulling the election of the Antipope Felix V., and the other in 1442, ordering the translation of the Council of Basil to Rome. Besides, Pallavicini states that the Acts of the Council of Florence sanctioned by the Pope and Cardinals are preserved in the archives of the Castle of St. Angelo; that an authentic copy of them was brought from Rome to Trent, and from them it appears that the decree regarding the inspired books was made by that Council. Moreover Father Justinian, a priest of the oratory, and afterwards Cardinal and Prefect of the Vatican library, published acts of the Council of Florence from which it is manifest that the Council continued till the year 1445.

4. But in Trent the theologians made a new and rigorous examination regarding the inspired books and traditions, in order to render an account of them to the fathers. The examen was private, and not to be registered in the Acts of the Council. Finally, the decree was made, in which as we there find, because the fathers believed that all the truths

divine writings, three questions were proposed. First, it
was asked whether all the sacred books as well of the New as
of the Old Testament should be approved. Secondly,
whether the books which we have of the Bible, should be
subjected to a new examination for approbation. Thirdly,
whether the sacred Scriptures should be divided into two
classes; that is, into those which were already regarded as
canonical and those which the Church appeared to have
already received as good and useful, but not as canonical;
such as the books of Proverbs and Wisdom.

2. With regard to the first point, all were of opinion that
the Council should approve of all the sacred books. And
with regard to the third, all rejected the above-mentioned
division, which was proposed in the Council by Bertan and
Seripando, and before the Council by Catejan, but strongly
reprobated by Melchior Cano, (De Loc. Theol. l. 2, c. 10,)
as inconvenient and inadmissible. But about the second
question, whether for the approbation of the sacred Books a
new examen should be made, there was greater difficulty.
Many, with Cardinal del Monte, and Cardinal Pacecco
objected to such an examination, saying that it was the
practice of the Church not to call in question definitions
already made. On the other hand, many maintained that
the examination should be made in order to give greater
authority to the truth, for the benefit of pastors and theologians, that thus they might be better able to confute the
errors of the false teachers. For, said they, theologians are
obliged not only to prove the truths of faith, but also to defend them against all adversaries; they added, that after
such an examination the heretics would not be able to say
that their arguments had not been even discussed.

3. The Bishop of Chioggia stated that in approving the
Scriptures and traditions it was not right to rest solely on
the decree which bore the name of the Council of Florence:
because, said he, this decree was not made by the Council,
since its last session was terminated in the year 1439, and

A DOGMATIC WORK

THE PRETENDED REFORMERS,

IN WHICH ARE EXPLAINED ALL THE POINTS OF FAITH DISCUSSED
AND DEFINED IN THE SACRED COUNCIL OF TRENT, &c.

FOURTH SESSION.

ON SCRIPTURE AND TRADITION.

SECTION I.

ON THE APPROBATION OF THE INSPIRED BOOKS AND APOSTOLIC TRADITIONS.

I PRAY my reader to observe that in this work the sessions
of the Council are not placed in the order in which they were
held from the first to the twenty-fifth, because in many of
the sessions there was no particular doctrine defined, and in
others there was no question of dogmas of faith; and, as I
have said in the preface, my object is to treat only of the
points of faith which the Council established against the
heretics. Hence we commence with the fourth session,
because it was in this session that the Fathers began to
examine the dogmatic articles which were attacked by the
innovators.

1. The Church never defines any dogma of faith which is
not founded on the sacred Scripture or tradition. Hence
the first care of the Council was to determine the true
canonical Scriptures, and the true apostolical traditions which
regard either faith or morals. The theologians therefore
were directed by the Council to make an exact examination
regarding the Scriptures and the traditions of the Church,
in order to give an account of them to the Fathers. This
examination was to be private, and not to be registered in
the acts of the Council. In the congregations preceding the
decree which was afterwards framed with regard to the

appertaining to the dogmas of faith are contained in the Sacred Scriptures, and in the traditions which were received from the mouth of Jesus Christ, by the Apostles, or dictated to them by the Holy Ghost, and which afterwards came down to our times, the Council declared that it received and venerated with equal piety and reverence, all the books of the New and Old Testament, and all the traditions which had been dictated by Jesus Christ or by the Holy Ghost, and had been preserved in the Catholic Church by an unbroken succession. "Omnes libros tam veteris quam novi testamenti, cum utriusque unus Deus sit auctor; necnon traditiones, ipsas, tum ad fidem, tum ad mores pertinentes, tanquam vel oretenus a Christo vel a Spiritu Sancto dictatas et continua successione in ecclesia catholica conservatas, pari pietatis affectu ac reverentia suscipit et veneratur."

5. Some objected to say that the Scriptures and traditions were received with the same piety and reverence, because, said they, although both came from God, still the latter have not the same stability as the former, since it appears that some of them have ceased. But the objection was generally rejected, and it was said in answer that both were equally the true word of God, and the foundations of faith, with this sole difference that the former were written, and the latter unwritten; that both are unchangeable truths, with the exception of the positive precepts and rites which are found in the Scripture as well as in tradition, and which are mutable laws. Hence in the decree, the Council declared that it received only the traditions which appertained to faith and morals, and before the formation of the decree, it was agreed that these only should be received without exception, and that the traditions which regarded rites should be received according to present customs. Peter Soave says, that, as many observed, the decree regarding traditions did not impose a strict obligation; because, on the one hand, the Council did not determine what traditions were to be received, and on the other, the anathema was fulminated

only against them who would knowingly and willingly despise the aforesaid traditions, "qui traditiones prædictas sciens et prudens contempserit." Hence he concludes that they who reject with reverence all traditions, do not transgress the decree. But in answer to Soave, Natalis Alexander says (Hist. Eccl. tom. 20, Sect. 16, 17, art. 2,) that his assertion is rash; because the Council declared that the Scriptures and the traditions were to be received with equal piety and reverence, "pari pietatis affectu ac reverentia suscipiendas." Hence as we cannot reject the Scriptures without temerity, neither can we without temerity reject the traditions. I pray the reader to peruse the observations which shall be made on tradition in the 8th section.

6. After the above mentioned declaration, was added (in the decree) the catalogue of all the books which were received as canonical by the Council. Soave has the temerity to assert that the Council approved of books which were apocryphal, or at least uncertain. But in answer to him, I say that they were approved only after a new and diligent examination. Besides, all the books, as has been already said, had been approved by the Council of Florence. Soave objects particularly against the approbation of the book of Baruch, which, he says, although it had never been reckoned among the inspired writings by the other Councils, was approved for no other reason than because lessons from it were read in the Church. But I answer that although the ancient councils had not placed this book on the catalogue of the canonical Scriptures they did not mean to reject it, but intended to include it in the book of Jeremias, to whom Baruch was amanuensis, as we read in the same book of Jeremias (c. 36,) and as is attested by St. Basil, St. Ambrose, Clement of Alexandria, St. John Chrysostom, St. Augustine, and the sovereign pontiffs, Sixtus I., Felix IV., and Pelagius I. (Bellarmin. lib. 1. de verb. Dei c. 8.) Besides, St. Cyprian, (lib. 2, contra Judæos, c. 5.) and St. Cyril, (lib. 10, contra Jul.)

quote it as the book of Jeremias, and other Fathers simply call it divinely inspired Scripture.

A certain author also has said that the Psalms should not be called by the general appellation of the Psalms of David, since, according to many, David was not the author of all the Psalms: but it was for this reason that the Council called them the *Psalter of David.*

7. In the end of the decree, we read: " Si quis autem libros ipsos integros cum omnibus suis partibus prout in ecclesia Catholica legi consueverunt et in veteri vulgata latina editione habentur, pro sacris et canonicis non susceperit, et traditiones prædictas sciens et prudens contempserit: anathema sit."

8. Soave objects, with certain adversaries, that in the first place the Council in the proceeding words " ordained that the traditions should be received without giving any means of ascertaining them," and secondly, that the Council had not commanded the reception, but only prohibited the contempt of the traditions, aud that therefore he who rejected them in respectful language did not contravene the decree of the Council. To the first objection, I answer that in this matter the Council imitated the sixth general Council, which abstained from declaring what were the true traditions. Besides there were just reasons why the Council did not declare in the decree on the Scripture and traditions, what traditions were to be held as as faith: for these were to be examined and declared in the future sessions, according as the occasion required. In answer to the second assertion, that there is no precept obliging us to receive the traditions, I say, that the precept is one thing, and the anathema another. That the council intended to command the faithful to receive the divine traditions, is evident: for in the decree the fathers declared that they received the Scriptures and the traditions with equal piety and reverence, "pari pietatis affectu ac reverentia." But with regard to the anathema, I say that a precept may be transgressed and not received in two

ways, either through weakness, or through contempt. The Council did not wish to pronounce an anathema against all who would violate the precept of receiving the Scriptures and traditions with equal respect, but only against them who, as the heretics do, would knowingly despise the traditions.

9. Soave also said that in receiving the traditions, the Council should also admit the ordination of deaconesses, and the popular elections of ministers, because these were apostolic institutions which lasted for several centuries, and, what is more important, that it should permit the use of the chalice to the laity, as was practised for 1400 years by all except the Latin Church. But I answer that the Council, as we read in the decree, spoke of and received only the traditions which continued till its own time; " quæ quasi per manus traditæ ad nos usque pervenerunt." The two first mentioned traditions had been given up for 800 years before the Council, and the third, regarding the chalice, had ceased for two centuries. With regard to the election of Ministers, we know that in the Council of Laodicea, which was held in the fourth century, it was declared "that the people should not be permitted to elect the persons who were to be promoted to the priesthood." (can. 3.) And long before, St. Paul in the Epistle to Titus, said: " For this cause I have left thee in Crete, that thou shouldst ordain priests in every city as I also appointed thee." (l. 5.) With regard to the use of the chalice, it is not true that it had been universally adopted until two hundred years before the Council: for St. Thomas, who lived three hundred years before the Council of Trent, disapproves of the custom in all the churches in which it then existed. (3 p. q. 18. art. 12.) Besides the Council of Constance, in the thirteenth session, declared that the use of the chalice had been long since abolished. Cardinal Bellarmine demonstrates that it ceased for 800 years, and that it was always held to be arbitrary, and not of precept in the Church. But this point shall be more fully examined in its own place.

C

SECTION II.

ON THE EDITION AND USE OF THE SACRED SCRIPTURES.

10. AFTER the decree regarding the reception of the canonical books and the apostolical traditions, the Council drew up the decree respecting the edition and use of the sacred Scriptures. In this decree the Vulgate edition was declared to be authentic, and was approved as such: " Statuit et declarat ut hæc ipsa vetus et vulgata editio, quæ longo tot seculorum usu in ipsa Ecclesia probata est in publicis lectionibus, disputationibus, prædicationibus et expositionibus pro authentica habeatur; et nemo illam rejicere quovis prætextu audeat vel presumat."

11. Against the approbation of the authenticity of the Vulgate, Soave objects that according to the opinion of Cardinal Cajetan, the infallibility of the Old Testament is derived from the Hebrew, and of the New Testament from the Greek text, but not from the Latin translation, the author of which was not infallible. But I answer that were the reason of Cajetan a valid one (his commentaries on the Scripture have been severely censured) we could not depend even on the present Hebrew or Greek text, but should trust only the originals of the Scripture, which were written by the prophets, evangelists, and Apostles; for all other copies have been liable to error. Hence I say that since God wished that the Scriptures should be an infallible rule of faith for all, he resolved to preserve in the Church, by his supernatural Providence, a version of the sacred writings, in a tongue understood by many, and which should be perpetual and free from every essential error regarding the dogmas of faith. Hence God has appointed on earth a manifest interpreter, that is the Church, or its head, who employing the care and

diligence which the condition of mortals permits, would point out a copy of the scriptures which Christians might unhesitatingly adopt.

12. And because the Vulgate edition in the Latin tongue (which is known universally to all theologians) had already begun to obtain the tacit approbation of the Church by its adoption, for several centuries, even from the time of St. Gregory, and had been received by the first luminaries of the Church— by St. Isidore, Bede, St. Remigius, St. Anselm, St. Bernard, Rabanus, Hugh of St. Victor, Robert the Abbot, and an immense number of other doctors,—the Council, in virtue' of the assistance promised to it by the Holy Ghost, declared that translation to be authentic, and free from all substantial error, leaving the Hebrew text of the Old Testament (which is very uncertain, because the points which have the signification of vowels, are supposed to have been omitted in the original), and the Greek of the new, all the authority which they merit. In the canon " Ut veterum," dist. 6, it is stated that we have the Hebrew version for the exposition of the old, and the Greek for the interpretation of the new law; but we ought to remember that this canon is to be attributed not to St. Augustine, (as Gratian says) although he adopts it (lib. 12, de doctr. Christ. c. 14, 15.) but to St. Jerome. (See Ep. 28. ad Lucillum.) But when St. Jerome laid down this canon, he had not prepared the Latin translation of the Scriptures. In his exposition of the inspired writings he must certainly have availed himself of the two original versions, but, as we find in the Gloss on the above mentioned canon, the holy doctor does not speak in the second prologue to the Bible as he did in his epistle to Lucillus.

13. But, continues Soave, if the Vulgate edition be correct and deserving of approbation, the other editions must be bad, and it is folly to make use of them. I answer that for us it is enough to know that the Vulgate is free from

errors in faith and morals, and that since the others have not been declared authentic, as the Vulgate has, it would be an error to prefer them to it. However the Council has given permission to the learned to explain the obscure passages which occur in the Vulgate, by means of the Hebrew and Greek texts. But after examining all these versions, the sense of many passages may remain obscure and doubtful, and will perhaps remain so till the end of the world.

14. But, says Soave, the Council should at least have declared in the Decree that the Vulgate would be revised and corrected. This objection was made in Trent and also in Rome; in submitting the decree, before its publication, to the consideration of the Holy See, the deputies of the Pope stated in their letter to Rome that against the approbation of the Vulgate it was objected that it contained many errors. The legates answered that these errors did not regard the substance of the dogmas, or of morals: and therefore they commended the resolution of the Pope to publish the Vulgate edition in a more correct form. But they were of opinion that it was not right to point out the inaccuracies which were but of little moment, lest the heteredox should thence take occasion to raise cavils which might confound the simple faithful. They also asserted that the Vulgate was never suspected of substantial errors, since it was conformable even to the most correct Hebrew and Greek versions; and that although in many passages there were obscurity and barbarisms, no one was forbidden to expound them in clearer and better language. Besides we ought to consider that the authors of the sacred volumes who wrote under the influence of divine inspiration, do not always relate facts and expressions along with all their individual circumstances and words: and this makes them sometimes appear to disagree in their narratives: but as the Holy Fathers and commentators remark, they substantially agree with each other. But even after the correction of the Vulgate, the church does not condemn those

who reject the more *pious* opinion, and hold that even in the Vulgate there are some accidental errors of little importance: for example that one tree, or animal is taken for another. This is held by Melchior Canus, (lib. 2. de loc. Theol. c. 13 concl. 1.) by Sixtus Senensis (Bibl. 5. c. ult) and others. But Elizalda remarks (de forma in quæst. rel. n. 44,) that it is not lawful to depart at pleasure, on every occasion from the Vulgate, but only in those passages on which our theologians are discordant, and regarding which there is no prohibition of the church.

15. Secondly, in the decree regarding the edition, and the use of the inspired writings the Council forbade all to wrest the sacred Scriptures to their meaning, in opposition to the sense in which the church understands them, or to the unanimous opinion of the Fathers: " Præterea......decernit ut nemo......in rebus fidei et morum......sacram Scripturam... contra sensum quem tenuit et tenet sancta mater Ecclesia (cujus est judicare de vero sensu et interpretatione Scripturarum) aut etiam contra unanimem consensum Patrum...... interpretari audeat, &c.

16. Soave appears to be astonished that the Council should impose any restraint on the manner of understanding the word of God, when Cardinal Cajetan, as he asserts, taught that new interpretations, even though contrary to that of the Fathers, ought not be rejected, unless they are opposed to other parts of Scripture, and to the doctrine of faith. But I answer that Cajetan, whose opinion on this point has been severely censured by Cano, (lib. 7. c. 3. et 4.) does not say that it is lawful to reject the uniform interpretation of the Fathers; he only says that we may give to the Scripture an interpretation different from all those which have been given by the Fathers when they disagree among themselves, so that a person remains doubtful which he ought to adopt, but not when the exposition of the Fathers is uniform. Justly indeed has the Council forbidden Christians to interpret the

divine word in opposition to the common opinion of the Fathers: for this has been always the ancient practice of the Church. Thus the Council of Ephesus, on the authority of the Fathers, condemned Nestorius, reproving his presumption in thinking that "he alone understood the Divine Word, and that all who had before expounded the Word of God had been ignorant of its meaning," Thus also, St. Jerome condemned the opinion of Helvidius, St. Basil, that of Amphiloteus, St. Augustine, that of the Pelagians and Donatists, St. Leo, that of Eutiches; Pope Agatho in the sixth Council censured the opinion of the Monothelites, and the Council of Florence, that of the Greeks.

17. Nor could this be otherwise; for had God permitted the early Fathers to have erred in the exposition of the sacred Scripture, he, (if I may use the expression) would have deceived us by permitting the sacred doctors to have understood the meaning of the Divine Word in a manner different from that which he intended. Hence we are bound to believe as a dogma of faith what the Doctors of the church have commonly approved as such: otherwise every one might doubt of the sense of every passage in the bible, however clear its meaning might be. But we must believe with the certainty of faith not only what has been defined by the Church, but also what appears to be clearly contained in the Scripture; otherwise before the definitions of the church, every one might doubt of any truth expressed in the sacred writings. We must then conclude that in what regards faith and morals, all the Fathers, when unanimous not in a mere opinion, but in teaching, cannot err without bringing into error the church, which is regulated by them. Hence the Council says: "let no one dare to interpret the Scripture in a manner contrary to the sense which the church holds, and to the unanimous consent of the Fathers." As then it is unlawful to expound the Scriptures in opposition to the sense of the church, which of its own nature is of faith,

so it is also forbidden to give them a meaning contrary to the unanimous interpretation of the Fathers. But before the decree was passed, the Bishop of Chioggia justly remarked that it is not forbidden to attribute a new meaning to texts of the sacred Scripture, as long as it is not opposed to the sense of the Church, or to the unanimous opinion of the Fathers.

18. Thirdly, in the decree it was forbidden, under pain of excommunication, to print or to sell the Holy Bible, or any of the sacred books, or annotations, or commentaries on them, without a previous examination and permission on the part of the Ecclesiastical superiors, or without the author's name, or (ementito prælo) that is, if the work be attributed not to the press in which it was printed but to another. It is also declared that the same prohibition extends to all who shall publish such books or give them to others, or keep them in their possession.

19. Cardinal Madruccio observed that it would be desirable to permit the Scriptures to be published in the vulgar tongue. But this was not deemed expedient, and it was thought sufficient to have them published in Latin, as well because, in the countries in which the Catholic Church flourishes, the Latin language was understood by those who were capable of interpreting the sacred writings, as also because many passages of the Bible are so obscure and equivocal that, should they fall into the hands of the people, they might suggest errors, or at least pernicious doubts.

SECTION III.

VARIOUS OBSERVATIONS ON THE CANONICAL BOOKS OF SCRIPTURE, WHICH THE READER WILL FIND USEFUL.

20. THE word *Canon* signifies a rule or catalogue of writings, and in this sense, it is here taken to mean a catalogue of the inspired books. The canonical books are divided into *protocanonical*, and *deuterocanonical*. The former are those that were always received in the Church as divine and inspired by God. The latter are the inspired books which were not always venerated as such, by all particular Churches, but were ultimately admitted among the sacred writings. The protocanonical books of the Old Testament are Genesis, Exodus, Leviticus, Numbers, Deuteronomy, Josue, Ruth, the four books of Kings, the two books of Paralipomenon, the first and second book of Esdras, the Psalms, Proverbs, the Canticle of Canticles, Isaias, Jeremias, Ezechiel, Daniel, and the twelve minor Prophets. The protocanonical books of the New Testament are the four Gospels of St. Matthew, St. Mark, St. Luke, and St. John, the Acts of the Apostles, the thirteen Epistles of St. Paul, one to the Romans, two to the Corinthians, one to the Galatians, one to the Ephesians, one to the Philippians, one to the Colossians, two to the Thessalonians, two to Timothy, one to Titus, and one to Philemon; also the first Epistle of St. Peter, and the first of St. John.

21. The deuterocanonical books of the Old Testament, are Esther, Baruch, the chapters of Daniel which contain the hymn of the three children, the history of Susanna, and of the dragon killed by Daniel; also the books of Tobias, of Judith, of Wisdom, Ecclesiasticus, and the first and second

book of Machabees. The deuterocanoncial books of the New Testament are the Epistle of St. Paul to the Hebrews, the Epistle of St. James, the second of St. Peter, the second and third of St. John, the Epistle of St. Jude, and the Apocalypse. To these are added the last chapter of St. Mark, and the history of the bloody sweat and of the apparition of the consoling angel in the gospel of St. Luke. Although these books have been always reckoned among the canonical Scriptures by the greater part of the church, they were not formerly received as such by some Catholics. But in the fourth session, the Council of Trent declared them to be divinely inspired.

22. The Calvinists and Lutherans reject six books of the Old Testament, viz. Tobias, Judith, Wisdom, Ecclesiasticus and the two books of Machabees. In the New Testament the Calvinists reject the Epistle of St. Jude, and the Apocalypse. But all the Councils and all the Fathers frequently quote these books as divinely inspired; and in their catalogues of the canonical Scriptures, the Sovereign pontiffs have given them a place. They were regarded as such by Origen, (Eus. lib.5. hist. c. 18) by St. Athanasius, (in synopsi) by St. Gregory Nazrinzen, (Carm. de Genuin. Scriptur.) by St. Cyril of Jerusalem, (catech. 4.) by the Council of Laodicea, (can. ult.) by the third Council of Carthage, (can. 47.) by St. Augustine, (lib. 2. de Doctr. Christi, cap. 8.) by Innocent the first, (Epist. ad Exsuper.) by Gelasius the First in the Council of Rome, by St. Isidore, (lib. 6. ethymol. c. 1.) by St. John Damascen, (lib. 4. de fide c. 18.) and finally as we have seen, by the Council of Trent, that is by the whole church. Surely this alone ought to be sufficient, since from the protocanonical books, it is evident that the Catholic Church is infallible in its decrees.

23. The Jews had many books in their canon which are not now in existence: such as the book *Bellorum Domini*, (ap. Num. 21.) the book *Justorum*, (ap. Jos. c. 10.) the

book *Verborum*, (ap. 3. Reg. 11.) and others. There were other books, such as Eldal and Medad, &c. which were not admitted into their canon. But St. Augustine (de civ. c. 38.) says that these were neither inspired nor canonical.

SECTION IV.

OBJECTIONS OF THE ADVERSARIES TO THE DEUTEROCANONICAL BOOKS.

24. WITH regard to the book of Baruch, our adversaries object that it is not found in the canon of any of the Fathers. But in answer, I say with Bellarmine (c. 8.) that it was not placed in the canon of the Fathers, because they believed that it was written by Jeremias, to whom Baruch was amanuensis, as we read in the 36th chapter of Jeremias. But all the Fathers have received the book of Baruch as divinely inspired, and have quoted passages from Jeremias, as may be seen in Bellarmine, (loc. cit.)

25. With regard to the book of Tobias, our opponents say that it is not found in the canon drawn up by Esdras. But I answer that it has been always received as divinely inspired by the Catholic Church, as appears from the Councils of Hippo and Carthage, and from the canon of Gelasius.

26. With regard to the Book of Judith, Luther and Grotius entertain doubts whether the narrative contained in it, is not fabulous; but the Holy Fathers have received it as true history, as is evident from the Council of Hippo held in the year 393, and from the Council of Carthage (anno 397), from one of the epistles of Innocent the first, (Epist. ad Exsuper), and from the Council held in Rome under Gelasius the First. The Anabaptists reject the book of

Esdras. But they err; for the Jews themselves received as divinely inspired the first seven chapters. It is true that some have doubted of the inspiration of the other seven chapters; but the generality of the Holy Fathers have maintained the veracity of the history of Esdras. Finally, this book is found in the Vulgate which has been approved by the Council of Trent. It is objected that the last seven chapters do not agree with the first. But I answer that the seven chapters which are the last in the Vulgate, are not in reality the last; some of them, viz. the 11th and 12th, belong to the beginning; others, such as the 13th, 14th, 15th, and 16th to the middle; and the tenth, to the end of the book. And St. Jerome placed them at the end, because he found them not in the Hebrew version, but only in the Vulgate.

27. Our adversaries object against the book of Tobias that it is not found in the canon of the Jews. I answer that Esdras did not place all the sacred writings in his canon, but the Catholic Church has always received this book as the inspired word of God; as is evident from the Councils of Hippo and Carthage, and from the canon of Gelasius. They also object that in this book it is said that Sara the future wife of the young Tobias lived in Rages, and in the fourth chapter, it is related that Gabel also dwelt there. But in the 6th chapter it is stated that when Tobias arrived at the dwelling place of Sara, the Angel sent Gabel from that place, to Rages. I answer that either in the kingdom of Media, there were two cities called Rages, or that the Rages mentioned in the third chapter was not the city but the territory of Rages, as we say that a person who lives in the Roman territory, lives in Rome.

28. Some have doubted whether the circumstances related in the book of Job really occurred. But the Greek and Latin Churches have held the truth of the narration of Job, and have venerated him as a holy man: and in Ezechiel (14, 14.) his name is mentioned with the names of the holy

men Noe and Daniel: "Etsi fuerint tres viri isti in medio ejus, Noe Daniel et Job." In our martyrology, his festival is fixed on the sixth of the Ides of May.

29. There are no objections to the canonicity of the Psalms, but with regard to their author there are two opinions; both are probable and held by respectable authors: the first is that David is the author of all the Psalms, the other that they were written by the authors whose names are found in the titles of the Psalms.

30. It has been doubted by some whether the book of Wisdom was written by Solomon. But the doubts are groundless, for from the book itself it is clear that Solomon was its author.

31. Against the canonicity of Ecclesiasticus it has been objected that it is not found in the canon of Esdras. But it has been already said that Esdras did not place all the inspired books in his canon. But the rulers of the Church and the principal Fathers have reckoned it among the sacred writings.

32. With regard to the book of Daniel some have entertained doubts about the inspiration of the Canticle of the three children, and of the history of Susanna, of Belus, and of the dragon, because they are not found in the Jewish canon. But the Catholic Church and the Fathers have received them as divinely inspired. It is objected that in the 6th chapter it is stated that Daniel was in the lions' den only for a single night, and that in the 14th chapter, it is said that he was there for 6 days. I answer that Daniel was thrown into the lions' den twice: first in Babylon, when he killed the dragon which the people adored, and then he was for six days in the den, as we read in the 14th chapter. On the second occasion he was cast into the den under Darius, because he had supplicated the divine aid against the edict of that sovereign, and then he was in the den only a single night, as is stated in the 6th chapter.

33. With regard to the first book of Macchabees, it

is objected that in the first chapter Alexander the Great was the first monarch of Greece, although it is certain that before him there had been several rulers over that country. I answer that the scripture does not speak of every sort of rule, but only of the monarchical sway, which Alexander was the first to exercise over the Greeks. It is also objected that in the 8th chapter, it is stated that the Romans annually appointed a magistrate whom all should obey, although at that time it was usual to appoint two consuls to govern the state. In answer I say that the scripture speaks thus, either because the Consuls presided in turn each month, or according to some, on every alternate day, or because the principal authority was vested in one of them.

34. With regard to the second book of Macchabees, our adversaries say, that in the first chapter it is stated that Antiochus died in the temple of Nanea, and in the 6th chapter of the first book it is said that he died in his bed. I answer that in the first chapter of the second book, the Scripture speaks not of Antiochus Epiphanes, but of Antiochus Soter, as he is called by Josephus, and the latter was in reality stoned in the temple of Nanea. But in the 6th chapter of the first book, the Scripture speaks of Antiochus Epiphanes, who died in Babylon.

35. It has been also objected that in the second chapter of the second book it is related that Jeremias concealed the ark in a cave, although we know that he was then in prison, and remained there till the destruction of the temple. I answer that Jeremias, knowing what was to happen, concealed the ark in the time of Joachim, and then he was free, and not confined to prison.

36. It has been objected against the epistle of St. Paul to the Hebrews, that it does not bear his name, and that its style is different from that of his other epistles. I answer that the Apostle omitted to give his name to that epistle because he knew that he was not acceptable to the Jewish

D

converts, in consequence of having insisted more frequently than the other Apostles, on the abolition of the Jewish law. The style is different from that of his other epistles, because, in that epistle St. Paul wrote in his native tongue, and therefore with elegance: but as St. Jerome remarks, the other epistles were written in Greek, with which the Apostle was not well acquainted.

37. With regard to the epistle of St. Jude it has been objected that he there quotes as a prophetical book, the book of Enoch, which is apocryphal. I answer that the entire book is not quoted, but only a single prediction made by Enoch, which was perhaps written in that apocryphal work, and which the Apostle knew to be true by a particular revelation.

SECTION V.

WERE THE SACRED SCRIPTURES INSPIRED NOT ONLY AS TO THE MATTER BUT ALSO AS TO THE WORDS.

St. Gregory says: " Ipse scripsit, et illius operis inspirator extitit." (Præf. in Job.) There are three opinions on this point. The first is that not only the sentiments but also the words were inspired by God. The second, that all the sentiments, but not all the words were inspired; this opinion is the most probable. The third is that many of the sentiments were inspired by God, and that others were added by certain authors, according to their own discretion, but this opinion is erroneous and impious. What is certain is that the entire substance as well of the Old as of the New Testament, was inspired by God: otherwise, says St. Augustine, "the whole authority of the Scriptures, and therefore our faith would totter: "Tota scripturarum vacillaret auctoritas,

ideoque et fides nostra." (Lib. 1. de doctr. Christ cap. 27.)
Hence St. Paul has called the scriptures " eloquia Dei,"
(Rom. 3.) and in his epistle to Timothy he says: " Omnis
scriptura divinitus inspirata." (c. 3.) This is also proved by the
tradition of the Fathers, by the authority of St. Ireneus (cont.
hæres. lib. 2. c. 47.) of Tertullian, (lib. de hab. mul. c.
23.) of St. Athanasius, (ep. ad. Marcellin.) of St. Basil,
(prœm. in Psal.) and of St. John Chrysostom, (hom. 21. in
c. 5. Gen.) This tradition is evident from the persevering
persuasion of Christians, regarding the New, and as appears
from the writings of Philo and Josephus, of the Jews regarding the Old Testament.

39. But that all the words of Scripture were not inspired
by God is held by St. Jerome, (ep. ad. Algasia,) and by St.
Augustine: "Si ergo quæritur," writes the latter, " quæ verba
potius dixerit Matthæus, an quæ Lucas, &c., nullo modo hinc
laborandum." (L. 2, de cons. Evang. c. 12.)   According to
the holy Doctor, it is enough that the sentiments be true,
since some of the sacred writers have followed one order, and
others have followed another. Hence, in citing certain texts,
Denis of Alexandria, Origen, St. Basil, St. Gregory of Nazianzen, St. Jerome, and other Fathers quote barbarisms which
certainly could not be dictated by God. The Vulgate is believed to be inspired by God in all the sentiments, but not in
all the words.

ANSWER TO SOME OF THE PRINCIPAL OBJECTIONS.

40. *First objection.* If all the sentiments were inspired
by God, the sacred writers would not be obliged to employ diligence and labour. But from the words of St. Luke, and the
author of the second book of Macchabees, this appears to be
false. I answer that not all, but only certain divine inspirations
exclude labour and diligence on the part of the sacred writers:
for God has not inspired all in the same manner; to some the
sentiments and the words were suggested by divine inspira-

tion, so that they did not stand in need of any reflection in order to write. But others were moved by God to take every precaution against falling into error, and in the mean time, he revealed to them things which they had forgotten or had not known.

41. *Second objection.* Many things in the Scriptures are contrary to the divine commands; such as certain imprecations which we find in the Psalms. " Effunde iram in gentes quæ te non noverunt," (Ps. lxxviii. 10.) and the like. But I answer that, as St. Augustine remarks, these were not imprecations dictated by the desire of revenge, but predictions of divine chastisement. " Non malevolentiæ voto ista dicuntur, sid spiritu prævisa prædicuntur." (In cit. Ps. 97.)

42. *Third objection.* There are certain useless things in the Scriptures which do not appear to be inspired by God, such as what the Apostle writes to Timothy: " Penulam quam reliqui Troade apud Carpum, veniens affer tecum." (2 Tim. iv. 13.) I answer that all the things which are contained in the Scripture are not equally useful, but none of them is useless, for they contribute to the integrity of the narrative, or serve for our instruction: thus the words of the Apostle teach us that we may meritoriously provide for human wants. St. Jerome says: " Quæcumque in scripturis levia et parva videntur, non minus esse a Deo inspirata quam creaturæ vilissimæ sint a conditore cœli et terræ." Ep. ad Philemon.

43. *Fourth objection.* Some things in the Scriptures are related as uncertain; thus in St. John we read: " There were six waterpots......two or three measures a piece."—ii. 6. I answer that in some places the Holy Ghost has not been pleased to declare certain circumstances, but wished to conform to the common usage in relating certain facts.

44. *Fourth objection.* The author of the second book of Macchabees asks pardon for his errors. I answer that there be speaks not of errors, but of defects in his style of writing.

" I will," he says, "here make an end of my narration; which
if I have done well, and as it becometh the history, it is
what I desired; but if not so perfectly, it must be pardoned
me."

SECTION VI.

ON THE SENSE OF THE SACRED SCRIPTURES.

45. The inspired writings have different senses: viz. the
literal and the mystic sense. The former is that which the
words plainly signify, and this sense alone supplies proofs
of faith. The mystic sense of any passage never affords
proofs of faith, unless when confirmed by another text which
explains the passage conformably to the mystic sense, or
when the Fathers commonly agree in expounding the passage in the mystic sense.

46. The mystic sense is that which is signified immediately by what the words express. Hence the mystic supposes
the literal sense. Thus St. John understands in the mystic
sense, of Christ, the passage in Exodus regarding the Paschal
Lamb. ("Nec os illius confringetis" 12, 46.) The mystic sense
is divided into the allegorical, which regards the mysteries of
faith; the analogical, which has reference to the eternal
beatitude, which we hope for; and the tropological, or
moral, which regards morals. There is also the accommodated sense; thus the words of our Lord to Magdalene,
" Maria optimam partem elegit," are accommodated to the
Blessed Virgin. The accommodated sense proves nothing,
since it was not intended by the Holy Ghost. It should be
observed that sometimes the same passage may have two
literal senses, for God can signify several things by the
same words.

47. It may be asked whether the meaning of the Scriptures is clear or obscure. The innovators say that all parts of the Scripture are clear; they hold this doctrine because they expound many obscure passages according to their own notions, and therefore say that they are all clear. But the contrary is evident from the Scriptures themselves. In St. Luke, xviii. 34, we read: " And they understood none of these things." And in the last chapter the same Evangelist says: " Then he opened their understanding that they might understand the Scriptures." And of the Epistles of St. Paul St. Peter says: " In which are certain hard things to be understood." (2 Pet. iii. 16.) This is also the doctrine of all the holy Fathers: it will be sufficient to quote St. Jerome and St. Augustine. In an epistle to Algasia, the former says of the Scripture: " Quæ tantis obscuritatibus obvoluta est." And the latter, in the 119th epistle to Januarius, writes: " in aliis innumeralibus rebus multa me latent, sed etiam ipsis sanctis scripturis multa nesciam plura quam sciam." That many passages of the Scriptures are obscure, is still more evident from the great diversity of interpretations which the Fathers and Catholic commentators have given to the same texts.

48. Against the obscurity of many parts of Scripture, the adversaries object from the words of Deuteronomy, xxx. 11: " This commandment that I command thee this day is not above thee:" I answer, that in this place it is not said that every precept is clear, but that the observance of every command understood according to the exposition of the Church, is not impossible, but possible and easy, with the assistance of grace. They also object from the text in Proverbs, " The commandment is a lamp, and the law is light," vi. 23; and from the words of the Psalmist, " The commandment of the Lord is lightsome, enlightening the eyes," xviii. 9. The meaning of these passages is, that the Divine commands, well understood, enlighten the mind and direct the

will to do good, but not that all parts of Scripture are clear.

49. The innovators say that although certain passages of the Scripture are obscure, the Lord gives each of the faithful a clear knowledge of their meaning. Behold the *private* interpretation of the heretics, which has produced such a variety of creeds. Hence, after all the provincial and national congresses and synods which they have held, they have never been able to draw up a formula 'of uniform belief: hence, every one knows, that among the reformers there are as many formulas of faith as there are individuals. This alone is sufficient to show that they are in error, and have not the true faith.

SECTION VII.

ON THE DIFFERENT VERSIONS OF THE SCRIPTURE.

50. ALL the books of the Old Testament were written in Hebrew. The books of the New Testament were written in Greek, except the Gospel of St. Matthew, the Epistle of St. Paul to the Hebrews, which was probably written in the Syriac language, mixed with Hebrew and Chaldaic words, and the Gospel of Saint Mark, which was probably written in Latin at Rome. Of the Old Testament there were many versions, that of Origen, of St. Lucian, of Theodotion, of Aquila, of Symmachus, and others: but the most celebrated was the Septuagint, which was made about 280 years before Christ, by King Ptolomy Philadelphus, the son of Ptolomy Lago, king of Egypt, and third king of Greece after Alexander the Great. He was introduced into Greece by Demetrius Philarchus, the philosopher. Wishing to enrich his library Ptolomy Philadelphus requested Eleazar, the High Priest, to send him a copy of the sacred writings, and a number of Hebrew doctors to translate them into Greek. Eleazar sent him seventy-two learned men, who made the version, which

was afterwards approved by the Jews and Greeks of Alexdria.

51. St. Ireneus, Clement of Alexandria, St. Augustine, along with Bellarmine and Baronius, were of opinion that these interpreters were inspired by the Holy Ghost; but this is denied by St. Jerome. Others say that they at least received aid from the Holy Ghost, not to fall into error.

52. Some have held, on the testimony of a certain pagan called Aristea, that the seventy-two interpreters were shut up in separate cells, that each might make his translation, and that when all the translations were compared they were found to agree. But St. Jerome rejects this narration, and says, (Præf. in Pentach.) " Nescio quis primus auctor septuaginta cellulas mendacio suo extruxerit:" the saint asserts that the seventy-two interpreters translated the sacred writings only after consulting among themselves. This is the opinion of Bellarmine, and of many learned moderns. Bellarmine and others remark, that at present the Septuagint version is so corrupt that it is quite different from what it was. However there is no doubt but the Apostles and the holy Fathers made use of that version: it is certain that at present it is not authentic, although Juenin (tom. i. pp. 75, 76) holds that it has been, and is still authentic.

53. With regard to the Latin versions of the Old Testament, the Vulgate, called by St. Augustine the Italic, and by St. Gregory the old version, was the most common. St. Jerome corrected it, and made two Latin translations of the entire of the Old Testament, except the Psalter, which he only corrected, and the books of Wisdom, of Ecclesiasticus, and of Machabees, which remain as they were in the old Latin version. The first translation was made from the Greek Septuagint version, and the second from the Hebrew text. The version of St. Jerome has been universally received in the western Church, and has been declared by the Council of Trent to be authentic, as being a version which

by means of Apostolical tradition has been approved as true by the long use of so many ages.

54. It is necessary to observe that the New Testament was not translated from the Greek into Latin by St. Jerome, but only purged from certain errors. This is held by Juenin, tom. i. p. 79, concl. 4. And Bellarmine says, (lib. 6, de verb. Dei. c. 7,) that the Greek version of the New Testament which St. Jerome prepared by order of St. Damasus is not at present perfectly safe, because it is not entirely free from corruption.

55. The heretics object against the Vulgate; first, that it differs from the Hebrew and Greek versions; and that on that account, Clement VIII. corrected the Vulgate, which had been published by Sixtus V. I answer that it does not differ substantially from them: and it is of little moment that it should disagree with them in a few places: for the learned say that through the negligence of the editors, defects have crept into the Hebrew and Greek versions. However the Greek and Hebrew versions are useful, inasmuch as they help us to discover the meaning of the words; and the Council of Trent, although it has preferred the Vulgate, has left them the authority which they had before. It is necessary to observe that in correcting the Vulgate, Clement VIII. changed not the sense, but only certain expressions in the edition of Sixtus V. But, as Clement says, the Vulgate even at present is not free from all accidental errors. But it has been defined that at present it is exempt from all substantial errors in faith and morals.

56. They object secondly, that the Council had no reason to prefer the Vulgate to the other editions. I answer that the use of the Vulgate in the Church for a thousand years was a sufficient reason for the preference. From the time of St. Gregory the Great, the Vulgate alone was used in the lessons and definitions of the Church, as appears from the works of St. Gregory, and from the acts of the councils.

57. They object thirdly that the Vulgate contains many errors which could not be corrected at the time of the Council of Trent. I answer that our adversaries have not been able to prove that it contains any error. And if through the neglect of editors any errors have crept into it, the sovereign pontiffs have corrected them. But if a few have been permitted to remain, they are of very little moment, and are not at all opposed to faith or morals, (sec. Juenin. tom. 1, p. 9, concl. 4.)

SECTION VIII.

IMPORTANT OBSERVATIONS ON TRADITIONS.

58. By tradition is understood the unwritten Word of God which the Church preserves and proposes to the faithful to be believed with the same certainty as the Sacred Scriptures. It is called tradition, because it is delivered not in writing, but from one to another, as it were from hand to hand, and passes from ear to ear by common narration or report. The written word of God is preserved on paper, and the unwritten, in the hearts of the faithful.

59. Traditions are of three kinds; Divine, Apostolical, and Ecclesiastical. The divine are those that come from God himself, or from Christ; such as the institution of the matter and forms of the sacraments. The apostolical traditions are those that come from the Apostles: these are of two kinds: for the traditions which they received from the mouth of Jesus Christ, or which were revealed to them by the Holy Ghost are divine traditions, and are different from the observances which the apostles, directed by the Holy Ghost, have left to the Church, such as the mixture of water with wine in the chalice; the fast of Lent, the observance of Easter and Pentecost, &c. The Ecclesiastical traditions are

the customs introduced in ancient times by the prelates, or by the faithful with the consent of the prelates, and which in time have acquired the force of laws, such as the recitation of the divine office by ecclesiastics, in holy orders, or holding a benefice, abstinence from flesh meat on Saturday, &c.

60. The innovators reject all traditions; but Catholics hold that there are real divine traditions, which along with the Scriptures are the foundation of faith. Hence the Council of Trent has taught that the Church holds in equal veneration the Scriptures and traditions. In the decree on the canonical Scriptures passed in the fourth session, the Council says: "Perspiciensque hanc veritatem et disciplinam contineri in libris scriptis et sine scripto traditionibus, quæ ab ipsius Christi ore ab apostolis acceptæ aut ab ipsis apostolis, spiritu sancto dictante, quasi per manus traditæ ad nos usque pervenerunt, orthodoxorum Patruam exempla secuti omnes libros tam veteris quam Novi Testamenti cum utriusque unus Deus sit auctor, necnon traditiones ipsas, tum ad fidem, tum ad mores pertinentes, tanquam vel oretenus a Christo vel a Spiritu Sancto dictatas et continua successione in ecclesia catholica conservatas, pari pietatis affectu ac reverentia suscipit et veneratur."

61. The divine traditions existed first in the state of the law of nature, that is from Adam till the time of Moses. There certainly must have been a certain rule of faith during that period. This rule of faith could not be taken from the Scriptures, because they were not then in existence. It was taken then from the tradition of Adam, who taught his children what God had revealed to him regarding redemption and the other mysteries of our salvation.

62. Under the *written law* promulgated by Moyses, the Jews, although they had several inspired books, were obliged to have recourse to tradition for the regulation of several things belonging to faith and morals. "Thou shalt,

said the Lord, tell thy son in that day, saying: This is what the Lord did to me when I came forth out of Egypt." (Exod. xiii. 8.) David said: "How great things he commanded our fathers, that they should make the same known to their children: that another generation might know them." (Ps. lxxvii. 6.) Thus not only the Scripture but the tradition of the fathers served to make known to the Jews the events which were to happen to them.

63. Finally, in the beginning of the evangelical law tradition was for several years absolutely necessary. For the Gospel of St. Matthew, which was the first book of the New Testament, was not published till eight years after the death of Jesus Christ, and all the other sacred writings were not published for many years after.

64. Even in our own times, traditions are necessary for several reasons. First, in order to distinguish the canonical from the apocryphal books: for the canonical books are not declared in any of the sacred Scriptures, nor as has been already said, can they be known from the private spirit. Hence all the holy Fathers say that we know the divine writings only from tradition. "Ex traditione didici," says Origen," de quatuor evangelis quod hæc sola, &c. (Ap. Euseb. hist. l. 6. c. 18.)

65. Secondly, traditions are necessary, that the Church may determine the true sense of the passages of Scripture by which are proved several dogmas of our faith, such as the Trinity of the divine persons, the consubstantiality of the Word with the Father, the procession of the Holy Ghost from the Father and the Son, the divine maternity of the Virgin Mary, the existence of original sin in all men, the real presence of Jesus Christ in the Eucharist. For the Socinians and other heretics deny that the Scriptures prove the doctrine of the Church on these mysteries.

66. Thirdly, they are necessary for the belief of several dogmas of faith which are held in common by Catholics,

Lutherans and Calvinists, against certain heretics: such as that the Divine Mother was always a virgin, which was denied by Helvidius: that baptism conferred on infants is valid, which is not admitted by the Anabaptists, and that baptism given by heretics is also valid, which was denied by the Donatists. With regard to these truths, there is no express declaration in the Scriptures; thus we know them from no other source than tradition.

67. Besides, the Apostles have not written all that they preached; and it is certain that they learned several things from the mouth of Jesus Christ. Hence they recommended to the faithful the traditions which they had communicated to them. "I praise you, brethren," says St. Paul, "that in all things you are mindful of me; and keep my ordinances as I have delivered them to you." (1 Cor. xi. 2.) And in another place he says: "Hold the traditions which you have learned, whether by word, or by our epistle." (2 Thes. ii. 14.) Hence on the latter passage, St. Chrysostom has written: "Hinc patet quod non omnia per epistolam, sed multa etiam sine litteris; eadem vero fide digna sunt tam illa quam ista."

68. The adversaries object first from the words of Deuteronomy: "You shall not add to the word that I speak to you, neither shall you take away from it," (iv. 2.) and also from the passage in St. Matthew: (xv. 3.) "Why do you also transgress the commandment of God for your tradition?" In answer to the first, I say that Moyses speaks not of a tradition, but of a precept. In the text from St. Matthew, our Lord said not for *my* tradition, but for *your* tradition; that is for a tradition invented by the Pharisees. Hence he added, "you have made void the commandment of God for your tradition."

69. Secondly, they object from the words of St. Paul to Timothy: "All Scripture inspired of God is profitable to teach, to reprove, to correct, to instruct in justice, that the man of God may be perfect, furnished to every good work."

E

(2 Tim. iii. 16, 17.)   Of what use, they ask, is tradition when the Scripture contains all things?   I answer that the Apostle says that the Scripture is profitable to teach, to reprove, &c., but he does not say that it is sufficient for every purpose.   Besides, St. Paul does not speak of all the sacred books taken collectively, but of each book in particular, and says that each is useful, but not sufficient to instruct us in all things that belong to faith and morals.

70. We know that the Councils have had recourse to tradition in order to determine the sense of the Scriptures. Theodoret states (hist. lib. i. c. 8,) that the first Council of Nice made use of tradition in the condemnation of Arius. The second Council of Nice, as appears from the sixth act, had recourse to tradition in defence of sacred images against the Iconoclasts.   The eighth Council, in the eighth act declared that the true traditions should be observed.

71. The holy Fathers also have uniformly held that the traditions should be regarded as the true word of God. This is the doctrine of the Greek Fathers, of St. Ignatius, (apud Euseb. hist. l. 1, c. 36.), of St. Ireneus, (l. 3, c. 4.) of Origen, (in c. 6, ad Rom.) of St. Basil, (l. de Sper. S. c. 27.) of St. John Chrysostom (loc. sup. cit.), and of St. Epiphanius, (de hæresibus, hær. 61.)   It is also the doctrine of the Latin Fathers; of Tertullian, (in lib. de præscr.), of St. Augustine, (lib. 5, de Bapt. c. 23.) and of Vincent of Lerins, who in the entire of his *Commonitorium* teaches that it is necessary to adhere to the traditions.

72. The adversaries object; first, that St. Cyprian did not believe that the tradition urged against him by Pope Stephen came from the apostles, but called it an ancient error, *vetustum errorem.*   I answer that St. Cyprian rejected the tradition to which St. Stephen appealed, because he thought that it did not originate with the apostles: but he certainly believed that it was necessary to hold the traditions which really descended from them.

73. Secondly, they object from the words of St. Jerome on the 23rd chapter of St. Matthew: " Hoc quia de Scripturis auctoritatem non habet, eadem facilitate contemnitur qua probatur." I answer that the Saint treated with contempt a certain objection, because it rested on the authority not of the Scripture, but of an apocryphal book, in which it was stated that the Zachary who had been killed by the Jews between the temple and the altar was the father of the Baptist.

74. Thirdly, they object that we cannot safely depend on tradition, because it is subject to change: thus the communion under both species, which had been in use for so many ages, has been abolished for four centuries. I answer that we speak of traditions which regard faith and morals, and which are infallible and immutable, and not of those which belong to discipline, and which may be changed for just reasons.

Finally, it is necessary to establish [the rules by which divine traditions are distinguished from those that are human. The heterodox reject tradition, because they say it is impossible to distinguish between true and false traditions.

RULES BY WHICH IT MAY BE KNOWN THAT A TRADITION IS HUMAN
AND NOT DIVINE.

First rule. What is found to have its origin in the opinion of some holy Father, or particular council, is not a divine tradition, even though it should be observed throughout the entire Church. For if we did not attend to this rule, we should have to admit without certain foundation, new revelations regarding faith or morals, which has been always abhorred and impugned in the Church by men the most attached to religion. " Mos iste," says Vincent of Lerins, " in Ecclesia semper viguit ut quo quis foret religiosior, eo promptius novellis ad-inventionibus contrairet." (Lib. 1. c. 5.)

Hence, the sovereign pontiffs, the Councils, and Fathers, have been most careful to reject all novelties or new doctrines on matters of faith, which differed from those that had been already received. This was well expressed in the words of the Apostle to Timothy: "O Timothy, keep that which is committed to thy trust, avoiding the profane novelties of words, and oppositions of knowledge falsely so called, which some promising, have erred concerning the faith." (1. Tim. vi. 20, 21.) Vincent of Lerins adds: "Quid est depositum? est quod tibi creditum est, non quod a te inventum; quod accepisti, non quod excogitasti." (loc. cit. c. 22.) By such pretended revealed novelties Montanus endeavoured to infect the Church.

Second rule. A doctrine which is found only in one particular Church should be considered not divine, but human: otherwise, as St. Augustine has demonstrated against the Donatists, the whole Catholic Church should be reduced to a corner of the earth. Hence, in such a case no regard should be paid to that particular Church.

Third rule. We ought not to regard as divine, a tradition which teaches a dogma on the authority of one, or of a few modern or ancient writers, though men of sanctity and learning, in opposition to the common opinion. The error of the Millenarians, that is that Christ after the resurrection of men would reign for a thousand years on earth along with the elect, was held by several of the Fathers, by Tertullian, St. Ireneus, and Lactantius (Euseb. hist. lib. iii. c. 39); but because it was contrary to the common opinion of the other Fathers, it was rejected.

SECTION IX.

RULES BY WHICH IT MAY BE KNOWN THAT A TRADITION IS DIVINE AND NOT HUMAN.

First rule. A dogma which is embraced by the whole Church ought to be considered as a divine tradition though it be not contained in the sacred Scriptures. Because the universal Church, which, according to the Apostle, (1. Tim. 3.) is the firm and infallible pillar of truth, cannot err. Hence Tertullian has written: "Quod apud multos unum invenitur, non est erratum, sed traditum." (de præsc.) Such is also the doctrine of St. Cyprian, (l. 3, epist. 13.) and of St. Jerome, in his writings against Vigilantius.

Second rule. The doctrine which the entire Church has defended in every age should be also regarded as a divine tradition: for, as at present, the Church cannot admit as divine what is human, so neither could she in preceding ages.

Third rule. We ought to believe that a practice which is observed by the whole Church, and which God alone could institute, is derived from apostolical tradition. It is thus that St Augustine proved that the practice of baptizing infants is a divine tradition: "Consuetudo matris ecclesiæ in baptizandis parvulis non est superflua deputanda nec omnino credenda, nisi apostolica esset traditio." (Lib. 10. de Gen. c. 23.) He says the same of the practice of not rebaptizing persons who were baptized by heretics. (Lib. 2, de Bapt. c. 7.) Melchior Cano says (de loc. l. 3. c. 4.) the same of several things which the Church does, and which it could not do if it had not received power from God through the tradition of the Apostles; such as to dispense in vows, and to relax oaths. It is also, as Juenin says, (t. 1. c. 3, 137.) by the tradition of the apostles that we know that a "matrimonium ratum et non consummatum" is dissolved by the solemn vow of religion. For it ought not to be supposed that in these things the Church has erred by usurping such powers without certain foundation.

Fourth rule. A practice which is known to be observed in the whole Church perpetually in every age, and does not appear to have originated in any Council, should be considered to be instituted by apostolical tradition, though it be of such a nature that it might have been instituted by the Church. "Quod universa tenet ecclesia," says St. Augustine, "nec conciliis institutum, sed semper retentum est, nonnisi auctoritate apostolica traditum rectissime creditur." (Lib. 4 de Bapt. c. 24.) Hence, theologians say that the fast of Lent is of apostolical institution.

Besides, Tertullian, (lib. de præscr.) and St. Ireneus (lib. 3. adv. hæres. c. 2.) say that when in the principal apostolical Churches in which there is an uninterrupted succession of Bishops, we find the tradition of any dogma, we ought to regard it as a divine tradition. In the third chapter of the work already quoted, St. Ireneus adds, that among the apostolical Churches in which the true tradition is preserved, the Roman Church holds the principal place. "In qua semper ab his qui sunt undique conservata est ea quæ est ab apostolis traditio." He afterwards enumerates all the Roman Pontiffs down to his own time, and adds: "Hac ordinatione et successione ea quæ est ab apostolis in Ecclesia traditio et veritatis proconizatio pervenit usque ad nos."

FIFTH SESSION.

ON ORIGINAL SIN.

1. THE difference between original and personal sin is that the latter is committed with a will which is physically our own, and the former was committed with a will which belonged physically to another, and morally to us. Original sin is in itself in the strict sense a mortal sin, transmitted by propagation to all the children of Adam. Hence David said: "For behold I was conceived in iniquities, and in sins did my mother conceive me." (Ps. l. 7.) The apostle says: "By one man sin entered into the world, and by sin death, and so death passed upon all men in whom all have sinned." (Rom. v. 12.) And in the Epistle to the Corinthians he writes: "If one died for all, then all were dead. And Christ died for all." (2. Cor. v. 14.) Thus the sin of Adam infected all his posterity, and brought death on all men.

2. Against the existence of original sin the Pelagians object from the text of St. Paul: "the law worketh wrath: for where there is no law there is no transgression." (Rom. iv. 15.) From these words, they infer that since infants cannot be bound by any law, they are incapable of prevarication. I answer that although they cannot transgress a law by a will which is physically their own, they are not incapable of violating a law by a will morally their own, in the will of Adam which contained the wills of all men.

3. The second objection against original sin, is taken from the following text: "We must be all manifested before the judgment seat of Christ, that every one may receive the proper things of the body according as he hath done." (2 Cor. v. 10.) Infants then, who have no sins of their own, shall

be saved. I answer that the preceding text is to be understood, not of infants who die without baptism before they
attain the use of reason, but of adults who have been baptized. Calvin excepts infants born of parents who have
faith, and says that they are saved, though they should die
without baptism. But this is false: for David was born of
parents who had faith, and he confessed that he was born
in sin. This, as we shall see, was also taught by the Council, in the fifth session (c. 4.); there the Fathers declared
that infants dying without baptism, though born of parents who
had been baptized, are not saved, and are lost, not on account
of the sins of their parents, but on account of the sin of
Adam, the progenitor of all men, "in whom all have sinned."

4. The third objection is taken from the words of Ezechiel;
"The son shall not bear the iniquity of the father." I
answer that this passage is to be understood of the actual
sins of our parents, and not of the original sin of our first
father, Adam, who contained in his will the wills of all his
descendants, with regard to the command by which God forbade him to eat the forbidden apple. Men sinned then in
Adam, not as the physical head of the human race, otherwise
we should be guilty of all his other sins, but as the moral
head, which represented all his children with reference to the
observance of that precept, in regard to which God (on
account of his supreme dominion over all his creatures) included the wills of all men in the will of Adam. This is
well expressed by saying that all men have sinned by the
sin of Adam, except Christ, who was not conceived by
natural generation, but by the operation of the Holy Ghost.

5. Before the formation of the decree regarding original
sin, it was suggested in the Council, that before the discussion
of the dogmas regarding justification, it would be necessary
to examine and define four points. 1. The nature of original
sin. 2. The manner in which original sin is propagated.
3. The evils caused by original sin. 4. The remedy by which

God repaired these evils. The suggestion was adopted by the Council.

With regard to the nature of original sin, it was said by some that it consists in the privation of the orignal justice in which Adam was constituted. Others said that this privation was not original sin, but the punishment of it. But Angelo Paschal, of the order of St. Dominick, and Bishop of Motola, quoted the authority of St. Thomas, to show that original sin is a defect opposed to original justice, which contained two parts: First, the subjection of the human to the divine will. Secondly, the subjection of all the powers of man to his will. Thus the defect opposed to the first was not the punishment of sin, but the guilt, which constituted the essence of original sin. The second defect and the others which followed in punishment of the first, were as it were the matter of original sin; thus original sin consists in concupiscence, or in the rebellion of the will as its material constituent, and in the privation of original justice as its formal constituent. This opinion was commonly approved. The Bishop of Bossa, who was also a Dominican, added that according to St. Thomas, although the essence of original sin consists in the privation of order, the subject of it was concupiscence, or the evil inclination to transitory goods.

6. With regard to the manner in which original sin is propagated in the descendants of Adam, it is necessary to distinguish the material, from the formal propagation, with regard to the punishment and guilt. The former takes place by generation; John Fonseca, Bishop of Castellamare, said that with regard to the punishment of original sin, God justly chastises the children of Adam by the depriving them of the advantages of original justice, as a king in punishment of the infidelity of a vassal, justly deprives him and his progeny of the possessions and honours which had been bestowed upon him. With regard to the guilt, the above-mentioned Paschal stated on the authority of St. Thomas,

that we are said to have sinned in Adam inasmuch as Adam contained in his fecundity the entire human race, and inasmuch as the choice of his will implied the happy or unhappy state of human nature: and therefore, by committing sin he caused his entire species to be born with the stain and with the deordination produced by his sin. Thus the personal stain of Adam contaminated his nature, but in us the stain of nature produces personal contamination.

7. With regard *to the evils caused by original sin*, Bertan said that it was certain that Adam received original justice and rectitude: had he preserved it, he would have obtained for himself and for us immortality, along with the other gifts of nature. But because he was disobedient to God, he lost the divine grace for himself and for us: the whole human race became disordered, the intellect was darkened and the will inclined to evil, and mankind were subjected to corporal and spiritual evils, particularly in the next life, where infants not baptized are certainly excluded from eternal beatitude.

8. With regard to the other pains endured by infants who die without baptism, there are many opinions; but there are three celebrated opinions. The first is that they suffer the pain of loss and of sense. The second, that they suffer the pain of loss, but not the pain of sense. The third, which is held by St. Thomas and Cardinal Sfrondati, that they suffer neither the pain of loss nor the pain of sense. In the Opuscle de malo, (qu. 5, art. 2,) St. Thomas holds as certain that they are free from the pain of sense: he gives the following reason for his opinion: " The pain of sense corresponds to the conversion to creatures; but in original sin there is no conversion to creatures; and therefore the pain of sense is not due to original sin;" for original sin does not imply an act. To this opinion the others oppose the doctrine of St. Augustine, who in several places appears to think that such infants are condemned to the pain of sense. But, I find that in

one place, the Saint declared that his judgment was suspended on this point: "Cum ad pœnam ventum est parvulorum, magnis, mihi crede, angustiis arctor, nec quidquid respondendum penitus invenio." (Lib. 5, contra Julian, c. 8, et epist. 28, ad Hier.)

9. With regard to the pain of loss, St. Thomas teaches (dist. 33, qu. 1, art. 2,) that, though infants dying without baptism are excluded from glory, they are not afflicted at the privation of the happiness of which they are incapable. Hence as a man does not feel pain at not being able to fly, so these infants are not afflicted at not being able to enjoy the glory which they never were capable of possessing, either by the principles of nature, or by their own merits. In another place, (De malo, qu. 5, art. 2,) the holy Doctor assigns another reason, viz. that the supernatural knowledge of glory is received only by actual faith, which transcends all natural knowledge: and therefore infants cannot suffer the pain of the privation of glory, since they never had any supernatural knowledge of it. Besides, in the place first quoted (in 2. sent. dist. 33. qu. 1. art. 2.), he says that infants who have died without baptism not only shall not suffer pain at their exclusion from eternal beatitude, but that they will even enjoy their own natural goods, and the divine goodness, inasmuch as they shall have a natural knowledge and a natural love of God: "Imo magis gaudebunt de hoc, quod participabunt multum de divina bonitate, et naturalibus perfectionibus." And he afterwards (Loc. cit. infra. ad 5.) adds, that though these infants are separated from God, as to the union of glory, "they are united to him by a participation of natural goods, and thus they will be able to enjoy him by natural knowledge and love."

10. But prescinding from this natural enjoyment which infants who have died without baptism, may possess, it is very equitable, and considering the divine mercy, to me it appears more probable that they receive neither reward nor

punishment in the other life: and from this opinion, St. Augustine himself does not dissent. (lib. 3. de lib. arb. c. 23.) " Non enim" he says, "timendum est ne non potuerit esse sententia media inter præmium et supplicium, cum sit vita media inter peccatum et recte factum." The same has been expressly taught by St. Gregory Nazianzen, and St. Gregory of Nyssa. " Parvuli," says the former, "nec cœlesti gloria nec supplicis a justo judice afficientur." (Serm. in. S. Lavacer.) And St. Gregory of Nyssa writes: " Immatura mors infantium demonstrat neque in doloribus et mœstitia futuros eos qui sic vivere desierunt." (Tract. de. Infant.) But let us return to the points examined by the Council.

11. With regard to the remedy by which God repaired the evils caused by original sin, it was commonly held that the remedy was baptism, which derives efficacy from the death of Jesus Christ, who, by his sanctifying grace, delivers us from sin. Some were of opinion that in speaking of the remedy, the interior faith of man should be united to the exterior washing; but because infants receive grace in baptism without such faith, it appeared that faith is not required universally for all, and therefore the proposition did not please the greater number of the fathers. Besides even in adults faith is necessary as a disposition, but not as a cause of justification. It was then decided, against the error of the Lutherans, that after baptism original sin ceases not only to be imputed, but even to exist. Hence in the Scripture baptism is called regeneration, which implies a passage from the state of death to that of life, in which men receive strength to perform acts of supernatural life.

12. The Lutherans hold that original sin is the same as concupiscence, and that because the latter remains in persons who are baptized, therefore, the sin also remains. This was disproved by several texts of Scripture, and particularly by the words of St Paul: " Our old man is crucified with him,

that the body of sin may be destroyed." (Rom. vi. 6.) Since then sin is destroyed by baptism, whilst concupiscence remains, it cannot be said that the sin consists in concupiscence. In the epistle of St. James we read: "Every man is tempted by his own concupiscence, being drawn away and allured. Then when concupiscence hath conceived it bringeth forth sin." (i. 14, 15.) If then concupiscence begets sin, it is not sin. It was also argued that he who is in sin, has not the proximate disposition for going to heaven. But it is certain that infants who are baptized, if they die before they attain the use of reason, go to heaven, and therefore they are not in sin. Hence when the apostle calls concupiscence sin, he does so only in a figurative sense, (as the Eucharist is called bread,) taking the cause for the effect. Sanfelice, Bishop of Cava, said that although it cannot be said that sin remains in us after baptism, still something of the nature of sin remains in concupiscence. But this opinion was generally reprobated.

After these preliminary discussions the Council drew up the decree, which was divided into five canons, and in which an anathema was pronounced against all who would hold the contrary.

1. Sacrosancta Tridentina synodus statuit ac declarat ...Adam, cum mandatum Dei in paradiso fuisset transgressus, statim sanctitatem et justitiam, in qua constitutus fuerat, amisisse, incurrisseque per offensam prævaricationis hujusmodi iram et indignationem Dei atque ideo mortem quam antea, illi comminatis fuerat Deus et cum morte captivitatem sub ejus potestate, qui mortis deinde habuit imperium, hoc est, diaboli totumque Adam......secundum corpus et animam in deterius commutatum fuisse.

2. Adæ prævaricationem non sibi soli, sed ejus propagini nocuisse; et acceptam a Deo sanctitatem et justitiam quam perdidit, non sibi soli, sed nobis etiam perdidisse; nec mortem et pœnas corporis tantum in genus humanum transfudisse, sed peccatum quod est mors animæ.

3. Hoc Adæ peccatum quod origine unum est, propagatione; non imitatione, transfusum omnibus, inest unicuique proprium, non per humanæ naturæ vires vel per aliud remedium tolli, sed per remedium unius mediatoris Domini nostri Jesu Christi; et ipsum Jesu Christi meritum, per baptismi sacramentum in forma Ecclesiæ rite collatum, tam adultis quam parvulis applicari.

4. Parvulos recentes ab uteris matrum baptizandos esse, etiamsi fuerint a baptizatis parentibus orti; eosque ex Adam trahere originale peccatum, quod regenerationis lavacro necesse est expiari ad vitam æternam consequendam.

5. Per Jesu Christi gratiam, quæ in Baptismate confertur, reatum originalis peccati remitti ac tolli totum id quod veram et propriam peccati rationem habet, illudque non tantum radi aut non imputari;......In renatis enim nihil odit Deus, quia nihil est damnationis iis qui vere consepulti sunt cum Christo per Baptisma in mortem......; ita ut nihil prorsus eos ab ingressu cœli remoretur. Manere autem in baptizatis concupiscentiam vel fomitem, S. Synodus fateri et sentire; quæ cum ad agonem relicta sit, nocere non consentientibus, sed viriliter per Christi Jesu gratiam repugnantibus, non valet; quinimo que legitime certaverit coronabitur. Hanc concupiscentiam quam aliquando Apostolus peccatum appellat ecclesiam catholicam nunquam intellexisse peccatum appellari quod vere et proprie in renatis peccatum sit, sed quia ex peccato est et ad peccatum inclinat.

14. At the end of the Decree the Council subjoined the following declaration: " Declarat tamen, S. Synodus, non esse suæ intentionis comprehendere, in hoc decreto, ubi de peccato originali agitur, beatam et immaculatam Virginem Mariam Dei genitricem; sed observandas esse constitutiones. Sixti Papæ IV. &c.

15. The Fathers made several observations on the tenor of this decree. It was at first stated in the decree, that by sin

Adam lost the sanctity in which he had been created (" in qua creatus fuerat.") The word created, (*creatus*,) was afterwards changed into constituted, (*constitutus*:) because it is a controverted point whether Adam had sanctifying grace at the very moment of his creation. Also in the fifth canon we find the words: " tolli totam id quod veram et propriam peccati rationem habet." Seripando wished to substitute for these, the words: "tolli totam rationem peccati." But the others were unwilling to change the words which had been already inserted in the canon.

16. There was a more tedious controversy about the words, " In renatis enim nihil odit Deus." Seripando said that God could not but hate concupiscence, which was the origin of sin, since it may be said that it is the concupiscible appetite that gains all victories for sin, and that on that account the holy Fathers inculcated the necessity of imploring the divine aid to resist concupiscence. But his reasons did not induce the Council to change the decree; because the words " Nihil odit Deus," meant a hatred of enmity, which cannot exist in God towards them who are born again to grace. The words, " In renatis," and not " in baptizatis," were used because a person may be baptized, and not be born again to grace, in consequence of not having, at baptism, the necessary dispositions. But God cannot hate in any way them who are made his own adopted children. However, some think that it may be said, that even in persons born again to grace, there is a defect which God hates with the hatred which is called the hatred of displeasure. But this opinion does not please others: for it is one thing to say that venial sins, which have their origin in concupiscence, are displeasing to God, and another, to say that concupiscence is in itself displeasing to him, after the Council had declared that concupiscence which was left to be combated, does not injure them who do not consent to it, but that on the contrary, it is profitable to all who resist it with fortitude.

17. It was stated also in the first draft of the decree that

the Council did not reprobate the scholastic opinion that
after baptism the material but not the formal part of original
sin remained.   But the fathers refused to admit this passage, because they wished to use the language of the ancient
Doctors rather than that of modern theologians, that thus
not only the doctrines but also the words might be received
with greater veneration.

18. Soave complains that the quiddity of original sin is not
declared in the decree, and says that the errors regarding
any matter cannot be censured unless its nature be first
known.   But I answer that what is necessary to be known
is that original sin renders us hateful to God and unworthy
of his grace, and of his glory.   As with respect to actual
sin it is enough to know that it deprives us of the divine
friendship, so it was neither useful, nor necessary to make
any further declaration regarding original sin.   But it is not
of any importance to know with certainty whether actual
sin consists in the bad act, or in the privation of rectitude.

19. Finally with regard to the exemption of the Blessed
Virgin from original guilt, the Council wished not to give
any decision, but to adhere to its original resolution of not
deciding scholastic questions.   The Bishop of Bitontium,
though a Franciscan, thought it better to leave the decree as
it stood.   Cardinal Pacecco proposed that after the words:
" declarat S. Synodus non esse suæ intentionis comprehendere, ubi de peccato originali agitur, B. Virginem," the
following words should be added: " quamvis pie credatur
ipsam fuisse conceptam sine peccato originali:" because, all
the religious orders (with one exception) and all the
universities regard the opinion in favour of the immaculate
conception as the more pious opinion, and adhere to it as
such: and still more because, in the general congregation
which was held before the session in which the decree was
framed, the majority were of his opinion.   But the
Dominicans opposed the proposition of Pacecco, saying that

if the belief of the immaculate conception were a pious belief, the disbelief of it should be impious. This argument was not conclusive; but although the majority of the Fathers held that the Divine Mother was conceived without sin, they thought it better to abstain from the use of words which would prejudice the opposite opinion, and the decree was drawn up in the words above mentioned.

20. Not content with the cautious reserve of the Council, Soave goes so far as to ridicule, as the offspring of popular ignorance, the opinion in favour of the exemption of the Virgin from original stain. He says that by excepting Mary among all men, the Council has rendered all the general propositions of the Scripture uncertain. If then, he says, Mary is not conceived in sin like all others, we must deny the truth of the words of the apostles: "And as in Adam all die, so also in Christ all shall be made alive." (1 Cor. xv. 22.)

21. But if, as Soave says, the Council deserves censure, it is necessary also to censure St. Augustine who has written: "Excepta itaque sancta Virgine Maria, de qua propter honorem Domini nullam prorsus, cum de peccatis agitur, habere volo quæstionem: unde enim scimus quod ei plus gratiæ collatum fuerit ad vincendum ex omni parte peccatum, quæ concipere et parere meruit eum quem constat nullum habuisse peccatum." (De nat. et grat. contra Pelag. d. 7, c. 35.) It is certain from the context that in this place, St. Augustine speaks of original sin, and that he exempts the Blessed Virgin from it: but granting that he speaks of actual sin, we have likewise in the Scripture the universal proposition that there is no man who does not sin." "For there is no man that sinneth not." (2. Par. 6. 36.) And St. James says: "In many things we all offend." (3. 2.) In these passages the Scripture does not except Mary: but St. Augustine makes an exception in her favour, because she had conceived and brought forth the Lamb without

F 2

spot.   And if St. Augustine pronounces her exempt even from venial sins, why could not the Council of Trent make an exception in her favour, in its decree regarding original sin, which is far more grievous than all venial sin.

The truth of an universal proposition is not incompatible with an exception of one particular object, which, because there is a special reason why it should not be comprehended, it is usual to mention in express terms whenever it is intended to include it.   On account of the concupiscence caused by the sin of Adam, no one is exempt from light faults, as appears even from many passages of Scripture. "Every man," says St. Paul, "is a liar," (Rom. iii. 4.) And St. John writes: "If we say we have no sin we deceive ourselves and the truth is not in us." (1 John i. 8.)   But still the Divine Mother, by a special privilege granted to her, was exempt from all such venial faults as the Council declared in the sixth session. (Can. 23.)   This supplies a strong argument in favour of the exemption of Mary from original guilt, for without such exemption she could not have been entirely free from all venial sins.

23. Soave also asserts, but the assertion is extremely silly, that the privilege of the divine maternity does not give any grounds for believing that the Blessed Virgin was free from original guilt: and he argues from the letter of St. Bernard (ep. 174.) to the Canons of Lyons, in which the holy Doctor says that if such an argument were valid, it should follow that the father of Mary and all her progenitors ought to be free from original sin.   But Soave is either mistaken or wishes to deceive: for St. Bernard does not say what Soave makes him say.   The saint only says that the Canons of Lyons should not celebrate on their own authority the festival of the conception, but should first obtain the approbation of the holy See; and that they argued badly in saying that since the nativity of Mary was kept as a festival, her conception should also be celebrated, because had she

not been conceived immaculate, she would not be born a saint. Hence St. Bernard answered them by saying that were such an argument a valid one, it would also prove that they ought to celebrate the birth of the father and of all the progenitors of Mary, because had they not been born, neither would she have been born. But the Saint never denied that (for the reason assigned by St. Augustin, that is because she was the mother of God,) privileges were given to Mary which were not bestowed on any other Saint.

24. We know that in his bull *Solicitudo*, which was published in 1661, Alexander VII. declared that the festival of the Conception of the Blessed Virgin was celebrated according to the pious opinion; the defenders of which hold that she was conceived immaculate from the first moment of her existence. The same Pontiff forbade, under the penalties imposed by Sixtus IV., to call into question or to interpret in any other sense, the favour shown to that opinion. Hence at present the Festival of the Conception of Mary is certainly celebrated by the Church according to the pious opinion; and it is forbidden to interpret the celebration of it in a sense different from that which the advocates of the pious opinion hold regarding the conception of Mary. From this we may infer that were St. Bernard living in our times, he would certainly write otherwise than he has written, and would certainly defend the pious opinion.

25. Cardinal Bellarmine says that the Blessed Virgin never contracted original guilt, but that she really sinned in Adam; and he adds that the opposite opinion is dangerous; because the Apostle asserts in several places, that all men have sinned in Adam. " In whom, he says, all have sinned" (Rom. v. 12.); and again: " For all have sinned; and do need the glory of God." (Rom. iii. 23.) In another place, he writes; " If one has died for all, then all were dead." (2. Cor. v. 14.) Bellarmine says that in the will of Adam, the will of all men, and consequently that of most holy Mary

was included. Thus by the sin of Adam, Mary contracted the proximate debt of original sin; and therefore, he says, that she sinned in Adam, but by a special privilege she was preserved from contracting the stain of sin.

26. But there are many learned authors who strenuously maintain that Mary was preserved from contracting either the debt or the guilt of sin. This opinion is defended by Cardinal Galatino, (de Arcal. l. 7. c. 18.) by Cardinal Cusano, (l. 8. exerc. 8.) by De Ponte, (lib. 2, Cant. ex. 10.) by Salazar, (de Virg. Concept, c. 7, s. 7.) by Catharinus, (de pecc. orig. c. ult.) by Navarino, (umbra virg. c. 10, ex. 28.) by Viva, (p. 8, de l. qu. 2, art. 3) by Cardinal de Lugo, Egidius, Richerius, and others. The reason which they assign, and which appears to be a probable one, is that since God has bestowed on this most noble creature, most special gifts of grace, we may piously believe that he has not included her will in the will of Adam, and that therefore she was preserved from contracting even the debt of sin.

27. This I say with regard to the debt of sin: but that most holy Mary has not contracted the stain of sin, I hold for certain, and this opinion is held as certain by Cardinal Everard, (in exam. theol.) by Du Vallius, (l. 2, qu. 2, de pecc.) by Rainaud, (Piet. Lugd. n. 29,) by Lossado, (disc. theol. de imm. conc. &c.) by Viva, (qu. prod. ad trut.), and by many others. To these may be added many of the Holy Fathers: " Suscipe me, says St. Ambrose, non de Sara, sed ex Maria, ut incorrupta sit virgo, sed virgo per gratiam ab omni integra labe peccati." (Serm. 22, in ps. 118.) Speaking of Mary, Origen says: " Nec serpentis venenosi afflatibus infecta est." (Hom. 2.) St. Ephrem writes: "Immaculata et ab omni peccati labe alienissima." (Tom. 5, orat. ad Dei. Gen. On the words of the angel to Mary: "Ave Maria gratia plena," St. Augustine has written: " Quibus ostendit ex integro (mark the expression *ex integro*) iram primæ sententiæ exclusam et plenam benedictionis gratiam

restitutam." (Sem. ii. in nat. Dom.) St. Cyprian or some other ancient author has written, (lib. de car. Chr. oper. de nat.): " Nec sustinebat justitia ut illud vas electionis communibus laxaretur injuriis, quoniam plurimum a cœteris distans, natura culpa." St. Amphilochius says: Qui antiquam virginem communicabat, nonsine probro condidit, ipse et secundam side nota et crimine fabricatus est." Tract. de Deip. Sophronius writes: " Virginem ideo dici immaculatam quia in nullo corrupta est." (In. epist. ap. Synod VI. tom. 3; p. 307. St. Ildelphonsus says: Constateam ab originali peccato immunem?" (Disp. de Virg. Mar.) St. John Damascene: " Ad hunc paradisum serpens aditum non habuit." (Orat. 2. de nat. Mar.) St. Peter Damian writes: " Caro virginis ex Adam sumpta maculas Adam non admisit." (Serm. de Asump. B. V.) St. Bruno has said: " Hæc est incorrupta terra illa cui benedixit Dominus, ab omni propterea peccati contagione libera." (In Ps. ci.) St. Bonaventure says: " Domina nostra fuit plena gratia præveniente in sua sanctificatione, gratia scilicet præservativa contra fœditatem originalis culpæ." (Serm. 2. de Asump.) St. Bernardine of Sienna writes: " Non enim credendum est quod ipse filius Dei voluerit nasci ex virgine et sumere ejus carnem quæ esset maculata aliquo orginati peccato." (Tom. 3. Serm. 49.) St. Lawrence Justinian says: " Ab ipsa conceptione (Maria) fuit in benedictionibus prævneta." (Serm. de annunt.) On the words, " invenisti gratiam," Idiota says: " Gratiam singularem, o dulcissima virgo, invenisti; quia fuerunt in te ab originali labe præservatio &c." (c. 6.) The same is taught by several other authors.

28. But there are two principal arguments in favour of this opinion. The first is the universal consent of the faithful. Father Egidius of the Presentation, of the order of Teresa says (de Præsent. Virg. q. 6. a. 4.) that all the religious orders adopt our opinion. And with regard to the Dominican order, which is the only one that has opposed it,

a modern author asserts that although 92 members of
that order have written against it, 133 have written in its
defence.

29. But that our opinion is in accordance with the
common sentiment of Catholics is shown above all by the
declaration of Alexander VII. in his celebrated bull,
" Solicitudo omnium Ecclesiarum," published in 1661, in
which he says: " Aucta rursus et propagata fuit pietas hæc
et cultus erga Deiparam......ita ut accedentibus academiis
ad hanc sententiam (that is the pious opinion that Mary was
preserved from all stain,) jam fere omnes Catholici eam com-
plectantur." And in reality it is maintained by the universities
of Sorbonne, of Salamanca, of Alcala, of Coimbra, of
Cologne, of Magunza, of Naples, and by many other
universities in which all who obtain degrees oblige themselves by oath to defend the immaculate conception of
Mary. The most learned Petavius urges this argument
taken from the common sentiment of the faithful. (Theol.
dogm. tom. 5. p. 2. l. 14. c. 2. n. 10.) And the celebrated
and learned Bishop D. Julius Torni writes (in adn. ad
Estium. l. 2. dist. 3. S. 2.) that this argument is convincing:
for in truth it is only by the common consent of the faithful that we are assured of the sanctification of Mary in her
mother's womb, and of her glorious assumption into heaven,
which St. Thomas holds as certain. Why then should not
the same common sentiment of the faithful, make us certain
of her immaculate conception?

30. Another argument still more convincing in favour of
Mary's preservation from original guilt is taken from the
celebration of the festival of the Conception of Mary by the
universal Church in the sense of the pious opinion, that
is in honour of her preservation from all stain at the first
moment of her conception. That the festival of her conception is celebrated in this sense, has been declared by
Alexander VII. in the Bull " sollicitudo omnium ecclesia-

rum." " Vetus est," says the Pontiff, "Christi" fidelium erga ejus B. matrem virginem Mariam pietas, sentientium ejus animam in primo instante creationis atque infusionis in corpus fuisse speciali Dei gratia et privilegio, intuitu meritorum Jesu Christi ejus filii, a macula peccati originalis præservatam immunem, atque in hoc sensu conceptionis festivitatem solemni ritu colentium et celebrantium." Thus even in ancient times the festival of the conception was celebrated in honour of the preservation of Mary from original stain, at the first instant in which God created her blessed soul, and infused it into the body. And Pope Alexander ordered the festival to be celebrated in this sense: " Nec non et in favorem festi et cultus conceptionis ejusdem Virginis Deiparæ, secundum piam istam sententiam exhibiti &c. (festivitatem) observari mandat."

31. And in addition to the penalties imposed by Sixtus IV., Alexander deprived of permission to preach or teach, and of active and passive voice, all who would call in question or interpret in a different manner, either in words or in writing, (he declared, that all books in which this should be done, were condemned) the favour shown to the above mentioned worship and pious opinion, either by assertions, or by proposing arguments against it and leaving them unanswered. Behold the words of the bull: " Insuper omnes qui præfatas constitutiones ita pergent interpretari ut favore per illas dictæ sententiæ et festo et cultui secundum illam exhibito frustrentur, vel qui hanc candem sententiam seu cultum in disputationem revocare aut contra ca quoquemodo, directe vel indirecte, quovis prætextu scripto seu voce, loqui, concionari, tractare, contra ea quidquam determinando aut asserendo, vel contra ea argumenta afferendo et insoluta relinquendo aut alio quovis excogitabili modo disserendo, ausi fuerint."

32. Hence, it is no longer lawful to say, as some before asserted, that the festival of the Conception is celebrated not in honour of Mary's preservation from guilt at the first

instant of her existence, but in honour of her sanctification in her mother's womb.

33. Besides it appears that it is no longer lawful to say, what Lewis Muratori asserted, viz., that the pious opinion is not certain, and that since the opposite is probable, it may happen that the Church will one day declare that Mary at the first moment of her conception had contracted the stain of sin. For, since the declaration of Alexander VII. that the feast of the conception is celebrated in honour of Mary's preservation from guilt at the first instant of her creation, it appears that the church cannot declare that she had contracted the stain of sin: for, by such a declaration the Church would pronounce that all past celebrations in honour of the immaculate conception were vain and false, because a false worship was paid to the virgin. But it is certain that the Church cannot celebrate a festival in honour of what is not holy: this is the doctrine of St. Leo Pope, (ep. decret. 4. c. 2.) of St. Eusebius, bishop, who has said that "in the apostolic see the Catholic religion was always preserved without stain." (Decr. 24, qu. 1. c. In sede,) and of all theologians, along with St. Augustine, (Serm. 95. et 113.) St. Bernard, (ep. ad Can. Lugd.) and St. Thomas, who proves from the celebration of her nativity by the Church, that she was sanctified before her birth. " The Church" says the saint, " celebrates the nativity of the Blessed Virgin: but the Church does not celebrate a festival except in honour of a saint: therefore the Blessed Virgin was sanctified in the womb." (3. p. qu. 27. a. 2.) Now if it is certain, as the Angelic Doctor holds, that Mary was sanctified in the womb because the Church celebrates her nativity, we ought also to hold for certain that Mary was preserved from sin at the first instant of her creation, since it is in this sense that the Church celebrates the feast of her conception.

34. It only remains to treat of the question which has been

so much disputed in our own times, viz. whether it is lawful
to make a vow to give one's life in defence of the immaculate conception of Mary. " Lamindo Pritanio, or Lewis
Muratori," in his celebrated work (De moderat. ingen.) and
other moderns, have denied the lawfulness of such a vow:
because, they say, no one can expose his life in defence of an
opinion which is not of faith, which rests on human authority
and may be false. But this opinion has not been yet defined by the Church to be certain; this could be done only by
means of tradition or of divine revelation. On the other
hand, several modern writers, and particularly the author of
the book entitled " Deipara, &c." hold the opposite opinion,
and with much greater probability. For it is necessary to
make a distinction between opinions merely human and
those that regard the worship of the Saints, and particularly of the Queen of Saints, and which in a certain manner
belong to faith. That this opinion regards the worship or
veneration of the Blessed Virgin is evident from the above-
mentioned bull of Alexander VII., in which he ordered the
feast of the conception to be celebrated in honour of Mary's
preservation from original stain at the first moment of her
creation. Besides, though this were a human opinion, it cannot
be said to be any longer purely human, but religious, as St.
Thomas teaches; since it regards worship in honour of the
Divine Mother, which worship is also referred to God. " Omnium virtutum opera," says the holy Doctor, " secundum quod
referuntur ad Deum, sunt quædam protestationes fidei per
quam nobis innotescit quod Deus hujusmodi opera a nobis
requirit, et nos pro eis remunerat; et secundum hoc possunt
esse martyrii causa." (2. 2. q. 124. a. 5.) The saint adds,
(ad 3.) " Quia bonum humanum possit effici divinum, si
referatur in Deum, ideo potest esse quodcumque bonum
humanum martyrii causa secundum quod in Deum refertur."
Every act of devotion towards the most holy Mary, and consequently to celebrate, as the Church requires, the feast of

G

her immaculate conception is certainly an act of religion; and therefore according to St. Thomas, such worship may be a just cause of martyrdom: since then it is lawful and meritorious in each person to give his life that he may not be hindered to give such veneration to the Blessed Virgin, much more will it be lawful and meritorious to suffer death in order to defend the object of this devotion, that is the immaculate conception of Mary, to which the devotion is referred. Hence in his work "De Canonizatione Sanctorum;" (lib. 1. c. 14.) after having shown that the Church favours our opinion regarding the immaculate preservation of the Blessed Virgin, and after having said that no one denies that this opinion is the more pious and the more religious, Benedict XIV. says: "Inter martyres ab ecclesia recensentur qui occisi fuerunt a tyranno vel quia sententiam magis religiosam exercebant, vel ne omitterent exercitium alicujus actus virtutis a quo tamen poterant sine peccato cessare." (n. 13.) Thus a satisfactory answer is given to the objection of Lamindo, that it is not lawful to lay down one's life in defence of the immaculate conception of the mother of God, because it is not of faith that she was conceived without stain.

SIXTH SESSION.

ON JUSTIFICATION. PROEMIUM.

1. Since it was necessary to treat in the Council of justification, which no preceding council had ever discussed, and which was the trunk from which almost all the errors of the modern heretics sprung, the Fathers resolved to examine the subject at full length, and with the greatest care. Hence it was said—first, that the books of the adversaries should be read with impartiality and with a disposition to censure what was false, and at the same time to approve of what was true. Secondly, that the theologians should first hold private conferences on the points to be examined, and after having digested them, should propose them to the Fathers. Thirdly, that the theologians should not sketch out any decree until after they had heard the sentiments of the Fathers. Fourthly, that on each point, the opinions of all the Fathers should not be taken together, but that each Father in particular should state his opinion.

2. It was then said that the subject matter might be divided into three heads. First, how is the passion of Jesus Christ applied to them who are converted to the faith, and what sort of grace do they afterwards merit? Secondly, what must a just man do in order to preserve himself in the state of grace? Thirdly, what is a person who loses sanctifying grace, able to do, what ought he to do, has he strength to recover the lost grace, and what resemblance does this second justification bear to the first? It was also said that it was necessary to treat of free will, since for the justification of adults their consent, which proceeds from free will, is necessary.

3. Hence they began to examine six points. 1. What is
the meaning and essence of justification? 2. What are the
causes of justification, that is, what does God do in im-
parting it, and what must man do in receiving it? 3. How
are we to understand the proposition of the Apostle, " man
is justified by faith?" 4. How do our works appertain to
justification, and how do the sacraments appertain to it?
5. What precedes, what accompanies, and what follows
justification? 6. By what authorities of scripture, of
tradition, of the Councils and Fathers, should the dogmas
to be defined, be sustained?

4. With regard to the first point all agreed that as to
the meaning of the word, justification is a passage from the
state of enmity with God to the condition of his friend and
adopted child; and that as to the essence, the formal
cause of justification is charity or grace infused into the
soul.   They also rejected the opinion attributed to the
master of the sentences, and which had been already censured in the schools, that is that it is not interior grace
which justifies, but only the external assistance of the Holy
Ghost.   With regard to the second point, some were of
opinion that our free will concurs not actively, but only passively to justification: this opinion was rejected as not being
a Catholic opinion.   With regard to the third point, all,
with few exceptions, agreed that man is justified by faith,
not as the immediate cause, but as a first remote disposition;
but with regard to the formal cause, it was said that faith
does not justify unless it is *informed* by the charity and
grace communicated to the soul by means of baptism or
penance.   With regard to the fourth and fifth points they
likewise agreed that works which dispose to justification have
merit only *de congruo;* that works performed, after justification and informed by grace merit *de condigno,*the preservation and augmentation of sanctifying grace, and the attainment of eternal life, but, as St. Paul has said, only with the

divine aid; "Yet not I, but the grace of God with me."—(1 Cor. xv. 10.)

5. When the Fathers came to the definition of the dogmas, the Legates were of opinion, that all the points should not be defined by way of canons and anathemas; because such definitions would only condemn false doctrines, but would not teach truth. Hence the decrees were divided into two classes: one taught catholic doctrine, the others condemned heretical errors. A copy of the draft was given to each of the fathers, and another sent to Rome. So many notes were added that it was necessary to draw it out a third time; it was afterwards considerably altered. The decrees were framed; but because they were obscure and too much encumbered with reasons, Seripando, the general of the Augustinians, was charged with the remodelling of them. He executed the task: but to his mortification, they were so much altered and corrected, that he could no longer recognise them as his own.

6. Finally, the decrees were proposed and confirmed in fifteen chapters, which we shall now treat of separately. We shall first notice what was said before the formation of the decrees. We shall then give the substance of the decrees, which were drawn up and published by the Council. We will afterwards introduce some annotations by Cardina Pallivicini on the words of the decrees. And finally we will adduce the canons of the Council, in which errors were condemned, and which correspond to each decree.

7. In the proemium of the chapters it is said, that since in modern times various errors regarding justification were spread abroad, the Council resolved to teach the truth according to scripture and tradition, and strictly forbade any one to assert or to believe the contrary. Hence it appears that the Council wished to declare to be of faith, what is contained in the decrees as well as what is contained in the canons.

8. The first chapter treats of the question whether the law

of nature or the Jewish law could justify a man without
grace. In that chapter we read: "Primum declarat sancta
synodus......quod cum omnes homines in prævaricatione
Adæ innocentiam perdidissent, facti immundi et......naturæ
filii iræ, quemadmodum in decreto de originali peccato expo-
suit, usque adeo servi erant peccati et sub potestate diaboli
ut non modo gentes per vim naturæ, sed ne Judæi quidem
per ipsam litteram legis Moysi inde liberari aut surgere
possunt." In the first draft, it was said, "*per legem*,"
but, for this expression, the words "*per litteram legis*,"
were substituted. It is necessary to know that at first
some wished to have "*nudam*," or "*solam*" added to
the word "*legem*," in order not to decide that the legal
observances were not meritorious; but the passage was not
altered, for the purpose of leaving untouched the common
opinion against the master of the sentences who, although
the Apostle has written that the doers of the law are
justified, (Rom. ii.), held that the sacraments, of the old law,
even as good works performed with faith and charity, did
not give sanctifying grace. Hence, the words "*per
litteram legis*" were justly substituted for "*per legem*,"
in order to condemn only what St. Paul condemned in his
epistle to the Romans, in which he reproves the Jews for
boasting against the Gentiles of their knowledge and observance of the letter of the law.

9. In the same chapter, the Council proceeds to say:
"Tametsi in eis liberum arbitrium minime extinctum esset,
viribus licet attenuatum et inclinatum." In the first
draft, the word was "*vulneratum*," which was afterwards changed into "*attenuatum et inclinatum*," words
less opposed to either of the two scholastic opinions, according to one of which the evil caused by original sin consists
in the mere loss of gratuitous gifts, and according to the
other, in some detriment to the state suited to human
nature. Others wished to have the words "*attenuatum*

et inclinatum," taken away altogether. Some wished to
add the words: "*cum subtractione bonorum gratui-
torum,*" saying that man's natural liberty remained as it
was before; and that if by liberty was understood that by
which man was before free from sin, it was extinct. But
the deputies answered that as to the first it was justly said
that free will was attenuated (*attenuatum*), since according
to St. Augustine the difficulty of doing good was one of the
evils of original sin. (Lib. 3, de lib. arb. c. 18). And, as
to the second, they said it was false, because man, even when
he rises by the divine grace from sin, co-operates with God
by his free will.

10. To this chapter belong the two following canons:
Can. 1. " Si quis dixerit hominem suis operibus, quæ vel
per humanæ naturæ vel per legis doctrinam fiant, absque
divina per Jesum Christum gratia posse justificari coram
Deo, anathema sit."

11. Can. 2. " Si quis dixerit ad hoc solum divinam
gratiam per Christum Jesum dari ut facilius homo juste
vivere ac vitam æternam promereri possit, quasi per liberum
arbitrium sine gratia utrumque, sed ægre tamen et difficulter,
possit, anathema sit."

12. The second chapter treats of the benefit of redemption. There the Council says: " Quo factum est ut cœlestis
Pater......Jesum Christum filium suum ante legem et legis
tempore multis sanctis Patribus declaratum et promissum...
ad homines miserit ut et Judæos, qui sub lege erant, redi-
meret, et gentes quæ non sectabantur justitiam, justitiam
apprehenderent, atque omnes adoptionem filiorum recipe-
rent."

13. In the third chapter, the Council adds: " Verum
etsi ille pro omnibus mortuus est, non omnes tamen mortis
ejus beneficium recipiunt, sed ii duntaxat quibus meritum
passionis ejus communicatur. Nam sicut revera homines,
nisi ex semine Abrahæ nascerentur, non nascerentur in-

justi......ita, nisi in Christo renascerentur, nunquam justifica-
rentur, cum ea renascentia per meritum passionis ejus, gratia
qua justi fiunt illis tribuatur."

14. The fourth chapter treats of justification. In that
chapter the Council says, that by the words of the Apostle,
" Justificationis impii descriptio insinuatur ut sit translatio
ab eo statu in quo homo nascitur filius Adæ, in statum
gratiæ et adoptionis filiorum Dei per secundum Adam
Jesum Christum, quæ translatio post evangelium promulgatum sine lavacro regenerationis aut ejus voto fieri non
potest."

15. In the fifth chapter, the Fathers speak of the obligation of adults to prepare themselves for justification, and of
the manner in which they obtain it: they say that without
the preventing grace of God, calling and assisting them, without any merit on their part, men cannot prepare themselves
to return to God: and that, on the other hand, they do not
obtain justification unless they dispose themselves by
assenting to, and co-operating with, grace. Hence they
say: "Ipsius justificationis exordium in adultis a Dei per
Jesum Christum præveniente gratia, sumendum esse; hoc
est ab ejus vocatione nullis eorum existentibus meritis......
ut per ejus excitantem atque adjuvantem gratiam......ad
suam ipsorum justificationem eidem gratiæ assentiendo et
co-operando disponantur; ita ut tangente Deo cor hominis
......neque homo ipse nihil omnino agat, inspirationem
illam recipiens, quippe qui illam abjicere potest, neque tamen
sine gratia Dei movere se ad justitiam......libera sua volun-
tate possit. Unde......cum dicitur: *convertimini ad me
......et convertar ad vos*, (Zach. i. 3.) libertatis nostræ
admonemur, cum respondemus: *Converte nos Domine ad
te et convertemur*, (Thr. v. 21.) Dei nos gratia præve-
niri confitemur." Father Pius, the general of the Conventuals, proposed that after the words *illam recipiens*, the
following words should be added: " *Cum sit in sua potes-*

tate illam non recipere." But it was thought better to retain the words "*Quippe qui illam abjicere potest,*" because to receive grace is not in our power, since God bestows it upon us without us; but it is in our power to reject grace. Peter Soave says that the words of the council: "*neque homo ipse nihil omnino agat, inspirationem illam recipiens; quippe qui illam abjicere potest,*" do not accord with the doctrine of the Apostle that it is grace that separates the vessels of wrath from the vessels of mercy. But I answer, that the doctrine of the Council is conformable to that of the Apostle: for it is certain that man has nothing which he has not received from God: hence his co-operation in receiving the divine inspirations is a gift of God who, as the Council says after St. Augustine, "voluit esse merita nostra quæ sunt ipsius dona." But Soave rejoins, and says, that if we can reject the inspirations of God, it is useless to say to him with the Church: "Ad te nostras etiam rebelles compelle propitius voluntates." I answer with Natalis Alexander, that the word *compelle* does not mean co-action, but only an efficacious motion or persuasion. It is in this sense we are to understand the text in St. Luke: "Go out into the high ways and hedges, and compel them to come in that my house may be filled."— (xiv. 23.)

16. Hence the third canon was drawn up in the following words: "Si quis dixerit, sine præveniente Spiritus Sancti inspiratione atque ejus adjutorio hominem credere, sperare, diligere aut pœnitere posse sicut oportet, ut ei justificationis gratia conferatur, anathema sit."

17. Can. 4. "Si quis dixerit liberum arbitrium a Deo motum et excitatum nihil co-operari assentiendo Deo excitanti et vocanti quo ad obtinendam justificationis gratiam se disponat ac præparet; neque posse dissentire, si velit, sed veluti inanime quoddam nihil omnino agere, mereque passive se habere, anathema sit." At first this canon did not con-

tain the words, *liberum arbitrium*, but merely the word
hominem. Hence some proposed that the words "universe
loquendo" should be introduced; for, they added, there
might be an extraordinary vocation which a man could not
resist; such, said they as, according to St. Augustine was the
vocation of St. Paul. But the Fathers refused to add the
clause: they only changed the word *hominem* into *liberum
arbitrium.* And in this they acted wisely: for in the case
of an extraordinary and necessitating vocation (if such were
ever given) the liberty of election would not remain; and
by using the words *liberum arbitrium*, the question was
not touched.

18. Can 5, " Si quis liberum hominis arbitrium post
Adæ peccatum amissum et extinctum esse dixerit, aut rem
esse de solo titulo, immo titulum sine re, figmentum denique
a satana invectum in Ecclesiam anathema sit."

19. Can. 6. " Si quis dixerit non esse in potestate hominis
vias suas malas facere, sed mala opera, ita ut bona, Deum
operari non permissive solum, sed etiam proprie et per se, adeo
ut sit proprium ejus opus non minus proditio Judæ quam
vocatio Pauli, anathema sit."

20. In the sixth chapter, the Council speaks of the
manner in which an infidel or sinner is disposed to receive
grace, by various steps or good acts, such as by faith, by
the fear of divine justice, &c. " Disponuntur ad ipsam
justitiam, dum excitati divina gratia et adjuti, fidem ex
auditu concipientes, libere moventur in Deum, credentes vere
esse quæ divinitus revelata et promissa sunt, atque illud in
primis, a Deo justificari impium per gratiam ejus, per
redemptionem quæ est in Christo Jesu; et dum, peccatores
se esse intelligentes, a divinæ justitiæ timore, quo utiliter
concutiuntur, ad considerandam Dei misericordiam se con-
vertendo, in spem eriguntur, fidentes Deum sibi propter
Christum propitium fore." Here it is necessary to observe
that on the words " *a divinæ justitiæ timore,* some one

remarked that the justification of the sinner takes its origin from hope, and not from fear; but the contrary opinion prevailed, because the sinner begins to desire justification through the remorse for sin, which molests him, and excites in him at the same time a dread of the divine chastisements, and therefore fear is the first sentiment excited in the mind of the sinner.

21. The decree continues: "Illumque, tanquam omnis justitiæ fontem, diligere incipiunt; ac propterea moventur adversus peccata, per odium aliquod et detestationem, hoc est per eam pœnitentiam quam ante baptismum agi oportet." These last words were inserted in order to distinguish this penance from that which is required for the sacrament of penance. It is also necessary to know that at first the act of love was not mentioned in the decree; but the Fathers wished to reckon it among the other acts, in the words, "*diligere incipiunt.*" For, as Pallavicini relates, the following words are found in a written statement of the theologians: "It appears right to unite with the act of faith and hope some act of love; for if repentance proceeded entirely from fear without a love of justice, and if the punishment alone, and not the offence offered to God were the motive of sorrow it would be fruitless."

22. To this sixth chapter belong the seventh and eighth canons: Can. 7. "Si quis dixerit opera omnia quæ ante justificationem fiunt, quacumque ratione facta sint vere esse peccata vel odium Dei mereri, aut quanto vehementius quis nititur se disponere ad gratiam, tanto eum gravius peccare, anathema sit."

23. Can. 8. "Si quis dixerit gehennæ metum, per quem ad misericordiam Dei, de peccatis dolendo, confugimus vel a peccato abstinemus, peccatum esse aut peccatores pejores facere, anathema sit."

24. In the seventh chapter, the Council declares the nature and causes of justification. We have already said

that in the beginning the Fathers discussed the question whether faith alone is sufficient for the justification of the sinner: but all agreed that faith is the first disposition, and that charity alone is the formal cause of justification.

25. The writings of the heretics of the northern countries, contain innumerable errors on justification. One of the principal errors from which they deduce many others, is that man is justified by faith alone: but this is contrary to the Scriptures, which require other acts along with faith. First, an act of fear: " For he that is without fear, cannot be justified." (Eccl. i. 28.) Secondly, an act of hope: " He that trusteth in the Lord shall be healed." (Prov. xxviii. 25.) Thirdly an act of love: "He that loveth not abideth in death." (1. John iii. 14.) " Many sins are forgiven her, because she hath loved much." (Luke. vii. 47.) Besides, to receive the grace of justification our own co-operation is necessary: for without works, our faith is dead, according to the words of St. James: " For even as the body without the spirit is dead; so also faith without works is dead." (2. 26.) Hence St. Paul has written: " And if I should have all faith, so that I could remove mountains, and have not charity, I am nothing." (1. Cor. xiii. 2.)

26. The innovators object from the words of the apostle: " We account a man to be justified by faith without the works of the law." (Rom. iii. 28.) But I answer that faith also is necessary for justification, but is not of itself sufficient: for, the abovementioned acts are expressly prescribed as necessary in the Scriptures themselves. They also object from the following words of St. Paul to the Galatians: " knowing that man is not justified by the works of the law, but by the faith of Jesus Christ." (ii. 16.) But the meaning of this passage is that man is not justified by the works of the old law, or by works performed without the grace of Jesus Christ.

27. They again object from the acts of the Apostles (c.

13.) and from the Epistle to the Romans (c. 10.) where it is said that all who believe are justified and saved. But these passages mean that all who believe are justified, provided they do not fail in the acts required as a disposition to justification.

28. The Archbishop of Sienna attempted in the Council to maintain that man was justified by faith alone: but he was heard with general displeasure. Sanfelice, Bishop of Cava, impertinently defended the same doctrine, saying, that when a man has faith, justification follows, and that charity is its companion, but not its cause: I say *impertinently*, for after having seen his opinion reprobated in the first congregation, instead of changing, he continued to defend it in the following congregation: but this redounded greatly to his dishonour. Monsignor Contarini, Bishop of Bellino, defended the same doctrine, asserting that the works which precede justification, and dispose men to receive it, are only the signs of faith: but in the following congregation he retracted what he had said.

29. They were strenuously opposed by many learned theologians, and particularly by the Bishop of Bitonto, who said that justification is attributed to faith, not as to a proximate cause, but as to the first beginning. Bertan said that men are justified not by faith, but through faith, so that our justice is not faith but is obtained by means of faith. The Bishop of Senagaglia demonstrated at length that faith is the door to attain to justification, but is not of itself sufficient to obtain it. He also said incidentally that in obtaining justification we do nothing more than abstain from placing obstacles, or from resisting the divine grace which prevents us. We know not in what sense he made this assertion: but it is certain that in receiving justification the will of man, as the fathers declared in the beginning, concurs not passively or negatively but actively. " Eidem gratiæ," said they, " libere assentiendo et co-operando disponamur." (c. 5.) And in the fourth canon it was condemned to say: " Liberum arbitrium

H

a Deo motum nihil co-operari assentiendo Deo excitanti quo ad obtinendam justificationis gratiam se disponat."

30. The abovementioned bishops of Sienna, of Cava, and Bellino, as they gave dissatisfaction by attributing all justification to faith, and nothing to other acts, so they were heard with disgust when they attributed justification entirely to the merits of Christ, and nothing to the works of man, which dispose him to receive justification. But on the other hand, the Archbishop of Matera was heard with great pleasure: he said that the works which dispose to justification, though they depend on grace, are also our works, and that in declaring that justification is the work of grace, the Councils did not intend to forbid us to say that it is also our work. In proof of this doctrine, he quoted St. Augustine (in Ps. 145.) and St. Basil (sum. mor.)

31. Bernard Diaz, Bishop of Calaorra, said that infidels do not dispose themselves by any work of their own to merit the grace of vocation, which is a pure gift of God: but when called, it is in their power to resist or obey the call: and that then, if they return to God and receive baptism with faith, hope, and a detestation of sin, they obtain the divine grace. Thus in two things God operates in us without us, in the vocation to virtue and in the infusion of justice. It depends on us to accept both the one and the other, but not without the divine aid: vocation by obeying it, and justice by wishing to receive it from God who offers it to us. And in the use of these two gifts we co-operate with God in such a way that our good works belong entirely to God and entirely to us: to God as the principal agent, and to us the secondary cause. And when it is said that infidels do not dispose themselves by any work of their own to merit vocation, it should be understood that they cannot dispose themselves to merit it either *de condigno* or *de congruo:* for to have merit *de congruo*, an act must be not only a natural, but also a supernatural good work, and this cannot be said of

the works of an infidel, who, because he is without faith, cannot perform supernatural good works.

32. The Bishop of Castellamare, said that our works, inasmuch as they proceed solely from us, have no merit with regard to eternal salvation; that inasmuch as they come from preventing grace, they have merit *de congruo*: and that when they proceed from sanctifying grace, and from our free will they merit *de condigno*, an augmentation of grace, and the attainment of glory on account of the divine promise, which may be inferred from the words of St. Paul: "There is laid up for me a crown of justice." (2. Tim. iv. 8.) He adds, that for the first justification, an act of faith is necessary: because without an act, the habit is not infused, and without the habit of faith no man is justified. For the second justification, the act is not required, because the habit exists, for it is not lost by the sinner. He stated that he meant to speak of an express and formal act of faith; for some exercise of faith is always necessary.

33. The decree of the Council which we find in the 7th chapter was then framed: there it is said that when sinners have the necessary dispositions, justification follows, by which, from being enemies of God, they become his friends, and heirs of heaven: "Hanc dispositionem seu præparationem justificatio ipsa consequitur, quæ non est sola peccatorum remissio sed et sanctificatio et renovatio interioris hominis per voluntariam susceptionem gratiæ et donorum; unde homo ex injusto fit justus, et ex inimico amicus, ut sit hæres secundum spem vitæ æternæ." The causes of justification are then enumerated: "Hujus justificationis causæ sunt: finalis quidem, gloria Dei et Christi ac vita æterna: efficiens vero misericors Deus......meritoria Jesus Christus qui......in ligno crucis nobis justificationem meruit et pro nobis Deo Patri satisfecit: instrumentalis item, sacramentum Baptismi quod est sacramentum fidei sine qua nulli unquam contingit justificatio: demum unica formalis causa

est justitia Dei non qua ipse justus est, sed qua nos justos facit ......et non modo reputamur sed vere justi nominamur et sumus, justitiam in nobis recipientes; unusquisque suam, secundum mensuram quam Spiritus sanctus partitur singulis prout vult et secundum propriam cujusque dispositionem et co-operationem. Quamquam enim nemo possit esse justus, nisi cui merita passionis Domini nostri Jesu Christi communicantur: id tamen in hac impii justificatione fit dum ejusdem sanctissimæ passionis merito per Spiritum Sanctum charitas Dei diffunditur in cordibus eorum qui justificantur atque ipsis inhæret. Unde in ipsa justificatione cum remissione peccatorum hæc omnia simul infusa accipit homo per Jesum Christum, cui inseritur, fidem, spem et charitatem. Nam fides, nisi ad eam accedat spes et charitas, neque unit perfecte cum Christo, neque corporis ejus vivum membrum efficit. Qua ratione verissime dicitur fidem sine operibus mortuam et otiosam esse; et in Christo Jesu neque circumcisionem aliquid valere neque præputium, sed fidem quæ per charitatem operatur. Hanc fidem ante Baptismi sacramentum ex apostolorum traditione catechumeni ab Ecclesia petunt cum petunt fidem, vitam æternam præstantem, quam sine spe et charitate fides præstare non potest, &c."

34. In this decree were condemned the errors of Luther, who denied the internal justifying form, and asserted that man never became just, but was only reputed just by the imputation of the extrinsic justice of Jesus Christ. But the Council declared: " Causa formalis est justitia Dei, non qua ipse justus est, sed qua nos justos facit......et non modo reputamur sed vere justi sumus."

35. Hence, according to the doctrine of the Council, grace is formally impressed on the soul by a certain interior gift, which is united and intrinsic to it, and thus it purifies and sanctifies it according to the expression of the Apostle: " And such some of you were, but you are washed, but you are sanctified, but you are justified." Hence grace does not

consist in the imputation of the justice of Jesus Christ, nor solely in the remission of sins, but also in the interior renovation of man, who by means of grace is stripped of the old Adam, and clothed with the new man Jesus Christ. Hence the Apostle has written: " Be renewed in the spirit of your mind; and put on the new man, who according to God, is created in justice and holiness of truth." (Eph. iv. 23, 24.) Behold how clearly the internal renovation produced by grace, is expressed in this passage: since by means of grace, man is changed from an enemy to the friend and adopted child of God, and is, in the language of the Scripture, even made an heir of heaven. For by the mere pardon of a rebel he does not become the friend, and the adopted, and well beloved child of his sovereign. This is the effect of divine charity, which makes us acquire the friendship of God, and become his adopted children. " The charity of God is poured forth in our hearts by the Holy Ghost who is given to us." (Rom. v. 5.) And in the eighth chapter, (v. 15.) the Apostle adds: " You have received the spirit of adoption of sons, whereby we cry Abba (Father)." Thus it is not true, as our adversaries say, that the justice of Jesus Christ renders men just because it is imputed to them, but because by virtue of the justice of Jesus Christ, grace is infused which renders them just.

36. The innovators object, first from the words of St. Paul, " Who of God is made unto us wisdom, and justice, and sanctification." Behold they say, how the Apostle teaches that the justice of Jesus Christ is imputed to us and renders us just. I answer that the justice of Jesus Christ is the meritorious cause of our justice, and that through his merits is given to us the grace which renders us just. And, as in saying that Jesus Christ is made unto us wisdom, the Apostle did not mean to say that the wisdom of Jesus Christ is imputed to us, but that the wisdom of Jesus Christ renders us wise; so in saying that he was made unto us justice, St. Paul did not mean that the justice of Jesus Christ imputed to us, rendered

us just, but that his justice, that is his merits render us just, by means of sanctifying grace, which, as St. Peter says, (2 ep. 1.) makes us partakers of the divine nature.

37. They also object from the words of the Psalmist; "Blessed are they whose iniquities are forgiven, and whose sins are covered. Blessed is the man to whom the Lord hath not imputed guilt." (Ps. xxxi. 1, 2.) Behold, they say, how sins are not taken away, but are covered, by not being imputed to the sinner. The meaning of the passage is that sins are covered in such a way that they are really taken away and cancelled: for when it is said that any thing is covered before God to whom all things are known, it is signified that that thing is entirely taken away and destroyed. This is the exposition given by St. Augustine, of the psalm just quoted: and was insinuated by David when he said: "And according to the multitude of thy tender mercies, blot out my iniquity." (Ps. l.) He implored the Lord not to cover but to cancel his sin. And when the Baptist pointed out Jesus Christ, he said: "Behold the lamb of God, behold him who taketh away the sin of the world." (John i. 29.) What is cancelled and taken away is not covered, but is entirely destroyed, and this arises from the impossibility of grace and sin existing together in the soul. Hence Ezechiel said, that sins taken away by penance are cancelled before God, so that he, as it were, loses the remembrance of them. "But if the wicked do penance for all his sins......living he shall live and shall not die. I will not remember all his iniquities that he hath done." (xviii. 21, 22.) In saying "happy is the man to whom the Lord hath not imputed guilt," David meant to say that he is truly happy whose sin is cancelled by divine grace, and to whom the Lord on that account does not impute, but remits, both the guilt and the punishment.

38. In the abovementioned decree of the seventh chapter, was reprobated the opinion of Seripando, who held that there are two kinds of justice, one intrinsic, the other ex-

trinsic; the former, he said, makes us pass from the state of sinners to that of the children of God, and then makes us perform good works in virtue of the divine grace; the latter is not intrinsic to us, and this is the justice and merits of Christ, which are imputed to us as our own, according to the measure which God pleases. He then said that the first justice without the second was not perfect nor sufficient to make us obtain glory. This he endeavoured to infer from the words of St. Paul: "The sufferings of this time are not worthy to be compared with the glory to come, that shall be revealed in us." (Rom. viii. 18.) From these words he argued that justification is caused by faith and not by works, since the first justification of passing from enmity with God to his friendship, is the effect of the pure mercy of the Saviour, and not the reward of works, which, being performed before works performed cannot be meritorious. With regard to the justification, after justification, he said, that the justice of man was not attributed merely to his works, but also to faith, since by faith the second justice of Christ, which supplies our defects, is applied to us.

39. Only five theologians, and among them three were of his own order, approved of this opinion of Seripando, that to attain eternal life, the imputation of the justice of Jesus Christ was necessary. All the others opposed it, and particularly Father Lainez, of the Society of Jesus, who produced a long written reply to Seripando. In answer to him these theologians said, among other things, that there are two sorts of causes: one that produce an effect, which for its conservation does not stand in need of them, for example, a son continues in existence independently of his father. The others produce effects which depend on their causes as well for their preservation as for their production: for example, the light always depends on the sun. In this second form we depend on God, who preserves as well our temporal life, as the spiritual life of grace. Neither are the two kinds of

justice, one intrinsic, and the other extrinsic, by the imputation of the merits of Jesus Christ, necesary for the attainment of eternal glory; but the same intrinsic justice which
is the effect of the merit of Jesus Christ, makes us rise from
sin, and afterwards makes us perform works of eternal life
which obtain for us the glory of eternity, on account of the
promise which God has made to us in consideration of the
merits of the Saviour. Hence they concluded that the grace
which is gratuitiously infused into our souls applies to us
perfectly the merits of Christ; and that therefore it is not
necessary that the extrinsic should supply the deficiency of
the internal justice, which, according to Seripando, is defective; since the intrinsic is a participation of the extrinsic
justice, or of the justice of Christ.

40. Bellarmine says (controv. 3. de. justif. lib. 1, c. 2. circa.
finem.)that this opinion of Seripando was held before by Pighius,
who likewise maintained that man is justified partly by intrinsic justice, and partly by the imputation of the justice of
Christ: but it is contrary to the words of the Council:
" Unica formalis causa (justificationis) est justitia Dei, non
qua ipse justus est sed qua nos justos facit.   Hence
Bellarmine says: " Si justitia inhærens est formalis causa
absolutæ justificationis, non igitur requiritur imputatio
justitiæ Christi, quæ justificationem alioqui inchoatam et imperfectam absolvat." He adds,that this opinion of Pighius was
certainly condemned in the tenth canon, in which it is forbidden to say that we are formally just by the justice of Christ.

41. The opinion of the Bishop of Bitonto was also condemned :in the justification of sinners he distinguished two
kinds of justification: the first was the remission of sin, the
second, the acquisition of justice: he then said that the
former was had by the imputation of the justice of Christ,
and that the latter, in which justice is acquired, is produced by grace interiorly infused into the soul at the very
nstant that we are delivered from the state of sin, and is

not exteriorly imputed to us through the merits of Christ, as the Lutherans hold. But Bellarmine says, (de justif. l. 1, c. 2, vers. Quod si concilium), that this opinion that there are two formal causes of justification, viz., the remission of sin, and the infusion of grace, is contrary to the doctrine of the Council, which declared in the seventh chapter that there is but one formal cause, which is solely the justice of God infused into the soul and inherent in it. He adds that the Council makes separate mention of the remission of sins and of the infusion of grace to point out the two effects of the same cause, that is the deliverance of the sinner from the state of enmity with God, and his passing to that of the divine friendship by means of justification.

42. Fourthly, it is necessary to observe, that because some were of opinion that justification was produced by grace, distinct from charity, whilst others held that it was caused by charity itself, without any other justifying grace, the Council, in order to leave the question undecided, used these words indifferently, now one and again the other.

43. Fifthly, some said that in this decree charity was declared by the words, "*fidem quæ per charitatem ope-ratur*," to be the formal cause of justification, though in the preceding chapter, charity was mentioned only as a preparation for justification. But, it was said in answer, that in the preceding or sixth chapter, the Fathers, by the words, *diligere incipiunt*, meant charity which is not accompanied with justice, or rather the beginning of charity; but in the seventh chapter they spoke of perfect charity, which justifies the soul.

44. Sixthly, Pallavicini remarks, that in this chapter it was the intention of the Council to establish the infused habit of justice and not the act: for when some one wished it to be more expressly declared that in justification grace was given as an infused habit, he was told in answer that it was sufficiently expressed in the words, " Charitas Dei

ipsis inhærens:" inherence implies stability, which belongs to a habit, and not to an act.

45. Peter Soave says, that the words of the Council, (c. vii.) "*Justitiam in nobis recipientes, unusquisque suam, secundum mensuram quam Spiritus Sanctus partitur singulos prout vult,*" contradict what immediately follows, "*et secundum propriam cujusque dispositionem et co-operationem.*" If, he says, dispositions on the part of man be necessary, God does not give justice *prout vult;* and if he gives it *prout vult,* it should not be said that he gives it *secundum propriam cujusque dispositionem.* I answer, with St. Augustine, that grace "*voluntatem hominis et præparat adjuvandam, et adjuvat præparatam.*" Hence, the Council justly said: "*Secundum mensuram, prout (Spiritus Sanctus) vult,*" and justly added: "*et secundam propriam cujusque dispositionem et co-operationem.*"

46. To this chapter (7) belong the following canons: Canon 9. "Si quis dixerit sola fide impium justificari, ita ut intelligat nihil aliud requiri quod ad justificationis gratiam consequendam co-operetur, et nulla ex parte necesse esse eum suæ voluntatis motu præparari atque disponi anathema sit."

Can. 10. "Si quis dixerit homines, sine Christi justitia per quam nobis meruit, justificari, aut per eam ipsam formaliter justos esse, anathema sit."

Can. 11. "Si quis dixerit homines justificari vel sola peccatorum remissione, exclusa gratia et charitate, quæ in cordibus eorum per Spiritum Sanctum diffundatur atque illis inhæreat, aut etiam gratiam qua justificamur, esse tantum favorem Dei, anathema sit."

47. In the eighth chapter the Council explains how we are to understand the expressions of the Apostle, that the sinner is justified by faith, and that he is justified gratuitously: "Arbitramur enim justificari hominem per fidem." (Rom.

iii. 28.) "Justificati gratis per gratiam." (Rom. iii. 24.)
The Council says: "Ut scilicet per fidem ideo justificari
dicamur quia fides est humanæ salutis initium, fundamen-
tum et radix omnis justificationis. Gratis autem justificari
ideo dicimur quia nihil eorum quæ justificationem præcedunt,
sive fides, sive opera, ipsam justificationis gratiam prome-
retur." In this passage the Council does not speak of merit
de congruo, but of merit *de condigno:* for when some
wished these words to be omitted, as being prejudicial to
works done through faith, it was said in answer that even
such works do not merit justification as due to them: hence
it appears that the Council spoke of merit *de condigno*.
And when the discussion took place on the manner in which
the words of the Apostle, "Justificati gratis per gratiam,
&c.," should be explained, some said that they ought to be
explained by saying that faith is a gratuitous gift of God;
but this did not please the Fathers, because even when a
sinner has faith, it is true to say that God justifies him gratuitously. Others wished to have it declared that *justification is effected without works:* but this was also rejected,
because besides faith, certain other works are necessary as a
disposition for justification. Hence the Council justly
approved the words above mentioned, in which it was denied
that works which precede justification have merit *de condigno*, but not that they have merit *de congruo*.

48. In the ninth chapter, the Council censures the
vain confidence of the innovators, that on account of it their
sins are remitted or have been remitted, and also the doctrine that no one is ever justified unless he believes with
certainty that he is justified. In that chapter the Fathers
declared that every one should be fearful, because no one
can know with the certainty of faith which cannot deceive
him, that he has obtained the divine grace. Thus, without
a special revelation from God, no one can believe, with the
certainty of divine faith, that God has pardoned his sins.

" Man knoweth not whether he be worthy of love or hatred."
(Eccl. ix. 1.)   Hence the Apostle said: my conscience does
not charge me with any present guilt: but I do not on that
account hold myself justified.   "I am not conscious to
myself of anything, yet I am not hereby justified." (1 Cor.
iv. 4.)   And the Prophet Jeremiah said: "The heart is
perverse above all things, and unsearchable, who can know
it?" (Jer. xvii. 9.)   Hence, no one who is certain of having
once rebelled against the divine majesty, can know with an
absolute certainty that his heart has been sincerely converted
again to God.

49. The innovators object, first from the words of the
Apostle: " The spirit himself giveth testimony to our spirit,
that we are the sons of God." (Rom. viii. 16.) But I answer
that the Holy Ghost gives us this testimony, not by divine
revelation, nor by infallible signs, but only by means of
certain conjectures which cannot produce any other than pre-
sumptive and moral certainty.   This is the doctrine of the
Holy Fathers. (See Bellarmine lib. 3, de Justif. c. 9, 10.)

50. Secondly, they say that Christian hope is compared to
an anchor, (Hebr. vi. 19.) on account of its unshaken firmness;
and they add, that this hope can never be firm unless we believe
with the most perfect certainty that our sins have been pardoned. We answer that, on the part of God, divine hope is not
only most certain, but even infallible, with the infallibility of
divine faith: hence it is thus defined by St. Thomas: " Hope
is a certain expectation of beatitude."   Yes, it is certain:
for as the holy doctor says, "it depends principally on the
divine omnipotence and mercy." (2. 2. qu. 18. a. 4.)   And
it is certain with the certainty of faith that these two attributes exist in God.   But the attainment of the object of
hope depends not only on God, but also on our own co-operation: in this we may fail if not at present, at least at
some future time, as the Council of Trent teaches in the
ninth chapter: " Quilibet, dum propriam infirmitatem

respicit, et de sua gratia dubitare potest." Hence in the twelfth and thirteenth chapters, the Council adds, that no one can promise himself with absolute certainty that he is in the state of grace, or that he will persevere in it.

51. However, Tournely justly says, that although sanctifying grace does not exclude all fear from the soul, still Christian hope is capable of expelling that excessive fear which tortures the souls of the just, and is sufficient to give them a moral certainty that they are the friends of God, and thus makes them enjoy a prudent peace of conscience, "Quo fit," he says, "ut legitima conscientiæ pace perfruantur." But this does not arise from their having the certainty of faith that they are in the state of grace, as the heretics say, but from the practice of charity towards God; this is the doctrine of St. Ambrose, St. Augustine, and St. Bernard, (in Cant.)

52. The innovators wrongly confound the certainty of faith with that of confidence, (confidence is the hope which arises from faith): but they err, for the certainty of faith excludes every doubt; but the certainty of confidence which rests not only on the divine promises, but also on our own co-operation, which may be wanting, can never be absolutely infallible. Hence it follows, as we have said, that without a special revelation no one can believe with the certainty of faith that he is in the state of grace, much less that he is predestined: these two errors were embraced and taught by Calvin.

53. Soave, in his history, conceals the arguments in favour of the doctrine of the Council, and puts forward reasons for the contrary error which ascribes to all the just a pretended certainty that they are in the state of grace. Among other things, he quotes the words of the Redeemer to the Paralytic: "Be of good heart, son, thy sins are forgiven thee." (Mat. ix. 2.) Behold, he says, how the paralytic, through the confidence of forgiveness, was pardoned. But I answer that

I

our Lord who gave the paralytic the gift of hope and faith,
gave him also the grace of charity, and repentance, by means
of which he received pardon.

54. Father Pius, general of the Conventuals, wished that
the Council would, in conformity with the doctrine of Scotus,
except a particular case in which it would be possible for
a person to believe with the certainty of faith that he was in
the state of grace. But the Archbishop of Nassia proved
at length that no one could have such certainty except by a
special revelation from God: since the Apostle, who had so
many proofs of being the friend of God, was fearful, and
said of himself: "I am not conscious to myself of anything,
yet I am not hereby justified." (1 Cor. iv. 4.) And Cardinal Pacecco quoted the text in the last chapter, (de purg.
can.), in which Innocent III. charged with temerity a certain
archbishop who wished to swear that his sins were forgiven.

55. Hence in this ninth chapter the Council says:
"Quamvis autem necessarium sit credere neque remitti
neque remissa unquam fuisse peccata, nisi gratis divina misericordia propter Christum, neminem tamen fiduciam et cer-
titudinem remissionis peccatorum suorum jactanti......pec-
cata dimitti dicendum est, cum apud hæreticos......contra
ecclesiam catholicam prædicetur vana hæc fiducia. Sed
neque illud asserendum est, oportere eos qui vere justificati
sunt, absque ulla omnino dubitatione apud semetipsos sta-
tuere se esse justificatos, neminemque......justificari nisi
eum qui certo credat se justificatum esse, atque hac sola fide
......justificationem perfici; quasi qui hoc non credit, de
Dei promissis deque mortis et resurrectionis Christi efficacia
dubitet. Nam sicut nemo pius de Dei misericordia, de
Christi merito deque sacramentorum virtute et efficacia dubitare debet, sic quilibet dum......propriam infirmitatem......
respicit, de sua gratia......timere potest; cum nullus scire
valeat certitudine fidei, cui non potest subesse falsum, se
gratiam Dei esse consecutum."

56. Notwithstanding this decree, Catherinus continued to maintain, as he did before, that in some particular case we might be able to believe with divine faith that a person is in the state of grace. He distinguished two sorts of faith, one catholic, that is universal, in the articles approved by the Church, and the objects of this faith, he said, cannot be false; so that when the Church proposes an object as of faith, that object can never be false. We may, he said, have another sort of faith regarding a particular object which depends at the same time on a dogma of faith, and on some truth known as certain by the light of nature. For example, it is certain that a person who is just baptized, is free from original guilt: on the other hand, I know that I have baptized an infant: I can then make an act of faith, since the object is really true, that the infant is free from sin, by applying to this particular case what the Church defines in general. But, although I can by that moral evidence believe that the infant is free from sin, still the object may possibly be false: for the liquid which I considered to be water might have been distilled from herbs, and invalid matter for the sacrament of Baptism. Such the reasoning of Catherinus.

57. Bellarmine (de justif. lib. 3, c. 3,) and Soto censure this opinion: they say that although it differs widely from the heresy of Luther, still it is justly considered to be erroneous: for the Council says: " Quilibet de sua gratia timere potest cum nullus scire valeat certitudine fidei se gratiam Dei esse consecutum." In answer to Soto, Catherinus said that the Fathers spoke of that kind of faith which can never be liable to error, such as Catholic faith, and that therefore, after the words *certitudine fidei*, they added, *cui non potest subesse falsum:* but that he spoke of particular faith, which might be liable to error, because its object was not declared by the Church. But Bellarmine says, that there is a contradiction in saying that a matter is revealed

by God; and that it can be false, since divine faith is absolutely infallible: whatever then can be false, can never be an object of faith.

58. To this chapter belong the twelfth, thirteenth, fourteenth, and twenty-eighth canons. Can. 12. "Si quis dixerit fidem justificantem nihil aliud esse quam fiduciam divinæ misericordiæ peccata remittentis propter Christum vel eam fiduciam solam esse qua justificamur, anathema sit."

59. Can. 13: "Si quis dixerit omni homini ad remissionem peccatorum assequendam necessarium esse ut credat certo et absque ulla hæsitatione propriæ infirmitatis et indispositionis peccata sibi esse remissa, anathema sit."

60. Can. 14. "Si quis dixerit hominem a peccatis absolvi ac justificari ex eo quod se absolvi ac justificari certo credat, aut neminem vere esse justificatum nisi qui credit se esse justificatum, ac hac sola fide absolutionem et justificationem perfici, anathema sit."

61. Can. 28. "Si quis dixerit, amissa per peccatum gratia, simul et fidem semper amitti; aut fidem, quæ remanet non esse veram fidem, licet non sit viva; aut eum qui manet sine charitate habet non esse Christianum, anathema sit."

62. In the tenth chapter, the Council treats of the augmentation of justification received by means of good works, and says: "Sic ergo justificati......euntes de virtute in virtutem, &c., per observationem mandatorum Dei et ecclesiæ, in ipsa justitia per Christi gratiam accepta, cooperante fide, bonis operibus crescunt atque magis justificeantur."

63. To this chapter belongs the following canon (24): "Si quis dixerit justitiam acceptam non conservari, neque etiam augeri coram Deo per bona opera, sed opera ipsa fructus solummodo et signa esse justificationis adeptæ, non autem ipsius augendæ causam, anathema sit."

64. In the eleventh chapter it is said, that the fulfilment of the commandments is necessary for salvation, and that man is able, with the aid of the divine grace, to observe them: "Nemo quantumvis justificatus, liberum se esse ab observatione mandatorum putare debet: nemo temeraria illa......voce uti, Dei precepta homini justificato ad observandum esse impossibilia. Nam Deus impossibilia non jubet, sed jubendo monet et facere quod possis, et petere quod non possis, et adjuvat ut possis." This sentence is taken from St. Augustine (de nat. et gr. c. 43.) except the last words *et adjuvat ut possis*, which are taken from other parts of the works of the saint, and were justly added to show that the impossibility of fulfilling the divine precepts can arise only from the neglect of prayer.

65. And, because the innovators objected against this doctrine, from certain passages of Scripture: such as that the just man falls daily, and that we should ask every day the forgrveness of our sins, the Council gave the following answer: "Licet enim in hac mortali vita quantumvis sancti in levia saltem et quotidiana, quæ venialia dicuntur, peccata quandoque cadunt, non propterea desinunt esse justi: nam ......justi ipsi eo magis se obligatos ad ambulandum in via justitiæ sentire debent, quo, liberati jam a peccato......pie viventes proficere possint &c., Deus namque sua gratia semel justificatos non deserit, nisi ab eis prius deseratur." Here Pallivicini remarks that the Council by these last words did not mean to say that God abandons us by taking from us the habit of grace, and dissolving the friendship which he had contracted with us, but intended to declare that unless we offend him, he does not abandon us by depriving us of his actual grace. And this he proves from the fact that in the first draft of the decree, there were other words which signified the actual grace of the divine aid, and not the habitual grace of the justifying form. In the first draft, it was said that such grace frequently prevents us from aban_

I 2

doning God, and sometimes is the cause why God returns to them who abandon him. These words could certainly be understood only of actual grace. And Pallavicini asserts that they were omitted for the sake of brevity.

66. It was then added: "Itaque nemo sibi in sola fide blandiri debet, putans fide sola se hæredem esse constitutum ......etiamsi Christo non compatiatur &c., Propterea Apostolus monet justificatos dicens......Castigo corpus meum et in servitutem redigo; ne forte cum aliis prædicavero ipse reprobus efficiar (1. Cor. ix. 27.) Item Petrus: satagite ut per bona opera certam vestram vocationem et electionem faciatis. (2. Ep. i. 10.)......Unde constat eos orthodoxæ doctrinæ adversari qui justum in omni bono opere saltem venialiter peccare, aut, quod intolerabilius est, pœnas æternas mereri; atque etiam eos qui statuunt in omnibus operibus justos peccare......si in illis mercedem quoque intuentur æternam, &c."

67. The following canons were then drawn up. (Can. 18.) " Si quis dixerit Dei præcepta homini, etiam justificatio et sub gratia constituto esse ad observandum impossibilia, anathema sit."

68. Can. 19: " Si quis dixerit nihil præceptum esse in Evangelio præter fidem, cætera esse indifferentia neque præcepta neque prohibita, sed libera; aut decem præcepta nihil pertinere ad Christianos, anathema sit."

69. Can. 20: " Si quis hominem justificatum et quantumlibet perfectum dixerit non teneri ad observationem mandatorum Dei et Ecclesiæ sed tantum ad credendum, quasi vero Evangelium sit nuda et absoluta promissio vitæ æternæ, sine conditione observationis mandatorum, anathema sit."

70. Can. 21: " Si quis dixerit Christum Jesum a Deo hominibus datum fuisse ut redemptorem cui fidant, non etiam ut legislatorem cui obediant, anathema sit."

71. Can. 25: " Si quis in quolibet bono opere justum saltem venialiter peccare dixerit aut quod intolerabilius est

mortaliter, atque ideo pœnas æternas mereri, tantumque ob id non damnari quia Deus ea opera non imputat ad damnationem, anathema sit."

72. Can. 31: " Si quis dixerit justificatum peccare dum intuitu æternæ mercedis bene operatur, anathema sit."

73. In the twelfth chapter the Council declares that it is temerity in any one to presume without a special revelation that he is predestined: " Nemo......præsumere debet ut certo statuat se omnino esse in numero prædestinatorum, quasi verum esset quod justificatus amplius peccare non possit; aut, si peccaverit, certam sibi resipiscentiam promittere debeat: nam, nisi ex speciali revelatione scire non potest quos Deus sibi elegerit.

74. To this chapter belong the 17th and 30th canons: "Si quis justificationis gratiam, nonnisi prædestinatis ad vitam contingere dixerit, reliquos vero omnes qui vocantur, vocari quidem, sed gratiam non accipere, utpote divina potestate prædestinatos ad malum, anathema sit." (Can. 17.)

Canon 30: " Si quis post acceptam justificationis gratiam cuilibet peccatori pœmtemti ita culpam remitti et reatum æternæ pœne deleri dixerit ut nullus remaneat reatus pœnæ temporalis exsolvendæ vel in hoc sæculo vel in futuro purgatorio, antequam ad regna cœlorum aditus patere possit, anathema sit."

75. In the thirteenth chapter, the Council speaks of the gift of perseverance. The innovators say that the grace of justification once obtained, cannot be lost. But this is clearly contrary to the Scriptures. "When the just man turneth himself away from his justice, and committeth iniquity, he shall die therein." (Ezech. xviii. 26.) In the same chapter (v. 24.) the prophet says: " But if the just man turn himself away from his justice, and do iniquity......all his justices which he hath done will not be remembered." In the Scriptures themselves, there are several examples of just men, (such as David, St. Peter, &c.) who by sin lost the grace of justification. Infants are certainly justified by

baptism: Calvin even says, but the assertion is heretical, that all the children of the faithful are born just, and adds that when adults are baptized, they cannot lose the grace of God nor be lost. But how many of them in their youth lose the divine grace! Experience shows too clearly that many fall away from justice. St. Paul says: "The unjust shall not possess the kingdom of God." (1. Cor. vi. 9.) In this place, St. Paul speaks of the sins of Christians. Hence it follows that every one who is baptized can forfeit innocence, and be lost. It also follows that the grace of justification is not given exclusively to the elect, as Calvin taught.

76. Against this doctrine our adversaries object from the words of St. John: "Whosoever is born of God committeth not sin, for his seed abideth in him, and he cannot sin." (1 John iii. 9.) The Apostle says that he who is born of God cannot sin, that is if he act as a child of God; for then the seed of God, that is, charity which cannot co-exist with sin, preserves him from sin; but St. John does not mean that he who is born of God cannot sin if he act as a child of Adam: for then he may fall into sin. It is thus St. Augustine explains the preceding passage of St. John.

77. The Council then says that all should hope in God for the gift of perseverance, but that they should also fear, lest they may lose it. " Similiter de perseverantiæ munere... nemo sibi certi aliquid absoluta certitudine polliceatur: tametsi in Dei auxilio firmissimam spem collocare et reponere omnes debent. Deus enim, nisi illi ipsius gratiæ defuerint, sicut cœpit opus bonum, ita perficiet, operans velle et perficere. Verumtamen, qui existimant stare videant ne cadant, et cum timore et tremore salutem suam operentur."

78. To this chapter correspond the 16th, 22nd, 'and 23rd canons. Canon 16. " Si quis magnum illud usque in finem perseverantiæ donum se certo habiturum absoluta et infallibili certitudine dixerit, nisi hoc ex speciali revelatione didicerit, anathema sit."

79. Canon 22. " Si quis dixerit, justificatum, vel sine spe-

ciali auxilio Dei in accepta justitia perseverare posse, vel
eum eo non posse, anathema sit." By this canon was also
condemned the opinion of John Fonseca, Bishop of Castela-
mare, who asserted that ordinarily a just man does not stand
in need of a special aid to observe the commandments; but
that for him the general assistance which is not withheld
from any one in a state of grace, is sufficient, and that a special help is required only when he has to fulfil any precept
of extraordinary difficulty.

80. Canon 23. " Si quis hominem semel justificatum
dixerit amplius peccare non posse neque gratiam amittere,
atque ideo cum qui labitur et peccat nunquam vere fuisse
justificatum; aut contra posse in tota vita peccata omnia
etiam venialia, vitare, nisi ex speciali Dei privilegio, quemadmodum de Beata virgine tenet Ecclesia, anathema sit."

81. The fourteenth chapter treats of the manner in which
they who have lost grace, may recover it: we there read:
" Qui vero ab accepta justificationis gratia per peccatum
exciderunt, rursus justificari poterunt......per Pœnitentiæ
sacramentum......etenim......Christus Jesus sacramentum
instituit Pœnitentiæ cum dixit: Accipite Spiritum Sanctum;
quorum remiseritis peccata, remittuntur eis, &c. Unde
docendum est Christiani hominis pœnitentiam aliam esse a
baptismali, eaque contineri non modo cessationem a peccatis
et detestationem eorum,......verum etiam eorumdem sacramentalem confessionem, saltem in voto et suo tempore faciendam, et sacerdotalem absolutionem: itemque satisfactionem
per jejunia, &c., non quidam pro pœna æterna, quæ cum
culpa remittitur, sed pro pœna temporali, quæ non tota
semper, ut in Baptismo fit, dimittitur illis, &c." The same
doctrine was defined in the Council of Florence in the
decree of Pope Eugenius.

82. The twenty-ninth canon was then drawn up: " Si
quis dixerit eum qui post Baptismum lapsus est non posse
per Dei gratiam resurgere, aut posse quidem, sed sola fide,

amissam justitiam recuperare sine sacramento Pœnetentiæ, prout sancta romana et universalis ecclesia, a Christo Domino et ejus apostolis edocta, hucusque professa est, servavit et docuit, anathema sit."

83. In the fifteenth chapter it is declared that grace but not faith is lost by every mortal sin. "Non modo infidelitate......sed etiam quocumque alio mortali peccato gratiam amitti, &c." Some proposed that the word *apostasia* should be substituted for *infidelitate:* but the latter was retained because it was opposed to the language of Luther, who used the word *infidelitate*.

84. The twenty-seventh canon was then framed: " Si quis dixerit nullum esse mortale peccatum, nisi infidelitatis, aut nullo alio, quamtumvis gravi et enormi, præterquam infidelitatis peccato, semel acceptam gratiam amitti, anathema sit."

85. Canon 28. " Si quis dixerit amissa per peccatum gratia, simul et fidem semper amitti; aut fidem quæ permanet non esse veram fidem, licet non sit viva; aut eum qui fidem sine charitate habet non esse Christianum, anathema sit."

86. The sixteenth chapter treats of merits and good works. For greater clearness, it will be useful to make a distinction between merit *de condigno*, and merit *de congruo*, and to explain the conditions of each. Merit *de condigno* is that to which, on account of a promise on the part of God, a reward is due in justice. Merit *de congruo* is that to which God grants a favour, not as due in justice but on account of a certain fitness or congruity.

87. For merit *de condigno*, three conditions are necessary: one on the part of the person who performs the work, another on the part of the work, and the third on the part of God. On the part of the person who performs the work, it is necessary that he be in the state of grace, and that he be in the state of probation. If he be separated from God

he can acquire no merit. "As the branch cannot bear fruit of itself unless it abide in the vine, so neither can you unless you abide in me." (John xv. 4.) He must also be in a state of probation. For after death man is out of the way and is no longer capable of merit or of demerit. Hence the Apostle exhorts us to do good during life, because after death we can gain no merit: "Behold now is the acceptable time; behold now is the day of salvation." (2 Cor. vi. 2.) "Whilst we have time, let us work good." (Gal. vi. 10.)

88. On the part of the work it is necessary, as Silvius and Suares hold, that it be good in itself, that it proceed from a supernatural motive, and that it be referred to God at least with a virtual intention when it is performed. Besides, it is necessary that it be performed, not through any absolute or relative necessity, but with full liberty: hence for merit, the liberty which consists in freedom from *co-action*, is not sufficient, as Jansenius erroneously taught. His doctrine was condemned as heretical in the third proposition extracted from his works.

89. On the part of God, a compact or promise is required, for God cannot be bound to give a reward, except by his own promise. St. Augustine says, (in Ps. 83,) "Debitorem Dominus ipse se fecit, non accipiendo, sed promittendo. Non ei dicimus: redde quod accepisti, sed redde quod promisisti."

90. With regard to merit *de congruo*, it is necessary that the work be good, free, and supernatural; but it is not necessary that the person who performs the work be in the state of grace, since the good work itself disposes him to receive sanctifying grace. Neither is a promise necessary on the part of God, for a supernatural good work has of itself a congruous efficacy to obtain from God the favour which is *de congruo* suited to it.

91. The Lutherans and Calvinists not only hold that

faith alone justifies the soul; but they also assert that the works of the just are not at all meritorious, that, on the contrary, they are real sins, because the sin of Adam renders sinful all the works of his descendants: however they say that such sins are not imputed to the just. But this doctrine is at variance with the words of our Lord: " Be glad and rejoice, for your reward is very great in heaven." (Mat. v. 12.) A reward corresponds to good works and to true merit.

92. They object from the words of Isaias. " All our justices are as the rag of a menstruous woman." (lxiv. 6.) I answer that there the Prophet spoke not of the works of the just, but of the iniquities of the Jews, in punishment of which they were all to fall into the hands of the king of Babylon. This is the exposition which St. Cyril gives of the preceding text. But that the works of the just are good is clear from the words of Jesus Christ: " Let your light shine before men, that they may see your good works and glorify your Father who is in heaven." (Mat. v. 16.) Hence St. Peter has written: " Wherefore brethren, labour the more, that by good works you may make sure your calling and election." (2 Peter i. 10.) If all works were sins the very exercise of faith itself by means of which alone the adversaries say, man is justified, would be sinful; it would also be a sin to ask pardon, or to say *forgive us our trespasses;* yet man would even be justified by sin itself when by means of that petition (which because it would be an act of fallen man, should be criminal,) he would obtain the pardon of his sins. What intolerable absurdities.

93. They rejoin and say, that merits on the part of man detract from the merits of Jesus Christ. I answer in one word that the merits of the just have efficacy not from themselves, but from the merits of Jesus Christ, from which proceeds whatsoever is good in them.

94. They also object from the words of Jesus Christ to

his disciples: "When you shall have done all these things that are commanded you, say: we are unprofitable servants; we have done that which we ought to do." (Luke xvii. 10.) From these words, they say, it appears that the works of the just are not truly meritorious. I answer, that our works are said to be unprofitable, not because they are not meritorious, but because without grace they would be of no value, and without a promise on the part of God, they would profit nothing to salvation: and the more so since in all our good works, we do what we are bound to do.

95. But let us now attend to the doctrine of the Council: "Justificatis......sive acceptam gratiam perpetuo conservaverint sive amissam recuperaverint......proponenda est vita æterna et tanquam gratia filiis per Christum Jesum misericorditer promissa et tanquam merces ex ipsius Dei promissione ipsorum meritis reddenda &c. Cum enim ille ipse Christus Jesus, tanquam caput in membra et vitis in palmites, in ipsos justificatos jugiter influat; quæ virtus bona eorum opera semper antecedit et comitatur et subsequitur, et sine qua nullo pacto Deo grata et meritoria esse possent; nihil ipsis justificatis amplius deesse credendum est quo minus plene divinæ legi satisfecisse et vitam æternam......si tamen in gratia decesserint, consequendam vere promeruisse censeantur &c. Ita neque propria nostra justitia, tanquam ex nobis propria statuitur, neque reputatur justitia Dei. Quæ enim justitia nostra dicitur quia per eam nobis inhærentem justificamur, illa eadem Dei est quia a Deo infunditur per Christi meritum......Licet bonis operibus merces tribuatur &c., absit tamen ut Christianus homo in seipso confidat vel glorietur, et non Domino; cujus tanta est erga homines bonitas ut eorum velit esse merita quæ sunt ipsius dona," &c. All the words of this chapter are taken either from the Scripture, or from the writings of the Saints, and particularly of St. Augustine.

96. To this last chapter correspond the twenty-sixth,

thirty-first, and thirty-second canons. (Can. 26.) " Si quis
dixerit justos non debere pro bonis operibus quæ in Deo
fuerint facta expectare et sperare æternam retributionem a
Deo per ejus misericordiam et Jesu Christi meritum, si bene
agendo et divina mandata custodiendo, usque in finem per-
severaverint, anathema sit."

97. Can. 31 : " Si quis dixerit justificatum peccare dum
intuitu, æternæ mercedis bene operatur anathema sit."

98. Can. 32: " Si quis dixerit hominis justificati bona
opera ita esse dona Dei ut non sint etiam bona ipsius justificati merita, aut ipsum justificatum bonis operibus, quæ ab
eo per Dei gratiam et Jesu Christi meritum cujus vivum
membrum est, fiunt, non vere mereri augmentum gratiæ,
vitam æternam et ipsius vitæ æternæ (si tamen in gratia
discesserit) consequutionem atque etiam gloriæ augmentum,
anathema sit."

99. From this canon we infer that the doctrine of the
innovators, viz. that all the just are equal in justice, is most
false: (Luther blasphemously asserted that his wife was as
holy as the Blessed Virgin.) St. John says that justice
may be increased: " He that is just, let him be justified
still, and he that is holy, let him be sanctified still." (Apoc.
c. 22.). Since then, each person may obtain an increase of
justice proportioned to his co-operation, all cannot be equal
in merit.

Can. 33. " Si quis dixerit per hanc doctrinam catholicam
de justificatione, a sancta synodo hoc præsenti decreto ex-
pressam aliqua ex parte gloriæ Dei vel meritis Jesu Christi
Domini nostri derogari, et non potius veritatem fidei nostræ,
Dei denique ac Christi Jesu gloriam illustrari anathema sit."

APPENDIX.—*On the manner on which operates.*

In our little congregation, we teach that in order to fulfil
the commandments, grace intrinsically efficacious is necessary,
and that every one can obtain this efficacious grace, with

the aid of the sufficient grace of payer, which is given to all.

100. Our system is this; that to do good and to fulfil the commandments sufficient grace, which only gives strength to do what is easy, is not enough, but that intrinsically efficacious grace which determines the will of man to do good, is necessary. We also say that this efficacious grace generally produces its effect by victorious delectation, but sometimes determines the consent of the will by other motives, such as hope, fear, &c. as St. Augustine teaches, saying that God draws men to himself by innumerable and admirable means. We also say that sufficient grace gives to all strength to pray actually if they wish (this is reckoned among the things that are easy) and that all who wish, can by prayer obtain all the efficacious graces necessary for the observance of all the commandments. All these things are explained at length in the book on prayer: here they are stated briefly.

101. It is certain that God wills the salvation of all: " Who," says St. Paul, " will have all men to be saved, and to come to the knowledge of the truth." (1 Tim. ii. 4.) And St. Peter writes: " Not willing that any should perish, but that all should return to penance." (2 Pet. iii. 9.) God complains, by the prophet Ezechiel, of them who voluntarily bring themselves to perdition. " Why will you die, O house of Israel......return ye and live." (18, 31, 32.) Hence, because he wills the salvation of all, the Lord gives to all the graces necessary to obtain eternal life. And we say that if he does not give to all efficacious grace, he at least gives them grace, by which, without the aid of any other grace, they may if they wish pray actually, and by prayer obtain every efficacious grace necessary to fulfil the law, and to be saved. This doctrine is maintained by Cardinal Norris, by Isambert, by Petavius, Thòmassinus, Cardinal du Perron, Alphonsus le Monie, and by several others to whom we shall hereafter refer, and at greater length and

professedly by Honoratus Tournely. (Præl. theol. t. 3, q. 7, a. 4, concl. 5, p. 553.)

102. Cardinal Norris (Jansen. error. calumnia sublata. c. 2, s. 1,) proves that every man in the present state has the help *sine quo*, that is the sufficient or ordinary grace, which, without requiring other aid, makes us pray, and thus obtain abundant and efficacious grace to fulfil the commandments: "Etiam in statu naturæ lapsæ datur adjutorium *sine quo*, secus ac Jansenius contendit; quod quidem adjutorium efficit in nobis actus debiles, nempe orationes minus fervidas pro adimplendis mandatis; in ordine ad quorum executionem adjutorium *sine quo* est tantum auxilium remotum, impetratorium tamen auxilii *quo*, sive gratiæ efficacis, qua mandata implentur." He adds, that if tepid prayer does not obtain efficacious grace, it at least obtains the grace to make more fervent petitions, which procure the efficacious graces we stand in need of. "Colligo ipsammet tepidam orationem fieri a nobis cum adjutorio *sine quo non*, ac ordinario concursu Dei, cum sint actus debiles, &c.; et tamen tepida oratione impetramus spiritum ferventioris orationis, qui nobis adjutorio *quo* donatur." This he confirms by the authority of St. Augustine, who on the seventeenth psalm has written: "Ego libera et valida intentione preces ad te direxi, quoniam ut hanc habere possem, exaudisti me infirmius orantem."

103. The same author says in the same place, that every one has the proximate power to pray, in order to obtain by prayer the proximate power to perform good works; and therefore all can pray if they wish, with the sole assistance of the ordinary grace without any other aid. Otherwise, says this most learned Cardinal, if for the proximate power to pray actually another power to obtain at least the grace of more fervent prayer, were necessary, for this power another grace should be required, and thus it would be necessary to proceed to infinity. "Manifestum est poten-

tiam ad orandum debere esse proximam in justo sive fideli: nam si fidelis sit in potentia remota ad simpliciter orandum (non enim hic loquor de fervida oratione), non habebit aliam potentiam pro impetranda oratione; alias procederetur in infinitum."

104. The most learned Denis Petavius asks why God imposes on us precepts which we cannot observe with the common or ordinary grace? Because (I answer with Du Valle and other theologians) the Lord, as the generality of the holy Fathers say, wishes that we have recourse to him by prayer. Hence I infer that we should hold as certain that every one has the proximate grace to pray actually, and by prayer to obtain greater help to do what he is unable to do with the aid of ordinary grace; otherwise God would have imposed upon us a law the observance of which would be impossible: the reason is evident.

105. To this I add another very strong reason: since God commands all actually to observe the commandments, it must certainly be supposed that he ordinarily gives to all at least the remote grace with which at least by prayer they can actually fulfil the law. In order then that the law be reasonable and that the reproof and punishment of all who transgress it, be just, it is necessary that every one have sufficient strength at least by means of prayer, actually to fulfil the commandments, and to pray actually without any other aid not common to all: otherwise were the proximate power to pray actually not given to all, it could not be said that every one has from God sufficient grace to enable him actually to fulfil the law. Hence Petavius (Theol. dogm. tom. 1, lib. 10, cap. 19, 20,) proves at length that with sufficient grace alone, without other aid, man performs actual good works; and he goes so far as to assert that to say the contrary would be *monstrous* (monstruosum esset), and that this is the doctrine, not only of theologians but of the Church. Hence, he concludes that the grace to observe

K 2

the commandments actually, follows prayer, and that God grants the gift of prayer at the very moment he imposes the command. " Donum istud quo Deus dat ut justa faciamus, effectum orationis subsequitur: et talis effectus legi comes datur." Hence, as the law is imposed on all, so the grace to pray, if they wish, is given to all.

106. Such is also the doctrine of Lewis Thomassinus (consensus scholæ de gratia, c. 8, tr. 3.) He first expresses his astonishment at those who say that the ordinary grace alone does not enable us to perform actually any good work, however small. He then concludes that to reconcile the two propositions that sufficient grace enables us to obtain salvation, and that efficacious grace is necessary for the observance of the entire law, we must, according to the doctrine of St. Augustine, say that sufficient grace enables us to pray actually, and to perform similar easy acts, by means of which we afterwards obtain efficacious grace to fulfil difficult precepts. St. Augustine says: " Eo ipso quo firmissime creditur Deum impossibilia non præcipere, hinc admonemur et in facilibus quid agamus, et in difficilibus quid petamus." (De nat. et grat. c. 69, n. 83.) On this text Cardinal Norris says: " Igitur opera facilia, sed minus perfecta, facere possumus absque eo quod magis auxilium a Deo postulemus; quod tamen in difficilibus petendum est." Thomassinus quotes the authority of St. Bonaventure, of Scotus and others on this point, and says: " Omnibus ea placuere sufficientia auxilia, vere sufficientia quibus asseritur quandoque voluntas, quandoque non."

107. The same is held by Habert, Bishop of Vabres and doctor of Sorbonne, who was the first that wrote against Jansenius. He says: " Censemus primo quod immediate cum ipso effectu consensus completi sufficiens (gratia) non habet habitudinem nisi contingenter vel mediate. Arbitramur proinde gratiam sufficientem esse gratiam disposi-

tionis ad efficacem, utpote ex cujus bono usu Deus postea gratiam completi effectus effectivam creatæ voluntati concedat." (Theol. Græcor. Patrum, lib. 2, c. 15, n. 7.) He quotes for this doctrine Gammacheus, Du Valle, Isambert, Peretius, Le Moine, and others. And in the same chapter (n. 3,) he says: "Auxilia igitur gratiæ sufficientis sunt dispositiva ad efficacem, et efficacia secundum quid, effectus videlicet incompleti impetrantis primo remote, propius ac tandem proxime, qualis est actus fidei, spei, timoris, atque inter hæc omnia, orationis. Unde celeberrimus Alphonsus Lemoinus gratiam illam sufficientem docuit esse gratiam petendi seu orationis, de qua toties B. Augustinus." Hence, according to this learned author, efficacious grace obtains its complete effect; but sufficient grace produces its effect either *contingently*, that is, it sometimes produces, and sometimes does not produce its effect; or *mediately*, that is, by means of prayer. He also holds that sufficient grace, according to the good use which is made of it, disposes a person to obtain efficacious grace. Hence he says sufficient grace is efficacious *secundum quid:* that is with regard to the beginning of the effect, but not with regard to its completion. Lastly, he says, that sufficient grace is the grace of prayer the use of which, according to St. Augustine, depends on ourselves. Hence we have no excuse when we neglect to observe a command for the fulfilment of which we have sufficient grace which, without any other help, enables us either to fulfil the precept, or at least to obtain by prayer additional aid to fulfil it. The reasoning of Habert is very just: he asserts that his doctrine was commonly held in the Sorbonne.

108. The author of the Theology for the use of the Seminary of Perigord, holds the same doctrine. (Tom. 2, lib. 6, qu. 3, p. 486.) He says that with the aid of sufficient grace, "aliquis potest bene agere et aliquando agit:" he adds: "nihil vetat ut ex duobus æquali auxilio præventis

faciliores actus, plenam conversionem præcedentes, sæpissime unus faciat, alius non." He afterwards writes: " Sic
quosdam pietatis actus, nempe humiliter Deum deprecari,
cum solo auxilio sufficienti facere (homo) potest et aliquando
facit, quibus se ad ulteriores gratias præparat:" he adds
that the order of divine Providence regarding the divine
graces is " ut priorum bono usui posteriores succedant."
He says in conclusion, that " by prayer for which the
sufficient grace given to all is most fully sufficient, men infallibly obtain" full conversion and even final perseverance.

109. This doctrine is also held by Charles du Plessis
d'Argentré, also a theologian of the university of Sorbonne,
(diss. de multipl. gen. gratiar.) he quotes more than a
thousand theologians who expressly teach that by sufficient
grace without other aid, a man performs easy works, and
that by performing good works with the aid of sufficient
grace, he obtains more abundant help for his perfect conversion. He adds that it is in this sense that we are
to understand the axiom received in the schools that " God
does not refuse grace (that is more abundant and efficacious
grace) to them who do what lies in their power," but in
this axiom it must be always understood that in doing
what lies in their power they act *viribus gratiæ*, that is of
sufficient grace.

110. This doctrine is held also by Cardinal d'Aguirre
(theol. S. Ans. t. 3, disp. 155 et 176) and by Father
Anthony Boucat (theol. Patrum diss. 3. sect. 4.) who
strenuously maintains that every one can by prayer without
additional aid, obtain the grace of conversion: and for this
opinion he quotes (besides Gammacheus, Du Valle,
Habert, Le Monie) Peter de Tarantasia Bishop of Toul,
Godert de Fonti, Henry da Gand, all doctors of Sorbonne,
along with Signor Ligni the regius Professor, who in his
treatise on grace demonstrates that sufficient grace gives

strength to pray and to do some works which are not difficult. Gaudentius Buontempi (in pallad. theol. de gratia,
d. 1. q. 1.) also shows that with the aid of sufficient grace
which is given to all who wish to avail themselves of it,
man obtains by prayer the efficacious grace which he
stands in need of. The learned Father Fortunato da Brescia
(corn. Jans. syst. confut. part 2, n. 225. p. 297.) teaches
the same: he holds that all have the mediate grace of
prayer to observe the commandments, and considers it
certain that St. Augustine held the same. Richard of St.
Victor also asserts that man sometimes consents to, and
sometimes resists the sufficient grace common to all.
Matthias Felicius, who wrote against Calvin, thus defines
the ordinary or sufficient grace: " Est motio divina qua
movetur homo ad bonum, nec alicui denegatur. Alii illi
acquiescunt, sicque ad gratiam habitualem disponuntur, alii
repugnant." Andrew Vega likewise says: " Hæc autem
auxilia quæ omnibus dantur, plerisque inefficacia vocantur,
quia non semper habent suum effectum sed aliquando a
peccatoribus frustrantur."

111. In one part of his theology Cardinal Gotti appears
not to dissent from us: for in answering the objection how
man can persevere if he wishes, though it is not in his power
to have the special aid necessary for perseverance, he says
that although this aid is not in his power, " still what man
can by the grace of God ask and obtain from God by
his grace, is said to be in his power: and in this manner
we can say that it is in the power of man to have the aid
necessary for perseverance, by obtaining it by prayers."
Hence as in order to verify that it is in the power of man
to persevere, it is necessary that he be able to obtain by
prayer, aid to persevere actually, without requiring any
other grace, so it is also necessary that by the aid of the sufficient grace common to all, he be able, without requiring
any other grace, actually to pray and by prayer to obtain

perseverance; otherwise it cannot be said that each one has
the grace necessary for perseverance, even the remote and
mediate grace by means of prayer.   This is the doctrine of
St. Francis of Sales: in his Theotimo, (tom. 2, lib. 2, c.
4.) he says that the grace to pray actually is given to
every one who wishes to avail himself of it, and from this
he infers that it is in the power of every one to persevere.
After having shown that to obtain the gift of final perseverance continual prayer is necessary, he adds: " Now
because the gift of prayer is freely promised to all who wish
to consent to the inspirations of heaven, it is by consequence
in our power to persevere."   The same is taught by
Cardinal Bellarmine: " Auxilium," he says, " sufficiens, ad
salutem pro loco et tempore mediate vel immediate omnibus
datur, &c., Diximus *mediate vel immediate ;* quoniam iis
qui usu rationis utuntur immitti credimus a Deo sanctas
inspirationes, ac per hoc immediate illas habere gratiam
excitantem, cui si acquiescere velint, possint ad justificationem disponi et ad salutem aliquando pertingere." (Tom.
4. controv. 3 de grat. lib. 2. c. 5.)   On the words of the
apostle, " God is faithful who will not suffer you to be
tempted above that which you are able," (1. Cor. 10. 13.)
St. Thomas says that God would not be faithful if he did
not grant to us (as far as regards himself) the grace by
means of which we may be able to obtain salvation.
" Non autem videretur esse fidelis, si nobis denegaret, in
quantum in ipso est, ea per quæ pervenire ad eum
possemus." (Lect. 1. in c. Ep. ad Cor.)   Besides, God
admonishes us in a thousand places of the holy Scriptures,
to repent and to have recourse to him by prayer, and promises to hear us if we have recourse to him.   " Turn ye at
my reproof: behold I will utter my spirit to you." (Prov.
i. 23.)   " Return ye and live." (Ezech. xviii. 32.) "Come
to me all you that labour and are burdened and I will
refresh you." (Mat. xi. 28.)   " Ask and it shall be given

you." (Mat. vii. 7.) Cardinal Bellarmine says (de grat. l. 2, c. 4.) that these exhortations, *turn ye*, *return*, *come*, *ask*, would be vain and mocking if God did not give to all at least the grace to pray actually if they wish.

112. If this doctrine were not true, how could the Council of Trent (sess. 6. c. 13.), reprove the heretics, who said that the observance of the commandments is impossible, and say: " Deus impossibilia non jubet, sed jubendo monet et facere quod possis et petere quod non possis, et adjuvat ut possis." After the Council had taught this doctrine, I know not how any one can say that to pray actually, the grace common to all is not sufficient, and that for actual prayer we stand in need of efficacious grace. Father Fortunato da Brescia justly says, that, if all did not receive grace to pray actually, and if an efficacious grace not common to all were necessary, it might be said that to pray would be in a certain sense impossible to many whom this efficacious grace necessary for prayer, would not be given. Hence the Council should not have said: " Deus monet petere quod non possis," for by these words it admonishes us to ask, that is to do an act for the performance of which we have not the actual aid without which it cannot be performed: hence the divine admonition to pray should be understood of praying actually without an additional grace not common to all. As the Lord admonishes us to do actually what we are able to do without additional grace, *monet et facere quod possis ;* so he likewise admonishes us to pray actually with the common grace which he gives to all, and without any new grace; this is expressed in the words: *et adjuvat ut possis.* This is precisely what St. Augustine wished to make us understand in the words already quoted above: " Eo ipso quo firmissime creditur Deum impossibilia non præcipere, hinc admonemsur et in facilibus quid agamus et in difficilibus quid petamus." (De nat. et grat. c. 69, n. 83.)

There the Saint demonstrates that if all have not strength to do what is difficult, they have at least grace to pray, if they wish, and by prayer to obtain it. I will propose the argument in a shorter form. The Council says that God does not impose commands the observance of which is impossible, because he either gives grace to observe them, or he gives the grace of prayer to obtain this aid, and he assists us to do either the one or the other. Now if it were true that the Lord does not give all the grace at least by means of prayer to observe all the commandments actually, we should admit the doctrine of Jansenius, that even the just have not the grace necessary for the actual fulfilment of some of the commandments.

113. Our doctrine is also confirmed by the holy Fathers, St. Basil, (lib. moral. summar. summa 62, c. 3,) says: "Uti tamen quis permissus est in tentationem incidere, eventum ut sufferre possit et voluntatem Dei per orationem petere." The saint then teaches that when any one is tempted, God permits the temptation that he may resist it by prayer for help to do the divine will. He therefore supposes that when man has not sufficient strength to overcome temptation, he has at least the common grace of prayer to obtain the additional help which he stands in need of. St. John Chrysostom writes: "Nec quisquam poterit excusari qui hostem vincere noluit, dum orare cessavit." (Hom. de Moys.) If any one had not grace to pray actually for efficacious grace to resist temptations, he would have an excuse for his defeat. St. Bernard says the same: "Who are we? or what strength have we? This God wished that seeing our deficiency, and that we had no other aid, we should run to his mercy with all humility." (Serm. 5, de Quad.) God then has imposed on us a law which our strength is not able to observe, that we may have recourse to him, and by prayer obtain strength to fulfil it; but if God refused to any one the grace to pray actually, to him

the observance of the law would be rendered utterly impossible. "But no," adds St. Bernard; "many complain that grace is wanting to them, but grace might far more justly complain that many are wanting to it." The Lord has greater reason to complain of us for being wanting to the grace which he bestows upon us than we have to complain that his grace is wanting to us. But none of the Fathers has taught this doctrine more clearly than St. Augustine has in so many parts of his works. In one place he says: "Therefore (God) imposes some precepts which we are unable to fulfil that we may know what we ought to ask from him." (Vide contra duas epist. Pelag.) "These are your own sins, for the knowledge of asking with profit is not taken away from any man." (lib. 3, de lib. arb. c. 19, n. 53.) Again he says: "What then is shown to us but that he who commands us to do these things grants us aid to ask, to seek, and to knock." (Lib. 1, ad Simp. q. 2.) In another place: "Take once and understand: are you not as yet drawn? Pray that you may be drawn." (Tr. 26, in Jo. n. 2.) In another place: "Let the man who is willing and unable, pray that his will may be sufficiently strengthened to observe the commandments: for he is thus assisted to do what he is commanded." (De orat. et lib. arb. tr. 10, n. 31, in fin.) These passages require no explanation. In another place the saint writes: "Free will is admonished by the commandments to ask the gift of God: but the admonition would be unprofitable to it if it did not first receive some love, that it might ask for the means of accomplishing what is commanded." (De grat. et lib. arb. c. 18.) Mark the words *some love:* behold sufficient grace by the aid of which man can obtain by prayer, grace actually to fulfil the commandments. Again he says: "Therefore he imposes the precept, that endeavouring to do what is commanded, and wearied by our own infirmity, we may know how to àsk the assistance of grace." (Ep.

L

89.) Hence the saint supposes that with the ordinary grace we cannot fulfil the commandments, but that we can easily obtain by prayer help to fulfil them. In another place: " It remains in this mortal life, not that a man fulfil justice when he wishes, but that with suppliant piety he turn to him by whose gift he can fulfil it." (Lib. div. qu. ad Simp., qu. 1, n. 14.) Since then, according to St. Augustine, nothing remains for man in this life but to turn to God, by whose gift he can observe the law, the holy doctor supposes as certain that every one has grace to pray actually: otherwise, if he had not efficacious grace, nor even the common grace of prayer, he would have no aid to fulfil the law, and to be saved.

114. But our doctrine is confirmed above all by the two following passages from St. Augustine. The first is: " It is certain that if we wish we observe the commandments; but because the will is prepared by the Lord, we must ask him to make us will so that by willing we may fulfil them." (De gr. et lib. arb. c. 16.) The saint says, that we observe the commandments if we wish; but that to have the will to fulfil them, we must ask the grace to will their observance, that by willing it we may observe them. The grace then to ask this sincere will to fulfil the commandments is given to all: otherwise if, for actually asking this will, efficacious grace not common to all were necessary, the man to whom this grace would not be given, could not have even the will to observe them.

115. The second text is that (lib. de corrept. et grat. c. 5,) in which the holy doctor answers the monks of Adrumetum, who said: If grace is necessary and is wanting to me, why do you correct me for not doing what I am unable to do? You should rather implore the Lord to give me this grace: *ora potius pro me.* In answer to them the saint said: You deserve correction, not because you do not do what you have not strength to do, but

because you do not pray for this strength. "Qui corripi non vult, et dicit; *ora potius pro me* ideo corripiendus est ut faciat etiam ipse pro se, (*idest*) ut oret etiam pro se." Now had not the saint believed that all received sufficient grace by which, without any other aid, they may pray actually if they wish, he could not have said absolutely that he who does not fulfil law, deserves correction because he did not pray. For the other might have replied: But I should not be corrected for not praying when I have not grace to pray actually. But St. Augustine always supposes as certain that they who have not efficacious grace to do good, have notwithstanding the grace to pray, and by prayer to obtain help to perform good works: "But," he says, "when they do not perform works, let them pray that they may receive what they do not as yet possess." Hence, in answer to the heretics, who inferred from the text, "No one can come to me except the Father, draw him," that no one can come to God whom God does not actually draw to himself, Bellarmine said: "We answer that from these words, it can only be inferred that all have not efficacious grace by which they actually believe; but not that they have not at least help by which they can believe, or certainly by which they can ask aid." (Lib. 2, de grat. c. 8.)

116. To conclude, our system which, as we have seen, has been held by so many theologians, well accords, on the one hand, with grace intrinsically efficacious, with which we infallibly but freely do good: for it cannot be denied that (as we observed when speaking of the system of Molina,) God can by his omnipotence move the hearts of men to wish freely what he wishes. On the other hand, in our system, we admit really sufficient grace common to all, by which, if he wishes to avail himself of it, every man will certainly obtain, by means of prayer, all the efficacious graces necessary for his salvation; but if he voluntarily

neglects to avail himself of it, these efficacious graces will be justly withheld from him. Neither will it profit him to say that he had not strength to overcome the temptation by which he was assailed; for if he wished to make use of the grace of prayer given to all, he would have easily obtained this strength by prayer, and would be saved.

117. But unless this sufficient grace is admitted, by which, without any other grace not common to all, every one can pray, and by prayer obtain efficacious grace to observe the law, I am unable to understand how sacred orators can exhort the people to return to God, if even the grace of prayer is refused to some. For the people might answer: Why do you exhort us to repentance? Ask God himself to convert us: for we have neither the immediate efficacious grace to return actually to God, nor the mediate sufficient grace to obtain it by means of prayer. I am likewise unable to conceive how the sacred scriptures can so strongly exhort men to listen to the divine inspirations if the grace of prayer be not granted to all: for they who are destitute even of the efficacious grace of prayer may say to God: Lord why dost thou tell us to do this? Do thou thyself make us do it; for thou knowest that we have not even the grace to ask thee to make us correspond to thy calls. Finally, I cannot comprehend how the reproof given to sinners in these words, "you always resist the Holy Ghost," (Acts. vii. 51,) can be just, if they do not receive even the remote grace necessary for actual prayer.

118. But in our system, which admits that the grace of prayer is common to all, every excuse is taken away from them who say that they had not strength to resist the attacks of the flesh and the devils; for if they had not actual strength to resist them, they had the grace of prayer by which they might have obtained efficacious grace, and have conquered all their enemies.

SEVENTH SESSION.

DECREE REGARDING THE SACRAMENTS.

ON THE SACRAMENTS IN GENERAL.

1. With regard to the sacraments in general, and Baptism and Confirmation in particular, the Fathers did not think it necessary to define the Catholic doctrine in separate decrees, as was done in the preceding session with regard to justification; they deemed it sufficient merely to condemn the opposite errors. Thirty-three canons of faith were framed; thirteen on the sacraments in general, fourteen on baptism, and three on confirmation.

2. In the proemium it was stated that for the complement of the doctrine promulgated on justification in the antecedent session it appeared congruous to treat of the holy sacraments, by means of which grace is communicated to us: and therefore the Council passed several canons condemnatory of errors contrary to faith. The canons are here transcribed: after each canon will be given the objections which have been proposed against it, and the observations which were made upon it.

3. Can. 3: " Si quis dixerit sacramenta novæ legis non fuisse omnia a Jesu Christo Domino nostro instituta; aut esse plura vel pauciora quam septem, videlicet Baptismum, Confirmationem, Eucharistiam, Pœnitentiam, Extremam Unctionem, Ordinem, Matrimonium; aut etiam aliquod horum septem non esse vere et proprie sacramentum, anathema sit."

4. Soave says that as to the number of sacraments, all the fathers agreed that there were seven, as well on account

L 2

of the authority of the Scholastics after the Master of the Sentences, as of the Council of Florence, and of the tradition of the Church of Rome. But he ought to have added the authority of the Greek Church, which although it was separated from the Roman Church for eight centuries, agreed perfectly with it upon this point. This he ought to have stated, in order to show more clearly that this truth has come to us from Jesus Christ and his apostles.

5. Soave, presuming as usual to instruct the Council, also says that it would have been advisable not to define that the sacraments were seven in number and neither more nor less: "*et non plura vel pauciora:*" because, said he, there are various opinions regarding the definition and essence of a sacrament, and therefore it was impossible to determine with accuracy and certainty, their quality and number. But I answer that for us it is enough to know that the sacraments are certain sensible signs made in the name of Jesus Christ, which when the requisite conditions take place, infallibly produce grace of themselves. Hence neither the benediction of an abbot, nor the creation of cardinals, nor the other functions mentioned by Soave are sacraments. Because they do not produce grace: neither is martyrdom a sacrament, since it is administered not in the name of Christ, but in order to insult him. But it is of little importance to know the quiddity of the sacraments, and in what their essence consists.

6. There were also some persons in the Council who advised the omission of the words: "*plura vel pauciora quam septem;*" because they had not been used by the ancient Doctors, nor by the Synod of Carthage, nor by the Council of Florence. But it was said in answer that in these times there were not two heresies, one of which asserted that there were only two or three real sacraments, and the other, that all the signs to which grace is promised in the Scripture, such as alms and prayer, are sacraments.

7. Can. 2: "Si quis dixerit ea ipsa novæ legis sacramenta sacramentis antiquæ legis ·non differre, nisi quia ceremoniæ sunt aliæ et alii ritus externi, anathema sit."

8. With regard to the truth of the Catholic doctrine on the difference between the sacraments of the old and new law, Soave endeavours to raise many doubts. The Catholic truth is that the sacraments of the new law produce grace, and that the sacraments of the old law only signify grace. Hence, it is an error to say, as the innovators do, that our sacraments are mere signs of grace; for they not only are signs, and signify grace, but like the clouds which are a sign and a cause of rain, they also produce grace. Hence, St. Paul called all the ceremonies of the old law "weak and needy elements, a shadow of things to come." (Gal. iv. 9, Col. ii. 17.) But on the other hand the Gospel assures us that by baptism, a man is born again to grace, that in the sacrament of Penance, sins are remitted, that in the Eucharist life is received, and that in the imposition of hands by a bishop, the holy Ghost is given. Hence it is evident that the sacraments are not barren signs, but are causes which produce the grace which they promise.

9. Can. 3: "Si quis dixerit hæc septem sacramenta ita esse inter se paria ut nulla ratione aliud sit alio dignius, anathema sit."

10. In this canon the words *nulla ratione* were inserted because Luther held that all the sacraments were equal, as he stated in a written document sent to the senate of Prague, in which he says: "One sacrament is not more excellent than another, since they all consist in the word of God." But this is contrary to the doctrine of St. Denis, of St. Ambrose, and Innocent the Third. (Cap. Cum. Marthæ. de celebr. missar.) In the Council it was said by some that each sacrament has some particular excellence, on account of which it is not inferior to the others: but the observation was disregarded.

11. Can. 4: Si quis dixerit sacramenta novæ legis non esse ad salutem necessaria, sed superflua; et sine eis aut eorum voto per solam fidem homines a Deo gratiam justificationis adipisci, licet omnia singulis necessaria non sint, anathema sit."

12. The heretics say that no sacrament is necessary, inasmuch as they hold that man is justified by faith alone, and that the sacraments only serve to excite and nourish this faith, which (as they say) can be equally excited and nourished by preaching. But this is certainly false, and is condemned in the fifth, sixth, seventh, and eighth canons: for as we know from the Scriptures, some of the sacraments are necessary *(necessitate medii)* as a means without which salvation is impossible. Thus, Baptism is necessary for all, Penance for them who have fallen into sin after baptism, and the Eucharist is necessary for all at least in desire *(in voto)*.

13. Soave says that at least the implicit desire of Baptism (the same holds for penance with regard to sinners) appeared to many of the fathers not to be necessary for justification: because Cornelius and the good thief were justified without having any knowledge of baptism. But Pallavicini says that this is a mere dream of Soave: for the theologians of Trent could not have adduced the example of Cornelius or of the good thief in defence of such an opinion, when every one knew that the obligation of Baptism did not commence till after the death of the Saviour, and after the promulgation of the Gospel. Besides who can deny that the act of perfect love of God, which is sufficient for justification, includes an implicit desire of Baptism, of Penance, and of the Eucharist. He who wishes the whole, wishes every part of that whole, and all the means necessary for its attainment. In order to be justified without baptism, an infidel must love God above all things, and must have an universal will to observe all the divine

precepts, among which the first is to receive baptism: and therefore in order to be justified it is necessary for him to have at least an implicit desire of that sacrament. For it is certain that to such desire is ascribed the spiritual regeneration of a person who has not been baptized, and that the remission of sins to baptized persons who have contrition, is likewise ascribed to the explicit or implicit desire of sacramental absolution.

14. In the fourth canon the words *licet omnia singulis necessaria non sint*, were afterwards inserted. By this canon it was intended to condemn Luther, who asserts that none of the sacraments is absolutely necessary for salvation, because as has been already said, he ascribed all salvation to faith, and nothing to the efficacy of the sacraments.

15. Can. 5: "Si quis dixerit hæc sacramenta propter fidem solam nutriendam instituta, anathema sit."

16. "Can. 6: "Si quis dixerit sacramenta novæ legis non continere gratiam quam significant, aut gratiam ipsam non ponentibus obicem non conferre, quasi signa tantum externa sint acceptæ per fidem gratiæ vel justitiæ, et notæ quædam christianæ professionis quibus apud homines discernuntur fideles ab infidelibus, anathema sit."

17. Can. 7: "Si quis dixerit non dari gratiam per hujusmodi sacramenta semper et omnibus quantum est ex parte Dei, etiamsi rite ea suscipiant, sed aliquando et aliquibus, anathema sit."

18. Can. 8: "Si quis dixerit per ipsa novæ legis sacramenta ex opere operato non conferri gratiam, sed solam fidem divinæ promissionis ad gratiam consequendam sufficere, anathema sit."

19. The errors condemned in these canons were justly condemned for the reasons assigned after the second canon.

20. Can. 9: "Si quis dixerit in tribus sacramentis, Baptismo scilicet, confirmatione, et ordine non imprimi characterem in anima, hoc est signum quoddam spirituale et indelebile, unde ea iterari non possunt, anathema sit."

21. On this dogma taught by the Catholic Church, regarding the character impressed on the soul by the three sacraments mentioned in the canon, viz., Baptism, Confirmation, and Order, which cannot be iterated, Soave refers to a passage in the works of Scotus, (in 4. dist. qu. 9.) in which this author says that our doctrine does not necessarily follow from the words of Scripture, or of the fathers, but is taken from the authority of the Church.   From the words of Scotus, Soave unjustly infers that he denies, though in a respectful manner, the truth defined by the Council.   This is a mere calumny, for although Scotus thinks differently on this point from other theologians, who commonly hold that this dogma is sufficiently proved from the fathers and the Scripture, it cannot be said or suspected that he either denied or doubted that the three abovementioned sacraments impress a character.   This truth is proved from several passages of Scripture, and particularly from the second epistle of St. Paul to the Corinthians, in which the Apostle says that God seals us and gives us a pledge of his inheritance.   "Who also hath sealed us, and given the pledge of the spirit in our hearts." (2 Cor. i. 22.)   It is still more clearly taught by the Greek and Latin Fathers (see Bellarmine de effect. sacram. lib. 2. c. 21.)   St. Augustine writes: "The sacrament of baptism is sufficient for the consecration which makes a heretic who is out of the Lord, guilty, because he has the character of the Lord.   The sacred doctrine teaches that he should be corrected, but not consecrated again." (Ep. 23.)

22. The heretics err in believing that the divine impressions are like the rights and possessions which men enjoy on earth.   These we ourselves acquire, and are conferred upon us only extrinsically: but the impressions of grace are supernatural, and are produced by God internally in the soul.   However some of the gifts of God are such that they may be cancelled, such as the grace of justification: but others are indelible, such as the gifts by which a man is

made a Christian, by which he is confirmed with the military seal of Christ, by which he receives power in the Church militant. These are called characters which cannot be obliterated even by sin.

23. Can. 10: " Si quis dixerit Christianos omnes in verbo et omnibus sacramentis administrandis habere potestatem, anathema sit."

24. This canon condemns the error of Luther who held that not only men, but also the angels and devils in human form, and all Christians were fit ministers of the sacraments; for he maintained that Baptism gives every man power over all the sacraments. This canon also condemns the error of Calvin, who denied that a layman can confer the sacrament of baptism, even in case of necessity. Hence in the canon it is justly said: " *Omnes in omnibus sacramentis habere potestatem:*" for in case of necessity a layman can administer baptism, and according to the true opinion which Bellarmine holds, the contracting parties alone (whatever others may say), are the ministers of the sacrament of matrimony. It is certain first that men alone and not angels can be the ministers of the sacraments: for to men alone this power was given by Jesus Christ, who said to them: " Going therefore teach ye all nations," &c., " Do this for a commemoration of me." " Whose sins you shall forgive they are forgiven them." It is certain, secondly, that in order to have power to administer all the sacraments it is not enough to be baptized. The Apostles were first baptized; afterwards, by the words already quoted, " Do this for a commemoration of me," the power of consecrating the Eucharist was given to them: and by the words " whose sins you shall forgive," &c., the power of absolving from sins was conferred upon them.

25. Can. 11: " Si quis dixerit in ministris, dum

sacramenta conficiunt et conferunt, non requiri intentionem saltem faciendi quod facit Ecclesia, anathema sit."

26. In this canon was condemned the opinion of Luther, who, in his book on the Babylonian Captivity, said that every sacrament is validly received as often as the minister pretends to confer, though he does not actually confer it, or as often as he pronounces the form in jest without the intention of administering the sacrament. For he maintained that the entire efficacy of the sacrament consists in the faith of the person who receives it, not in the sacrament itself, and still less in the intention of the minister.

27. Ambrosius Cathèrinus defended in the Council the celebrated opinion, that for the validity of a sacrament it is enough that the minister confer it seriously though he should have no intention of conferring it. This opinion had been before maintained by Peter de Palude, and Sylvester da Prierius. According to Catherinus, if in conferring baptism the minister of the sacrament intend only the material washing of the infant, provided he does it seriously, the baptism is valid. His principal reason is that otherwise if sacraments conferred in such a manner were not valid, all baptisms and sacramental absolutions, and, what is more important, all ordinations of priests and bishops, on the validity of which so many other ordinations depend, would be doubtful.

28. Speaking of the opinion of Catherinus, Bellarmine does not hesitate to say: " I do not see in what it differs from that of the heretics." Pallavicini asserts that it is false; because it is contrary to the common opinion of theologians, who at least require in the minister the implicit intention of conferring the sacrament: but not condemned because the Council in the eleventh canon, which has been just quoted, only declared that it is necessary for the

minister to have the intention of doing what the Church does. Hence, when the minister confers the sacrament externally and seriously as it is usually administered in the Church, the opinion cannot be said to be condemned by this canon. In reality Catherinus continued to defend it after the Council, and many defend it at present. However it is a very hard thing to say that a sacrament is valid when the minister intends positively not to confer it. With regard to the sacrament of penance in particular we have the words of our Lord, " Whose sins you shall forgive, they are forgiven them, and whose *sins* you shall retain they are retained." (John xx. 23.) These words denote that for the validity of absolution the priest must have a real intention of absolving. Besides St. Thomas (3 p. q. 64, a. 8,) teaches that since the actions of the sacraments may be referred to several ends; for example the washing in baptism may be referred either to the removal of corporal or spiritual uncleanness; hence the end of the action must be determined by the intention of the minister. Behold the words of the holy doctor: " Sicut ablutio aquæ quæ fit in Baptismo potest ordinari et ad munditiam corporalem et ad sanitatem spiritualem et ad ludum et alia hujusmodi; et ideo oportet quod determinetur ad unum, idest ad sacramentale effectum, per intentionem abluentis." (Loc. cit.)

29. The adversaries object from what the Angelic Doctor afterwards says in answer to the second objection: " In verbis autem quæ profert (minister) exprimitur intentio Ecclesiæ, quæ sufficit ad perfectionem sacramenti." But Gonet answers that in this passage St. Thomas intended only to say that it is not necessary that the minister manifest externally his intention of wishing the sacrament to produce its effect, because "in the words which he pronounces, the intention of the Church is expressed." This is still more clear from what St. Thomas says in the tenth

article, where he asks whether a direct intention in the minister is necessary for the validity of the sacrament? He answers in the following words: "Intentio ministri potest perverti dupliciter. Uno modo respectu sacramenti puta cum aliquis non intendit sacramentum conferre sed derisorie aliquid agere: et talis perversitas tollit veritatem sacramenti, præcipue quando suam intentionem exterius manifestat." The case is otherwise, says the saint, if the minister should intend to confer the sacrament for a bad end, for example, if he should intend to pervert it to the purposes of witchcraft, &c. Mark the words, "Cum aliquis non intendit sacramentum conferre:" hence St. Thomas requires absolutely, for the validity of the sacrament, that the minister have the intention of conferring the sacrament. But he says that the sacrament is valid if the minister has the intention of conferring it, even though his intention be criminal. The only distinction, therefore, which he makes is between the minister's having and not having the intention of conferring the sacrament. And in another place he says expressly: " Si minister non intendat sacramentum conferre, non perficitur sacramentum."

30. To this I add the condemnation of the following proposition by Alexander VIII.: "Valet Baptismus collatus a ministro qui omnem ritum externum formamque baptizandi observat, intus vero in corde suo apud se resolvit: non intendo facere quod facit Ecclesia." (Prop. 28.) The advocates of the opposite opinion say that this condemnation does not fall on their doctrine since the proposition may be understood even of a jocose external rite. But I answer that to assert the validity of a sacrament conferred by a jocose external rite, without any intention of administering the sacrament, had been already condemned by the Council of Trent, and therefore this second condemnation would be useless. I answer, secondly, that the above-mentioned proposition was held not by the heretics but by

Catholic authors, and particularly by John Maria Scribo-
nius (summa theol. disp. 1, de sacram. q. 6,) who held the
validity of the sacrament when it was administered not in
a jocose but in a serious manner, without an intention on the
part of the minister: and this was the proposition which
was condemned.   Benedict XIV. (de synodo, lib. 7. c. 4.)
says that the opinion of Catherinus was at least greatly
weakened by the condemnation of the above-mentioned
proposition; he concludes that though it were probable, a
person would certainly sin by acting on it in the administration of any sacrament.   For the sacrament would be
doubtful; and should therefore be repeated conditionally.

31. With regard to the inconvenient consequences urged
against our doctrine by Catherinus, Pallavicini says, that
though the intention of the minister were not necessary, the
same inconveniences might occur in other ways.   For example, in administering the sacrament of penance the
priest, because he pronounces the words of absolution in a
low voice, could easily omit an essential word, and thus
could leave all his penitents in their sins.   The minister of
baptism could easily do the same, by intentionally corrupting
the form: and from the invalidity of this sacrament,
which is the gate of all the sacraments, would follow the invalidity of many sacramental absolutions and ordinations.
Hence we must have recourse to divine Providence, which
prevents such destruction of souls; besides such sacrileges
bring no temporal advantage to those who would be guilty
of them.   With regard to the sacrament of baptism, which
is the most necessary, there were ancient and modern theologians, such as Alexander d'Ales and Gabriel Durando, who
say, along with St. Thomas (3 p. q. 64, a. 8, ad 2,) that
were such a case to happen God would supply for infants,
and their own faith and desire of baptism would supply for
adults.   Pallavicini says that in such cases grace would
be infused not by the sacrament, or in virtue of a divine

promise, but only through the mercy of God, who would not permit our confidence to be deluded by the malice of the ministers of the sacraments.

32. Can. 12. "Si quis dixerit ministrum in peccato mortali existentem, modo omnia essentialia quæ ad sacramentum conficiendum aut conferendum pertinent servaverit, non conficere aut conferre sacramentum, anathema sit."

33. The error condemned in this canon was first held by the Donatists, and afterwards by John Wickliff, by whom it was strenuously defended. It is certainly an error: because, according to the words of St. John, " he it is that baptizeth with the Holy Ghost," (i. 33.) Jesus Christ is the principal author of the sacraments, and, therefore, as often as the minister does all that is essential to the validity of the sacrament, the sacrament is valid; besides the power of administering the sacraments is a power of jurisdiction which is granted not for the benefit of the person who obtains it, but of the person who receives the sacrament, and therefore is not lost by the sin of the minister.

34. Can. 13. "Si quis dixerit receptos et approbatos ecclesiæ catholicæ ritus in solemni sacramentorum administratione adhiberi consuetos, aut contemni aut sine peccato a ministris pro libito omitti aut in novos alios per quemcumque ecclesiarum pastorem mutari posse, anathema sit."

35. There is no doubt but the Church has power to institute and to change the rites and ceremonies to be employed in the administration of the sacraments, as the Council of Trent itself declared in the twenty-first session, (c. 2): "Hanc potestatem," says the Council, "perpetuo in Ecclesia fuisse ut in sacramentorum dispensatione, salva illorum substantia, ea statueret vel mutaret quæ suscipientium utilitati seu ipsorum sacramentorum venerationi pro rerum, temporum et locorum varietate magis expedire judicaret." But this power belongs only to the Church: hence she has justly forbidden any change in her rites:

otherwise, as St. Augustine says, (epist. 54, alias 108,) by the novelties of different ministers, the common order and peace of the Church would be disturbed.

On Baptism.

36. Can. 1. " Si quis dixerit Baptismum Joannis habuisse eandem vim cum Baptismo Christi, anathema sit."

37. In the Council some were unwilling to admit the preceding canon without some alteration; because, the Scripture declares that the Baptism of John was given for the remission of sins. They were, perhaps, induced to adopt this opinion, by the words of St. Luke regarding St. John the Baptist: " And he came into all the country about the Jordan, preaching the baptism of penance for the remission of sins." But it was said in answer, that according to the interpretation of the Fathers, the Baptism of John was for the remission of sins not by its own efficacy, but according to hope through the Baptism of Christ, for which it was a preparation, and of which it was a figure. This the Baptist himself insinuated in these words: " I indeed baptize you with water, but there shall come one mightier than I, the latchet of whose shoes I am not worthy to loose; he shall baptize you with the Holy Ghost and with fire." (Luke iii. 16.)

38. Can. 2. " Si quis dixerit aquam veram et natu-ralem non esse de necessitate Baptismi, atque ideo verba Domini nostri Jesu Christi—*nisi quis renatus fuerit ex aqua et Spiritu Sancto*—ad metaphoram aliquam detor-serit, anathema sit." This canon is condemnatory of the error of many heretics, and also of Luther, who when asked whether in the case in which water could not be had, it was lawful to baptize in milk or beer, answered that what-ever can be called a bath, is sufficient for baptism. " Quid-quid balnei nomine nuncupari potest, illud esse aptum ad baptizandum." (In Sympos. colloqu. c. 17.) Now baths

may be made of milk and beer; but such matter is certainly not sufficient for baptism.

39. Can. 3. "Si quis dixerit in Ecclesia Romana quæ omnium ecclesiarum est magistra, non esse veram de Baptismi sacramento doctrinam, anathema sit."

40. Can. 4. "Si quis dixerit Baptismum qui etiam datur ab hæreticis in nomine Patris, et Filii, et Spiritus Sancti, cum intentione faciendi quod facit Ecclesia, non esse verum Baptismum, anathema sit."

41. Soave says that in the ancient Church persons baptized by heretics were not rebaptized: he is right; but the reason which he assigns is false, viz. that the heretics did not use the matter and form which are now deemed essential, because in the early ages nothing was known about matter and form. This reason is most false. If Soave means to say that the early Christians had no knowledge of the terms —matter and form, I say that it is of no importance whether they understood the terms or not. It is sufficient that they had a knowledge of what is signified by these words. But if he intends to say that in ancient times the essential requisites for baptism, which are now called matter and form, he is most rash in ascribing to the early Christians gross ignorance of the Gospel, which expressly teaches that water is the matter of Baptism, and that the form is, "I baptize thee in the name of the Father, &c."

42. However with regard to the form, Bellarmine remarks (l. 3, c. 3, de baptismo) that we cannot evidently infer from the Gospel alone, that the words, "I baptize thee in the name of the Father, and of the Son, and of the Holy Ghost," is the true form of baptism: and that it is necessary to have recourse also to the tradition and authority of the Church, which has declared that these words are the form of that sacrament.

43. Can. 5. "Si quis dixerit Baptismum liberum esse, hoc est non necessarium ad salutem, anathema sit."

44. In the Council two points were disputed: first, what was the remedy in the old law for the salvation of infants who died before they attained the use of reason. In his book of disputations, Luther said that the sacraments which gave grace were instituted immediately after the sin of Adam. Several theologians thought this proposition not deserving of condemnation with regard to the salvation of infants: because, according to St. Augustine, we must suppose that in all times God had instituted some remedy for infants that should die in their childhood. Now because it did not produce its effect through the merit of the infants, and because (as many think) it should require some sensible oblation, this remedy appeared to have the property of a sacrament: that it was a sacrament was held by several scholastics. Hence, as Pallavicini says, it was deemed better not to decide the point.

45. The second point was whether they should condemn the opinion of Cajetan, who thought that in the new law there should be some remedy for the salvation of infants that die in the womb. He said that a person who would give the benediction in the name of the most holy Trinity to infants in danger of death in the womb, could not be censured. He added, "who knows but the divine mercy will accept such a baptism, on account of the desire of the parents." In order to save this opinion from censure, Seripando said that were it not true, faith would be more efficacious before the gospel than at present, since according to St. Gregory, faith produced then what the water of Baptism produces now. But Dominicus Soto pronounced the opinion to be an heretical error, and St. Pius V. ordered it to be expunged from Cajetan's work. For to say that heaven is open to him who is not baptized, or has not the desire of baptism, appears to be clearly opposed to the words of Jesus Christ: "unless a man be born again of

water and the Holy Ghost, he cannot enter into the kingdom of God." (Johu iii. 5.) In answer to Seripando, I say that at present it is easier to procure water and a person to administer baptism, than it was then to have true faith, which, according to the common opinion, was not sufficient to save infants before birth; Gerson went so far as to say that it may be presumed that God dispenses with the necessity of Baptism on account of the prayers of the parents. I answer that we should not believe that God extends such mercy beyond the limits which he has revealed in the Scripture, but only according to the course of natural causes.

46. Can. 6: " Si quis dixerit baptizatum non posse, etiamsi velit, gratiam amittere, quantumcunque peccet, nisi nolit credere, anathema sit." This canon corresponds to the twenty-third canon of the sixth session on Justification.

47. Can. 7: " Si quis dixerit baptizatos per Baptismum ipsum solius tantum fidei debitores fieri, non autem universæ legis Christi servandæ, anathema sit." This corresponds to the nineteenth canon of the same sixth session.

48. Can. 8: " Si quis dixerit baptizatos liberos esse ab omnibus, S. Ecclesiæ præceptis quæ vel scripta vel tradita sunt, ita ut ea observare non teneantur, nisi se sua sponte illas submittere voluerint, anathema sit." This corresponds to the twentieth canon of the sixth session.

49. Can. 9: "Si quis dixerit ita revocandos esse homines ad Baptismi suscepti memoriam ut vota omnia quæ post Baptismum fiunt, vi promissionis in Baptismo ipso jam factæ irrita esse intelligant, quasi per ea, et fidei quam professi sunt detrahatur et ipsi Baptismo, anathema sit."

50. The words " *vota omnia quæ post Baptismum fiunt,*" were inserted, because it was thought that as it was a probable opinion that all antecedent vows were cancelled by religious profession, the same might be held with regard to vows made before Baptism.

51. Can. 10. " Si quis dixerit peccata omnia quæ post Baptismum fiunt, sola recordatione et fide suscepti Baptismi, vel dimitti vel venialia fieri, anathema sit."

52. Can. 11: " Si quis dixerit, verum et rite collatum Baptismum iterandum esse illi qui apud infideles fidem Christi negaverit, cum ad pœnitentiam convertitur, anathema sit."

53. Can. 12: " Si quis dixerit neminem esse baptizandum, nisi ea ætate qua Christus baptizatus sit, vel in ipso mortis articulo, anathema sit."

54. Can. 13: " Si quis dixerit parvulos, eo quod actum credendi non habent, suscepto Baptismo inter fidelis computandos non esse, ac propterea, cum ad annos discretionis pervenerint, esse rebaptizandos, aut præstare omitti eorum baptisma quam eos non actu proprio credentes baptizari in sola fide Ecclesiæ, anathema sit."

55. Can. 14: "Si quis dixerit hujusmodi parvulos, cum adoleverint, interrogandos esse an ratum habere velint quod patrini eorum, dum baptizarentur, polliciti sunt; et ubi se nolle responderint suo esse arbitrio relinquendos nec alia interim pœna ad Christianam vitam cogendos, nisi ut ab Eucharistia aliorumque sacramentorum perceptione arceantur donec resipiscant, anathema sit."

56. It is well known that, as Chalon says (hist. de sacram. l. 1. c. 11.) the practice of administering Baptism by triple immersion continued from the time of the Apostles till the fourteenth century. Hence St. Thomas, who lived in the thirteenth century, considered it a grevious sin to baptize otherwise than by immersion. (3 p. q. 66. a. 7, 8.) In the administration of Baptism the entire body was immersed in the water. Females were baptized at a time and place different from the time and place at which men were baptized. In entering and leaving the font, females were covered by their godmothers, and men by their godfathers, with a certain linen garment which they afterwards preserved as a

memorial of the benefit conferred upon them. These garments were called *Satane*. St. Gregory permitted the Spaniards to baptize by infusion: hence, for just reasons, and particularly on account of the injury done to infants by immersion, infusion began from that time to be substituted. However Father Chalon justly thinks that in ancient times infusion was adopted, in several cases: for example when dying persons, or martyrs confined to prison were to be baptized. And St. Cyprian (see Chalon loc. cit.) when asked by a Bishop if persons who at baptism were only sprinkled with water, should be called Christians, answered in the affirmative.

57. Here I think it right to notice several things regarding baptism, the knowledge of some of which will be useful, and of others, necessary. Among the heretics opposed to baptism were the Gnostics, who rejected everything sensible, and the Manicheans in the third century, because they said that water came from the evil principle. The Paulianists and certain Arians corrupted the form of baptism by mutilating the invocation of the three divine persons. That the true form contained a distinct invocation of the three divine persons, appears from tradition, as St. Justin, Tertullian, and St. Basil assert (See Father Chalon. Hist. de sacr. c. 13). Hence the Council of Nice declared that baptism is null when given in any other form. Tournely (de Bapt.) answers all the objections which the unbelievers take from expressions of some of the Fathers who appeared to think otherwise; and solves the difficulty arising from certain words of St. Ambrose, by showing that in using these words, the saint spoke not of the form of baptism, but of the profession made by catechumens. The form used by the Greeks is different from that which is used in the Latin church. The words used by the Greeks are, " Servus Dei baptizatur, *or* baptizetur in nomine Patris, amen, in nomine Filii, amen, et Spiritus Sancti, amen."

This form is certainly valid for the Greeks: for it was approved by Eugene IV. in the decree for the instruction of the Armenians. The form used in the Latin church is that which we have in the ritual. " Ego te baptizo in nomine Patris, et Filii et Spiritus Sancti. Amen." The words " in nomine Patris et Filii et Spiritus Sancti," are certainly essential and necessary, since they were prescribed by Christ himself. " Euntes...docete omnes gentes, baptizantes eos in nomine Patris et Filii et Spiritus Sancti." (Mat. xxviii. 19.) Hence St. Augustine has written: " Quis nesciat non esse Baptisma Christi, si verba, evangelica, quibus symbolum constat, illic defuerint?" (6 de bapt., c. 25.) With regard to the words, " Ego te baptizo," some ancient authors, such as the Master of the Sentences, Præpositus, Peter Cantor, &c., said that these words were not always used in the church in the administration of Baptism: for, said they, Baptism is valid if the following words be pronounced: " In nomine Patris, et Filii et Spiritus Sancti, Amen." Others say that the words *Ego et baptizo*" have been always used, but have not been always essential. But Juenin shows that they have been always used and always essential, as appears from the chapter: " Si quis extra, de baptismo," of Alexander VII. There it is said: " Si quis puerum ter in aqua merserit in nomine Patris et Filii et Spiritus Sancti, Amen; et non dixerit: *Ego te baptizo*, puer non est baptizatus." Besides the following proposition was condemned by Alexander VIII. in 1690: " Valuit aliquando baptismus sub hac forma collatus: In nomine Patris &c. prætermissis illis: *Ego te baptizo*." The word *te* is also necessary as Juenin justly holds; (ibid. q. 3.): but not the word *Ego* or *amen*, although these cannot be omitted without sin. The baptism would be valid, if for the word *baptizo* the minister of the sacrament should substitute the word *abluo, lavo* or the like; but he would not be excused from sin.

58. Our adversaries object from a passage in the Acts of the Apostles, in which it is said that baptism was first given in the name of Christ. "Baptizetur unusquisque vestrum in nomine Christi." (Act. ii. 38,) and from the eighth chapter (v. 12.) "In nomine Jesu Christi baptizabantur viri ac mulieres." I answer that the words *in nomine Jesu Christi* mean that the persons to whom allusion is made were baptized not with the baptism of the Baptist, but with the baptism instituted by Christ. These words are thus expounded by St. Augustine: "In nomine Jesu Christi," says the Holy Doctor," jussi sunt baptizari, et tamen intelliguntur non baptizati, nisi in nomine Patris et Filii et Spiritus Sancti. Cur non sic audis de Filio Dei; *omnia per ipsum facta sunt*, ut et non nominatum intelligas ibi etiam Spiritum Sanctum ?" (l. 2, contra Max. c. 27.) Nor is our doctrine opposed to the answer of Pope Nicholas I. to the Bulgarians, in which he said that persons baptized by a certain Jew were validly baptized, "Si in nomine S. Trinitatis vel tantum in nomine Christi (sicut in actibus Apostolorum legitur) baptizati sunt (unum quippe idemque est ut S. exponit Ambrosius), rebaptizari non debent." For I say that Pope Nicholas had been asked not about the form, but only about the minister of baptism, and therefore he alludes only in a passing way to the form. "A quodam Judæ," says the Pontiff, "nescitis utrum christiano, an pagano, multos in patria vestra baptizatos asseritis, et quid de iis agendum consulitis." The adversaries add that St. Ambrose has written, that for baptism the invocation of one person of the Trinity is sufficient. "Qui unam dixerit," says the saint, "Trinitatem significavit. Si Christum dicas, et Deum Patrem, a quo unctus est Filius: et ipsum, qui unctus est, Filium; et Spiritum, quo unctus est, designasti." (l. i. de Spir. S. c. 3.) I answer that there St. Ambrose treats not of the form of baptism, but of its effect, which he says should be attributed to each person of the Trinity, and thus the saint intends to prove that in

acts *ad extra* what is attributed to one of the persons of the Trinity is understood to be attributed to the others.

59. Besides it is necessary to observe that because they are in a state of pure innocence, persons just baptized are, according to the constant persuasion of the holy Fathers and of the Church, free from all guilt and punishment, so that were they to die immediately after baptism they would be instantly admitted into heaven. Hence, Father Chalon says that many deferred baptism till death, because they believed that by receiving baptism at death, they should be exempt from all responsibility. Peter Lombard (lib. i. sent. d. 17,) has said that baptized infants are not just by intrinsic justice, but by the love which God bears them: but such imputative justice of Lombard has been commonly rejected by divines after the example of the Council of Trent, in which (sess. 11, can. 6.) it was condemned to say that man is justified not by the internal justice which God communicates to him, but by the external imputation of the justice of Jesus Christ. If a person in the state of sin should receive baptism without a detestation of his sin, all his faults shall be remitted as soon as he repents of them: for the sacrament will then revive, and produce its effect as if it had been originally received with the requisite dispositions.

60. It is necessary also to know that in ancient times when there was any notable doubt about the validity of baptism, it was repeated, as Father Martene proves against some who denied it, by showing that this was practised for more than 800 years. Every one knows that persons baptized by heretics should not be rebaptized, as St. Stephen declared against the opinion of St. Cyprian, and as was afterwards defined in the Council of Nice. Hence, in writing against the Donatists, who rebaptized persons who had been baptized by heretics, St. Augustine has solved all the difficulties proposed by St. Cyprian.

61. Till the sixth century, baptism was ordinarily conferred

N

by Bishops alone, as Father Chalon relates, (c. 17.) so that according to this author, in order to baptize in the churches of their titles, the Cardinals used to ask the permission of the Pope. When the people in the rural districts embraced the faith, it was necessary to permit priests to baptize in their churches. It is however, probable, as a certain author says, that bishops were the ordinary ministers of baptism, as long as the custom of baptizing only adults continued in the Church, but not after the custom of baptizing infants was introduced. In the ninth tome of his history, Tillemont says, that there is no doubt, but in the Latin Church laymen, according to the common doctrine of the Church taught by Tertullian, St. Jerome, and St. Augustine, administered baptism in cases of necessity: but he says that in the Greek Church, St. Basil and St. Cyprian appear to doubt whether this should be done. However, he adds that the reason why the Greek Church did not give express permission to laymen to baptize in extreme cases, was perhaps because it was apprehended that they might abuse it. In the work already quoted, (c. 17,) Father Chalon says that in the course of time, the Greeks themselves laid aside their doubt, and admitted that in case of necessity, all could baptize.

62. The custom of anointing the crown of the head with the chrism is most ancient; for although it was not universal, it is mentioned by Innocent the First in his decretal to the Bishop of Eugubio. The ceremony of putting in the hand of the Neophytes a lighted candle is also most ancient, it is mentioned by St. Ambrose (lib. de lapsu virg. c. 5,) and by St. Gregory Nazianzen, (Orat. de Bapt.)

63. In ancient times adults were confirmed with the holy chrism on the forehead, as soon as they came from the sacred font: they then assisted at mass, at which they received the communion. This practice is mentioned by St. Augustine (serm. 127.); and according to the Roman Ritual, it lasted till the twelfth or thirteenth century.

Father Chalon (c. 18.) asserts that this practice exists at present among the orientals. The Eucharist was not given to infants lest they should reject it: but, as St. Cyprian says, (lib. de lapsis) a small portion of the consecrated chalice, was given to them. And in the twelfth century, as Hugh of St. Victor advised (l. i. de sac. c. 20), in order to prevent every inconvenience, the priest used to dip his finger in the sacred blood, and put it into the mouth of the infant, saying: "May the body and blood of Jesus Christ preserve thy soul unto eternal life." From this practice, the author of the notes to the history of Father Chalon, (note 66) infers that even then it was believed that under one species alone the body and blood of Jesus Christ were contained.

On Confirmation.

1. Can. 1. "Si quis dixerit confirmationem baptizatorum otiosam cæremoniam esse et non potius verum et proprium sacramentum, aut olim nihil aliud fuisse quam catechesim quamdam qua adolescentiæ proximi fidei suæ rationem coram Ecclesia exponebant, anathema sit."

2. Can. 2. "Si quis dixerit injurios esse Spiritui Sancti eos qui sacro confirmationis chrismati virtutem aliquam tribuunt, anathema sit."

3. Can. 3. "Si quis dixerit sanctæ confirmationis ordinarium ministrum non esse solum episcopum, sed quemvis simplicem sacerdotem, anathema sit."

4. Be it observed on the word *ordinarium*, which was added to the preceding canon, that some were of opinion that the above-mentioned article should be omitted; because we know from the Council of Florence, that the sovereign Pontiffs have sometimes given simple priests power to confirm with chrism consecrated by a bishop. We also know that St. Gregory stated in a letter to the bishop of Cagliari, (lib. 4, ep. 26) that he gave this power to the priests of

those places in which there were not bishops. But on the
other hand Nobili, bishop of Acci, said that in the Council
of Florence the fact was mentioned, but the article was
not defined: and he held that the ministers of the sacraments appointed by Christ could not be changed. This was
the opinion also of Durandus, of Major, and of Adrian VI.,
but before he became Pope. For after being raised to the
chair of St. Peter, he granted to the Franciscans in the Indies
the power of administering confirmation: and this privilege
is preserved in the convent of St. Francis in Siviglia. A
similar privilege was given to the Friar Minors by John
XXII. Nicholas IV., Eugene IV., Leo X., and lastly by
Benedict XIV., in the bull *Eo quamvis tempore*, dated
May 4th, 1745.

5. Soave endeavours to throw discredit on the Council
for admitting this canon; and says that it appears strange
that the Fathers should depend on the epistle of St.
Gregory. If, he adds, this epistle had been lost, the Church
would have held the opposite. I answer that the conduct
of St. Gregory accords with the subsequent and antecedent practice, and which had been adopted before his time
in the Oriental Church, in which priests confirm infants
immediately after baptism, as Peter Arcudius states in the
second book of his *Concordia*. Nor is there any force in
the reply of Soave, that for six hundred years before the
time of St. Gregory we do not find in any book mention
made of such dispensation. For, in the first place, we find
it mentioned by the ancient author of the book *of Questions
regarding the New and Old Testament* (qu. 101.),
which has been ascribed to St. Augustine, and also by
another ancient author of comments on the epistle of St.
Paul to the Ephesians (c. 4.), attributed to St. Ambrose.
Besides, I say that several practices of the early ages were
not committed to writing, but were handed down by tradition to succeeding generations; and therefore the heretics,

because they reject tradition, have denied several dogmas of faith. Moreover we certainly should not suppose that so learned a man as St. Gregory would grant dispensations in this matter without being warranted to grant them by Scripture or tradition. Hence the Council prudently added to the abovementioned canon, the word *ordinarium*, which had been before adopted by the Council of Florence.

6. Thus it has been the constant practice in the western Church that Bishops alone should administer the sacrament of confirmation. In ancient times, confirmation was also given by the Chorepiscopi, but only by those who had received episcopal consecration, and not by the others who were but simple priests. We also find that the Popes granted the power of administering confirmation to certain Abbots, to the Abbot of Montecassino and others. But in an epistle to Decentius, Innocent I. expressly prohibited priests to give confirmation even to infants: " With regard," he says, "to the sealing (confirmation) of infants, it is manifest that this is permitted to no one but to bishops." Pope Gelasius says the same (Ep. 12, c. 6.). This was also forbidden by the Council of Constance, in the condemnation of the twentieth article of Wiclef, by the Council of Florence, and finally by the Council of Trent in the third canon. And should it be ever mentioned in history that the unction was given by priests, this must be understood of extreme unction, or of the unction of the crown of the head, or of the unction which was formerly given to converted heretics. It can only be admitted that the power of giving confirmation, as extraordinary ministers, has been sometimes granted to priests by the sovereign pontiffs, as has been already said with regard to the priests of Sardinia, and as is at present enjoyed by the Franciscan missionaries through the concession of Adrian II. Benedict XIV. has granted the same privilege to the guardian of the holy land. But this permission is

granted only by a particular dispensation of the Pope: without such dispensation the confirmation would, as Benedict XIV. says, (de synodo. lib. 7, c. 7, et seq.) be not only unlawful, but invalid. However in the East, priests were accustomed, even before the heresy of Nestorius, to administer confirmation. This custom commenced in Alexandria in Egypt, and was afterwards diffused through the other Oriental Churches, and continues till the present day, and was finally approved by three pontiffs, Leo X., Clement VII., and Alexander VIII., who declared that the Greeks should not be disturbed in the practice of this rite. Hence it is supposed that to prevent the separation of the Greeks, who are known to be so tenacious of their rites, from the Church of Rome, the Popes have granted this dispensation.

7. It will be useful here to make some additional observations regarding the sacrament of confirmation. From ecclesiastical history, it appears that the Lutherans and Calvinists were the first who denied that confirmation is a sacrament. But that it is a sacrament is very clear from the Acts of the Apostles (viii. 14.) where we find that St. Peter and St. John were sent to give the Holy Ghost (that is the sacrament of confirmation) to the Samaritans who had been baptized by Philip the deacon. And from the time of the apostles, it has been constantly administered by the bishops of the Church. "They," says St. Cyprian, "who are baptized, are presented to the prelates of the Church, that by our prayer and by the imposition of hands, they may receive the Holy Ghost, and be perfected with the seal of the Lord." (Ep. 13.) Tertullian also writes: "As soon as we leave the sacred font of baptism, we are anointed with blessed oil. They then impose hands upon us and give us the benediction, invoking the Holy Ghost." (de Bapt. c. 7.) The same has been taught by St. Jerome, St. Hilary, St. Augustine, and others. This appears also from the sacramentary of St. Gregory, published by Father Menard,

and from the manuscripts of the secretary of Pope Gelasius, who occupied the chair of St. Peter more than nine hundred years ago.

8. With regard to the matter of confirmation, it is certain that balsam is necessary *as a matter of precept;* but that it is necessary *for the validity of the sacrament* is denied with probability by Sotus, Navarre, Juenin, the Continuator of Tournely, and others, resting on the chapter (Pastoralis de Sacram. non iter.) in which Innocent III. being asked whether confirmation, conferred with oil alone, was valid, answered that "nothing was to be repeated, but that what was incautiously omitted should be carefully supplied." However, it is more commonly held that balsam is necessary for the validity of the sacrament: this is taught by Bellarmine, Gonet, the author of the Theology of Perigord, by Concina, and others, along with St. Thomas, (3 p. q. 72, a. 2.) and the Roman Catechism. (n. 7.) It is proved from the Council of Florence, in which it was stated that the matter of confirmation is chrism. *composed of oil and balsam.* In answer to the passage quoted from Innocent III. the advocates of the latter opinion say, with the Gloss, that there it is said that *nothing is to be repeated,* because "what is not done before is not said to *be repeated.*" This answer is not satisfactory. Hence, as Ferrari says, (bibl. v. Confirmatio, n. 10.) on the authority of a decree of the Sacred Congregation of the Council, the first opinion does not cease to be sufficiently probable. But since, without balsam, the validity of the sacrament would be at least dubious, the confirmation should be repeated conditionally. Along with the balsam the Greeks add about forty kinds of sweet scented spices and perfumes. We do not find it stated that during the entire of the fourth century any day was fixed for the consecration of the chrism: but in the fifth century the custom of consecrating it on holy Thursday was introduced, and was after-

wards established, as we find in the Sacramentary of Gelasius: at present the same day is fixed in the Greek rituals.
Cardinal Lambertini says, (De fest. par. 1, p. 257) that in
ancient times there were three masses on holy Thursday;
in the first penitents were reconciled, in the second the
chrism was consecrated, and the third was celebrated in
honour of the solemnity.   In Greece the chrism was consecrated only by the three patriarchs; but in the west it
was consecrated in his own diocess by every Bishop, assisted
by twelve priests, and by seven deacons, as has been declared by Innocent III. and as is practised at present.   The
Bishop is assisted by so many priests and deacons, because
formerly such was the number of ministers that formed the
college which served the bishop in his cathedral for the
benefit of the entire diocess.   The benediction of the oil for
catechumens and for the sick, is more ancient than that of
the chrism: for greater convenience these three benedictions are given at the same time.   In the Roman Order we
find that the chrism was given in the church or in the
sacristy.

9. The form of confirmation that has been used in the
Latin Church, at least from the twelfth century, consists in
the words, "N., signo te signo crucis, et confirmo te Chrismate salutis in nomine Patris, et Filii et Spiritus Sancti.
Amen." But before that time the form was various: towards
the eighth century the form of the Roman order was shorter:
it was in these words: " Confirmo te in nomine Patris et
Filii et Spiritus Sancti." Amalarius mentions another form
still shorter ,which consisted in the words: "In nomine Patris
et Filii et Spiritus Sancti." In England the invocation of
the most Holy Trinity was omitted: in the pontifical of
of Elbert, bishop of York, who lived about the middle of
the eighth century, the following form was given: " Receive
the sign of the holy cross along with the chrism of salvation
in Jesus Christ our Lord, unto eternal life, amen." In the

Sacramentary of Gelasius, whilst he signed the forehead of the person to be confirmed, the bishop said: " The sign of the cross unto eternal life, amen." Gelasius lived more than nine hundred years ago. In the oriental churches the form, as was prescribed by the Council of Constantinople, was: " Signaculum doni Spiritus Sancti." These words were said by the minister of the sacrament whilst he anointed the forehead of the person to be confirmed. The bishop anoints with chrism, not only the forehead, but also the eyes, the ears, &c., saying at the same time several prayers. In other churches not in the east, various forms were used.

10. In ancient times, till the thirteenth century, whenever the bishop baptized either adults or infants, he gave them confirmation immediately after baptism. This practice is followed even at present in the oriental church, as Father Chalon relates (c. 3.): but there is no proof that it is universal. According to the Roman catechism, confirmation is not given to children, till they attain the age of twelve, or at least of seven years: however Benedict XIV. (de synod. lib. 7, c. 10.) says that it may be given to children before that age when they are in danger of death, or if the bishop should be obliged to be absent for a long time.

11. Father Chalon writes (c. 10, en fin.) that in the Greek Church we do not find that in giving confirmation, the bishop imposes hands except in anointing with the chrism: this practice accords with the opinion of the theologians who hold that the anointing with chrism includes the imposition of hands. But with regard to the Latin Church, he says that all the latin authors, and all the sacramentaries and rituals prescribe the unction of the forehead along with the accompanying words.

12. I am unwilling to omit in this place, the explanation of the great question regarding the matter and form of confirmation, on which I have written at length in my moral theology; here I shall be as brief as possible. There are

various opinions, but two of them are more commonly held. The first is, that in this sacrament there are two partial matters, and two partial forms. The first matter is the imposition of hands by the bishop at the beginning, when he extends his hands towards the persons to be confirmed, and the first form is the prayer which he then recites : the second partial matter is the unction with chrism, by the bishop, of the forehead of the person to be confirmed, and the second form consists in the words : " Signo te, signo crucis, &c." This opinion is held by Merbesius, Juenin, Habert, Genettus, Du-Hamel, &c.; Tournely thinks it probable.

13. The second opinion which appears to be commonly held, is that the matter of confirmation consists in the unction with chrism, along with the accompanying imposition of hands. This opinion is adopted by St. Thomas (3 p. qu. 72, art. 2), and in the first lesson on the 6th chapter of the epistle to the Hebrews, in which he says that the matter of confirmation is the imposition of hands, which accompanies the unction. This opinion is maintained by an immense number of divines; by St. Bonaventure, by Estius, Waldensis, Cabassutius, St. Antonine, Bellarmine, Silvius, who even says that it is of faith that the matter of confirmation consists entirely in the unction with chrism, by John Lawrence Berti, who strenuously defends it as certain: it is also held by Scotus, Gonet, Collet, by the Continuator of Tournely, by the author of the *Theologia Petrocorensis*, by Soto, Frassen, Antoine, Peter Demarca, and many others quoted by Witasse, who asserts that it is the opinion of all the Thomists and Scotists. The Roman catechism says (s. 7), that the chrism of oil and balsam is the sole matter of confirmation, and adds : " Quod autem ea sit hujus sacramenti materia tum sancta Ecclesia et concilia perpetuo docuerunt, tum a quamplurimis S. Patribus traditum." I have maintained with Bellarmine, that this

opinion is morally certain; that it is so will appear from the arguments which I shall adduce.

14. No one doubts that for confirmation, both the unction with chrism, and the imposition of hands are necessary. But this imposition is that which accompanies the unction, as we learn from the declaration of Innocent III. (Can. unic. de sacr. uncto, s. Per frontis). There the Pontiff says: "Per frontis chrismationem manus impositio designetar: quæ alio nomine dicitur confirmatio; quia per eam Spiritus Sanctus ad augmentum datur et robur." The word *designatur* should not be taken to mean the same as *significatur aut figuratur*, but to signify the same as *signatur, assignatur, aut, habetur confirmatio:* this is evident from the words which immediately follow: "Unde cum cæteras unctiones simplex sacerdos valeat exhibere, hanc nonnisi summus sacerdos, idest episcopus, debet conferre: quia de solis apostolis legitur (quorum vicarii sunt episcopi) quod per manus impositionem Spiritum Sanctum dabant." Here the Pontiff quotes the words of the Acts of the Apostles (c. 8, v. 17), where it is related that St. Peter and St. John confirmed the Samaritans (who had been already baptized) by imposing hands upon them. "Tunc imponebant manus super illos, et accipiebant Spiritum Sanctum." Immediately after these words he adds: "Cujus adventum per unctionis ministerium designatur." By saying then that bishops alone can give the unction because the Apostles alone imposed hands, he says by consequence, that that imposition of hands was the same for the unction, which the unction is now for the imposition of hands. Thus bishops by giving the unction now do the same as the Apostles did by imposing hands; otherwise we must say that the Apostles changed the matter of confirmation. But, as Bellarmine justly remarks, this cannot be said; since the matter and form could be instituted only by Christ, and cannot be altered by others.

15. This is confirmed by another canon of the same Pope, which is still more clear on the point. (cap. 4, Quanto, de consuetud.)   There he says: " Ut est sacramentum confirmationis, quod, chrismando renatos, soli debent episcopi per manus impositionem conferre." Mark the words, " Chrismando......per manus impositionem:" then to impose hands with the chrism is the same as to confirm.   It is also proved by the profession of faith of the Emperor Paleologus, which we find in his letter to Gregory X., and which was quoted and approved in the 2nd Council of Lyons.   In that profession of faith we find these words: " Aliud est sacramentum confirmationis, quod per manuum impositionem episcopi conferunt chrismandis renatis."

16. To all this may be added the declaration of Eugene IV., which was approved by the Council of Florence. " Secundum sacramentum," says the Pontiff, " est confirmatio cujus materia est chrisma confectum ex oleo et balsamo......per episcopum benedictum.   Forma autem est: Signo te signo crucis, et confirmo chrismate salutis, in nomine Patris et Filii et Spiritus Sancti, Amen." Hence several authors say that according to this definition it is of faith that the unction by the bishop is the sole matter, and the accompanying words the sole form of confirmation.   I also add the declaration of Benedict XIV., in his encyclical letter to the archbishops and bishops of the Greek rite (Tom. 4, Bullar, n. 54, p. 225, s. 51) in which he says of the two opinions, first: " Unicuique licet sequi partem quæ placuerit:" that is, that it is lawful to adopt the first opinion that there are two partial matters and forms, and this is the more secure: or to adopt the second opinion, or that the unction by the hand of the bishop is the sole matter and that the accompanying words are the sole form. But in the fifty-second section he declares expressly that it is beyond dispute that confirmation is conferred whenever the minister applies the unction and pronounces the accom-

panying form: "Est extra controversiam, in ecclesia latina (he had already declared the same regarding the Greek Church), confirmationis sacramentum conferri, adhibito sacro chrismate oleo olivarum balsamo commixto, ductoque signo crucis per ministrum in fronte suscipientis dum idem minister formæ verba profert.

17. Let it be here observed that in the Bull "Etsi pastoralis," (n. 57, t. 1, bull. s. 3. n. 4.) Benedict XIV. declared that persons living among the Greeks, who refuse, or neglect, to receive confirmation when it is in their power to receive it, should be admonished by their bishops, that such omission or neglect is a grievous sin. "Monendi sunt ab ordinariis locorum eos gravis peccati reatu teneri, si cum possint, ad confirmationem accedere renuunt ac negligunt." The same should certainly be said of persons living among the Latins.

THIRTEENTH SESSION.

ON THE SACRAMENT OF THE EUCHARIST.

1. In this session, the Fathers resolved to teach, as they had done in the session on justification, the true doctrine concerning the Eucharist, that the faithful might know what they were obliged to believe regarding this sacrament. Hence, in the proemium, it was stated, that, because they wished to extirpate the errors regarding this sacrament, and to expound the doctrine which the Church, instructed in the beginning by Jesus Christ, and afterwards enlightened by the Holy Ghost, had always held, and shall for ever hold, the Fathers forbade any one to believe, teach, or preach otherwise than they taught.

2. Soave says that the Thomists as well as the Scotists maintained that the Church had declared their particular opinions to be of faith. But this was contrary to the intention of the Fathers, as appears from the acts, and from the definitions themselves, which were drawn up in words which could not prejudice the opinions of any of the schools. And, therefore, as we shall see, the Council wished to decide nothing regarding the mode of the sacramental presence of Jesus Christ, or regarding the question whether the grace infused by receiving communion under both species, is equal to, or greater than that which is communicated when the Eucharist is received only under one species.

3. Soave also asserts that the Italians, through fear of being covered with shame by the superior learning of the German and Flemish divines, complained of the order made

by the persons who presided, that the points of doctrine should be established by the authority of Scripture and of the Fathers. But Pallavicini says that the assertion of Soave is false; because, in the preceding sessions, the Italians had displayed their erudition by frequent quotations from the Scriptures, Councils, and Fathers, and that among them there was a Melchior Cano, a Sotus, a Seripando, a Catherinus, a Salmeron, and a Lainez, who pledged himself not to quote the words of any author which he had not read in the original.

4. In the first chapter, it is defined in the following words, that in the Eucharist, the body and blood of Jesus Christ are truly, really, and substantially contained under the consecrated species of bread and wine. "Docet S. Synodus in Eucharistæ sacramento post panis et vini consecrationem Jesum Christum, verum Deum atque hominem, vere, realiter ac substantialiter sub specie illarum rerum sensibilium contineri. Nec enim inter se pugnant, ut ipse Salvator semper ad dexteram Patris in cœlis assideat juxta modum existendi naturalem, et ut multis......aliis in locis sacramentaliter præsens sua substantia nobis adsit." In this definition the Council wished to leave untouched the question between the Thomists and Scotists, whether one and the same body can by the divine power exist in several places with the same mode with which it naturally exists only in one place. "Ita enim majores nostri omnes......apertissime professi sunt hoc sacramentum in ultima cœna Redemptorem nostrum instituisse, cum post panis vinique benedictionem se suum ipsius corpus illis præbere ac suum sanguinem disertis......verbis testatus est; quæ verba, a sanctis evangelistis commemorata et a S. Paulo repetita, cum propriam illam......significationem præ se ferant secundum quam a Patribus intellecta sunt indignissimum flagitium est ea......ad fictitios tropos,......contra universum Ecclesiæ sensum detorqueri: quæ tanquam columna et firmamentum

veritatis, hæc ab impiis hominibus excogitata commenta......
detestata est."

5. The sacrament of the Eucharist had never been
impugned till the ninth century: about that period a certain
John Scotus began to teach that the Eucharist was but a
figure. In the eleventh century, Berengarius defended the
same heresy: he retracted several times and afterwards
relapsed into various errors: but was finally reconciled at
death with the Catholic Church in 1088. But it was
only in the sixteenth century that the sect was formed
which has constantly opposed the dogma of the Eucharist.
The first who impugned it, was Carlostad, Archdeacon of
Wirtemberg, in Saxony. Ecolampadius, a monk of the
order of St. Bridget, and Zuinglius, a parish priest, adopted
the same error. They were afterwards joined by Bucer
and Calvin, who, as Father Chalon has written, asserted
that the Eucharist is not even a sacrament, but a mere external commemoration. Luther denied the transubstantiation
of the bread and wine into the body and blood of Christ,
and abolished private masses: but he said that without
rejecting the gospel he could not deny the real presence of
the body and blood of Jesus Christ in the Eucharist.

6. It will be useful in this place to examine part by
part the words of this first chapter. The Council says:
vere, realiter et substantialiter." *Vere*, to exclude the
figurative presence of Jesus Christ, which was taught by
the Sacramentarians; the figure is opposed to the truth,
and therefore the word *vere* was used. *Realiter*, to exclude the imaginary presence; because the heretics say
that the flesh of Jesus Christ is not corporally present as it
is in heaven, but as faith apprehends it, that is as if it were
present. Calvin does not refuse to say that the real
body of Jesus Christ is in the Eucharist, but he will not
admit that it is really present. The Council also says:
substantialiter, to exclude the presence of mere efficacy or

virtue to which Calvin reduced the presence of the real body of Jesus Christ, saying that the Eucharist does not contain the substance of the body of Jesus Christ, but its virtue or efficacy, by which the Lord communicates himself and his goods to us. But we say that it contains the entire substance of his body into which the substance of the bread is converted. Hence, we say, as shall be soon explained more fully, that under the species of bread the body of Christ neither occupies place, nor has natural extension, but that, as St. Thomas teaches, (4. p. q. 76, a. 1, ad. 3.) it is sacramentally present after the manner of a substance, precisely as the substance of bread was before the consecration.

7. The Council also says: "Nec enim hæc inter se pugnant, ut Salvator in cœlis assideat juxta modum naturalem, et ut multis......aliis in locis sacramentaliter præsens sua substantia nobis adsit ea existendi ratione quam verbis exprimere vix possumus." The Council then teaches that the body of Jesus Christ is in heaven according to its natural mode, but that his sacramental substance is present in many other places. Thus the consecrated host, and every particle of it contains the very body of Jesus Christ, which is seated in heaven. And this we must believe because God is omnipotent, and because he himself has revealed it, saying: *This is my body.* It matters not that we are unable to comprehend how this can be? Were we to regulate the mysteries of faith according to our limited understanding, we would soon deny more than one of these mysteries, and particularly the mysteries of the Trinity and Incarnation: for we cannot comprehend how three persons are the same substance, and how in a single person there are two natures, one divine and the other human.

8. The heretics say that although God is omnipotent, he cannot do things which are in themselves repugnant and contradictory: such (they say) as would be to make a human

body be present in the Eucharist without its extension and qualities: for God cannot deprive things of their essence: and it is essential to a body to have extension and quantity. I answer that God cannot take away its essence from any thing; but he can take away a property from the essence: he cannot deprive fire of its essence, but he can deprive it of the property of burning, as he did with regard to the three Hebrew children. Thus also, although he cannot make a body exist without extension and quantity, he can make it exist without occupying place, without being divisible, and so as to be entire under every minute part of the visible species which contain it, with an extension not natural, but miraculous and substantial. It is thus, precisely, that the body of Jesus Christ is present in the Eucharist; for this implies that the body is present in substance, that is, that as the substance of the bread was before under its own species, and did not occupy place, and was entire in every part of the species, so the body of Christ, into which the substance of the bread is converted, does not occupy more place than the substance of the bread occupied before, according to its dimension: and thus it is entire in each part of the species as the entire substance of the bread was in each part before the consecration. This is the doctrine of St. Thomas: "Tota substantia corporis Christi continetur in hoc sacramento post consecrationem, sicut ante consecrationem continebatur ibi tota substantia panis." (3. p. q. 76, a. 1.) the Saint adds (ibid. ad 3.): "Propria autem totalitas substantiæ continetur indifferenter in pauca vel magna quantitate; unde et tota substantia corporis et sanguinis Christi continetur hoc sacramento."

9. The body of Christ is not in this sacrament, as in place *definitive,* so that being there it cannot be in another place; nor is it there *circumscriptivè,* that is, according to the measure of the proper quantity corresponding to the quan-

tity of place. Hence the place in which the body of Christ is, is not a vacuum, neither can it be said to be filled with the substance of the body of Christ, since it is filled with the sacramental species which occupy that place, at least by a miracle, as they miraculously subsist after the manner of a substance.

10. Nor can it be said that the body of Christ is in the Sacrament, in a moveable manner; for since it is not there as in place, the Lord is not moved in this sacrament, according as the place is changed; but he can be moved only by accident, on account of the species under which he is contained: so that according to the motion of the species, it may be said, that Christ, who is contained under them, is moved. Thus when the human body is moved, the soul, which is not capable of existing in place, is also moved by accident.

11. And here it is necessary to observe, that when the species are corrupted, the body of Christ ceases to remain under them, not because it depends on them, but because this sacrament is instituted in such a manner, that Christ remains under the species as long as they exist, and ceases to remain under them when they cease to exist, just as God ceases to be the Lord of the creatures that cease to exist. This is the doctrine of St. Thomas. " Quibus (speciebus)," says the holy Doctor, " cessantibus, desinit esse corpus Christi sub eis; non quia ab eis dependeat, sed quia tollitur habitudo corporis Christi ad illas species, quemadmodum Deus desinit esse Dominus creaturæ deficientis." (3 p. q. 76, art. 5, ad. 3.)

12. In the same chapter the Council says: " Post panis vinique benedictionemse suum corpus illis præbere......perspicuis verbis testatus est; quæ verba a sanctis evangelistis commemorata, et a S. Paulo postea repetita, cum propriam significationem præ se ferant, secundum quam a Patribus intellecta sunt flagitium est ea a quibusdam pravis hominibus

ad fictitios tropos......contra......Ecclesiæ sensum detorqueri." *Post panis vinique benedictionem:* these words
are against the Lutheran ubiquists, who hold, that even before the consecration, the species contain the body of the
Lord. They are also against the Calvinists, who say that
the Eucharist is not a union of the faithful with Christ by
means of his body and blood, but only a sign of such union,
which was before effected by means of faith; and therefore
they maintain that the Eucharist is not made a sacrament
by the consecration of the priest, but by the Evangelical
promise contained in the discourse of the Redeemer.

13. *Perspicuis verbis testatus, est, &c.* These words
of Jesus Christ we find in the gospels of St. Matthew, (c. 26);
of St. Mark, (c. 14); and of St. Luke, (c. 22). The words
are: "Take and eat: this is my body." They were afterwards repeated by St. Paul, in the first epistle to the Corinthians, (c. 11). St. Cyril exclaims: " Since he has said
of the bread: *This is my Body*, who will ever dare to
doubt it? And since he himself has said: "*This is my
blood*, who will say that it is not his blood?" (Catech.
mystag. 4.) It is a certain rule, commonly received by all
the Fathers and theologians, that the words of Scripture
should be taken in their strict sense, whenever a clear absurdity does not follow from the literal meaning; for
if we could explain all the words of Scripture in the tropical
and figurative sense, it would be impossible to draw a convincing proof of any dogma from the inspired writings.

14. This doctrine of the Eucharist was afterwards confirmed by the same Apostle, when, speaking of the use of
this sacrament, he said: " The chalice of benediction which
we bless, is it not the communion of the blood of Christ?
And the bread which we break, is it not the partaking of
the body of the Lord?" (1 Cor. x. 16.) These words show
very clearly, that the Eucharist contains the true body and
blood of Jesus Christ. The Apostle taught the same doc-

trine, when he said: " But let a man prove himself; and so let him eat of that bread, and drink of the chalice. For he that eateth and drinketh unworthily, eateth and drinketh judgment to himself, not discerning the body of the Lord." (1 Cor. xi. 28, &c.) Mark the words, " *not discerning the body of the Lord.*" If we had to venerate only the figure of the body of Christ, St. Paul would not have condemned with so much severity, those who communicate in the state of sin: he declares them deserving of eternal death, inasmuch as by communicating unworthily, they do not discern the body of Christ from earthly food.

15. Oh God, how great the malice and ingratitude of men! The Lord wished to bestow upon us this infinite gift of his love, in which he gives himself entirely to us: " Divitias sui erga homines amoris velut effudit," says the Council. But men are unwilling to be grateful to him, and seek, in many ways, to distort to another meaning, the words of the Lord, " this is my body." Some say that the pronoun *hoc* means *hîc*. But how can this be? If the word *hoc* is taken as adjective, it cannot agree with bread (panis), which is of the masculine gender, but must agree with the word body (corpus), which is *neuter*. Nor does it matter that the pronoun *hoc* and the verb *est* have no signification till the words *corpus meum* are pronounced: for it not unfrequently happens that in many propositions the antecedent words have not their signification till the proposition is complete. If the word *hoc* is taken as a substantive, as St. Thomas understands it (3 p. qu. 78, a. 5), then *tò hoc* does not signify this body or this bread, but signifies, this thing or this substance contained under these species of bread, is my body.

16. Others, among whom is Zuinglius, distort the sense of the word *est*, and say that it means the same as *significat;* they take an example from Exodus: " Est enim phase (idest transitus) Domini," xii. 11, in which the pas-

chal lamb, along with the ceremonies prescribed, *was* not, (as the inspired writer says), but *signified* the passage of the Lord. This most silly interpretation of Zuinglius, has had but few followers, for in our case, it is altogether improper; it can be admitted only when the word *est* cannot have its own signification.

17. The Sacramentarians say, that the word *corpus* means the figure of the body. But this interpretation, as has been already said, is at variance with the common rule, that the words of Scripture should be taken in the literal sense, when it does not involve a manifest absurdity. Besides, this exposition is clearly opposed to the following words of St. Paul, who, after the words " *hoc est corpus meum,*" adds, " *quod pro vobis tradetur.*" (1 Cor. ii. 24.) Our Lord did not deliver up to his passion the figure of his body, but his true body. Speaking of his blood, the Redeemer said: " *Hic est enim sanguis meus novi testamenti qui pro multis effundetur in remissionem peccatorum.*" (Matt. 26.) Then the blood of Jesus Christ was to be shed: the blood is shed, and not the figure of the blood.

18. Besides, the truth of the real presence of the true body and blood of the Lord, in the sacrament of the altar, is confirmed, and evidently declared in the sixth chapter of St. John. The innovators err in saying, that that chapter has reference only to the Incarnation of the Saviour. It is true that the entire chapter does not regard the Eucharist, but it is certain that from the fifty-second verse, the Redeemer, as Calvin himself admits, (Inst. lib. 4, c. 17, s. 1.) speaks of the holy sacrament. This is proved first by the words: " The bread that I will give is my flesh, for the life of the world." (John vi. 52.) Had our Lord spoken of the manducation by faith alone, as the innovators say, he would not have said, I *will* give, for such manducation existed at all times. Even in the old law, the faithful figuratively eat Jesus Christ, by means of faith. He said : " I

will give," because he then promised to give us his flesh in the sacrament, which he afterwards instituted at the last supper. He said: "*that I will give*," says the angelic Doctor, because this sacrament had not been as yet instituted......But he does not say: it signifies my flesh, but "it is my flesh, because what is taken is truly the body of Christ." (Lect. 9 in Jo.) Besides, had our Lord intended to speak in that place, only of the spiritual manducation by faith in his incarnation, he would not have said, *the bread that I will give*, but *the bread that I have given*, for he had already taken flesh, and many had already believed in him. This is also confirmed by the following words: "*My flesh is meat indeed, and my blood is drink indeed.*" (John vi. 56.) The distinction between meat and drink can occur only in the sacramental manducation of the body and blood of Christ; for in the spiritual manducation by faith, which is altogether internal, meat and drink are the same thing.

19. This is also proved from what the Capharnites said, when they heard the words of Jesus Christ, and from his answer to them. " How," said they, " can this man give us his flesh to eat?" (v. 53.) They in reality, departed from our Lord. " After this many of his disciples went back; and walked no more with him." (verse 67.) Now, if the Eucharist did not really contain the flesh of Jesus Christ, he could have instantly removed their agitation and doubts, by saying, that men should eat his flesh, merely by faith. But no, he answered absolutely: " Except you eat the flesh of the Son of Man, and drink his blood, you shall not have life in you." (verse 54.) And to the twelve Apostles who remained with him, he said: " Will you also go away?" St. Peter answered: " Lord, to whom shall we go? Thou hast the words of eternal life. And we have believed and have known, that thou art Christ the Son of God." (John vi. 68, &c.) To confirm the truth of the real presence, the Saviour

said: "For my flesh is meat indeed, and my blood
is drink indeed." (verse 56.)   Had he not given us his
true flesh and his true blood in the Eucharist, the use of
these words would be altogether improper.   Although the
Council has not declared, in an express canon, that in this
sixth chapter of St. John, the Redeemer spoke of the real
manducation of his flesh, still, in several places, for example, in the second chapter of this Session, and in the first
chapter of the 21st Session, it quotes several texts from this
chapter of St. John, to prove and confirm the truth of the
Eucharist.   Besides, in the second Council of Nice (act 6),
from the words, *except you eat the flesh of the Son of
Man, &c.*, it was proved that in the sacrifice of the altar,
the true and real body and blood of Jesus Christ are
offered.

20. Against our doctrine, Picenino the preacher, objects
from the words of St. Augustine, where speaking of the text
of St. John, " except you eat the flesh of the Son of Man,
&c;" the holy Doctor says, that the flesh of the Lord is a
figure, by which we are commanded to preserve the remembrance of his passion: " Figura est præcipiens passione do-
minica esse communicandum." (l. 3, de doctr. ch. c. 16.)
I answer, that there is no doubt but the *Eucharist
has been instituted in commemoration of the passion, as
the Evangelists tell us: " Do this for a commemoration
of me." And St. Paul says: " As often as you shall
eat this bread,.........you shall show the death of the
Lord." But it is necessary to make a distinction with
regard to the figures which we find in the scriptures;
some of them are mere figures, for the words cannot be understood in the strict sense, such as when it is
said of Christ that he is a *door*, a *lion*, a *vine*, &c.   Other
figures are truths which the words express, and at the
same time, figures of other mysteries which they signify, as
when the Apostle said: " Abraham had two sons: the one by a

bondwoman, and the other by a freewoman.........which things are said by an allegory—for these are the two testaments." (Gal. iv. 22—24.) Behold Abraham had two sons, Isaac and Ismael, who were really his sons: but they were at the same time, a figure of the Old and New Testament. The same is true of the sacrifice of Isaac, and of the spoliation of the Egyptians. Thus, in the scriptures, figures consist sometimes in the words alone, and at other times in a fact, which is at the same time, a real fact and a real figure. This is precisely the case with regard to the flesh of Jesus Christ in the Eucharist; it is the true flesh of Jesus Christ, and at the same time, a figure which reminds us of his passion. And this is what St. Augustine meant when he called the flesh of our Lord a figure. For how could the holy Doctor intend to say, that the flesh of Jesus Christ was a mere figure, when he asserts so frequently in his works, that the Eucharist contains the true body and blood of Christ? In one place in particular, he says: " We receive with a faithful heart and mouth, Jesus Christ giving us his flesh to be eaten, and his blood to be drunk." (Lib. 2, c. 9, adv. leg. et prop.) In another place, he says: " The bread which you see on the altar, sanctified by the word of God, is the body of Christ; the chalice, or what the chalice contains, sanctified by the word of God, is the blood of Christ." (Ser. 83, de diver. nunc. 227.)

21. The adversaries object also, from the answer of our Lord to the Capharnites, when after he had foretold the institution of the sacrament of the Eucharist, they said: " How can this man give us his flesh to eat?" (John vi. 53.) In answer to them, the Saviour said: " It is the spirit that quickeneth; the flesh profiteth nothing." (v. 64.) Hence, say the innovators, the real manducation of the flesh of Christ is unprofitable; it is only the spiritual manducation by faith that profits the soul. To this objection St. Augustine gives the following answer: " Non prodest quidquam, sed quomodo illi intellexerunt, quomodo in cadavere

P

caro dilaniatur et in macello venditur, non quomodo spiritu vegetatur, caro non prodest sola: accedat spiritus et prodest multum." (Tr. 26 in Jo.) Thus it profits nothing to eat mere dead flesh, such as is sold in the market, separated from the spirit, that is from the soul and divinity of Jesus Christ. It was in this sense the Capharnites understood the words of Jesus Christ. But on the other hand, the sacramental manducation of his flesh profiteth much. The error then of the Jews consisted not in thinking that our Lord wished to give us his flesh to eat, but in conceiving that we were to eat it, as we eat flesh sold in the market.

22. But of what use is it to the heretics to bring forward clear texts of Scripture, passages from the Fathers, and evident reasons, when by separating from the Catholic church, they have lost the way of arriving at the truth? All their errors arise from their determination not to submit to the judgment of the church, which God has declared to be the pillar and the ground of the truth. They say that the Holy Ghost enlightens every christian with the knowledge of the truths which he has to believe. But, with regard to this sacrament of the Eucharist, I ask, were not Luther and Zuinglius christians? Luther says that the Eucharist contains the real body of Jesus Christ, Zuinglius asserts that it does not contain the real body, but only the sign of the body of Christ. Now, which of the two holds the truth, and which of them should we follow? On the other hand, we Catholics have the Holy Church, which in so many Councils teaches us that the species of bread, after the consecration, really contains the body of Jesus Christ: why should we not believe it? Thus we have been taught first by the Council of Alexandria, which was afterwards approved by the second Œcumenical Council. Thus we have been taught by the second Council of Nice, and by the 7th Œcumenical Council (act. 6, tom. 3, in fin.) in which it was condemned as erroneous to say that the Eucharist contains

only the figure of the body of Jesus Christ. "Dixit," says this council, " accipite, edi̱te hoc est corpus meum......non autem dixit: sumite, edite imaginem corporis mei." Thus we have been taught by the council held in Rome, under Gregory VII. in 1079, in which Berengarius abjured his heresy, and made his profession of faith, acknowledging that by the consecration, the bread and wine are substantially converted into the body and blood of Christ. Thus we have been taught in the fourth Council of Lateran, under Innocent III. in 1215, in which the Fathers declared (c. 1): " Credimus corpus et sanguinem Christi sub speciebus panis et vini veraciter contineri transubstantiatis pane in corpus et vino in sanguinem." Thus we have been taught by the Council of Florence, in these words: " Substantiam panis in corpus Christi converti, &c." (In doct. de sacr. c. 4.) Thus in fine we are taught by the Council of Trent (Can. 1, Sess. 13): " Si quis negaverit," says the Council, in ss. Eucharistiæ sacramento contineri vere, realiter, et substantialiter corpus et sanguinem una cum anima et Divinitate Domini nostri Jesu Christi ac proinde totum Christum; sed dixerit tantummodo esse in eo ut in signo vel figura aut virtute, anathema sit." *In signo,* as Zuinglius said: *in figura,* as Ecolampadius held; *in virtute,* as was maintained by Calvin, who asserted that the Eucharist contained the body of Jesus Christ, in as much as it contained the virtue of making us communicate with the body of Jesus Christ.

23. In the second chapter the Council speaks of the love which Jesus Christ has shown us, in the institution of the Eucharist, and of the fruits which souls receive from this great sacrament. " Salvator noster discessurus ex hoc mundo ad Patrem sacramentum hoc instituit, in quo divitias divini sui erga homines amoris velut effudit. Sumi autem voluit tanquam animarum cibum, quo alantur et confortentur viventes vita illius qui dixit; *qui manducat me, et ipse vivet propter me.*" (Jo. vi. 58); " et tanquam anti-

dotum, quo liberemur a culpis quotidianis, et a peccatis
mortalibus præservemur. Pignus præterea id esse voluit
futuræ nostræ gloriæ et symbolum illius corporis, cujus ipse
caput existit, et nos membra, &c."

24. To this chapter corresponds the fifth canon, in
which it is condemned to say, that the principal fruit of the
Eucharist is the remission of sins, or that no other fruit re-
sults from it: " Si quis dixerit vel præcipuum fructum ss.
Eucharistiæ esse remissionem peccatorum, vel ex ea non
alios effectus provenire, anathema sit."

25. In the third chapter, it is said that the other sacraments confer grace when they are received, but that in the
Eucharist, even before its reception, the author of grace is
contained; for, by the efficacy of the words of consecration,
his body is present under the species of bread, and his
blood under the species of wine; his body is also under the
species of wine, and his blood under the species of bread,
along with his soul under each species, by virtue of the natural connexion which exists between them, and also along
with the divinity which is likewise present under each species, on account of the hypostatic union of the Word with
the body and soul of our Lord. Hence Jesus Christ is contained entirely under one species, as well as under both,
and under each part of them. " Commune est......Eucha-
ristiæ cum cæteris sacramentis, symbolum esse rei sacræ et
invisibilis gratiæ formam visibilem: verum illud in ea excel-
lens et singulare reperitur quod reliqua sacramenta tunc
sanctificandi vim habent cum quis illis utitur, at in Eucharistia ipse sanctitatis auctor ante usum est; nondum enim
Eucharistia de manu Domini apostoli susceperunt cum vere
tamen ipse affirmaret corpus suum esse quod præbebat. Et
semper hæc fides in Ecclesia Dei fuit, statim post consecrationem verum Domini corpus verumque ejus sanguinem sub
panis et vini specie una cum ipsius anima et divinitate existere; sed corpus sub specie panis et sanguinem sub vini specie

ex vi verborum; ipsum autem corpus sub specie vini, et sanguinem sub specie panis, animamque sub utraque, vi naturalis illius connexionis et concomitantiæ qua partes Christi Domini qui......resurrexit......inter se copulantur; divinitatem porro propter admirabilem illam ejus cum corpore et anima hypostaticam unionem. Quapropter......totus...... Christus sub panis specie et sub quavis ipsius speciei parte, totus item sub vini specie et sub ejus partibus existit."

26. To this chapter corresponds the third canon: " Si quis negaverit in venerabili sacramento Eucharistiæ sub unaquaque specie et sub singulis cujusque speciei partibus, separatione facta, totum Christum contineri, anathema sit."

27. John Emilian, bishop of Tuy, proposed that the words *separatione facta*, should be added to the preceding canon, because it was held by some that Jesus Christ is not contained under every particle of the host, whilst it remains entire. The archbishop of Cagliari and others opposed the addition of the preceding words, because by their insertion, the opposite opinion would be implicitly condemned. However, the Council thought it right to add the words, because otherwise, the first opinion would be censured, and by their insertion, both opinions would remain untouched. Hence, it is certain, that it is not of faith that Jesus Christ is present, whole and entire under every part of the host before it is divided. Soave therefore errs, in saying, that from the addition of the above-mentioned words, *it appears to follow necessarily that our Lord is not entire in each part, before the division of the host.* For, from the addition of the words, *separatione facta*, it can only be inferred, that it is not heresy to say, that Christ is not entire in each part of the host before it is divided: but it is silliness to say that what is not condemned as heretical, is defined to be true.

28. To the third chapter also belongs the fourth canon: " Si quis dixerit, peracta consecratione, in admirabili Eucharistiæ sacramento non esse corpus et sanguinem Domini

nostri Jesu Christi, sed tantum in usu, dum sumitur, non autem ante vel post, et in hostiis seu partibus consecratis, quæ post communionem reservantur vel supersunt, non remanere verum corpus Domini, anathema sit."

29. In this canon was condemned the error of Luther, who said that Christ is not present in the Eucharist before or after the reception of the sacrament. In a letter to Simon Wolferinus, (l. 3, c. 1.) he said that the body of Christ is in the Eucharist from the beginning of the *Pater noster* in the mass, and remains in it during all the time that is necessary for the faithful to communicate without difficulty or haste. But I ask Luther, if there was no one to communicate at mass, or if by any accident the person who wished to communicate, should retire, would not the body of the Lord, which was present in the host, remain there without being received? Justly then has the Council taught that the body of Christ is present under the consecrated species, even when the sacrament is not received. In teaching this doctrine the Council rested on the most ancient tradition of the Church, and on the words of Jesus Christ, who, by saying that the Eucharist was his body, before the disciples received it, has assured us that he is present in the holy sacrament, even before its reception. Soave says that the reason which the Council has assigned in the third chapter, is not sufficient to prove that Jesus Christ is present in the Eucharist before its use, because the very *handing* of it to the person who communicates, is an action which appertains to the use of the sacrament. I answer that it is not true that all the actions which belong to the use, are the use of the sacrament; for it may happen that a person who intended to communicate will afterwards abstain from communion; and in such a case, it cannot be said, that the Eucharist has been used or received, but in that case Jesus Christ would be present under the Eucharistic species.

30. In the fourth chapter, the Fathers speak of transub-

stantiation, and say, that because Jesus Christ had said that what he held in his hands under the appearance of bread, was his body, the Church has always believed, and now declares, that by the consecration, the entire substance of the bread and wine is converted into the body and blood of Jesus Christ, and that this conversion, the Catholic Church properly calls *transubstantiation.* " Quoniam autem Christus......corpus suum id quod specie panis offerebat, vere esse dixit, ideo persuasum semper in Ecclesia Dei fuit, idque nunc denuo S. hæc Synodus declarat, per consecrationem panis et vini conversionem fieri totius substantiæ panis in substantiam corporis Christi et totius substantiæ vini in substantiam sanguinis ejus; quæ conversio convenienter et proprie a sancta Catholica ecclesia *transubstantiato* appellatur."

31. To this fourth chapter the second canon corresponds: " Si quis dixerit in sacro-sancto Eucharistiæ sacramento remanere substantiam panis et vini una cum corpore et sanguine Domini nostri Jesu Christi; negaveritque conversionem totius substantiæ panis in corpus, et vini in sanguinem, manentibus dumtaxat speciebus panis et vini, quam quidem conversionem Catholica ecclesia aptissime transubstantionem appellat, anathema sit."

32. Since it is certain, that by means of the words *hoc est corpus meum*, the Eucharist contains the body of Jesus Christ, the word *hoc* indicates the whole substance of the thing present, which is the body of our Lord, and not the substance of bread which had been before under the species. If the substance of bread remained, the word *hoc* (this) could not be used; but the Son of God should have said *hic* (*here*), or *in hoc* (*in this*). This is confirmed by the words of our Lord, in the 6th chapter of St. John: " The bread that I will give is my flesh." (verse 52). If the substance of bread remained, Jesus Christ could not have said, that the bread was his flesh; but he should have said that his flesh was in the bread.

33. But here Soave sallies forth, and says that the Council appears to have fallen into a contradiction: because on the one hand, it declared in the first chapter that the conversion of the bread into the body of Christ, could scarcely be expressed in words, and in this fourth chapter it says that this conversion is properly called transubstantiation. Since then he says, this conversion may be designated by an appropriate name, it should not be said that it cannot be expressed in words. To this objection, Pallavicini justly answers that the union between the Divine Word and the humanity of Christ is said to be ineffable, and still it is called *an hypostatic union.* Many epithets may be properly applied to an object, though none of them will explain its nature so as to render it fully intelligible to the human intellect. Thus the Council says that the conversion of the substance of bread into that of the body of Christ, can *scarcely be explained in words;* because we cannot comprehend, and much less can we explain, how one of these substances is converted suddenly and totally into the other, and how the species of bread and wine remain visible and tangible only with the substance of the body and blood of our Lord, who is neither tangible nor visible in the sacrament. However, it does not follow from this that the conversion of the bread into the substance of the body of Christ, cannot be properly called *transubstantiation*: since, as we call the transition of a body from one figure to another, *transfiguration*, and its passage from one form to another, *transformation*, so the passage of one substance into another, while the species of the former remain, is justly called *transubstantiation.* And, if, as Cicero has said (lib. 3, de finib. in princ.), it is lawful to invent new words in order to express things which are singular, much more is it allowable, and even necessary to do so in theology, which teaches several points of doctrine that are singular and new to the human intellect.

34. With regard to the mode of *transubstantiation*, whether it takes place by the annihilation of the substance of bread, or by *adduction*, or by uniting to the species, the body of Christ, we say with St. Thomas, that transubstantiation does not take place in any of these ways, but that it is reproductive of the body of our Lord: because by the words of consecration the body of Jesus Christ is instantly reproduced in the Eucharist, as if it then began to exist. Hence, the Holy Fathers say that in the Eucharist the body of Christ is as it were created. I say *as it were;* because, as St. Thomas says (3, p. qu. 75, a. 7.), in creation what has not existence passes into a state of existence; but in the Eucharist the substance of bread is converted into the substance of the body of Christ.

35. In the fifth chapter, the Council speaks of the worship of latria, with which we ought to adore Jesus Christ in the consecrated host: hence, it approves of the custom of celebrating every year the festival of this mystery, and of carrying the blessed sacrament in procession to be adored by the people, and to remind them of the great benefit bestowed upon them in the Eucharist. "Omnes Christi fideles pro more in catholica ecclesia semper r ecepto, latriæ cultum huic SS. Sacramento......exhibeant &c. declarat præterea S. Synodus, pie......inductum fuisse ut singulis annis peculiari quadam......die......hoc ven. sacramentum singulari......solemnitate celebraretur utque in processionibus ......illud per vias......circumferretur......cum christiani... ...singulari quadam significatione gratos testentur animos erga......Dominum......pro tam......divino beneficio, quo mortis ejus......triumphus representatur, &c."

36. To this chapter the 6th canon corresponds: "Si quis dixerit in S. Eucharistiæ sacramento Christum Dei Filium non esse cultu latriæ, etiam externo, adorandum atque ideo nec festiva celebritate venerandum neque in processionibus secundum laudabilem Ecclesiæ ritum et consuetu-

dinem solemniter circumgestandum vel non publice ut ado-
retur populo proponendum, et ejus adoratores essi idololatras,
anathema sit."

37. Soave says that it was observed in the Council, that
the language of the fifth chapter, in which the Fathers say,
that the worship of latria should be given *to this* most
holy sacrament, is very incorrect; because the *sacrament*
does not mean the thing containing; and therefore he says,
that in the sixth chapter this mode of speaking was corrected, by saying that we should adore the Son of God in
this sacrament. But in answer to this groundless supposi-
tion of Soave, I say, that in the sacraments of the new law,
theologians distinguish three things: the *sacramentum
tantum*, which signifies something sacred and occult, or is
the visible sign which signifies the invisible grace conferred by
the sacrament, and this is the strict signification of the word
sacrament; secondly, the *res sacramenti*, that is the thing
signified, or the effect of the sacrament, which in the Eucharist is the refection of the soul; thirdly, the *sacramentum et res*, and in the Eucharist this is the body of Christ,
which is signified by the sacramental species, and also signifies the grace conferred on the soul. Thus, in the Eucharist the body of Christ is not distinct from the sacrament, since the Eucharist is a compound of the body of
Christ, and the sacramental species. In order then to be
obliged to adore the Eucharist, with the worship of *latria*,
it is enough to know, that the body of Christ is a part of
this compound. Thus, of itself the humanity of Christ
does not merit the worship of latria, because it is a creature; but still we adore Jesus Christ with this worship, because he is a compound which contains the divinity. In
the Eucharist our adoration is directed, not to the species,
but to Jesus Christ, who is contained under the species.

38. In the 6th chapter, the Fathers commend the practice of preserving this sacrament in the tabernacle, and of

bringing it to the sick. " Consuetudo asservandi in sacrario Eucharistiam adeo antiqua est ut eam sæculum etiam Nicæni concilii agnoverit. Porro deferri ipsum......ad infirmos......multis in conciliis præceptum invenitur, et vetustissimo Ecclesiæ more est observatum. Quare sancta hæc synodus retinendum omnino salutarem hunc et necessarium morem statuit."

39. To this chapter the 7th canon corresponds: " Si quis dixerit non licere Eucharistiam in sacrario reservari, sed statim post consecrationem adstantibus necessario distribuendam, aut non licere ut illa ad infirmos honorifice deferatur, anathema sit."

40. Here the heretics exclaim and say: " how can the body of Jesus Christ be multiplied in so many places in which the sacrament is preserved? But let them attend to what the Council has said in the first chapter, viz.: that Jesus Christ is in heaven according to his natural mode of existence, but on earth his substance is present in the Eucharist, in a sacramental manner; in a manner which we can neither express nor comprehend, but must believe to be possible and true, because he himself has revealed it. The body of Christ is present in the Eucharist, by the conversion of the bread into its substance; hence, as the conversions of bread into another substance, can be multiplied a thousand-fold, so likewise its conversion into the substance of the body of our Lord, may be multiplied without any multiplication of Jesus Christ. A single sound, without being multiplied, is found in the ears of all who hear it. The sun, without being multiplied, is found in the eyes of all who behold it. And thus, the body of our Lord, without being multiplied, may be present under all the species of bread which are consecrated. The mode is certainly miraculous, and is not intelligible to us: but the effect of faith is to make us believe what we are not able to comprehend.

41. The seventh chapter treats of the obligation

contained in the words of St Paul, " *let a man prove him-self*," by which all who know that they are guilty of mor-tal sin, are bound to go to confession before they receive communion. " Communicari volenti revocandum est in memoriam......præceptum; Probet semetipsum homo (1 Cor. xi. 28). Ecclesiastica consuetudo declarat eam probatio-nem necessariam esse ut nullus sibi conscius mortalis pec-cati, quantumvis sibi contritus videatur, absque præmissa sacramentali confessione ad Eucharistiam accedere debeat. Quod......etiam a sacerdotibus......servandum......modo non desit illis copia confessoris. Quod si, necessitate ur-gente sacerdos absque prævia confessione celebraverit, quam-primum confiteatur."

42. To this chapter the 11th canon corresponds: " Si quis dixerit solam fidem esse sufficientem præparationem ad sumendum ss. Eucharistiæ sacramentum, anathema sit."

43. This canon is against the error of Luther, who said that the spiritual manducation alone gives life, and that this life is given, not by the application of the sacrament, but by the faith of the person who receives it. But this is false, for, as the Apostle has said with regard to Baptism (Eph. v.) the sacraments of themselves, by the external application, confer grace. It is true that faith is necessary, in order to obtain life in receiving the Eucharist, but it is necessary as a disposition, and not as a cause of grace; for the sacrament is of itself always efficacious. Let us pro-ceed with the words of the same canon: "Et ne tantum sacramentum indigne......sumatur, statuit atque declarat ipsa s. synodus illis quos conscientia peccati mortalis gravat, quantumcumque etiam se contritos existiment, habita copia confessoris necessario præmittendam esse confessionem sa-cramentalem. Si quis autem contrarium docere, prædicare vel pertinaciter asserere seu etia m publice disputando defen-dere præsumpserit, eo ipso excommunicatus existat."

44. On this canon several discussions took place in the

Council. With regard to the phrase, "*habita copia confessoris*," the word *sacerdotis* was found in the first draft of the canon, but afterwards the word *confessoris* was substituted in its stead, in order not to imply that there was an obligation of going to confession to a priest who had not faculties to absolve. Some expressed a doubt of the obligation of confession imposed by the Council, and said that contrition, with the desire of going to confession at a seasonable time, was sufficient. Others, among whom was Melchior Cano, said that they did not approve of the opinion of Cajetan, Paludanus, Richardus, and others, who denied the necessity of confession, although, according to Hugo, Eusebius, Nicephorus, and St. Cyprian, the contrary appeared from the tradition of the Church: hence, they thought that this opinion should be condemned as erroneous, but not as heretical. This was done ; the Church declared that it was necessary to go to confession before communion, but the opposite was not condemned as heretical.

45. In the 8th chapter the Council distinguishes three uses of the Eucharist: the *sacramental* alone, or the reception of the holy communion in the state of sin: the *spiritual* alone by faith, without receiving the sacrament; and the *sacramental* and *spiritual*, which consists in receiving the communion with the requisite dispositions. Hence, the Council declared that it was the perpetual custom of the Church, that the laity should receive the Eucharist from the hands of a priest, and that priests should administer it to themselves. "Quod usum recte......Patres nostri tres rationes hoc sacramentum accipiendi distinxerunt: quosdam enim docuerunt sacramentaliter dumtaxat id sumere, ut peccatores; alios tantum *spiritualiter*...qui voto...illum coelestem panem edentes, fide viva, quæ per dilectionem operatur, fructum ejus...sentiunt : tertios *sacramentaliter* simul et *spiritualiter*; hi autem sunt qui ita se prius pro-

Q

bant et instruunt ut vestem nuptialem induti ad divinam hanc mensam accedant......Semper autem in ecclesia Dei mos fuit ut laici a sacerdotibus communionem acciperent, sacerdotes autem celebrantes seipsos communicarent, qui mos tanquam ex traditione apostolica descendens, jure ac merito retineri debet," &c.

To this chapter corresponds the 10th canon: " Si quis dixerit non licere sacerdoti celebranti seipsum communicare, anathema sit."

46. In the preceding canon (9) an anathema was pronounced against all who would deny that, according to the chapter, Omnis utriusque sexus (XII de pœnit. et rem.), every christian is obliged to communicate at least at Easter. Hence the Council declared: " Si quis negaverit omnes et singulos Christi fideles utriusque sexus, cum ad annos discretionis pervenerint, teneri singulis annis saltem in paschate ad communicandum, juxta præceptum, S. matris Ecclesiæ anathema sit."

47. Soave states that one of the theologians of the Council said that the obligation of communicating at Easter should not be pronounced to be of faith, because it would be a strange thing to declare an ordinance of the Church to be of faith. But the Council pronounced an anathema against any one who would deny the obligation of communicating at Easter. Some one said that the condemnation of the opposite doctrine should be accompanied with some explanation, because the precept by which the obligation was imposed, was not divine, but ecclesiastical. Another said that the doctrine was schismatical, rather than heretical. But in the end all agreed to condemn it with an anathema; and justly, says Pallavicini; for as they who ordinarily omit to hear mass on Sundays and holidays of obligation, or who eat meat on Friday and Saturday, are suspected of being wanting in faith; so they who deny that we are obliged to obey the precept

of the Church, by which all are commanded to communicate every year, are also suspected of failing in faith.   For it is presumed that they do not believe that the Church has received power to impose such precepts, although it is certain, from the Scriptures and apostolical tradition, that God himself has communicated to his Church authority to command what she deems to be in some measure necessary for attaining eternal salvation.

FOURTEENTH SESSION.

ON THE SACRAMENT OF PENANCE.

1. The first chapter treats of the necessity and institution of the sacrament of penance, and it is there said that penance has been always necessary for persons who have fallen into mortal sin: but that it was not a sacrament till Jesus Christ, after his resurrection, gave the Holy Ghost to his disciples, saying: " Receive ye the Holy Ghost; whose sins you shall forgive, they are forgiven them; and whose *sins* you shall retain, they are retained." By these words all the Fathers have, by common consent, understood that the power of remitting and retaining sins has been communicated to the Church, and therefore the Council condemns those who, by a distorted interpretation, explain these words of the power of preaching the Gospel.

2. It is an error to say that the Novatians and Montanists have utterly denied the sacrament of penance: they only said that the Church has not power to absolve from certain very enormous sins. However, Luther, Zuinglius, and Calvin, reject this sacrament; for although they admit a certain reconciliation with regard to persons who fall into sin after baptism, they deny that priests have power to remit sins. At first, Luther admitted only three sacraments (lib. de captiv. Babil.): " Tantum tria pro tempore ponenda; Baptismus, Pœnitentia et Panis." But afterwards, in the same work, he reduced penance to baptism, and thus reduced the three sacraments to two. " Baptismum et Panem," he says, " cum in his solis et restitutum divinitus signum et promissionem remissionis peccatorum videamus; nam Pœnitentiæ sacramentum signo visibili et

divinitus instituto caret." In his other works he afterwards admitted penance to be a sacrament. Zuinglius (lib. de vera et falsa relig.) rejects it altogether; Calvin (lib. 4, instit. c. 19, s. 15), Beza (in conf. fid. c. 7.) and their followers also deny that penance is a sacrament. But from the words already quoted: "Receive ye the Holy Ghost; whose sins you shall forgive," &c. (John xx. 22, 23), it is proved that penance is a sacrament; for we see that it has been instituted by God, that grace has been promised to it, and that it is a sensible external sign, which consists in the words of absolution (see Bellarmine tom. 3, de Pœnit. lib. 1, c. 10).

3. Calvin says that the words "whose sins you shall forgive," &c., regard the remission of sins which is granted to sinners when they are converted by baptism, or by preaching. But we answer, that Jesus Christ gave to the apostles and their successors the power of forgiving the sins of infidels by baptism, and of christians by penance: and, according to the exposition of St. Chrysostom, Theophylactus and St. Ambrose (l. 1, de Pœn. c. 2), the words above quoted, in their strict sense, signify the power of the keys which is exercised with regard to the faithful. Tertullian says that there are two gates for receiving pardon— viz.: baptism and penance. In the discourse *de absolutione*, St. Cyprian (or another ancient author) says the same. This is also taught by St. Jerome (lib. 1, contra Pelag.), by St. Augustine (epist. 180, ad Honor.), by St. Chrysostom (de sacerdot.), by St. Cyril (lib. 12, in Jo. c. 56), by St. Leo (ep. 91, ad Theodor.), and Theodoret (ep. divini., decret. c. de Pœn). But it is still more clearly proved from the decree of Lucius III. (*Ad abolendam* extra, de hær.), and from the Councils of Florence and Trent. Hence, were this doctrine not true, the whole church would have been in error for so many centuries, which is impossible: since Jesus Christ has promised to his

Q 2

Church, that " the gates of hell shall not prevail against it" (Matt. xvi. 18).

4. Calvin says also that the words *remittur eis* do not imply a promise, but only an encouragement to hope for pardon. He says the same of baptism and the other sacraments. But he speaks inconsiderately: for clearer language than the words *Ego te baptizo*, *Ego te absoluto*, could not be used to signify justification, and in reality they justify a person who has the requisite dispositions, though he should neither hear nor understand them.

5. Thus the Calvinists have rejected the sacrament of penance altogether. The Lutherans have not destroyed it entirely, but have mutilated and explained it in such a manner, that they have badly left the name, as well because they have no longer legitimate priests; as because they say that sins are remitted only through faith, and that Jesus Christ has given no other power to the apostles and their successors than that of proclaiming to sinners the Divine promise of pardon, and of afterwards declaring to them, in the sacrament of penance, that their sins are forgiven through the merits of the Saviour. This declaration might be made not only by priests, but also by laymen, by women, and even by infidels.

6. But the Catholic Church, in the Council of Trent (Sess. 14, c. 6), teaches that Jesus Christ has communicated to priests a real judicial power to absolve and to retain sins. " Quorum remiseritis peccata, &c., quorum retinueritis, &c. He did not say, " quibus denuntiaveritis peccata esse remissa, &c. (John xx. 23.) It is true that, for·the justification of a sinner who has contrition, and cannot find a confessor, a desire of sacramental absolution is sufficient: such desire is included in contrition. But for the remission of sins committed after baptism, absolution is always necessary *in re vel in voto :* and, as St. Ambrose says, in giving absolution, the priest, as the Vicar of

Christ, by the power delegated to him by Christ himself, truly remits sins. "Impossibile videbatur per Pœnitentiam peccata dimitti: concessit hoc Christus apostolis suis; quod ab apostolis ad sacerdotes transmissum est." (Lib. 2, de Pœnit. c. 2.)

7. Kemnitius objects that in the sacrament of penance the matter, that is, the element, is wanting. Of this we shall speak at greater length in explaining the third chapter, where we shall treat of the parts of Penance. For the present, we shall say briefly, in answer to Kemnitius, that in all the sacraments matter of the same quality is not necessary; such, for example, as the water used in baptism. In the other sacraments it is sufficient that there be an external sign which represents their spiritual effect, according to the nature of each sacrament: and it matters not whether the sign can be perceived with the sense of sight, or with the sense of hearing, by the person who receives the sacrament. Hence, as St. Augustine says (l. 2, c. 3, de doctr. Christi.), in Penance in which the external sign consists, in the confession of the penitent and in the absolution of the priest, the strict nature of a sacrament is not wanting. Nor can any difficulty arise from the words of the holy doctor: "Accedit verbum ad elementum et fit sacramentum," (tr. 80, in Joan.) for this the saint says only of baptism.

8. Kemnitius also objects that the sacrament of penance has no foundation in the early Fathers, and that it rests solely on the ancient practice of public penance, in which confession was required and punishments for sin imposed. But, granting that the first reconciliations of persons who had fallen into sin were made by public penance, might not these reconciliations which included contrition, confession, and the words of absolution pronounced by a priest, be sacraments?

9. Hence, in the first chapter, the Council says: "Si ea in regeneratis omnibus gratitudo erga Deum esset ut justitiam in Baptismo ipsius gratia susceptam, constanter

tuerentur, non fuisset opus aliud ab ipso Baptismo sacramentum ad peccatorum remissionem esse institutum. Quoniam autem Deus, dives in misericordia, cognovit figmentum nostrum, illis etiam vitæ remedium contulit qui se postea in peccati servitutem......tradidissent, sacramentum videlicet Pœnitentiæ, quo lapsis post Baptismum beneficium mortis Christi applicatur.   Fuit quidem pœnitentia universis hominibus qui se mortali aliquo peccato inquinassent quovis tempore ad gratiam......assequendam necessaria, illis etiam qui Baptismi sacramento ablui petivissent, ut perversitate ......emendata, tantam Dei offensionem, cum peccati odio et pro animi dolore detestarentur......Porro nec ante adventum Christi pœnitentia erat sacramentum, nec est post adventum illius cuiquam ante Baptismum.   Dominus autem sacramentum Pœnitentiæ tunc præcipue instituit cum a mortuis excitatus insufflavit in discipulos suos dicens: *Accipite Spiritum Sanctum : quorum remiseritis peccata, remittuntur eis ; et quorum retinueritis, retenta sunt.*   Quo tam insigni facto et verbis tam perspicuis potestatem remittendi et retinendi peccata, ad reconciliandos fideles post Baptismum lapsos, apostolis et eorum legitimis successoribus fuisse communicatam, universorum Patrum consensus semper intellexit.   Et Novatianos, remittendi potestatem pertinaciter negantes (*that is with regard only to some enormous sins*), magna ratione ecclesia catholica tanquam hæreticos explosit atque condemnavit.   Quare verissimum hunc illorum verborum Domini sensum sancta hæc Synodus probans et recipiens, damnat eorum commentitias interpretationes qui verba illa ad potestatem prædicandi verbum Dei et Christi evangelium annuntiandi, contra hujusmodi sacramenti institutionem, falso detorquent."

10. To this chapter are added the first and third canons. First canon: " Si quis dixerit in catholica ecclesia Pœnitentiam non esse vere et proprie sacramentum pro fidelibus

quoties post Baptismum in peccata labuntur ipsi Deo reconciliandis a Christo Domino institutum, anathema sit."

11. Can. 3: "Si quis dixerit verba illa Domini Salvatoris: *Accipite Spiritum Sanctum: quorum remiseritis peccata, remittuntur eis; et quorum retinueritis, retenta sunt*, non esse intelligenda de potestate remittendi et retinendi peccata in sacramento Pœnitentiæ, sicut ecclesia catholica ab initio semper intellexit, detorserit autem, contra institutionem hujus sacramenti, ad auctoritatem prædicandi Evangelium, anathema sit."

12. Peter Soave proposes three objections; the first is, that the other sacraments were shadowed in the law of Moses, and that, therefore, it appears strange that Jesus Christ should have instituted the sacrament of penance without having prefigured it in any way. But St. John Chrysostom, (lib. 3, de sacerd.) points out an express figure of this sacrament in the Old Testament: " To remove the leprosy of the body," says the saint, "or to speak more correctly, not to remove, but declare it removed, was permitted only to the Jewish priests: but to our priests it is given not to declare the removal of corporal leprosy, or of spiritual uncleanness, but to remove altogether the stains of the soul. To this figure, St. John Fonseca, bishop of Castellamare, alluded in the Council when he spoke on this point.

13. The second objection is, that in the Gospel the obligations and actions of this sacrament are not specially mentioned. Pallavicini says in answer, that if all the articles of faith were clearly expressed in the Gospel, there would have been but few heretics. With regard to the mystery of the Trinity, several Councils were necessary, in order to declare the true doctrine of faith. This shows the necessity of having recourse to tradition, and still more to the Vicar of Christ, who is the infallible interpreter of tradition and Scripture.

14. The third objection is, that penance was instituted

by the words " *Quorum remiseritis peccata*," &c., and
that, therefore, in the form, the word *remitto* should be
used rather than *absolvo*. I answer, that as Cardinal
Lugo says, (disp. 2, de pœnit.) either is sufficient; but the
latter is prescribed by an ecclesiastical law, and a person
who would not use it would be guilty of sin; for the Church
and the Council recognise the institution of this sacrament
not only in the words which I have quoted from St. John,
but also in the words, " Quæcumque alligaveritis super terram erunt ligata et in cœlo, et quæcumque solveritis super
terram, erunt soluta et in cœlo." The exercise of the power
conferred by these words, appears to be better expressed
by the word *absolvo*, than by the word *remitto*, because
the former expresses more clearly the judicial act which the
confessor performs in giving absolution.

CHAPTER II.—ON THE DIFFERENCE BETWEEN
PENANCE AND BAPTISM.

15. In the second Chapter, the Council treats of the
difference between Penance and Baptism, and says, that
the former differs from the latter, and is necessary for
those who have fallen after Baptism. There the Council
also declared that in Baptism the guilt and punishment of
sin are remitted; and that in Penance the guilt is remitted,
but the penalty is remitted only after many tears and
labours. Behold the words of the Council: " Cæterum
hoc sacramentum multis rationibus a Baptismo differre dig-
noscitur: nam præterquamquod materia et forma .... lon-
gissime dissidet, constat certe Baptismi ministrum judicem
esse non oportere, cum Ecclesia in neminem judicium exer-
ceat qui non prius in ipsam per Baptismi januam fuerit in-
gressus. *Quid enim mihi*, inquit Apostolus, *de iis qui
foris sunt judicare !* 1 Cor. 1 in fin. Secus est de domes-
ticis fidei, quos Christus Dominus lavacro Baptismi sui

corporis membra semel efficit: nam hos, si se postea crimine aliquo contaminaverint, non jam repetito Baptismo,
cum id in ecclesia Catholica, nulla ratione liceat, sed ante
hoc tribunal tanquam reos sisti voluit, ut per sacerdotum
sententiam non semel sed quoties ab admissis peccatis ad
ipsum poenitentes confugerint, possent liberari. Alius est
praeterea Baptismi, alius Poenitentiae fructus; per Baptismum enim, Christum induentes, nova prorsus in illo efficimur creatura, plenam et integram peccatorum omnium
remissionem consequentes, ad quam tamen novitatem et
integritatem per sacramentum Poenitentiae sine magnis
nostris fletibus et laboribus, divina id exigente justitia, pervenire nequaquam possumus: ut merito Poenitentiae laboriosus
quidam Baptismus a ss. Patribus dictus fuerit. Est autem
hoc sacramentum Poenitentiae lapsis post Baptismum ad
salutem necessarium ut nondum regeneratus ipse Baptismis."

16. To this chapter the second canon corresponds: Si
quis, sacramenta confundens, ipsum Baptismum Poenitentiae
sacramentum esse dixerit, quasi, haec duo sacramenta dis-
tincta non sint, atque ideo Poenitentiam non recte secundam post naufragium tabulam appellari, anathema sit."

CHAPTER III.—ON THE PARTS OF PENANCE.

17. In the third chapter the Council treated of the parts
and of the fruits of this sacrament, and declared that the
words of the priest, " *ego te absolvo a peccatis tuis*," to
which are laudably added certain prayers, not essential to
it, are the form of the sacrament of penance, in which its
efficacy consists. The Council also declared that the acts
of the penitent—that is, contrition, confession, and satisfaction, are, as it were the matter of this sacrament, that
they are required by divine institution for the integrity
of the sacrament, and for the full remission of sins, and
are therefore called the parts of penance. But with

regard to its efficacy, the substance and effects of this sacrament consist in reconciliation with God, which pious christians, who devoutly confess their sins, sometimes receive with great spiritual consolation. The Council then condemns the opinion of those who say that faith and the terrors of conscience are the parts of penance. Behold the words of the Council: "Docet præterea S. Synodus sacramenti Pœnitentiæ formam, in qua præcipue ipsius vis sita est, in illis ministri verbis positam esse: *ego te absolvo*, &c.; quibus quidem de ecclesiæ sanctæ more preces quædam laudabiliter adjunguntur, ad ipsius tamen formæ essentiam nequaquam spectant, neque ad ipsius sacramenti administrationem sunt necessariæ. Sunt autem quasi materia hujus sacramenti ipsius pœnitentis actus, nempe contritio, confessio et satisfactio. Qui, quatenus in pœnitente ad integritatem sacramenti ad plenamque peccatorum remissionem ex Dei institutione requiruntur, hac ratione Pœnitentiæ partes dicuntur. Sane vero res et effectus hujus sacramenti, quantum ad ejus vim et efficaciam pertinet, reconciliatio est cum Deo: quam interdum in viris piis et cum devotione hoc sacramento percipientibus conscientiæ pax et serenitas cum vehementi spiritus consolatione consequi solet. Hæc de partibus et effectu hujus sacramenti sancta synodus tradens, simul eorum sententiam damnat qui Pœnitentiæ partes incussos conscientiæ terrores et fidem esse contendunt."

18. To this chapter the fourth canon corresponds (Can. 4): "Si quis negaverit ad integram et perfectam peccatorum remissionem requiri tres actus in pœnitente, quasi materia sacramenti Pœnitentiæ, videlicet contritionem, confessionem et satisfactionem, quæ tres Pœnitentiæ partes dicuntur: aut dixerit duas tantum esse Pœnitentiæ partes, terrores scilicet incussos conscientiæ, agnito peccato, et fidem conceptam ex Evangelio vel absolutione, qua credit quis sibi per Christum remissa peccata, anathema sit."

19. Luther censures Catholics for teaching that sorrow
for our sins without faith is sufficient for this sacrament.
But he errs; for the Catholic Church teaches that we must
believe that in this sacrament God, through the merits of
Christ, pardons the sins of all who are disposed for it by
contrition, which no one can have without faith; but not
the faith which Luther requires: it is heresy to say, that
to obtain pardon, it is enough for the sinner to believe
firmly that his sins are forgiven. But we shall soon return
to this point. There is no truth in the assertion of Luther,
that our Church teaches that we ought to be always uncertain of pardon, and to doubt whether Christ has died for
the atonement of our sins. No, we have no doubt but
Christ has died in order to obtain our pardon; neither have
we any doubt that in the sacrament of penance, through
his merits, sins are forgiven; we are only uncertain whether
we ourselves have the requisite dispositions; and therefore
we say that it is heresy to assert that we ought to believe
firmly that our sins are forgiven, whenever we believe that
they are pardoned.

20. There are three opinions held by heretics regarding
the parts of penance. The first is that of Luther, who
asserts (lib. contra bull. anticr.) that there are two parts of
penance—viz.: contrition and faith. By contrition, he
means the terrors of conscience, excited by the threats of
the law. By *faith*, he understands a certain confidence of
the forgiveness of sins on account of the promise which,
according to him, has been promulgated in the Gospel. He
pronounced to be heretical the doctrine of the Lovanians,
who (prop. 27) taught that contrition, confession, and satisfaction, are parts of the sacrament. This opinion of
Luther was held by Melancton, the Centuriators of Mag-
deburg, by Kemnitius, and other followers.

21. The second opinion is maintained by those who, to
contrition and faith, add a third part, which consists in

B

all the good works that are performed after justification, along with the purpose of abstaining from sin, which they call *new obedience*.

22. The third opinion is that of Calvin, who (Inst. lib. 3, c. 3, s. 8), along with Theodore Beza, held, that there are two constituent parts of penance—viz.: *mortification*, or abstinence from sin, and *vivification*, or care to lead a good life.

23. With regard to the opinion of Luther, we say that the terrors excited by the law cannot be a part of the sacrament. This terror is indeed one of the things which prepare the sinner for justification, as the Council teaches (sess. 6, c. 6). But it cannot be a part of penance, since the consideration of chastisement is not repentance for sin, although it leads to repentance, according to the words of the Apostle: "I am glad, not because you were made sorrowful, but because you were made sorrowful unto penance." (2 Cor. vii. 9,) Had the sorrow of the Corinthians been true penance, St. Paul would have rejoiced at it. Hence, in his comment on this passage, St. John Chrysostom says: "Non gaudeo de tristitia, gaudeo de fructu." I rejoice not at the sorrow, but at the fruit—that is, at the penance which followed from it. Besides, the dread of punishment frequently arises, not from repentance, but from self-love, which makes us afraid of chastisement. The devils "believe and tremble." (St. James ii. 19.) And how many sinners are there who, during their sinful course, fear the divine vengeance, and still continue to lead a bad life! Besides, many repent of their sins, not on account of the punishment due to them, but through the love they bear to God, as Jesus Christ said of Magdalene: "Many sins are forgiven her because she hath loved much." (Luke vii. 47.) Since then sin may be remitted without these terrors of conscience, they are not a part of penance.

24. Secondly, the *faith*, or confidence of pardon, which

Luther requires as a part of the sacrament, is also a disposition for penance, and even necessary for it, but is not a
part of penance. The adversaries argue in favour of their
opinion from the words "repent and believe the Gospel."
(Mark i. 15.) But this text is unfavourable to them; for
it distinguishes faith from penance. The Redeemer did not
say *repent believing*, but *repent and believe*. The parts
of penance proceed from penance: faith does not arise from
penance, but precedes it. "The men of Ninive believed
in God, and they proclaimed a fast, and put on sackcloth
from the greatest to the least." (Jon. iii. 5.) But how
can any one believe that his sins are forgiven unless he has
first repented of them? The holy Fathers thus define penance: "Præterita peccata plangere et plangenda non
admittere." (S. Greg. hom. 34). "Commissa flagitia con-
demnare." (S. Ambros. in ps. 37.) When we say that
faith is necessary for the remission of sins, we mean to
speak of the Catholic faith, which teaches that God pardons
sins through the merits of Jesus Christ, as the Council of
Trent says (sess. 6, c. 6), but not of the heretical faith that
faith (or confidence) and a certain belief of pardon justifies
the sinner, and is therefore a part of penance.

25. With regard to the second opinion, that all the good
works which are performed after justification, are parts of
penance, on account of the purpose of leading a good life
for the future, I say that such a purpose is necessary for
justification, and appertains to penance, since without it contrition cannot be real. But neither this purpose, nor any
other good work, performed after justification, is a part of
penance. Many of the good works which penitents perform, proceed from charity towards God, or from a love of
justice, or from devotion, and therefore cannot be parts of
penance.

26. With regard to the opinion of Calvin, that *mortification* and *vivification*, or abstinence from sin and

zeal for virtue, are the two parts of penance, I say that it is likewise false. Calvin confounds penance with justification: he even makes justification precede penance, since he says that penance is the fruit of faith, which (according to him) justifies the sinner. But, according to the Scriptures, penance precedes justification. "If the wicked do penance for all his sins,......I will not remember all his iniquities." (Ezech. xviii. 21, &c.) "Except you do penance, you shall all likewise perish." (Luke xiii. 5.) "Be penitent... that your sins may be blotted out." (Acts iii. 19.) Since then penance precedes justification, much more should it precede the *mortification* and *vivification* of Calvin, which, according to him, are the fruits of justifying faith.

27. The adversaries say that contrition cannot be a part of the sacrament, since it is internal, and not sensible. I answer, that it is not sensible in itself, but it is rendered sensible by the confession of sins, by the petition for absolution, or by some other external sign. Nor is it of any moment that the sacrament is sometimes received without confession by persons who are deprived of their senses; for with regard to such persons, confession made then, or before, by some external signs, is a true confession, and is sufficient for the sacrament. The adversaries say that even confession cannot be a part of the sacrament, because it is a sign of sins committed, but not of grace, or of the remission of sins. I answer that confession without absolution, is not a sign of grace; but when united with absolution, or with the form of the sacrament, *ego te absolvo, &c.*, it is certainly a sign of grace. Thus, by itself, water in baptism is not a sign of grace; but when united with the form, *ego te baptizo, &c.*, it is a sign of grace. In order then that in the sacraments the matter be a sign of grace, it is sufficient that, when united with the form, it signifies grace.

28. Our adversaries also object that Judas fulfilled the

three parts of penance, by contrition, confession, and satisfaction, and that still his sin was not forgiven. I answer, that Judas had none of the parts of penance: in him we find neither contrition, nor confession; for, in order to be parts of penance, these must be accompanied with the hope of pardon through the merits of Jesus Christ. But this hope he had not; neither did he make satisfaction, for the voluntary destruction of his own life was an act, not of satisfaction, but of despair.

29. Kemnitius objects that a hypocrite might pretend to perform the three parts of penance which we require, and might therefore receive the pardon of his sins. But this is false; for they only obtain forgiveness who receive this sacrament with sincerity, and not through hypocrisy; since, without sincerity, the best part of the sacrament—viz., true contrition, would be wanting.

30. But, with regard to the parts of penance, we have also to contend with certain Catholics, whose opinion, though very different from the doctrine of the heretics, appears to be improbable. Scotus says (in 4 sent. d. 14. q. 4)that the absolution alone constitutes the entire essence of the sacrament of penance: and in this he is followed by Ukam, Almain, John Major, and others. But although they deny that contrition and confession are essential parts of the sacrament, they admit that they are necessary parts, not as essential, but conditional, without which the sacrament would be null and void. And in answer to the objection, that in their opinion there would be no sensible sign in the sacrament of penance, they say that this sign is found in the sound of the words of absolution. But the contrary opinion is commonly held by divines, along with St. Thomas (3, p. qu. 90, a. 2, 3) and this opinion appears certain from the words of the Councils of Florence and of Trent. With regard to the sacrament of penance, the Council of Florence says: "Quartum sacramentum est Pœnitentiæ, cujus quasi materia sunt actus pœnitentis [that is, as the Council

afterwards adds], cordis contritio cum proposito non peccandi de cætero, oris confessio et satisfactio pro peccatis."
The Council then mentions the form: "*ego te absolvo a
peccatis tuis.*" To this we may add that Lucius III. (c.
Abolendam, de hæret.) called the sacraments, Baptism, Confession of sins, and Matrimony: if confession did not belong to the essence of the sacrament of penance, the Pontiff would not have called this sacrament confession of sins.

31. The Council of Trent (c. 3.) says that the acts of the
penitent, viz., contrition, confession, and satisfaction, are
the parts of Penance, and asserts that they are, *as it were,
the matter* of the sacrament: Behold the words of the
Council: "Sunt autem quasi materia hujus sacramenti
ipsius pœnitentis actus, nempe contritio, confessio, et satisfactio; qui, quatenus in pœnitente ad integritatem sacramenti,
et ad plenam et perfectam peccatorem remissionem ex Dei institutione requiruntur, Pœnitentie partes dicuntur." Thus immediately after saying that the acts of the penitent are *as it were
the matter* of the sacrament, the Council calls them the
parts of penance, and says that by divine institution they
belong to the integrity of the sacrament, and are required
for the full remission of sins. From the words of the
Council, Juenin argues: "Sacramenti vero partes sunt illi
intrinsicæ; atque materia intrinsica et materia ex qua, idem
omnino sunt; ergo illi actus sunt materia ex qua sacramenti Pœnitentiæ, quos concilium Tridentinum asseruit esse
quasi illius materiam, esse debent illius partes." (Tom. 7, P.
303, concl. 2.) Hence, Bellarmine justly says (c. 15.) that
Scotus and the others have adopted their opinion because
they wrote before the Council of Florence and Trent, in
which these things were more accurately explained, and
adds: "Quod si hoc tempore superessent, sine dubio
Ecclesiæ definitioni ac sententiæ acquiescerent." Bellarmine says that the opinion that the acts of the penitent are
as it were the matter of this sacrament, and the absolution
of the priest the form, is most true: and he asserts that it

is the opinion of St. Thomas, Richardus, Durandus, and of the generality of divines. (In. 4, sent. dist. 14.) The rite of imposing hands on the penitent, is most ancient, but, as St. Thomas says (opusc. 22, de forma absol.), it is certain that it does not belong to the essence of the sacrament.

32. A certain concealed partizan of Scotus (Morelli, the author of the compendium of Pallavicini, &c. s. 220.) says: "The Council calls the three acts of the penitent not *the matter*, but *as it were the matter* of the sacrament, and thus confirms the opinion of Scotus that they are not really the matter, but circumstances necessary for the sacrament." But this author errs: for others commonly think that the Council had not any intention whatever of confirming the opinion of Scotus, and that by the words it used, it confirmed the common opinion that the three parts and not the absolution alone, are essential to the sacrament. Besides, in the passage quoted from his works, Scotus speaks very confusedly; among other things, he says: "Pœnitentiæ est absolutio pœnitentis facta certis verbis, &c." Bellarmine says that the absolution is an act of the priest, but the penance is not an act of the priest, but of the penitent, and as we shall hereafter see, the sacrament is, according to the doctrine of St. Thomas, composed of both.

33. But why has the Council said that the three acts of the penitent are *as it were the matter*, and why has it not called them the matter of the sacrament? Bellarmine answers that the Council of Trent has called these acts, "quasi materia, non quod non sint vere materia, qualem sacramenta requirunt; sed quod non sint res aliqua solida ac tractabilis, qualis in aliis sacramentis cernitur." To this question the Roman catechism gives the following answer: "Sed quia ejus generis materiæ non sunt quæ extrinsecus adhibeatur, ut aqua in Baptismo, et chrismatio in confirmatione." Because, adds the catechism, no other sensible sign is required for the matter of the sacrament than that which the words

of the form declare: and of this kind precisely are the acts of the penitent. Besides, it cannot be said of any sacrament that the matter is strictly and physically the matter of the sacrament.

34. The adversaries say in reply that the Council calls the acts of the penitent *quasi materia*, and the parts of Penance, inasmuch as they are necessary for the integrity of the sacrament, and for the full remission of sins; but not because they intrinsically compose the sacrament, as water composes Baptism. In answer to this argument, Juenin says that were it a valid one, it might be also said that the acts of faith, hope, and charity might also be called the *quasi materia* of Baptism, because these acts are necessary, in order to receive sanctifying grace in Baptism. He also says that in speaking of the dispositions necessary to receive grace in Baptism, or in the other sacraments, the Council has never said that these dispositions are, as it were, the matter and parts of the sacrament. Hence, in saying that the acts of the penitent are, *as it were the matter* and parts of Penance, the Council certainly meant not that they are mere dispositions, but real parts of the sacrament.

35. The Scotists also object that the sacrament ought to be a sign of the effect which it produces: the effect of Penance is the remission of sins, which is signified not by contrition nor by confession, but only by the absolution, and therefore, the strict essence of the sacrament consists in the absolution alone. I answer that as by giving absolution, the priest signifies that he remits sin, so by an humble confession, and by contrition for the offences he has offered to God, the penitent signifies that he withdraws from sin: hence St. Thomas says (3, p. q. 86, a. 6.) that although the sacramental efficacy resides principally in the power of the keys by which the priest absolves the sinner, it also resides in the acts of the penitent, inasmuch as God makes use of them to signify and to produce justification. Behold the

words of the holy Doctor: "Omne autem sacramentum producit effectum suum non solum virtute formæ sed etiam virtute materiæ: ex utroque enim est unum sacramentum. Unde sicut remissio culpæ fit in Baptismo, non solum virtute formæ, sed etiam virtute materiæ (scilicet aquæ principalius tamen virtute formæ ex qua et ipsa aqua virtutem recipit; ita etiam et remissio culpæ est effectus Pœnitentiæ, principalius quidem ex virtute clavium, quas habent ministri, ex quorum parte accipitur id quod est formale in hoc sacramento, secundario autem ex vi actuum pœnitentis pertinentium ad virtutem pœnitentiæ; tamen prout hi actus aliqualiter ordinantur ad claves Ecclesiæ; et sic patet quod remissio culpæ est effectus pœnitentiæ secundum quod est virtus, principalius tamen secundum quod est sacramentum."

36. They moreover object that the acts of the penitent cannot be the matter of the sacrament of Penance, since among them we reckon satisfaction, without which confession may be valid, as happens in the case in which the penitent is unable to perform the satisfaction. I answer that satisfaction is a part of Penance, but is not altogether essential; it is the integral matter by which Penance is completed. It is also essential though inadequate matter, so that if the penitent had not the intention of fulfilling it, the sacrament would be altogether null.

37. In the fourth chapter, the Council speaks of contrition. Luther and Calvin said that contrition is the fruit of justifying faith, and therefore they denied that it is a part of penance. Luther also said that true contrition is not a hatred and detestation of past sins, but a love of justice and a new life, and he added that the sorrow which a person feels for past sins, "makes him a hypocrite, and even a greater sinner, &c. The best penance is a new life." From this error Kemnitius and Calvin kept aloof: and because the Scriptures were too clear on the point, they

held that in order to obtain pardon the sinner must hate the evil he has done. " Be converted to me with all your heart, in fasting and weeping and in mourning. And rend your hearts and not your garments, and turn to the Lord your God; for he is gracious and merciful." (Joel ii. 12, &c.) " There is none that doth penance for his sin, saying: What have I done?" (Jer. viii. 6.) " I will recount to thee all my years in the bitterness of my soul." (Isa. xxxviii. 15.) All the holy Fathers inculcate the same doctrine. St. Cyprian says: " Dolentes peccata vestra perspicite." (Serm. de laps.) The same is taught by St. Ambrose (lib. 2, de Pœnit. c. 10.), by St. John Chrysostom (lib. 1. de compunct.), by St. Jerome (in c. 31, Hier.), by St. Augustine (Ench. c. 65.), by St. Gregory (hom. 24, in Evang.), and others.

38. There is no doubt but contrition necessarily includes the purpose of leading a new life: this purpose is not a part of the sacrament but it always accompanies contrition. Several authors say that for the validity of the sacrament an implied purpose is sufficient: but Bellarmine (de Pœnit. l. 2, c. 6.) along with Peter Lombard, Alexander de Ales, St. Thomas, and the generality of divines, holds that the purpose should be explicit and formal: and because there is question of the validity of the sacrament, this opinion should be followed, on account of the proposition condemned by Innocent XI. (Prop. 1.) Besides in the definition of contrition the Council expresses the purpose. " Contritio est detestatio &c., cum proposito non peccandi de cætero."

39. Notwithstanding all the clamour of the innovators, the Council declared in the fourth chapter that, *contrition is a detestation for sin committed, with a purpose of sinning no more.* The Council says that contrition has been always necessary in order to obtain pardon, and that it prepares men for the remission of sins, if it be united with confidence in the divine mercy, and with a desire of

doing all that is necessary for the reception of the sacrament. The Council then teaches that contrition is not a mere cessation from ʳthe commission of sin along with a beginning of a new life; but that it is also a hatred of past sin. In this chapter it is also said that although contrition is sometimes perfected by charity, so that it reconciles the sinner with God, before the reception of the sacrament, still the reconciliation is always ascribed to contrition on account of the desire of the sacrament, which it always at least implicitly contains. It is also said that imperfect contrition, called *attrition*, which commonly arises from the consideration of the turpitude of sin, or from the fear of hell, and the divine chastisements, when it excludes the will of sinning, and is accompanied with the hope of pardon, is a gift of God by which the penitent prepares the way to his own sanctification. And although without the sacrament, this attrition is incapable of justifying the sinner, still it disposes him to receive sanctifying grace in the sacrament. Hence, the Council adds: some have falsely calumniated Catholic writers, as if they taught that the sacrament of penance confers grace on penitents without any good motion on their part, a doctrine which has never been taught or held by the Church. Finally the Council says in this chapter that it is false to say that contrition is extorted or forced, or not free and voluntary.

40. Behold the words of the Council (c. 4): "Contritio quæ primum locum inter dictos pœnitentis actus habet, animi dolor ac detestatio est de peccato commisso, cum proposito non peccandi de cætero. Fuit autem quovis tempore ad impetrandam veniam peccatorum hic contritionis motus necessarius: et in homine post Baptismum lapso ita demum præparat ad remissionem peccatorum, si cum fiducia divinæ misericordiæ, et voto præstandi reliqua conjunctus sit quæ ad rite suscipiendum hoc sacramentum requiruntur. Declarat igitur sancta Synodus hanc contritionem non solum cessationem a peccato et vitæ novæ propositum et inchoa-

tionem, sed veteris etiam odium continere juxta illud: *Projicite a vobis omnes iniquitates vestras in quibus prævaricati estis, et facite vobis cor novum et spiritum novum.* Et certe qui illos sanctorum clamores consideraverit: *Tibi soli peccavi, et malum coram te feci: Laboravi in gemitu meo, lavabo per singulas noctes lectum meum; Recogitabo tibi omnes annos meos in amaritudine animæ meæ;* et alios hujus generis, facile intelliget, eos ex vehementi quodam anteactæ vitæ odio et ingenti peccatorum detestatione manasse. Docet præterea, etsi contritionem hanc aliquando charitate perfectam esse contingat, hominemque Deo reconciliare priusquam hoc sacramentum actu suscipiatur, ipsam nihilominus reconciliationem ipsi contritioni, sine sacramenti voto, quod in illa includitur, non esse adscribendam. Illam vero contritionem imperfectam quæ attritio dicitur quoniam vel ex turpitudinis peccati consideratione, vel ex gehennæ et pœnarum metu communiter concipitur, si voluntatem peccandi excludat cum spe veniæ, declarat non solum non facere hominem hypocritam et magis peccatorem, verum etiam donum Dei esse, et spiritus sancti impulsum, non adhuc quidem inhabitantis, sed tantum moventis quo pœnitens adjutus viam sibi ad justitiam parat. Et quamvis sine sacramento Pœnitentiæ per se ad justificationem perducere peccatorem nequit, tamen eum ad Dei gratiam in sacramento Pœnitentiæ impetrandam disponit. Hoc enim timore utiliter concussi, Ninivitæ, ad Jonæ prædicationem, plenam terroribus pœnitentiam egerunt, et misericordiam a Domino impetrarunt. Quamobrem falso quidam calumniantur catholicos scriptores quasi tradiderint sacramentum Pœnitentiæ absque bono motu suscipientium gratiam conferre: quod nunquam Ecclesia docuit nec sensit. Sed et falso docent contritionem esse extortam et coactam, non liberam et voluntariam."

41. To this chapter the fifth canon corresponds. (Can. 5): "Si quis dixerit eam contritionem quæ paratur

per discussionem, collectionem et detestationem peccatorum, qua quis recogitat annos suos in amaritudine animæ
suæ, ponderando peccatorum suorum gravitatem, multitudinem, fœditatem, amissionem æternæ beatitudinis et
æternæ damnationis incursum, cum proposito melioris vitæ,
non esse verum et utilem dolorem nec præparare ad gratiam,
sed facere hominem hypocritam et magis peccatorem,
demum illam esse dolorem coactum et non liberum ac volun-
tarium, anathema sit."

42. Here we may introduce the great question whether
for the reception of the sacrament of Penance, attrition is
sufficient, and whether it should include *inchoate love*. With
regard to inchoate love, it is necessary to know that in 1667
Alexander VII. published a decree, in which he forbade
under pain of excommunication: "Ne quis audeat alicujus
theologicæ censuræ alteriusve injuriæ nota taxare alterutram
sententiam, sive negantem necessitatem aliqualis dilectionis
Dei in attritione ex metu gehennæ concepta, quæ hodie
inter scholasticos communior videtur; sive asserentem
dictæ dilectionis necessitatem." At present theologians
agree in affirming that attrition is sufficient for the sacrament, but that it should include inchoate love. For it is
certain that one of the dispositions necessary for the justification of the sinner is, as the Council of Trent teaches
(sess. 6, c. 6), that "Deum tanquam justitiæ fontem diligere incipiat, ac propterea moveatur adversus peccata per
odium aliquod et detestationem." But must this inchoate
love be predominant charity, with which a person loves
God above all things, as is held by Juenin, Merbesius,
Habert, Morino, Concine, and Antoine? It is very commonly held by theologians that such predominant charity
is not necessary for the sacrament of penance: this is the
opinion of Gonet, Melchior Cano, of the author of the
Theologia Petrocorensis, of Tournely, Collet, Cabassutius,
Wigandt, and of an immense number of other divines.

Benedict XIV. (de synod. lib. 7, c. 13, ex n. 6,) asserts that, since the Council of Trent, all the schools have adopted this opinion. The reason is, that were the love of God *above all things* required, the sacrament of penance would be not a sacrament of the *dead*, but of the *living*, because all penitents would come in the state of grace to receive it. For, as St. Thomas teaches (suppl. q. 5, a. 3), all contrition which arises from predominant charity, cancels sin, and is true contrition. And this happens whenever the loss of grace displeases the soul more than the loss of every other good. And since it is true contrition, however remiss it may be, it destroys sin in the soul. "Quantumcuncque parvus sit dolor, dummodo ad contritionis rationem sufficiat, omnem culpam delet." Here St. Thomas speaks of contrition without the sacrament of penance. In another place he says: "Per solam contritionem dimittitur peccatum; sed si, antequam absolvatur, habeat hoc sacramentum in voto" (Quodlib. 4, a. 1). This we also know from the words of the Council: "Etsi contritionem hanc aliquando charitate perfectam esse contingat hominemque Deo reconciliare priusquam hoc sacramentum actu suscipiatur," &c. Nor can it be said that by contrition, *perfected by charity*, the Council meant not remiss, but intense, fervent and ardent charity. For fervour does not belong to the essence of contrition, or to its perfection, but, as St. Thomas says, only to its state or mode; since it is a circumstance which is added by accident to the substance of contrition: "plus et minus non variant speciem."

43. And that by contrition *charitate perfectam*, the Council did not mean intense charity, but merely contrition, which proceeds from predominant charity, appears from the context; for the Council distinguishes *perfect* contrition, which springs from charity (*charitate perfectam*), from *imperfect* contrition, which arises from the consideration

of the turpitude of sin, or from the fear of hell. " Illam vero contritionem imperfectam quæ attritio dicitur, quia vel ex turpitudinis peccati consideratione vel ex gehennæ vel pœnarum metu concipitur." Of the latter the Council says that though it is a gift of God, and disposes the sinner to receive sanctifying grace, it does not produce grace without the aid of the sacrament. That all contrition, though it be remiss, sanctifies the soul, is certain; for it is a formal act of charity; and charity cannot exist in the soul with sin and with hatred of God, as is evident from so many passages of Scripture: " I love them that love me." (Prov. viii. 17.) " He that loveth me, shall be loved of my Father." (John xiv. 21.) " Every one that loveth is born of God." (1 John iv. 7.) This is the common doctrine of the Holy Fathers and of Theologians. St. Thomas says: (2, 2. q. 45. a. 4.) " Charitas non potest esse cum peccato mortali." Here the Saint cannot mean intense charity; for in another place he says: " Actus peccati mortalis contrariatur charitati, quæ consistit in hoc quod Deus diligatur super omnia." (2. 2. q. 24, a. 12.) He also says that perfect, or intense charity, does not differ in its essence from imperfect charity: " Charitas perfecta et imperfecta non differunt secundum essentiam, sed secundum statum." (2. 2. q. 44, a. 8, ad 2.)

44. This is still clearer from the condemnation of the following proposition of Baius, by Gregory XIII.: " Charitas illa quæ est plenitudo legis non semper est conjuncta cum remissione peccatorum." (Prop. 32.) The love which is the *fulfilment of the law*—that is, which is sufficient for the fulfilment of the precept of charity, is certainly that by which we love God above all things, as all theologians hold along with St. Thomas, who, in explaining the precept—" *Thou shalt love the Lord thy God with thy whole heart*," says: " When we are commanded to love God with our whole heart, we are given to understand that we ought to love him above all things." Since then pre-

dominant charity, however remiss, cannot exist with sin, it is certain that all contrition, which is also a formal act of charity, cancels sin. Hence, if the inchoate love, required in attrition, be predominant love, all sinners would go to confession in the state of grace, and the confessor, in giving them absolution, would only declare them absolved. This was the doctrine of Luther. But the adversaries say no; because the sinner is always absolved by virtue of the sacramental absolution which he had a desire to receive. But we answer, that then the sacrament of penance would never produce its effect of remitting sin at the time of its actual administration: but it is the property of every sacrament to produce its effect when it is actually administered; and we should neither assert nor think without clear proof that such a difference exists between penance and the other sacraments. With regard to the question, whether inchoate love, which is not perfect, and predominant charity, but only the beginning of love, is, according to the words of the Council, "*Deum diligere incipiunt,*" required as a disposition for justification, I admit that it is necessary, and I say that this beginning of love is intrinsically and actually contained in all attrition; because it is contained as well in the fear of the divine chastisements; "The fear of God is the beginning of his love," (Eccl. xxv. 16,) as in the hope of pardon and beatitude, according to the words of St. Thomas: "Ex hoc quod per aliquem speramus bona, incipimus ipsum diligere" (1. 2. q. 40, a. 7). Pallavicini mentions (lib. 8, c. 13) that some said in the Council that to the words *diligere incipiunt*, the words *per actum charitatis* should be added; but the Council refused to add these words.

45. But prescinding from the arguments already adduced, our opinion is proved from the words of the Council. Luther, as we have already seen, said that attrition conceived from the fear of hell, makes us greater sinners.

But this is not true. Were a person to detest sin through fear of hell, so that he would continue to commit sin if there was no hell, such fear would render him more guilty; but if, as the Council says, he excludes the will of sinning, and hates his sins on account of the torments of hell, which he has merited, he not only does not sin, but, according to the doctrine of the Council, he performs a good act, which is a gift of God, and an impulse of the Holy Ghost, and disposes him to obtain sanctifying grace in the sacrament. "Et quamvis sine sacramento Pœnitentiæ per se ad justificationem perducere peccatorem nequeat, tamen eum ad Dei gratiam in sacramento Pœnitentiæ impetrandam disponit." It is true that in the first draft the word *sufficit* was used, but the Fathers had no difficulty in substituting for it the word *disponit.* The meaning of the two words was substantially the same, since (as Gonet and other theologians say) it appears that the Council could not mean by the word *disponit*, a remote disposition. For it had before declared that attrition, conceived from the fear of hell, &c., is a gift of God, and an impulse of the Holy Ghost, and consequently a disposition to justification. Hence, in saying "tamen ad Dei gratiam in sacramento inpetrandam disponit," it appears that the Council must mean a proximate disposition. This is more clear from the context; for had the Council, by the word *disponit*, understood a remote disposition, it would have incongruously said: "et quamvis sine sacramento ad justificationem perducere nequeat, tamen ad Dei gratiam in sacramento impetrandam disponit." It should have rather said: "et quamvis sine sacramento non disponat ad gratiam, tamen in sacramento disponit ad illam impetrandam." Since then the Council said: "and although without the sacrament attrition cannot bring the sinner to justification," we may infer, by connecting the phrases, that it intended to say, that in the sacrament attrition justifies the sinner, and consequently that it

s 2

meant, by the word *disponit*, a proximate, and not a remote, disposition.

46. This appears still more clearly from what the Council adds almost immediately: "Quamobrem falso quidam calumniantur catholicos scriptores, quasi tradiderint sacramentum Pœnitentiæ absque bono motu suscipientium gratiam conferre; quod nunquam Ecclesia Dei docuit, nec sensit." Luther and the other heretics have never charged Catholics with saying that grace was given to those who had contrition, but only with teaching, in opposition to the doctrine of Luther, that grace is given to those who have attrition on account of having a good motion, which disposes them to receive sanctifying grace in the sacrament. "Tristitia," said Luther, "ob fœditatem peccatorum, amissionem beatitudinis, &c., magis facit peccatorem; et tales indigne absolvuntur." Hence, he censures those "qui vocant attritionem hanc proxime (non remote) disponentem ad contritionem." It was certainly in this sense the Council spoke when it said: "*ad gratiam impetrandam disponit*;" otherwise we must say that in the same chapter it spoke in one sense at one time, and in another at another. Thus the author of the Theologia Petrocorensis solidly argues, and I do not see how our adversaries can answer his argument. To this may be added the doctrine of St. Thomas on Baptism. The dispositions for receiving grace in baptism are the same as those that are necessary for justification in the sacrament of penance. St. Thomas says: "Ad hoc ut homo se præparet ad gratiam in Baptismo, præexigitur fides, sed non charitas; quia sufficit attritio præcedens, etsi non contritio." (In 4, sent., dist. 6, q. 1, art. 3, ad 5.)

47. I have written all these things in my moral theology, but it was necessary to repeat them in this place. But this question is of little practical importance; for there is no doubt but a penitent should endeavour as much as possible

to obtain more perfect contrition in preparing for this sacrament, in order to secure the remission of his sins; and the confessor should on his part suggest to his penitents more perfect acts of contrition and charity. But our opinion gives reason not to despair of the salvation of certain sinners, whose sins are so great in number and enormity, as to excite doubts whether, in receiving the sacrament of penance, they have predominant charity. There are many other questions connected with this subject which belong to moral rather than to dogmatic theology: these I have treated in my moral theology.

CHAPTER V.—ON CONFESSION.

48. In the fifth chapter the Council treats of confession, and says that the Church had always understood that in the institution of this sacrament God had also ordained a full and entire confession of sins, since Jesus Christ has for this purpose left priests as his vicars, that they, as judges, should remit or retain sins. Now, in such judgment they could not give or refuse absolution to penitents, nor prescribe satisfaction without having a distinct knowledge of their sins; and therefore christians are bound to confess even the hidden sins with which their conscience charges them, along with all the circumstances which change the species of the sins. But although it is a laudable practice to confess venial sins, they may be omitted in confession, and may be cancelled by other means. The Council also says that the public confession of sins, though not commanded like secret confession, is not forbidden—that it is an error to say that confession is an invention of the Council of Lateran—that the precept of confession was not imposed by that Council, which only ordained that each of the faithful should go to confession at least once a year, in the time of Lent, as is the practice. Behold the

words of the Council: "Ex institutione sacramenti Pœnitentiæ, jam explicata, universa Ecclesia semper intellexit
institutam etiam esse a Domino integram peccatorum confessionem, et omnibus post Baptismum lapsis jure divino
necessariam existere; quia D. N. Jesus Christus e terris
ascensurus ad cœlos sacerdotes sui ipsius vicarios reliquit,
tanquam præsides et judices, ad quos omnia mortalia
crimina deferantur in quæ Christi fideles ceciderint; qui
pro potestate clavium, remissionis aut retentionis sententiam
pronuntient. Constat enim sacerdotes judicium hoc incog-
nita causa exercere non potuisse, neque æquitatem quidem
illos in pœnis injungendis servare potuisse, si in genere
dumtaxat, et non potius in specie ac sigillatim sua ipsi
peccata declarassent. Ex his colligitur oportere a pœnitente omnia peccata mortalia, quorum post diligentem sui
discussionem conscientiam habet, in confessione recenseri,
etiam occultissima illa sint et tantum adversus duo ultima
decalogi præcepta commissa, quæ nonnumquam animum
gravius sauciant, et periculosiora sunt iis quæ in manifesto
admittuntur; nam venialia quibus a gratia Dei non excludi-
mur et in quæ frequentius labimur, quamquam recte et
utiliter citra omnem præsumptionem in confessione dicantur,
quod piorum hominum usus demonstrat, taceri tamen citra
culpam multisque aliis remediis expiari possunt. Verum
cum universa mortalia peccata etiam cogitationis, homines
filios iræ, et Dei inimicos reddant, necesse est omnium etiam
veniam cum aperta et verecunda confessione a Deo quærere.
Itaque dum omnia quæ memoriæ occurrunt peccata Christi
fideles confiteri student, procul dubio omnia divinæ misericordiæ ignoscenda exponunt, qui vero secus faciunt et
scienter aliqua retinent, nihil divinæ bonitati per sacerdotem
remittendum proponunt. Quod ignorat, medicina non curat.
Colligitur præterea etiam eas circumstantias in confessione
explicandas esse quæ speciem peccati mutant; quod sine
illis peccata ipsa neque a pœnitentibus integre exponantur

nec judicibus innotescant, et fieri nequeat ut de gravitate
criminum recte censere possint, et pœnam quam oportet
pro illis pœnitentibus imponere: unde alienum a ratione est
docere circumstantias has ab hominibus otiosis excogitatas
fuisse, aut unam tantum circumstantiam confitendam esse,
nempe peccasse in fratrem. Sed et impium est confessionem
quæ hac ratione fiere præcipitur, impossibilem dicere, aut
carnificinam illam conscientiarum appellare: constat enim
nihil aliud in Ecclesia a pœnitentibus exigi quam ut postquam quisque diligentius se excusserit et conscientiæ suæ
sinus omnes et latebras exploraverit, ea peccata confiteatur
quibus se Dominum et Deum suum mortaliter offendisse
meminerit; reliqua autem peccata, quæ diligenter cogitanti
non occurrunt, in universum eadem confessione inclusa esse
intelliguntur pro quibus fideliter cum propheta dicimus: *Ab
occultis meis munda me Domine.*   Ipsa vero hujus confessionis difficultas ac peccata detegendi verecundia gravis
quidem videri possit, nisi tot tantisque commodis et consola-
tionibus levaretur quæ omnibus digne ad hoc sacramentum
accedentibus per absolutionem certissime conferuntur.
Cæterum, quoad modum confitendi secreto apud solum
sacerdotem, etsi Christus non vetuerit quin aliquis, in vindictam suorum scelerum et sui humiliationem, cum ob
aliorum exemplum, tum ob Ecclesiæ offensæ ædificationem,
delicta sua publice confiteri possit, non est tamen hoc
divino præcepto mandatum; nec satis consulte humana
aliqua lege præciperetur ut delicta, præsertim secreta, publica
essent confessione aperienda.   Unde cum a ss. et antiquissimis Patribus magno unanimique consenu secreta confessio
sacramentalis, quæ ab initio Ecclesia sancta usa est et modo
etiam utitur, fuerit semper commendata manifeste refellitur
inanis eorum calumnia qui eam a divino mandato alienam
et inventum humanum esse atque a Patribus in concilio
Lateranensi congregatis initium habuisse docere non veren-
tur: neque enim per Lateranense Concilium Ecclesia sta-

tuit ut Christi fideles confiterentur, quod jure divino necessarium et institutum esse intellexerat, sed ut præceptum
confessionis saltem semel in anno ab omnibus et singulis,
• cum ad annos discretionis pervenisssent, impleretur; unde
jam in universa Ecclesia, cum ingenti animarum fidelium
fructu, observatur mos ille salutaris confitendi sacro illo et
maxime acceptabili tempore quadragesimæ; quem morem
hæc sancta synodus maxime probat et amplectitur, tanquam
pium vel merito retinendum."

49. To the fifth chapter is added the sixth canon, in
which the Council says: "Si quis negaverit confessionem
sacramentalem vel institutam vel ad salutem necessariam esse
jure divino: aut dixerit modum secrete confitendi soli sacerdoti quem Ecclesia catholica semper observavit et observat,
alienum esse ab institutione et mandato Christi et inventum
esse humanum, anathema sit."

50. To the 5th chapter the seventh canon also appertains (Can. 7): " Si quis dixerit in sacramento Pœnitentiæ
ad remissionem peccatorum necessarium non esse jure divino
confiteri omnia et singula peccata mortalia quorum memoria
cum debita et diligenti præmeditatione habeatur, etiam
occulta et quæ sunt contra duo ultima decalogi præcepta, et
circumstantias quæ peccati speciem mutant; sed eam confessionem tantum esse utilem ad erudiendum et consolan-
dum pœnitentem et olim observatum fuisse tantum ad satisfactionem canonicam imponendam; aut dixerit eos qui
omnia peccata confiteri student nihil relinquere velle divinæ
misericordiæ ignoscendum; aut demum non licere confiteri
peccata venialia, anathema sit."

51. Some say that the Novatians, Montanists, and Wic-
lefites, have denied that penance is a sacrament; but this
is not true. They only denied that the Church had power
to absolve from certain enormous sins, but not from the sins
which are ordinarily committed. However, the head of
this heresy was the impious Montanus, who, because he

could not obtain a bishoprick, began to rave about the year 171, and to pretend to the gift of prophecy. He was joined by two females, Priscilla and Maximilla, who also assumed the character of prophets. He had a great number of followers, but was condemned by two Councils. He said that the Church can remit light, but not grievous, sins. This we learn from a work written by Tertullian (de pudie. c. 2.) after he had become a disciple of Montanus who, through the instrumentality of Novatus, was chosen pope by three bishops, and was the first anti-pope.

52. John Wicleff said that there is no foundation for this power in the Holy Scriptures, and that it was given to priests by the pope in the Council of Lateran. Erasmus, of Rotterdam, said the same. (adnot. ad ep. Hier. ad Ocean. et adnot. ad cap. 19, Actor.) The Calvinists have entirely rejected confession from the number of the sacraments. The Lutherans, too, have, not totally, but partially, rejected the sacrament of penance. Luther had a thousand opinions on this point, but at length, in the Smalcaldic articles, he said that the confession of sins is useful, but not necessary, because it is enough to confess our sins to God; much less, he says, is it necessary to explain the number of grievous sins. Melancthon taught the same doctrine in the Confession of Augsburgh. Calvin (lib. 3, inst. c. 4, s. 7,) does not doubt but confession is of divine precept, and that the practice of it was most ancient; but he says that it can be easily proved that in the early ages the practice was free, and not obligatory. Kemnitius says that it is sufficient to accuse ourselves in general of all our sins without explaining them.

53. But the necessity and obligation of confessing mortal sins is sufficiently declared in the words—" Whose sins you shall forgive, they are forgiven," &c. (John xx. 23.) Our adversaries deny that the power of forgiving and retaining sins was given by these words, and say that this passage is to be understood of the ministry to preach for-

giveness, or damnation to sinners. However, to bind and to loose do not signify to denounce and to declare, but to impose bonds, and to remove them. And how can these bonds be taken away if the judge does not know them? Priests are regarded as judges by the Holy Fathers: By St. John Chrysostom, (lib. 3, de sacerd.), by St. Gregory Nazianzen, (orat. ad cives) by St. Ambrose, (lib. 1, de pœnit c. 2,) by St. Jerome (ep. ad Heliod.), by St. Augustine (lib. 20, de civ. Dei c. 9), by St. Innocent I. (ep. 1. ad Decent. c. 7), and by St. Gregory. (hom. 26, in Evang.) If the priest forgives sins, not by absolving the sinner, but by announcing the divine promise to pardon sin, the deaf and persons deprived of their senses, could not be absolved. But that these are absolved, we know for certain from the Council of Orange (c. 12), and from the fourth Council of Carthage, from St. Augustine (lib. 1, de adult. c. ult.), and St. Leo (ep. ad Theod.). Besides, if absolution were not a judicial act, but a mere promulgation of the divine promise, priests would not be necessary for this promulgation: it might be made by a layman, by a woman, and even by an infidel. This the heretics are not unwilling to admit; but it is contrary to the doctrine of all the ancients, and to the custom of all churches.

54. The necessity of confession appears from several passages of Scripture. It is proved from the words of St. John: "If we confess our sins, he is faithful and just to forgive us our sins," &c. (1 John i. 9.) This text must be necessarily understood of sacramental confession, since it is only to sacramental confession that the pardon of sins has been promised. "Whose sins you shall forgive," &c. For if, in every confession made to God, sins were remitted, how could it be said, "whose sins you shall forgive," &c.? And how could priests retain, or bind, if, by confessing his sins to God, the penitent were absolved from them by God himself?

55. Secondly, it is proved from the words: "And many of them that believed, came confessing and declaring their deeds." (Acts xix. 18.)   By their *deeds*, Luther understands the miracles which the faithful performed; but this exposition is rejected by the heretics themselves, because it is utterly at variance with the words of the Evangelist. Kemnitius says that the faithful confessed some of their sins, but not all.   Calvin says the same; but the words *"confessing their deeds"* cannot be properly understood of the confession of *some* of their sins.   Calvin says: "Hoc semel legimus confessos esse: papæ lex quotannis repeti debet."   But we are not to suppose that because it is recorded once that the faithful confessed their sins, they did not confess them at other times.

56. It is proved, thirdly, from the text of St. James: "Confess your sins one to another." (Ep. v.¡16.) Calvin says (inst. l. 4, c.1, 22.) that here the apostle speaks of the confession which a christian should make to an offended brother, in order to obtain pardon; but in another place he acknowledges that the words of St. James regard the power of the keys. Melancton says that St. James speaks of the confession which a person makes to a spiritual man, in order to obtain instruction from him, and to procure his prayers.   Such the manner in which these new masters understand the words of the apostle: however, the Holy Fathers have not understood them in this sense, but have explained them of the sacramental confession which is made to priests: and justly, for immediately after having commanded the priests to anoint the sick with oil, that their sins might be pardoned, the apostle says: "Confess your sins one to another." Hence, it appears that the confession should be made to the priests, of whom he had just spoken, otherwise the words, *"confess your sins,"* would be either useless, or unconnected.

57. From the works of the Holy Fathers it is clear

T

that sacramental confession was practised in the first ages
of the Church. From the writings of St. Ireneus, who
lived in the second century, it appears that it was even
then usual to confess even secret sins. (Lib. 1, adv. hær.
c. 9.) Tertullian, who lived in the same century, says that
the *exomologesis* consists in confessing to God our own
sins, that by confession we may obtain penance to appease
the anger of God. He then adds: " Presbyteris advolvi,
et caris Dei adgeniculari." (Lib. de pœn. c. 9.) Thus he
counsels christians to kneel down at the foot of the priest,
and afterwards exhorts them not to be ashamed to do it:
" Plerosque hoc opus ut publicationem sui suffugere, pudoris
magis memores quam salutis." (Ib. c. 10.) Origen, who
also flourished in the same century, after mentioning several
means by which sins are remitted in the Church, says:
" The seventh means is, when the sinner is not ashamed to
declare his sin to a priest, and to ask a remedy." " Cum
non erubescit sacerdoti Domini indicare peccatum suum, et
quærere medicinam." (Hom. 11, in Levit.) St. Basil
writes: " Ut vita corporis aperiunt iis qui rationem qua ea
curanda sunt, teneant, eodem modo peccatorum confessio
fieri debet apud eos qui ea possint curari." (In reg. brev.
resp. 229.)

58. Besides, St. Gregory of Nyssa says: " Audacter
ostende illa quæ sunt recondita animi arcana, tanquam
occulta viscera." (Orat. in eos qui al. acerb judic.) St. Ambrose writes: " Si vis justificari, fatere delictum tuum;
solvit enim criminum nexus verecunda confessio peccatorum." (Lib. 2, de pœn. c. 6.) Paulinus, the author
of the life of the saint, relates that " quotiescumque illi aliquis ob percipiendam pœnitentiam lapsus suos
confessus esset, ita flebat ut flere illum compelleret." St.
Jerome says: " Si quem serpens diabolus occulte momor-
derit, si vulnus suum magistro noluerit confiteri, magister
prodesse non poterit......Quod ignorat medicina non curat."

(In c. 10, Eccl.) In the year 440, in a letter to certain
bishops of the Campagna Felice, who wished to compel
penitents to confess their sins publicly, St. Leo said: "Re-
moveatur tam improbabilis consuetudo, ne multi a pœnitentiæ remediis arceantur: sufficit enim illa confessio quæ
offertur sacerdoti, qui pro delictis pœnitentium precator
accedit." (Ep. 136.) To the authority of these Fathers
we may add that of St. Cyprian, (ep. 16, l. 3, ad Pleb.) of
St. Athanasius, (serm. in verba, Profecti in pagum,) of St.
Hilary (can. 18, in Mat.) of St. John Chrysostom, (hom.
30, in Genes.) and others. On the words of St. James,
"Confess your sins one to another," St. Augustine writes:
"Eges sacerdotis, qui mediator sit apud Deum tuum
salubri judicio; alioquin responsum divinum quomodo con-
summaretur: Confitemini alterutrum peccata vestra? In
another place, (hom. 49, ex Levit.) addressing them who
say, it is enough for me to repent in my heart, God will
then pardon me, the saint writes: "Nemo sibi dicat novit
Deus qui mihi ignoscit quid in corde ago. Ergo sine causa
sunt claves datæ Ecclesiæ Dei? On the same words of
St. James, "Confess your sins one to another," St. Bernard says: "Nempe homines hominibus, qui potestatem
absolvendi habent." (Lib. med. c. 9.) He afterwards adds:
"Dedit nobis ministerium reconciliationis, pro Christo ergo
legatione fungimur." The legate who is sent by a prince
with power to pardon rebels, cannot exercise his power
unless he hears from the mouth of the guilty the crime
which they have committed: hence the power of reconciling
sinners with God includes the power of enquiring into the
state of their consciences.

59. The necessity of confession is also proved from the
Ecumenical Councils, which have regarded it as commanded
by a divine precept. In the sixth Council (can. 102,) it is
said: "Oportet autem eos qui solvendi et ligandi potestatem a Deo accepere, peccati qualitatem considerare......et

sic morbo, convenientem adferre medicinam." The Council
of Laodicea (can. 2,) says: "Pro qualitate peccati pœnitentiæ tempus tribuendum est." In the Latin church sacramental confession has been commanded by several Councils:
by the third Council of Carthage (can. 1), of Challon
(Cabilonensis), Worms, and others, and, finally, by the
Council of Lateran, under Innocent III., (can. 21) by the
Council of Constance, (sess. 8,) by the Councils of Florence and Trent. Thus, if confession had not been of
divine precept, the Church would have been in error, at
least for the space of four centuries. According to St.
Augustine, the common practice of the Church affords an
additional proof of the necessity of confession; for the
saint (lib. 4, de bapt. c. 24,) lays it down as a certain maxim
that, what is practised in the Church for a long time, and
is not found to have been established by any positive law
of the Church, should be believed to be of divine institution. This rule is particularly applicable to confession, in
which we do not find that any dispensation was ever
granted by the Sovereign Pontiff.

60. Kenmitius (in censur. ad cap. 5, Trid.) persists in
saying, that by confession, the ancient Fathers meant not
sacramental confession, but the confession which a christian
makes to God, or to a neighbour, in order to obtain forgiveness of an offence. But to see that Kemnitius is in error
it is sufficient to give a glance at the passages we have
quoted from the Holy Fathers. However, he acknowledges
that the Fathers commended the confession which was
made to priests, and adds, that some expressions of the
Fathers appear favourable to the necessity of sacramental
confession. Calvin does not deny it, but says (inst. lib. 3,
c. 4, s. 7,) that for the faithful there was not a precept of
sacramental confession before the constitution (Omnis
utriusque sexus, &c.,) of the Council of Lateran under
Innocent III. But, as has been already said, Calvin errs;

for the law of confession was not enacted by Innocent. He only determined the time at which the faithful should fulfil it—that is, he ordained that they should, according to what had been before prescribed by Pope Innocent I., Leo I., and·Zephyrianus, go to confession at least once a-year.

61. It is necessary to know, that although in the first ages auricular confession was practised, confessors would frequently recommend their penitents, for their greater humiliation, to confess some secret sin publicly, when the public confession would not cause scandal, nor render the sacrament odious. Behold what Origen says on this point: "Proba prius medicum cui debeas causam languoris exponere......ut ita demum si quid ille intellexerit talem esse languorem tuum qui in conventu Ecclesiæ exponi debeat, ex quo et cæteri ædificari poterunt et tu facile sanari, illius consilio procurandum est." (Hom. 2, in Ps. 37.) But in the East this practice ceased in the fifth century on the following occasion: a certain noble lady in Constantinople confessed to the penitentiary that she had sinned with a certain deacon, and without his advice or permission confessed her sin publicly, and also published the name of her accomplice: this gave great scandal, and excited a tumult among the people, who drove the deacon out of the Church. The Archbishop Nectarius, the predecessor of St. John Chrysostom, was so much grieved that he abolished the office of penitentiary, and forbade all the faithful to make a public confession of their hidden sins, or to do public penance for secret transgressions. Thus the public confession of secret sins was forbidden: and in a short time the prohibition passed from the eastern to the western Church.

62. Hence, Calvin, (inst. lib. 3, c 4, s. 7.) and Thomas Waldensis err in saying that the law of auricular confession was instituted not by Christ, but by the Bishops, and only in certain places. Calvin asserts that it is related by Sozomen that on account of the scandal caused by the public con-

T 2

fession of a lady who had sinned with a deacon, Nectarius, archbishop of Constantinople, abolished auricular confession; he adds that from that time the practice of confession ceased in the oriental churches. From this Calvin concludes that had auricular confession been of divine precept, Nectarius would not have dared to prohibit it. But, as I have already said, he errs: for we know from the same Sozomen, from Socrates, and Nicephorus that on the occasion of the Novatian heresy, the Bishops appointed a priest to the office of penitentiary, that he might preside over public penitents who were to make a public confession of their sins. Thus, as may be inferred from the writings of St. Chrysostom, (hom. 8, de pœn.) the bishops intended, not that the faithful should not make a confession of their sins, but that they should not confess them publicly. Nor was it the duty of the penitentiary to order penitents to publish all their sins, but only those which were public and required public penance. Sozomen attests that the prohibition of Nectarius to make a public confession of secret sins continued in all the western Churches. And St. Leo asserts that the practice of publicly confessing occult sins never existed in Rome: hence, the Holy Pontiff reproves (ep. 80, ad epis. Cam.) certain bishops who wished to introduce that custom.

63. The permission which, according to Sozomen and Socrates, Nectarius gave to each of the faithful to partake of the sacred mysteries according to his conscience, (secundum suam conscientiam ad sacra mysteria participanda accederet,) did not imply that each person could without going to confession, receive the Eucharist, even though he had been guilty of a grievous sin which had not been confessed, but that without being obliged to present himself to the public tribunal of the Church, each person might go to communion according to his conscience; that is (as Bellarmine says, l. 3, c. 14.) if he were in the state of sin he should confess it privately, if he were free from sin, he might communicate.

64. It remains to answer some other objections of the heretics against auricular confession. Calvin objects from a passage of St. Chrysostom (in ps. 50.) " Si confunderis dicere alicui quæ peccasti, dicito quotidie ea in anima tua : non dico ut confitearis conservo tuo qui exprobret; dicito Deo, qui curat ea. Cave, homini dixeris, ne tibi exprobret." (Hom. 4, in Ez.) In answer I say that in this passage the holy Doctor wished to confirm the prohibition of Nectarius his predecessor, against the public confession of secret sins, but did not intend to interfere with auricular confession. This may be inferred from other passages in the writings of the Saint. " Non cogo te in medium prodire theatrum; mihi soli dic peccatum privatim." (Hom. cit. 4.) Before these words he says: " Cave homini dixeris, ne tibi exprobret." In public confessions it was usual to upbraid the penitent with his guilt, as we learn from Origen: " Exprobrent eum confitentem." (Hom. 2, in Ps. 37.) St. Chrysostom says *cave*; had he intended to forbid secret confession, he would have gone farther than the innovators, who admit that the confession at least of some more grievous sins is most useful. When the holy doctor said *dicito Deo qui ea curat*, he spoke not of sacramental confession, but of the public confession which penitents were before accustomed to make for their own confusion; and it is this kind of confession that he forbids. But St. John Chrysostom in a thousand places exhorts to private confession " Ultro sibi persuadeant curationi sacerdotum se se submittere oportere." (lib. 2, de sacerd.) In another place he reproves those who through shame, omit to confess their sins privately, and says: " Commisisti aliquod scelus: hominis cœlas, non Deum, et nihil curas." (Hom. 33, in Jo.)

65. Calvin objects also from the text of Ezechiel (c. 33.): " Quotiescumque ingemuerit peccator......omnium iniquitatum ejus......non recordabor." This passage is ordinarily quoted in these words: but in reality they are not found in

the Scripture. The passage to which Calvin alludes is taken from the eighteenth chapter (v. 21, 22.) of Ezechiel, "Si autem impius egerit pœnitentiam ab omnibus peccatis suis......vita vivet, et non morietur; omnium iniquitatum &c." On the text which he has quoted, Calvin says: "Huic verbo qui audet aliquid adjicere non peccata ligat, sed Dei misericordiam." He then concludes that repentance alone without confession is sufficient. In answer I say that the words *egerit pœnitentiam* are to be understood of penance which has all the requisite conditions, that is which includes the acts of faith, hope, charity, and contrition, along with the desire of Baptism or confession.

66. Calvin also objects that at present the remission of sins is not different from what it has always been: but auricular confession has not always been practised: therefore it is not necessary for our reconciliation with God. I answer that even baptism has not been always in use: it did not belong to the law of Moyses: are we then to conclude that even baptism is not necessary for salvation? But if on account of the words of Christ: "Nisi quis renatus fuerit ex aqua et Spiritu Sancto, non potest introire in regnum Dei." (Jo. 3, 5.) Baptism is necessary in the new law, so on account of the words of the same Saviour: "Quorum remiseritis peccata remittuntur eis; quorum retinueritis, retenta sunt," (Jo. 20, 23.) confession is likewise necessary. On these words of the Redeemer, Peter Soave, speaking in the name of the Germans, (according to his custom of putting into the mouth of others his own censures on the Council,) makes four objections. First, he says that the obligation of making a full confession of all mortal sins along with the circumstances which change the species, does not clearly follow from the judicial power which Christ has given of remitting and retaining sins; because Christ has distinguished not two classes of sins, one to be remitted and the other to be retained, but two classes of men, to one of which, viz.,

the penitent, sins are forgiven: to the other, that is the persons who have not the requisite dispositions, their sins are retained. I answer, that the words, "whose sins you shall forgive, they are forgiven, and whose sins you shall retain, they are retained," signify, principally, two classes, not so much of penitents as of sins—the one to be remitted, the other to be retained. But granting that in the text there is no distinction made between sins, but only between penitents, it would even in that case be necessary to confess each mortal sin along with the circumstances which change the species; for, without such confession, the confessor could not know sufficiently whether a penitent has an affection to sin—whether he is resolved to remove all proximate occasions, and whether he is disposed to receive the medicinal penance, which ought to be imposed upon him. Soave objects, secondly, that the Apostles and their disciples were ignorant of the circumstances which change the species of sin; and that even at the present day men would perhaps be ignorant of them, if Aristotle had not made the distinction; and from this an article of faith has been framed. I answer, that the knowledge of certain circumstances which change the species of sin, is not peculiar to Aristotle; it is found among the rude and illiterate. For example, all know that the murder of a parent is a sin, not only against justice, but also against filial piety. Besides, the Council only says that the penitent, after a diligent examination of conscience, " ea peccata confiteatur quibus se Deum mortaliter offendisse meminerit; reliqua autem peccata quæ diligenter cogitanti non occurrunt, in universum eadem confessione inclusa esse intelliguntur." Hence, a person who does not know, or does not advert to the malice of a circumstance which changes the species, is not obliged to confess it. Thirdly, he objects that it is inconstancy or ignorance to condemn those who say that the absolution is the exercise of a naked ministry to declare that sins are forgiven, and afterwards to recognise in priests the character of a judge, since the office of judge is only to declare the guilt of delinquents. He adds, that it cannot be said that, by the priest, sinners are made just, but that it is better to say that their punishment is remitted, and that they return to their former state. I answer, that the office of a judge, delegated by a prince with power to grant or refuse pardon, or the remission of punishment to criminals, with a knowledge of the cause, is not only to declare them guilty, or innocent, but also to pronounce the sentence at the very time the favour is granted or refused: and this is the office of a priest who hears confessions. And that priests have the power not only of declaring that sins are remitted, but also of absolving from them, we know from the words of Christ (Matt. c. 18, John c. 20); for the words to *loose* and to *remit* do not imply a mere naked ministry to declare, but also a judicial act, by which sentence of absolution is pronounced after the cause has been examined. Soave objects, fourthly, that the reason which the Council assigns for the necessity of confessing the species of sins—viz., that the priest may be able to impose suitable penance, is false. First, because in reality light penances are imposed for the most grievous sins. Secondly, because the Council itself declares that satisfaction may be made to God by voluntary mortifications, or by bearing patiently the pains sent to us by God. Thirdly, because the priest cannot sufficiently measure the amount of punishment to be endured in purgatory. I answer, that the Council forbids confessors to impose light penance for very grievous sins, and commands them to proportion the penance imposed to the grievousness of the sins of the penitent: " Debent, pro qualitate criminum et pœnitentium facultate, salutares et convenientes satisfactiones injungere."

67. Kemnitius objects from the text: " As the Father

hath sent me, I also send you." (John xx. 21.)　Christ, he says, granted pardon to sinners without hearing their sins.　I answer, that by the words just quoted, the Apostles were sent to reconcile sinners, but in a manner different from that in which Christ absolved them.　He absolved them with an absolute power; he saw the bottom of their hearts, and knew whether they had contrition or not: but, in order to know the dispositions of penitents, the Apostles required a confession of their sins, or a manifestation of their conscience; and for this purpose Christ gave them the power of loosing and binding.　Christ pardoned Magdalene without baptism, but he commanded the Apostles to baptize all who were converted to the faith: "Baptizantes eos in nomine Patris," &c.

68.　Kemnitius also says: then the new law is more severe than the old, which did not impose so grievous an obligation as that of confession.　I answer, that the new law cannot be said to be more severe than the old, because it contains a single precept, or even a few precepts, more severe than those of the old law.　The old law was far more severe, inasmuch as it imposed so many ceremonial and judicial precepts, which are not obligatory in the new law.　Besides, to the precepts of the old law there was not annexed the promise of grace, which Christ our Lord has several times promised to his followers, and with which they can easily fulfil all his commands.　Hence, the old law was called a law of fear, and the evangelical law is called a law of charity: and to a christian, animated and assisted by charity, what precept can be difficult?

CHAPTER VI.—ON THE MINISTER OF THE SACRAMENT AND ON ABSOLUTION.

69.　In the sixth chapter the Council condemns those who attribute the power of the keys to any one except

bishops and priests, and say that public sins are forgiven by
public correction, and that secret sins are remitted by making
a confession to any christian. The Council also teaches
that a priest, in the state of sin, can validly administer
this sacrament; and that it is an error to say that bad
priests are deprived of the power of validly absolving from
sin. It also declares that absolution is not the exercise of
a naked ministry to preach the Gospel, or to declare that
sins are forgiven, but a judicial act, by which the priest
pronounces sentence, by giving or refusing absolution to
the penitent. Hence, for the remission of his sins, the
faith of the penitent, by which he considers himself absolved,
although he has not contrition, and although the
priest should not intend to act seriously, or to absolve him, is
not sufficient. Behold the words of the Council : " Circa
ministrum autem hujus sacramenti, declarat s. synodus,
falsas esse, et a veritate Evangelii penitus alienas doctrinas
omnes quæ ad alios quosvis homines, præter episcopos et
sacerdotes, clavium ministerium perniciose extendunt, putantes
verba illa Domini : "*quæcumque alligaveritis
super terram, erunt alligata et in cœlo ; et quorum
remiseritis peccata, remittentur eis ; et quorum
retinueritis retenta sunt :* ad omnes Christi fideles indifferenter
et promiscue, contra institutionem hujus sacramenti
ita fuisse dicta utquivis potestatem habeat remittendi
peccata, publica quidem per correptionem, si correptus
acquieverit; secreta vero per spontaneam confessionem
cuicumque factam. Docet quoque etiam sacerdotes
qui mortali peccato tenentur, per virtutem Spiritus sancti in
ordinatione collatam, tanquam Christi ministros, functionem
remittendi peccata exercere, eosque prave sentire qui in
malis sacerdotibus hanc potestatem non esse contendunt.

Quamvis autem absolutio sacerdotis alieni beneficii sit
dispensatio, tamen non est solum nudum ministerium vel
annuntiandi Evangelium vel declarandi remissa esse peccata,

sed instar actus judicialis quo ab ipso velut a judice sententia pronuntiatur. Atque ideo non debet pœnitens adeo sibi de sua ipsius fide blandiri ut etiamsi nulla adsit contritio, aut sacerdotis animus serio agendi et vere absolvendi desit, putet tamen se propter suam solam fidem vere et coram Deo esse absolutum: nec enim fides sine pœnitentia remissionem ullam peccatorum præstaret, nec is esset nisi salutis suæ negligentissimus qui sacerdotem jocose absolventem cognosceret, et non alium serio agentem requireret."

70. To this chapter the sixth canon corresponds: "Si quis dixerit duas tantum esse Pœnitentiæ parte, terrores, &c., et fidem conceptam ex Evangelio vel absolutione, qua credit quis sibi per Christum remissa peccata, anathema sit."

71. In accordance with the error condemned in this canon, Luther taught that the minister should give absolution. In the catechism of Luther, where he speaks of the form of the sacrament of penance, the minister, after having heard the confession of the penitent, is directed to say to him: "*Dost thou believe that the remission of sins which I give thee is forgiveness from God?*" When the penitent answers in the affirmative, the minister says: "*By the command of Christ I pardon thee thy sins.*"

72. Let it be observed that, with regard to the form of this sacrament, or the form of absolution, the Greeks use the deprecative form: and Juenin says that before the twelfth century the Latins also used the deprecative form, as appears from several rituals and sacramentaries: but the Council of Trent has declared that the form is not valid, unless it be in the indicative mood: *Ego te absolvo a peccatis tuis.* But how could the deprecative form be valid formerly among the Latins, and at present among the Greeks, although it is now invalid among the Latins? Juenin justly answers (tom. 7, p. 383, de Pœnit.), that the

Church can change the forms of the sacraments, not substantially, but with regard to the mode, by annexing something as a condition, without which the sacrament would
not be valid: for Jesus Christ himself has entrusted the
administration of the sacraments to the prudence of the
Church, which has prescribed the indicative form to express
the act of jurisdiction, which priests exercise in administering this sacrament.

CHAPTER VII.—ON JURISDICTION, AND THE RESERVATION OF SINS.

73. In the seventh chapter it is said that the absolution
of priests, who have not ordinary or delegated jurisdiction
over their penitents, is null and void. It is also said that
the Pontiff and bishops have justly reserved certain very
grievous sins; but that in the article of death every priest
can absolve the faithful from all sins and censures; that,
however, except in the article of death, penitents should go to
their superiors in order to obtain absolution from reserved
cases: " Quoniam igitur natura et ratio judicii illud exposcit
ut sententia in subditos dumtaxat feratur; persuasum semper
in Ecclesia Dei fuit et verissimum esse synodus hæc confirmat
nullius momenti absolutionem eam esse debere quam sacerdos
in eum profert in quem ordinariam ut subdelegatam non habet
jurisdictionem. Magnopere vero ad christiani populi disciplinam pertinere ss. Patribus nostris visum est ut atiociora
quædam et gravia crimina non a quibusvis, sed a summis
dumtaxat sacerdotibus absolverentur. Unde merito ponti-
fices maximi, pro suprema potestate sibi in Ecclesia universa tradita, causas aliquas criminum graviores suo
potuerunt peculiari judicio resesvare. Nec dubitandum est,
quando omnia quæ a Deo sunt, ordinata sunt, quin hoc
idem episcopis omnibus in sua cuique diœcesi, in ædificationem tamen non in destructionem, liceat pro illis in subditos, tradita super reliquos inferiores sacerdotes auctoritate,

præsertim quoad illa quibus excommunicationis censura annexa est. Hanc autem delictorum reservationem consonum est divinæ auctoritati non tantum in externa politia, sed coram Deo vim habere. Verumtamen pie admodum, ne hac occasione aliquis pereat, in eadem Ecclesia Dei custoditum fuit ut nulla sit reservatio in articulo mortis; atque ideo omnes sacerdotes quoslibet pœnitentes a quibusvis peccatis et censuris absolvere possunt; extra quem articulum sacerdotes cum nihil possunt in casibus reservatis, id unum pœnitentibus persuadere nitentur ut ad superiores et legitimos judices pro beneficio absolutionis accedant."

74. Thus for the absolution of certain very grievous sins, the Council requires that penitents have recourse to a superior, who, as being in a more exalted station, may be better able to admonish them, and to impose upon them salutary penances proportioned to their guilt. Hence, the opinion of those who say that persons who are ignorant of a reservation, do not incur it, does not, as I have said in my Moral Theology, appear to be sufficiently probable: for I say that reservation is not a punishment, nor has it the nature of a punishment with regard to penitents, but is a subtraction of jurisdiction from confessors, that on certain very grievous sins a more accurate judgment may be pronounced by the superiors, who have the faculties to absolve even from reserved sins.

CHAPTER VIII.—ON SATISFACTION.

75. In the eighth chapter, the Council declares that it is false to say that God does not pardon the guilt of sin without also remitting the entire punishment due to it. It also declares that voluntary sufferings satisfy for sins not through their own merit, but through the merits of Christ, through which God accepts them. And therefore, the Council directs priests to impose salutary penances proportioned to the

enormity of the sins, and the strength of the penitent: to
take care not to enjoin very light penance for very grievous
sins: but to impose penance calculated not only to preserve
the new life, but to punish past sins. The Council also
declares that such penances do not diminish the satisfaction
of our Lord Jesus Christ. " Demum quoad satisfactionem,
quæ ex omnibus Pœnitentiæ partibus, quemadmodum a
Patribus nostris Christiano populo fuit perpetuo tempore
commendata, ita una maxime nostra ætate summo pietatis
prætextu impugnatur ab iis qui speciem pietatis habent,
virtutem autem ejus abnegarunt, S. Synodus declarat
falsum omnino esse et a verbo Dei alienum culpam a
Domino nunquam remitti, quin universa etiam pœna con-
donetur; perspicua enim et illustria in sacris litteris exempla reperiuntur quibus, præter divinam traditionem, hic
error quam manifestissime revincitur.   Sane et divinæ
justitiæ ratio exigere videtur ut aliter ab eo in gratiam
recipiantur qui ante Baptismum per ignorantiam deliquerint,
aliter vero qui, semel a peccatis et dæmonis servitute liberati
et accepto Spiritus sancti dono, scienter templum Dei violare
et Spiritum Sanctum contristare non formidaverint; et
divinam clementiam decet ne ita nobis absque ulla satis-
factione peccata dimittantur ut, occasione accepta, peccata
leviora putantes, velut injurii et contumeliosi Spiritui Sancto
in graviora labamur, thesaurizantes nobis iram in die iræ.
Proculdubio enim magnopere a peccato revocant, et quasi
fræno quodam coercent satisfactoriæ pœnæ, cautioresque et
vigilantiores in futurum pœnitentes efficiunt: medentur
quoque peccatorum reliquias, et vitiosos habitus male
vivendo comparatos contrariis virtutum actionibus tollunt;
neque vero securior ulla via in ecclesia Dei unquam ex-
istimata fuit ad amovendam imminentem a Domino pœnam
quam ut hæc pœnitentiæ opera homines cum vero animi
dolore frequentent.   Accedit ad hæc quod dum satisfaciendo
patimur pro peccatis, Christo Jesu, qui pro peccatis nostris

satisfecit, ex quo omnis nostra sufficientia est conformes efficimur, certissimam quoque inde arrham habentes quod, si compatimur et conglorificabimur. Neque vero ita nostra est satisfactio hæc quam pro peccatis nostris exsolvimus ut non sit per Christum Jesum: nam ex nobis, tanqnam ex nobis nihil possumus, eo co-operante qui nos confortat, omnia possumus: ita non habet homo unde glorietur sed omnis gloriatio nostra in Christo est, in quo vivimus, in quo movemur, in quo satisfacimus, facientes fructus dignos pœnitentiæ, qui ex illo vim habent, ab illo offeruntur Patri, et per illum acceptantur a Patre. Debent ergo sacerdotes Domini, quantum spiritus et prudentia suggesserit, pro qualitate criminum et pœnitentium facultate, salutares et con-venientes satisfactiones injungere: nisi forte peccatis con-niveant, et indulgentius cum pœnitentibus agant, levissima quædam opera pro gravissimis delictis injungendo, alienorum peccatorum participes efficiantur. Habeant autem præ oculis ut satisfactio quam imponunt non sit tantum ad novæ vitæ custodiam et infirmitatis medicamentum, sed etiam ad præ-teritorum peccatorum vindictam et castigationem; nam claves sacerdotibus non ad solvendum dumtaxat, sed ad ligandum concessas etiam antiqui Patres et credunt et docent; nec propterea existimarunt sacramentum Pœnitentiæ esse forum iræ vel pœnarum, sicut nemo unquam catholicus sensit, ex hujusmodi nostris satisfactionibus vim meriti et satisfactionis Domini nostri Jesu Christi vel obscurari vel aliqua ex parte imminui: quod dum novatores intelligere nolunt ita opti-mam pœnitentiam novam vitam esse docent ut omnem satisfactionis vim et usum tollant."

76. Luther and Calvin say that God does not exact any punishment in satisfaction for sins after he has pardoned them, but the Council teaches, as we have seen, that after the remission of the guilt, the obligation of making satisfaction for the temporal punishment, even in the next life, fre-quently remains, if full satisfaction is not made in this life.

The pains of the next life satisfy *de condigno ;* the pains of this life satisfy only *de congruo,* as theologians, resting on the words of Daniel—" Redeem thou thy sins with alms," (iv. 24,) commonly hold.   According to the tradition of the Holy Fathers, the word *sin* includes the debt of punishment. (See Bellarmine, lib. 4, c. 9.)   And we know that in opposition to the doctrine of Luther and Calvin, David, after he had been assured by the prophet Nathan that his sin was forgiven, was punished with the death of his son. " Nathan said to David, the Lord also hath taken away thy sin; thou shalt not die.   Nevertheless, because thou hast given occasion to the enemies of the Lord to blaspheme, for this thing, the child that is born to thee shall surely die." (2 Kings xii. 13.)   This the prophet foretold, and the event verified the prediction.

77. The temporal punishment which remains, may be redeemed by voluntary good works, as the Council teaches. Luther admits, but Calvin denies this doctrine. It is proved by the example of the Ninevites, who, by their penitential works, prevented the subversion of their city, which was threatened by the prophet Jonas. (cap. ult.) Hence, after absolution, priests properly prescribe as penance, fasts, prayers and alms; and thus we understand how the confessor binds the penitent, since, to impose penance, belongs to the power of the keys, as is taught by St. Leo (ep. 91, ad Theod.), and by St. Cyprian. (serm. de laps.)

CHAPTER IX.—ON SATISFACTORY WORKS.

78. In the ninth chapter the Council adds, that the divine benignity is so great, that in consideration of the merits of Jesus Christ, God is willing to accept, in satisfaction for sins, not only voluntary works of penance offered to him, or those which the confessor has imposed, but also the divine chastisements, provided we bear them with

patience. " Docet præterea tantam esse divinæ munificentiæ largitatem, ut non solum pœnis sponte a nobis pro vindicando peccato susceptis aut sacerdotis arbitrio pro mensura delicti impositis, sed etiam, quod maximum amoris argumentum est, temporalibus flagellis a Deo inflictis, et a nobis patienter toleratis, apud Deum Patrem per Christum Jesum satisfacere valeamus.

79. Here I insert a brief notice of many ancient practices regarding the sacramental confession, which have been collected by Father Chalon in his history of the sacraments. In ancient times, bishops alone administered the sacrament of Penance; but when impeded by a just cause, they entrusted this office to secular and even to regular priests: but ordinarily the confession was made only to bishops, or sometimes to bishops and their senate or presbytery, as is stated by Mabillon, (tr. della conf. 40, sec. 3.) who mentions many instances in which confessions were thus made. After the Novatian schism the office of penitentiary was instituted: but after its abolition by Nectarius, parish priests (called *proprii sacerdotes*) were appointed to hear confessions as well in the cities as in the villages; and they alone administered the sacrament of penance. Religious were afterwards permitted to hear confessions: to this the parish priests objected: but the cause of the religious was defended by Albertus Magnus, by St. Thomas, and St. Bonaventure, who maintained that under the words *proprio pastore* used by the Council of Lateran in the canon "Omnis utriusque sexus," (de pœn. et rem.) was included every priest approved by the ordinary. On this point there were various decisions: Innocent IV. forbade the faithful to confess their sins to any one except their own pastors, or without at least having obtained his permission. Alexander the Fourth condemned those who held that the bishops could not give faculties for hearing confessions against the will of the parish priest. This decision was confirmed by

Clement IV., who notwithstanding the dissent of the parish priests, gave faculties to the Franciscans. Alexander V. in a special bull extended these faculties to all the mendicant orders. Gerson wrote against this bull and maintained that the pope could not deprive parish priests of their exclusive right to hear confessions; hence, all the Mendicants were banished from the university of Paris. But finally the Council of Trent ordained (sess. 28, de ref. c. 15.) that no one could hear confessions without the permission of the bishop; and thus an end was put to the controversy.

80. In ancient times some confessed their sins to deacons or other ecclesiastics; but such confessions were not sacramental confessions. Formerly, in several places deacons and other ecclesiastics heard confession and gave absolution: but this was an abuse, and was prohibited by the bishops and by several synods. St. Basil (interrog. 228.) expressly forbade his nuns to confess their sins to any one but a priest.

81. The following was the ancient mode of going to confession. The penitent came: the priest said certain prayers over him: he then made the penitent sit near him (as is at present done in the Greek Church), and heard his confession, interrogating him first regarding his faith. The penitent then knelt down and entreated the priest to recommend him to God, and remained prostrate on the ground for a considerable time, making acts of sorrow for his sins. Then the confessor made him stand up, and gave him penance: the penitent prostrated himself again, and the confessor read over him seven prayers which are found in the penitentials. Both of them then went to the church: the confession was not made in the church but in a place exposed to public view: confessions were heard in private houses only in cases of sickness. But in the time of St. Peter Damian all confessions were heard in the church before the altar, and there the penitents recited many psalms and pray-

ers, and then retired to perform the penance before they received absolution. But in the beginning of the thirteenth century this discipline was changed. All this is stated by Father Chalon (cap. 8.): he takes it from Alcuin the preceptor of Charlemagne in the eighth century, (lib. de div. offic.) and from Brocard of Worms. (lib. 19.) We find the same in the ancient Roman Order. (Apud. Biblioth. Patr. tom. 10.)

82. The stations of penitents began towards the end of the third century. There were four of them: the *weepers*, the *hearers*, the *prostrate*, and the *standers*; as St. Basil expressly mentions, (lib. 2, c. 2.). But to understand this, it is necessary to know, as Fleury says in his ecclesiastical history, (c. 35.) that in the beginning the churches were composed of a portico through which there was an entrance into a square court surrounded by pillars, like a monastic cloister: in the middle of the court there was a fountain: there the poor stood before the door of the church. At the extremity there was a double porch from which there were three doors into the church. Within the church, at the entrance was the baptistery, and at its extremity was the sacristy, which was called the *secretary*, and also the *treasure*. Along the church there were little cells for those who wished to pray apart from the people, as there are at present chapels in our churches. The church was divided by two rows of columns: towards its extremity to the east, was the altar, behind which was the presbytery where the priests recited the office along with the bishop, who sat at the end of the church, opposite to the door. Before the altar there was a balustrade or chancel. In the middle of the church stood the pulpit, to which there was an ascent on two sides: for it was used for the public lessons. There was likewise a pulpit for the Gospel, and another for the Epistle.

83. With regard to the stations mentioned above, it is related in the canon ascribed to St. Gregory Thaumaturgus

that the station of the *weepers* was outside the church: there they implored of all who entered to intercede in their favour.   The *hearers* stood within the door of the church, and were permitted to go as far as the pulpit, the place for the people was between the pulpit and the chancel of the altar.   The *hearers* remained standing to listen to the Scriptures, to Sermons and Instructions: but when the recital of the prayers commenced, they were sent out along with the catechumens.   As soon as they left the church, the doors were locked, and the mass commenced along with chaunting of the Symbol and the prayers for the oblation of gifts.   The *prostrates* were also excluded from the church during the mass.   They were called *prostrates*, because hands were imposed on them, and many prayers recited over them, while they lay prostrate before their expulsion from the church.   This second station was of long duration: it lasted at least for seven years. The *hearers*, who belonged to the third station, were permitted to listen to the lessons and sermons.   Finally, the *standers* were permitted to hear mass, but in a separate place, and were deprived of communion: hence, they partook only of the prayers of the sacrifice.   Among these, there were certain persons who had committed grievous sins, but were not subjected to canonical penance, and also persons who spontaneously came forward to accuse themselves with great sentiments of compunction.

84. With regard to the form of the sacrament of Penance, Father Morino (See Tournely tom. 2, q. 9, concl. 3,) proves by a great number of authorities, that, as has been already said, the form, until the twelfth century was deprecative: "*Dominus te absolvat*," &c. to which many prayers were added: in reciting them, the priest held his hand on the head of the penitent.   We find the same stated by St. Ambrose, (l. 8, c. 8, 10, 11,) and by St. Leo. (epist. 83.) Father Chalon says, (l. 2, c. 32,) that this appears from all

the penitentials, whether Greek or Latin. Peter Cantor, who flourished towards the end of the twelfth century, gives the deprecative form. In the Sum of d'Ales, we find the deprecative and indicative form. And St. Thomas wrote an opuscle in favour of the indicative form, in which he says that we cannot contradict the words of Jesus Christ: "Quidquid solveritis, &c.," The Doctors of Paris decided that the form *ego te absolvo* should be used. Because the priest in the tribunal of penance performs the office of judge: and therefore, it strictly belongs to him to pass sentence. But the Council of Trent has decided (sess. 14, c. 3) that the essential words of absolution are; *ego te absolvo a peccatis tuis*, and that the accompanying prayers are useful but not necessary. However the Greeks have preserved the deprecative form, which is also approved by the Church. (Sec. n. 71.)

85. By the canons a priest, if he should violate the seal of confession, is deposed and condemned to live as a pilgrim during his whole life. (Can. Sacerdos. 1, caus. 33, qu. 3, dist. 6.) Gratian says that this canon was passed by Gregory the Great: but Morino ascribes it to Gregory VII., or to some Pope who lived about that time. And in the Council of Lateran under Innocent III. (Extrav. de pœn. et rem.) it is ordained that such a priest should not only be deposed but should also be shut up in a monastery.

86. In ancient times all were obliged to go to confession in the beginning of Lent, as appears from the ancient rituals. Formerly there were, as Brocard attests (lib. 19, c. 5.), three Lents in the Latin Church. The principal one was before Easter, the second during Advent, before the festival of Christmas, and the third for the forty days before the feast of St. Martin. Afterwards they were reduced to two, one before Easter, the other in Advent, and finally to that which preceded Easter: but the fast on the quarter tenses still continued to be of precept.

87. In the thirteenth century great penitentiaries were appointed in the various dioceses, with faculties to absolve from reserved cases.   But even before that time sins were reserved to the pope or bishops, as Peter Cantor, and Fleury (Hist. tom. 2, p. 259.) attest.

88. Formerly, it was disputed whether absolution given from a distance was valid.   Suares held that it was: (de pœnit. d. 19. sect. 3.) but Clement VIII. on the 20th of July, 1692, forbade priests to receive the confession of an absent person in writing, and prohibited penitents to receive absolution from a distance.

89. Formerly penances were not left to the discretion of the confessor, but should be imposed according to the penitential canons which were registered in the penitentials, and public and private confessions were regulated in the same manner, except that public penance should be performed in public.   In the eighth century, in which public penance was altogether abolished, various writers composed penitential books in which were explained the species of sins, and the punishments corresponding to them according to the canons of the Councils, and the customs of the principal churches, along with the formulas of absolution and other prayers.   Among them the most celebrated were the Roman penitential, the penitential of Bede, and that of Theodore.

90. Public penance was prescribed for public sinners but only on account of sins of the first class, from which even when secret, penitents were not, as Father Chalon says (c. 6.), absolved until after they had performed canonical penance. Public sinners were compelled even by excommunication to perform public penance.   Father Chalon says (c. 7.) that some secret sinners through humility submitted to public penance, but without publishing their sins.   However, they were permitted to do this only once.   This discipline did not continue longer than the seventh century.   From that time the practice of imposing canonical penance several

times, on public sinners, commenced. In the Council of Nice (can. 12.) it was said that greater indulgence might be shown to fervent penitents. And the recommendations of the martyrs and confessors who suffered for the faith, would obtain the remission of a part of the penance. These recommendations were called *libelli commendatitii* which were sometimes presented by the deacons, and were afterwards examined by the bishops. This privilege of the martyrs commenced before the time of Tertullian, it was recognised in the year 176, or 177, in the persecution of Marcus Aurelius, and ceased only with the martyrs. In the three first centuries ecclesiastics in holy orders were subjected to public penance, when guilty of public sins. And after being deposed they could never again enter upon the exercise of their orders even after they had done public penance. After the third century this was restrained to minor ecclesiastics. (Chalon. lib. 2, c. 18, 19.) And public sinners, even after having performed public penance, were incapable of receiving holy orders. But this did not hold for persons who had voluntarily subjected themselves to public penance. In the west, but not in the east, public penitents were also excluded from military and magisterial offices, from traffic, from contracting matrimony, and from the use of marriage. But all this ceased in the fourteenth century along with the use of public penance. (Chalon. l. 2, c. 16.)

CONTINUATION OF THE FOURTEENTH SESSION.

ON THE SACRAMENT OF EXTREME UNCTION.

1. After treating of the sacrament of penance the Council lays down the doctrine on the sacrament of extreme unction, which the Fathers regarded as the final complement of life which in Christians should be a perpetual penance. The Council adds that as God in his goodness has provided us during life with various means of defence against all the assaults of our enemies, so he has not left us unprovided with special arms in the last combat, at death, when hell exerts all its strength for our destruction.

CHAPTER I.—ON THE INSTITUTION OF THE SACRAMENT OF EXTREME UNCTION.

2. In this chapter, the Fathers declare, that the sacred unction of the sick has been instituted as a true and real sacrament, as is insinuated in the Gospel of St. Mark, and as was afterwards promulgated by St. James, the Apostle, in these words: "Is any man sick among you? Let him bring in the priests of the church, and let them pray over him, anointing him with oil in the name of the Lord. And the prayer of faith shall save the sick man: and the Lord shall raise him up, and if he be in sins they shall be forgiven him." From these words, the church, instructed by apostolical tradition, teaches that oil blessed by a bishop is the matter of this sacrament: for the unction represents the grace with which the soul of the sick man is invisibly anointed. The form of this sacrament consists in these

words: " Per istam unctionem, &c." Behold the words of
the Council: " Instituta est autem sacra hæc unctio infir-
morum tanquam vere et proprie sacramentum novi Testamenti, a Christo D. N. apud Marcum quidem insinuatum
(c. 6, v. 12, et. seq.) per Jacobum apostolum et Domini
fratrem fidelibus commendatum ac promulgatum: *Infir-
matur*, inquit, *quis in vobis? inducat presbyteros
Ecclesiæ, et orent super eum, ungentes eum oleo in
nomine Domini ; et oratio fidei salvabit infirmum et
alleviabit eum Dominus ; et si in peccatis sit, dimittentur
ei.*" Quibus verbis, ut ex apostolica traditione per manus
accepta, Ecclesia didicit, docet materiam, formam, proprium
ministrum et effectum hujus salutaris sacramenti. Intellexit
enim Ecclesia materiam esse oleum ab episcopo benedictum ;
nam unctio aptissime Spiritus Sancti gratiam, qua invis-
sibiliter anima ægrotantis inungitur, repræsentat; forma
deinde esse illa verba: *Per istam unctionem, &c.*

3. To this chapter corresponds the first canon in which
the Council says: " Si quis dixerit Extremam Unctionem
non esse vere et proprie sacramentum a Christo Domino
institutum, et a B. Jacobo apostolo promulgatum, sed ritum
tantum acceptum a Patribus aut figmentum humanum
anathema sit."

4. Thus in this first chapter the Council teaches that the
sacrament of Extreme Unction is in the true and strict
sense of the word, a sacrament which was insinuated in
the Gospel of St. Mark, (vi. 12, &c.) in these words: " And
going forth they preached that men should do penance; and
they cast out many devils, and anointed with oil many that
were sick, and healed them," and which was promulgated by
St. James. Hence, it was not instituted but only promulgated
by St. James: this sacrament, as well as all the others were
instituted by Christ. But whether Christ instituted this
sacrament immediately or through St. James, is a disputed
question: neither of the opinions regarding this point is of

faith, since the Council of Trent only says, that this sacrament was instituted by Christ, and this is certainly of faith. It appears to be more probable that it was instituted immediately by Christ, since the Council ascribes only the promulgation of it to St. James: "Instituta est sacra hæc unctio......a Christo Domino tanquam sacramentum novi Testamenti, apud Marcum quidem insinuatum, per Jacobum autem fidelibus promulgatum." With regard to the time of the promulgation of the sacrament of Extreme Unction, Tournely thinks it more probable (Comp. de sacr. Extr. unct. t. 2, p. 30, q. 2.) that it was promulgated after the institution of penance, because, according to the language of the Fathers, it is *perfective* and *consummative* of that sacrament.

5. Luther and Calvin have abolished Extreme Unction, and have called it a popish superstition. But, as has been said, the Council declared it to be a real sacrament, in which we find the three essential requisites which constitute a sacrament. First, in Extreme Unction there is a sensible sign in the unction with oil: secondly, there is a promise of grace, "if he be in sins, they shall be forgiven him:" thirdly, there is a divine institution "anointing him with oil in the name of the Lord:" and since it was merely promulgated by St. James, it must have been instituted by Christ, to whom alone the institution of the sacraments belongs.

6. Calvin objects that in his chronicle, Sigebert relates that the Extreme Unction was instituted by Innocent I. But how can we give credit to the statement of Sigebert, when Innocent himself (ep. 1, c. 8.) asserts that the Extreme Unction of the sick is a real sacrament, and does not insinuate in the most remote manner that it was instituted by him? Sigebert himself attests the same. All the facts asserted by the heretics, are suspected of falsehood.

7. It is also objected that in the first ages, the persons who related the death of the saints, do not mention that they received this sacrament at the end of life. But they have not mentioned that the saints received the Eucharist, which all the faithful used certainly to receive before death. It is enough to know, as Possidius says in the life of St. Augustine, that it was a common maxim of the saints that no one should die without signs of penance: " Sacerdotes absque digna pœnitentia exire de corpore non debere." Under the word penance was also included the reception of this last sacrament.

8. The adversaries object also that St. James attributes the effect of extreme unction to the prayer of faith: "and the prayer of faith shall save the sick man." Were it a sacrament, they say, the effect would be attributed to the unction as the matter of the sacrament, and to the prayer merely as the form. But they err, for in truth the effect is ascribed simply to the unction and prayer, " *anointing him in the name of the Lord.*" Immediately after these words, the apostle says: " *and the prayer of faith shall save the sick man.*" The words *the prayer of faith*, should not be taken *subjectively*, of the faith of the priest, but *objectively* or of the faith of the whole church, since that prayer contains the object of faith, which is the sacrament.

9. From the Council we also know the matter of extreme unction: the remote matter is oil of olives, as is evident from the Euchology of the Greeks, and from the sacramentary of St. Gregory. For the word *oil*, strictly speaking, signifies olive oil, as we find in the Roman Catechism: " ex olearum baccis tantummodo expressum." (part. 2, n. 9.) The other oils are not simply oils, but are called oils with an *adjunct*, for example of flaxseed, nut, &c. Nor can any difficulty arise from its being called chrism, by Innocent I., for by that term he meant any

2 x

unction whatever. But according to Tournely, (tom. 2, de extr. unct. p. 17.) if it should ever happen that the olive oil was found to be mixed with balsam, like the oil of catechumens, it would be fit matter for the sacrament in case of necessity.

10. It is also necessary to know that although the Greeks use oil blessed by a priest, the Latins must get the oil blessed by a bishop. However, the pope can give simple priests power to bless the oil, as appears from the decree of Clement VIII. (See my Moral Theology, lib. 6. n. 709, dub. 3.) With regard to the question whether the benediction or consecration of the oil is necessary for the validity of the sacrament, Juenin says (tom. 7, de extr unct. 424, qu. 1.) that it is evident that among the Greeks the benediction is only of precept, but is never prescribed as necessary for the sacrament. Other very learned theologians, such as Bellarmine, Estius, &c., hold that it is necessary for the validity of the sacrament: Sambovius along with others to whom Tournely appears to adhere (tom. 2, de sacr. p. 15.) denies its necessity, and answers the arguments of Bellarmine. But when there is question of the validity of the sacrament, it is not lawful except in case of necessity, to use doubtful matter. But if there were a deficiency of consecrated oil, a portion of unblessed oil, but less in quantity than what is blessed, may be mixed with it, as appears from the chapter, "Quod in dubiis de consecr."

11. The *proximate* matter is the unction itself, which in the Latin Church must be made on the eyes, the ears, the nostrils, the lips, the hands, the soles of the feet, or near these parts, and on the loins with regard to men (but not with regard to women), who can be moved without danger, as is directed in the Sacramentary of St. Gregory, and in the Roman ritual. In cases of necessity when there is not time to anoint the other senses, it is sufficient to anoint one, which can be more easily anointed, saying:

" indulgeat tibi Deus quicquid per sensus *deliquisti*," for
St. James only says: *let them anoint.* But as Tournely
justly says (t. 2, de. extr. unct. p. 21, q. 3.) after St.
Thomas, when there is time, it is not lawful to omit any
of the abovementioned unctions. In ancient times the sick
were ordinarily obliged to go to the church, in order to receive
this sacrament: of this, Father Chalon mentions several examples. (lib. 3, c. 3.) St. Cesarius supposes that this
practice was common in the church, and therefore the
sacrament was not deferred to the extremity of life. This
is practised at present by the Trappists.

12. From the Council we also know that the form of
this sacrament consists in the words: "*Per istam
unctionem*, &c.*" This is the form which was prescribed by
Eugene IV. in his instruction to the Armenians: "Per
istam unctionem et suam piissimam misericordiam indulgeat
tibi Deus quidquid deliquisti per visum, odoratum, gustum,
tactum, auditum, gressus, lumborum delectationem." This
form is given in the decree of Eugene IV. and in the
Roman ritual. But Father Chalon (Cit. lib. 3, c. 1.) states
that in ancient times there was a great variety with regard
to this matter: he even relates many instances in which
only one part of the body was anointed. For the validity
of the sacrament, the words *per istam sanctam unctionem*
&c., are not necessary; neither is it necessary to mention
all the senses, the words: " indulgeat tibi Deus quidquid
per sensus deliquisti," are sufficient. I have said that the
other words are not necessary for the validity of the sacrament: but except in cases of necessity, they cannot be omitted
without sin. The form used by the Greeks is different; it
expresses the particular effects of the sacrament. Juenin
says (de Extr. unct. p. 22, qu. 2.) that some of the Latin
Churches formerly adopted the indicative form: *Ungo te
oleo*, &c., and states that according to St. Thomas, St.
Bonaventure, and others, this was the Ambrosian form

which was used at Milan: *Ungo te oleo sanctificato in
nomine Patris*, &c.   But the form which is universally
used at present in the Latin Church, is the deprecative
form givèn above; and this, Juenin also asserts, (p. 25, q.
2, v. 3.) has been always used in the Greek Church.

CHAPTER II.—ON THE EFFECT OF THIS
SACRAMENT.

13. In the second chapter the Council distinguishes the
res et effectus: the *thing* (res) of the sacrament is the grace
of the Holy Ghost: the effect (effectus) is what the Council
afterwards explains: " *Res porro et effectus* hujus sacramenti illis verbis explicatur: *et oratio fidei salvabit
infirmum, et alleviabit eum Dominus : et si in peccatis sit, dimittentur ei.* Res etenim hæc gratia est
Spiritus Sancti cujus unctio delicta, si quæ sint adhuc expianda, ac peccati reliquias abstergit; et ægroti animam
alleviat et confirmat, magnam in eo divinæ misericordiæ
fiduciam excitando; qua infirmus sublevatur et morbi in-
commoda ac labores levius fert, et tentationibus dæmonis
calcaneo insidiantis facilius resistit, et sanitatem corporis
interdum, ubi saluti animæ expedierit, consequitur."

14. Thus the effects of the sacrament are principally
three: first the remission of sins along with the removal of
the relics of sin: secondly, the divine aid to enable the
sick man to bear with greater patience the inconveniencies
of his infirmity, and greater strength to resist the last
attacks of the enemy: thirdly, this sacrament also gives
corporal health, when it is expedient for the salvation of
the soul.   The Thomists hold that the restoration of corporal
health is produced *ex opere operato :* but Estius contends
that it is produced *ex opere operantis*, that is in virtue of
the public prayers of the church by which the oil is consecrated. (See Tournely de extr. unct. p. 56, q. 7.)

15. It is disputed whether the remission of sins is a direct primary effect of the sacrament; Tournely, (de extr. unct. 49, q. 1.) along with Sotus and other Thomists affirm absolutely that it is, and argue in favour of their opinion, from the words of St. James, *si in peccatis fuerit, dimittentur ei*, from the words of the Council, *cujus unctio delicta si quæ sint adhuc expianda abstergit*, and also from the words of the form : *indulgeat tibi Deus quidquid......deliquisti &c.*

16. Secondly, it is disputed whether the remission of sins is the simple primary effect. There is no doubt but it is the primary, but not the simple and sole effect: for it is united with two other secondary effects, viz., the removal of the relics of sin, and the alleviation of the sick man. By the relics of sin are meant the propensity to evil, tepidity in the practice of virtue, and darkness of mind: for Extreme unction is given by way of a perfect cure, and as the complement of penance.

17. It is disputed also whether the direct primary effect of this sacrament is to remit only venial, or also mortal sins. Sambovius maintains the affirmative, (de extr. unct. disp. 5, a. 1.) and says that although Extreme unction is a sacrament of the living, still, because it is the complement of penance, its primary effect is to remit venial, and its secondary effect is to remit even mortal sins. But Juenin justly impugns this opinion. (de extr. unct. p. 3, q. 4.) The opinion of St. Thomas is the more probable: he holds that the sacraments of the living, such as Confirmation, Eucharist, Order, and Extreme unction, remit grievous sins not directly, but by accident, when the person who receives the sacrament has attrition, which he considers to be contrition, and cannot receive another sacrament. Behold the words of the Angelic Doctor regarding the Eucharist: " Potest tamen hoc sacramentum operari remissionem peccati (mortalis): forte enim primo si (suscipiens sacramentum) non

fuit sufficienter contritus, consequetur per hoc sacramentum gratiam charitatis, quæ contritionem perficiet et remissionem peccati." (3, p. q. 69, a. 3.)   The saint says the same of extreme unction. (3, p. q. 30, a. 1.)   This opinion of St. Thomas is adopted by Gonet, Cardinal Bellarmine, Concina, Suares, and most commonly by the other divines. They justly argue in favour of their opinion, from the words of the Council of Trent: " Si quis dixerit sacramenta novæ legis......gratiam non ponentibus obicem non conferre, anathema sit." (Sess. 7, can. 6.)   He who receives the sacrament with contrition, which he considers to be such, certainly does not place any obstacle to the reception of grace.

CHAPTER III.—ON THE MINISTER OF EXTREME UNCTION; AND ON THE TIME IT SHOULD BE GIVEN.

18. In the third and last chapter, the Council declares that the minister of Extreme unction is a bishop, or priest, and that the persons to whom it should be administered are sick persons in danger of death.   It also declares that Extreme unction may be received a second time by those who recover from their illness, and relapse into the same danger.   The Council moreover censures those who assert that Extreme unction ceased when the grace of miraculous cures ceased in the primitive Church.   It likewise declares that the contempt of this sacrament is a most grievous sin. " Jam vero quod attinet ad præscriptionem eorum qui et suscipere et ministrare hoc sacramentum debent, haud obscure fuit illud etiam in verbis prædictis traditum: nam et ostenditur illic proprios hujus sacramenti ministros esse Ecclesiæ presbyteros, quo nomine, eo loco, non ætate seniores aut primores in populo intelligendi veniunt, sed aut episcopi aut sacerdotes ab ipsis rite ordinati per impositionem manuum

presbyterii. Declaratur etiam esse hanc unctionem infirmis adhibendam, illis vero præsertim qui tam periculose decumbunt ut in exitu vitæ constituti videantur; unde et sacramentum exeuntium nuncupatur. Quod si infirmi post susceptam hanc unctionem convaluerint, iterum hujus sacramenti subsidio juvari poterunt, cum in aliud simile vitæ discrimen inciderint. Quare nulla ratione audiendi sunt, qui contra tam apertam et dilucidam apostoli Jacobi sententiam docent hanc unctionem vel figmentum esse humanum vel ritum a Patribus acceptum......nec promissionem gratiæ habentem; et qui illam jam cessasse asserunt, quasi ad gratiam curationum dumtaxat in primitiva Ecclesia referenda esset; et qui dicunt ritum et usum quem S. Romana Ecclesia in hujus sacramenti administratione observat Jacobi apostoli sententiæ repugnare, atque ideo in alium commutandum esse; et denique qui hanc extremam unctionem a fidelibus sine peccato contemni posse affirmant. Hæc enim omnia apertissime pugnant cum perspicuis tanti apostoli verbis; nec profecto ecclesia Romana, aliarum omnium mater et magistra, aliud in hac administranda unctione, quantum ad ea quæ hujus sacramenti substantiam perficiunt, observat quam quod B. Jacobus præscripsit. Nec vero tanti sacramenti contemptus absque ingenti scelere et ipsius Spiritus Sancti injuria esse posset."

19. To this chapter are added the third and fourth canons. Can. 3. " Si quis dixerit Extremæ unctionis ritum et usum quem observat S. Romana ecclesia repugnare sententiæ B. Jacobi apostoli, ideoque eum mutandum, posseque a christianis absque peccato contemni, anathema sit."

20. Canon 4: " Si quis dixerit presbyteros Ecclesiæ, quos B. Jacobus adducendos esse ad infirmum inungendum hortatur non esse sacerdotes ab episcopo ordinatos, sed ætate seniores in quavis communitate, ob idque proprium

extremæ unctionis ministrum non esse solum sacerdotem, anathema sit."

21. Thus from the Council we know that the ministers of extreme unction are not laymen, nor the elders among the people, as Calvin held, but as Estius demonstrates (In ep. pag. 1142, col. 1,) and as the holy Fathers taught, only they who have been raised by the episcopal or sacerdotal dignity. In the New Testament the word *presbyteri* means solely the ministers of the church: besides St. James speaks of priests who remit sins; but the power of remitting sins has never been granted to laymen. Moreover the Council says that this is clearly contained in the words of St. James. In the fifth century, some admitted that priests are the ministers of this sacrament, but absurdly excluded bishops; and this they attempted to prove from the epistle of Innocent I., to Decentius: but they erred, for Innocent himself in that letter expressly mentions bishops. The Council also (cap. 3,) says that bishops as well as priests are ministers of Extreme unction.

22. Every priest can administer extreme unction validly, because, for the administration of this sacrament, the power of jurisdiction is not necessary; the power of order is sufficient. I have said *validly :* for in order to administer it lawfully, a priest must have either the ordinary jurisdiction of a bishop, or of a parish priest, or must have delegated jurisdiction from them, as is prescribed in the first Clementine. (de privileg.) But if a priest who has such jurisdiction cannot be had, is it lawful for any priest, even though a religious, to administer the sacrament? Navarre answers in the negative. (in man. c. 27, n. 101.) But the opposite opinion is more probable, and is held by Silvius, Sotus, and may others along with Tournely. (de. Extr. unct. p. 35, q. 2.) Nor is this opinion opposed to the decree of Clement, (Dudum. de sepultur.) in which religious were

forbidden, under pain of excommunication, to violate the rights of parish priests: for this prohibition regarded religious who, under the pretext of their privileges, wished to perform the office of parish priests, but did not extend to cases of necessity, in which extreme unction should be given, and when the legitimate minister could not be found. To this may be added the authority of St. Charles Borromeo, who, in the Council of Milan, ordained: " Si porro is (parochus) impeditus aut alias in mora est, mortisque periculum instat, hoc sacramentum sacerdos alius administret.

23. For the administration of extreme unction, the Greeks require seven priests, as appears from their Euchologies, or five, or three, as Renaudot states (tom. 7, de sacram.): but they do not wait until the sick man is at the point of death. Father Chalon says, that formerly when seven priests anointed a sick man, a lamp containing seven candles was prepared, and that each priest lighted his own candle, and then, with the sign of the cross and reciting many prayers, they anointed the sick man. Even among the Latins, in ancient times, several priests were called to anoint the sick, as appears from the Sacramentary of St. Gregory. But for several centuries extreme unction has been administered in the Latin Church by a single priest. This practice is not opposed to the words of St. James, " *let him bring in the priests:*" for in the Scripture the plural is frequently used for the singular number. Thus St. Matthew and St. Mark say, that the robbers who were crucified with our Redeemer, reviled him, although, as we read in St. Luke, (xxiii. 39) only one of them blasphemed our Lord: " Unus autem de his, &c."

24. In his history of the Sacraments, (lib. 3, c. 1.) Father Chalon relates that formerly the extreme unction was administered promiscuously by one priest or by several, as appears from the ancient rituals. (apud Martene 1, 2, c. 7, a. 4.) He also says that sometimes all the priests

y

anointed the sick man, each reciting the form corresponding to the sense which was anointed: that sometimes one anointed one part, and another another part, each reciting the form peculiar to that part. He likewise mentions in the same chapter many instances in which the sacrament was administered by a single priest. He adds, that before the sick man was anointed, it was usual to put sackcloth and ashes under him, or at least over him: both the sackcloth and ashes were blessed. This was practised especially in Italy.

25. With regard to the persons who are capable of receiving extreme unction, there is, as Arcudius (lib. 5, de Extr. Unct. c. 4) and Goarius think, an universal practice among the Greeks of anointing even those that are in health. The same is stated by Leo Allatius, (l. 3, de cons. eccl. c. 16, n., 3) who says: "Non tantum infirmos, sed sanos quoque homines extrema unctione, et sæpius, Græci inungunt." Arcudius holds that the Greeks consider this unction of persons in health to be a real sacrament: but this is denied by Goarius and Juenin, (p. 39, q. 1,) who says that at the time of Innocent I. even among the Latins, it was usual to anoint persons with oil blessed by the bishop in order to remove diseases; but no one believes that this unction was regarded as a sacrament. But St. James expressly says, that the sick are the persons to whom extreme unction should be given. "Is any one sick among you? Let him bring in the priests," &c. Hence it is not lawful to give this sacrament to persons in health, (such as those who are under sentence of execution,) even though they should be near death. And the Council of Trent clearly points out the sick as the persons who should be anointed: "Declaratur etiam esse hanc unctionem infirmis adhibendam, illis vero præsertim qui tam periculose decumbunt ut in exitu vitæ constituti videantur." But Benedict XIV. observes in his bull (53, s. 46, tom. 4, Bullar.) that this sacrament should be given

to the sick while they have the use of reason: " dum sibi
constant, et sui compotes sunt:" the priest ought not to wait
for the last moment of life, when the dying have no longer
the use of their senses. Hence the Roman catechism says:
" Gravissime peccant qui illud tempus ægroti ungendi observare solent cum jam, omni salutis spe amissa vita et sen-
sibus carere incipiat." (de extr. unct. s. q.) Hence,
Juenin justly says that the sick, who are in danger of
death, may be anointed though they have not reached the
end of life: " Numerari debent omnes qui perculose laborant, sive in exitu constituti videantur, sive non." This
clearly follows from the words of the Council: " Unctionem
infirmis adhibendam, illis vero præsertim qui in exitu vitæ
constituti videantur." The word *præsertim* shows that
the extreme unction may be given even to those who have
not reached the end of life. Hence theologians commonly
teach that this sacrament may be lawfully administered
whenever the sickness is accompanied with the danger of
death, even though the danger be not proximate. Hence,
in the abovementioned bull Benedict XIV. says: " Ne sacramentum extremæ unctionis ministretur bene valentibus,
sed iis dumtaxat qui gravi morbo laborent." And among
those to whom extreme unction may be given, St. Charles
Borromeo justly says that we ought to reckon decrepid old
persons, who suffer great languor, although they do not
labour under any other infirmity.

26. This sacrament should not be given to children who
have not attained the use of reason, nor to persons who
have been foolish from their birth; for such persons have
never been guilty of actual sin. But it may be given to
children who have completed their seventh year, and to
fools who have had some lucid intervals.

27. With regard to the dispositions necessary for receiving this sacrament, which is one of the sacraments of

the living, it is necessary that the sick man be in the state
of grace; and should he be in the state of sin, he ought to
have contrition, and ought to have a moral certainty that
his contrition is real, otherwise he should go to confession;
Juenin, Tournely, and Concina absolutely require confession,
but other authors only require contrition.   In ancient times
extreme unction was given before the viaticum; Father
Chalon (l. 3, c. 2,) says that Pope Leo IX., who lived
in the eleventh century, received it in this manner; he also
mentions examples of persons who received it after the
viaticum.   But, according to Juenin, the practice of the
Latin churches has been, for several centuries, to receive the
viaticum before the extreme unction.   However if a person
wishes to receive both at the same time, the extreme unction should, according to the Parisian ritual (as is reasonable) be given first, and then the viaticum, that the sacrament of extreme unction may first produce its effect of remitting sin; but the extreme unction should be given first
only when the sick man is not in danger of dying without
the eucharist.   See Juenin, p. 7, de Extr. unct. qu. 8, p. 234.

28. Father Chalon (l. 3, c. 7,) relates that formerly in
several places the unction was repeated for seven days.
But the Council teaches that extreme unction can be repeated
only when the sick man recovers and afterwards relapses
into similar danger of death.   " Quod si infirmi post
susceptam unctionem convaluerint, iterum hujus sacramenti
subsidio juvari poterunt, cum in aliud simile vitæ discrimen
inciderint."   The Council afterwards adds: " Quare nulla
ratione audiendi sunt qui illam (unctionem) jam cessasse
asserunt, quasi ad gratiam curationum dumtaxat in primitiva ecclesia referenda esset."

29. That the reader may more easily understand what
the Fathers say in this place, I will repeat what they teach
in the first chapter on the institution of this sacrament.

" Vere et proprie sacramentum a Christo D. N. apud Marcum quidem insinuatum, per Jacobum autem commendatum ac promulgatum." As we have said at the commencement of the treatise on this sacrament, the Council teaches that the extreme unction was insinuated or prefigured in the cures of corporal maladies, which the disciples of our Lord performed before the institution of this sacrament, by anointing the sick with oil: " Et ungebant oleo multos ægros, et sanabant." (Marc. 6, 13.) Calvin maintains that in the words, *anointing him with oil in the name of the Lord*, St. James spoke of the unction of which St. Mark speaks, and which was performed by the disciples who had the gift of healing the sick by anointing them with oil. From this error Calvin deduces another, viz., that since the gift of miraculous cures has ceased, the unction of the sick has also ceased, and is at present not a sacrament but a useless and superstitious ceremony. But he errs: for the unction of which St. James speaks, is that which is performed by priests: but all, even the laity, might perform the unction mentioned by St. Mark: besides the priesthood had not been then instituted. Nor is it true that when the gift of miraculous cures ceased, the extreme unction ceased: for from its first institution, this sacrament has been always administered in the church, as Origen, (hom. 2, in Levit.) St. Chrysostom, (de sacerdot.) Pope Innocent I., (ep. ad Decent.) and St. Gregory, (Sacramentar.) attest. And of this all the rituals that have been since published, make express mention. However Father Chalon, (lib. 3, c. 1.) relates that on account of the persecutions, this sacrament was seldom given in the three first centuries, and this is very probable.

30. Finally the Council says that in a Christian the contempt of this sacrament is a great crime: " Nec vero tanti sacramenti contemptus absque ingenti scelere et ipsius Spiritus Sancti injuria esse posset." But it is disputed

2 r

whether a Christian who, without any contempt for the
sacrament, voluntarily refuses to receive extreme unction
is guilty of a grievous sin.   According to the more common
opinion he does not sin grievously: and this is held by St.
Thomas, (in 4, sent. dist. 2, q. 1, a. 1, q. 3, ad. 1.) by
Estius, Silvius, Sambovius, Navarre, and many others.   Of
the extreme unction and Confirmation St. Thomas says:
" non sunt de necessitate salutis."   But the opposite
opinion, which is maintained by Concina, Habert, Juenin,
and St. Bonaventure, is not improbable: they say that there
is a positive precept in the words of St. James: " Let him
bring in the priests of the Church, and let them pray over
him, anointing him with oil in the name of the Lord."
This argument does not fully convince me, since the words
do not denote a certain precept: but I say that at death
every one is obliged to receive this sacrament, on account
of the charity which he is bound to practise towards himself.   For, although a sick man may be fortified by other
means, still at death his mind is very weak, and feels a
difficulty in making good acts, and as the Council of Trent
says, the assaults of the devil are then more violent: " Nullum tempus est in quo vehementius (adversarius) omnes
suæ astutiæ nervos intendat ad perdendum nos quam cum
impendere nobis exitum vitæ perspicit."   The Council adds
that in this sacrament, the Lord has prepared for us a
certain most powerful aid: " tanquam firmissimo quodam
præsidio (nos) munivit."   I know not then how a sick man
who in such danger of eternal perdition, voluntarily deprives
himself of so powerful a help to conquer hell, can be excused from a grievous sin against charity towards himself,
in exposing himself to the danger of yielding to temptation
in that last contest with the enemy.

TWENTY-FIRST SESSION.

ON COMMUNION UNDER BOTH SPECIES, AND ON GIVING COMMUNION TO INFANTS.

1. In this session the Council lays down the doctrine which the faithful should hold on the two abovementioned points, and forbids any one to believe or teach otherwise. In the first chapter the Council declares that laymen and ecclesiastics who do not consecrate the Eucharist, are not obliged to communicate under both species, since it is certain that communion under one kind is sufficient for salvation. " S. synodus, a Spiritu Sancto......edocta atque Ecclesia judicium et consuetudinem secuta, declarat et docet nullo divino præcepto laicos et clericos non conficientes obligari ad Eucharistiæ sacramentum sub utraque specie sumendum: neque ullo pacto, salva fide, dubitari posse quin illis alterius specei communio ad salutem sufficiat. Nam etsi Christus......hoc sacramentum in panis et vini speciebus instituit et apostolis tradidit, non tamen illa institutio et traditio eo tendunt ut Christi omnes fideles statuto Domini ad utramque speciem accipiendam adstringantur. Sed neque ex sermone illo, apud Joannem 6, recte colligitur utriusque speciei communionem præceptam esse; namque qui dixit: " *Nisi manducaveritis carnem Filii hominis, et biberitis ejus sanguinem non habebitis vitam in vobis*, (Jo. 6.) dixit quoque: *Si quis manducaverit ex hoc pane vivet in æternam, &c., Qui manducat hunc panem vivet in æternam*. (Jo. ibid.)

2. To this chapter the first canon corresponds: Can. I. " Si quis dixerit ex Dei præcepto vel necessitate salutis omnes et singulos Christi fideles utramque speciem sanctissimi Eucharistiæ sacramenti sumere debere, anathema sit."

3. In the second chapter, the Council says that in the administration of the sacraments, the church has always had power to make the regulations and changes which it judged to be most expedient, according to the various circumstances which might occur. And, therefore, although at the commencement of Christianity, it was usual to receive communion under both kinds, still the Church has for just reasons established the practice of communion under one species only. " Præterea declarat hanc potestatem perpetuo in Ecclesia fuisse ut in sacramentorum dispensatione......ea statueret vel mutaret quæ pro......rerum temporum et locorum varietate magis expedire judicaret. Id autem Apostolus non obscure visus est innuissi cum ait, (1 Cor. iv. 1.) *Sic nos existimet homo ut ministros Christi et dispensatores mysteriorum Dei*......Quare......licet ab initio......, utriusque speciei usus fuisset, tamen, mutata consuetudine justis causis hanc consuetudinem sub altera specie communicandi approbavit et pro lege habendam decrevit," &c.

4. To this chapter the second canon corresponds. Can. 2: " Si quis dixerit sanctam ecclesiam catholicam non justis causis et rationibus adductam fuisse ut laicos, atque etiam clericos non conficientes, sub panis tantummodo specie communicaret, aut in eo errase, anathema sit."

Peter Soave objects that by this canon the Council founds a dogma of faith on a human fact, that is, that the church has made a decree to be observed as a human law, and by the divine law we are obliged to believe that decree to be a just one. I answer that the Council has not founded a dogma on a human fact, but on a certain principle, that as the Church cannot err in matters of faith and morals, so it cannot be induced, without a just cause to make laws regarding the administration of the sacraments.

5. In the third chapter, the Council declares that under one of the species Jesus Christ is received whole and entire, along with the true sacrament; and that, therefore, with regard to the fruit of the Eucharist, they who receive it under one kind alone, are not defrauded of any grace necessary for salvation: "Insuper declarat......fatendum esse etiam sub altera tantum specie totum atque integrum Christum verumque sacramentum sumi; ac propterea quod ad fructum attinet, nulla gratia necessaria ad salutem eos defraudari qui unam speciem solam accipiunt."

To this third chapter the third canon corresponds: Can. 3: "Si quis negaverit totum et integrum Christum, omnium gratiarum fontem et auctorem, sub una specie sumi, quia ut quidam falso asserunt, non secundum ipsius Christi institutionem sub utraque specie sumatur, anathema sit."

7. In the fourth chapter, the Council teaches that infants are not under any obligation whatever of receiving the communion: since they received sanctifying grace in baptism and cannot lose it at that age. And although for a just cause suited to the time, the ancient Fathers gave the Eucharist to infants, we must certainly believe that they did not do so because it was necessary for salvation. "Denique S. Synodus docet parvulos usu rationis carentes nulla obligari necessitate ad......Eucharistæ communionem; siquidem, per Baptismi lavacrum regenerati, adeptam gratiam in illa ætate amittere non possunt. Neque ideo tamen damnanda est antiquitas, si eum morem aliquando servavit: ut enim SS. illi Patres sui facti probabilem causam pro illius temporis ratione habuerunt, ita certe eos nulla salutis necessitate id fecisse......credendum est."

8. To this fourth chapter, the fourth Canon corresponds. Can. 4: "Si quis dixerit parvulis, antequam ad annos

discretionis pervenerint, necessarium esse Eucharistiæ communionem, anathema sit."

9. At the end of this session the Council reserved to another time, at which an occasion would offer, the examination and definition of two points which had been before proposed: first, whether the use of the chalice should be altogether forbidden to the faithful who do not celebrate mass; and secondly, whether it ought not for just reasons to be occasionally granted to an individual, or to a certain nation or kingdom, under certain conditions.

10. In this session Alphonsus Salmeron showed that it was certain that the use of the cup could not be of divine precept, since the church had for a long time prohibited it to the laity, as he proved from the Councils of Constance and Basil, and from all the writers of the preceeding five hundred years. He added that even in ancient times the chalice was not given to all, as appears from several histories and works of the Fathers. He answered the objections of the adversaries by saying that although our Lord at the last supper gave the Eucharist to the disciples under both kinds, saying to them, *bibite ex eo omnes,* still he addressed these words only to the disciples. Nor are we obliged to imitate all the actions of the Redeemer, in all their circumstances, but only when we are commanded by the Scripture or by the tradition of the church. He also said that the Gospel of St John (c. 6.) does not command the use of the chalice; for in that chapter the communion is sometimes mentioned under both kinds, and sometimes under the species of bread alone.

11. In his history Father Chalon says that at present the orientals administer the body and blood with a spoon; but formerly the blood, as St. Cyril of Jerusalem says, (Catech. 5. myst.) was taken from the chalice itself. Afterwards the practice was, as Brocard attests, (lib. 5, c.

3,) to give a consecrated particle dipped in the blood.
This was prohibited by Pope Urban in the Council of Clermont: according to Father Chalon (c. 7.) this manner of communicating continued till the twelfth century; from that
period the practice of communion under both species began
to be abolished. St. Thomas says (3, p. q. 80, a. 12, ad
2.) that in his own time, it was abolished, and the Council
of Constance expressly forbade it. Pope Pius the fourth
granted the use of the chalice to Germany; but as Cardinal
Bona relates, the concession was revoked by St. Pius the fifth.
Monsignor Bossuet says in his treatise on communion, (Ps.
165.) that in ancient times, the communion was given
only under the species of bread, on certain days, such as on
Good Friday.

12. Salmeron also said that they who receive the sacrament under one species, do not receive less than those who
receive it under both species; since even under one of the
species Christ is contained entirely, as had been defined by
the Councils of Constance and Florence. With regard to
the question whether a person receives as much grace by
receiving under one species as by receiving under both, he
said that in his opinion equal grace would be received in
both cases; and he endeavoured to prove his opinion by
several reasons. He added that this was not connected
with the article under discussion, since it depended entirely
on the will of God.

13. A certain brother Amante of the order of Servites,
and theologian of the bishop of Sebenico, in order to defend
the opinion that greater grace was received from communion under both species than from communion under one, went
so far as to say that the blood is not a part of human nature,
but the first aliment, and that therefore the blood of Christ
was not contained under the species of bread. But he was
severely censured by the others, and compelled to retract his

expressions, and to say that he had proposed this objection in order to refute it.

14. On the other hand a certain Portuguese undertook to defend that even priests who consecrate the Eucharist, are not bound by a divine precept to receive under both kinds: but all the others opposed his proposition, and in refutation of it, advanced several reasons which are given by Pallavicini; Cardinal Lugo also gives them, (de Euch., di sp. 19, Sect. 8.) and in the same place refutes Raphael de Volterra, who said that Innocent VIII. dispensed the Norwegian priests from the obligation of receiving under both kinds.

15. In a word, all agreed that he who receives under one kind does not receive less than the person who receives under both species. As to the effect of grace conferred by the sacrament, some maintained that he who receives both species receives greater grace, because the sacraments produce what they signify, according to their signs; and when the signs are multiplied, the grace is multiplied. But the greater number were of opinion that by virtue of the sacrament, equal grace was infused in both cases.

16. With regard to infants, it was asked whether it was commanded by a divine precept to give them communion. All answered in the negative, since the Eucharist is given by way of food, the nature of which is to restore what is lost by heat, that is by the disorder of the human passions: and this loss does not take place in infants, who have not free will. However, some few said that the communion increases grace in some measure in infants; but this the others denied, because infants communicate altogether in material manner and without any disposition. They added that in ancient times the Eucharist was given to infants not to produce an augmentation of grace, but to preserve them from the effects of witchcraft, or from being possessed by devils. Finally with regard to the question whether it was expedient to

grant to any nation, for example to the Germans, the use of the chalice, the imperial delegates who urged the concession were told that the point would be better examined and determined at a future time; it was afterwards refused, to the dissatisfaction of the delegates.

17. In the end of the second chapter, the Fathers added the following words with regard to the administration of the Eucharist under one kind: " Quam reprobare aut sine ipsius Ecclesiæ auctoritate pro libito mutare non licet." These words were added, because it was said by some that in several countries, such as Cyprus, Candia, and Greece, the use of the chalice was retained: but in answer to them it was said that it was granted to these countries by the Church as a special privilege; and therefore these last words were added in order not to offend those who had obtained the privilege.

18. Soave says that it appears extraordinary that the Council, although it had made four articles of faith to which anathemas were annexed, could not decide the question regarding the use of the chalice which was one of ecclesiastical law, and which appeared to some to be the point which should be treated first, because if the use of the chalice were granted, there would be an end to all the disputes. But Pallavicini says in answer that all this reasoning is fallacious: for as it was easy to see that there is no divine precept commanding the use of the cup, so it was doubtful whether it was expedient to grant or forbid it. Nor is it true, that had it been granted, the disputes would have ceased: for although the Church had granted the use of the cup, the innovators would not cease to question its power to permit or prohibit communion under both kinds.

19. Soave also says that by declaring that the faithful in receiving only under the species of bread are not defrauded of any necessary grace, the Council appeared to confess that they lose some grace which is not necessary, and as it were doubted whether human authority could put an

z

obstacle to the superabundant grace of God: for this appears
to be contrary to charity.   Pallavicini answers that from
the declaration that Christians to whom the cup is prohibited,
are not deprived of any necessary grace, we cannot argue
that the Council meant to admit that they are deprived of
any grace which is not necessary.   It often happens that a
person affirms or denies a proposition in circumstances in
which it may be affirmed or denied, without any reference
to what would happen if such circumstances did not exist.

20. With regard to the assertion that the Church has
not power to deprive the faithful of the superabundant
grace of the sacraments, (this is what Soave means to
assert) or that though it had the power it would violate
charity by depriving them of that grace, I answer that the
Church should not regard the sole augmentation of grace in
those who receive the Eucharist, but rather the veneration
of the sacrament.   Otherwise it would have done wrong in
prohibiting communion, and the celebration of mass on
Good Friday, and in prohibiting priests to celebrate mass
several times on the same day.   Peter Soave moreover
says that two things gave occasion to much discussion.   The
first was the obligation imposed by the Council to believe
that antiquity did not consider the communion of infants
necessary.   For where there is a question of what is past, the
authority which cannot alter what has happened, has no
weight.   On the other hand he says that St. Augustine in
nine places treats at length of the necessity of the Eucharist
for infants, and adds that the Roman Church itself has
several times defined it to be necessary for their salvation:
he also quotes the epistle of Pope Innocent, in which this
doctrine is clearly taught.   He adds that some persons in
the Council expressed their surprise that the Fathers by
their declaration that communion is not necessary for infants
would expose others to the danger of saying that either
Pope Innocent or the Council had fallen into error.

21. But Pallavicini says in answer: if Soave understood that the Church cannot declare to be faith, the truth of a past fact which is not subject to its jurisdiction, he proves himself to be as ignorant as he is incredulous of the authority of the Church. For it is certain that the Church can declare to be faith that that has not actually happened, which God assures us in the Scriptures, could not happen; for example that a saint in glory has not fallen into hell. Now since it is revealed in the Scriptures that the Church is the pillar and ground of the truth, the Council resting on this revelation could have defined that the Church has not erred by believing that communion was necessary for the salvation of infants. Besides the Council did not treat in this place of the opinion which the ancient Fathers held regarding the communion of infants, but said that as these Fathers had probable reasons for their conduct, according to the circumstances of the times, so we should certainly believe that they did not give communion to infants, because they thought it necessary for their salvation. As to the authority of St. Augustine, and the epistle of Pope Innocent I., Pallavicini confesses that St. Augustine, particularly in two places, holds that the Eucharist is as necessary as Baptism; but he says that it is well known for a long time in the schools, that the holy doctor understood the sixth chapter of St John, not only of sacramental communion, but also of the mystical incorporation of the soul with Christ by means of Baptism and faith. And thus St. Augustine refuted Julian who, as the Pelagians did also, denied the necessity of baptism for admission into heaven; and thus he proved the existence of original sin. This is the interpretation which St. Thomas (3, p. q. 80, art. 9, ad. 3.) gave of the words of St. Augustine. And in reality how could St. Augustine mean to say that children who die after baptism without receiving the Eucharist, could relapse into sin without any fault of their own? The

following is the passage from the letter of Innocent I., (which is the twenty-first among the decretals, and was directed to the Fathers of the Council of Milevis: " What you say is preached by them, *(by the Pelagians)* that the rewards of eternal life are given to infants even without baptism is very foolish: because unless they eat the flesh of the Son of man and drink his blood, they shall not have life in them." Behold how Innocent intended to say that in baptism the flesh of Jesus Christ is eaten. These expressions of St. Augustine and of Innocent were fully discussed in Trent: and Erasmus was charged with temerity in saying that they should be understood of the Eucharist.

22. The second point which, according to Soave, gave occasion to a long discussion, was the canon in which the Fathers declared it to be heresy to say that the Church was not induced by just reasons to withhold the use of the chalice. Soave says that this is to found a canon of faith on a human fact. He also asserts that some persons in the Council were surprised to hear it said that we are bound to observe the decrees of the Church only as human laws, and that we are obliged to believe that by the divine law these decrees are just; he adds that things which change every day were made articles of faith. In answer, Pallavicini says: " Supposing it to be of faith that the Church cannot err in matters of faith and morals, it is also of faith that in making laws regarding the dispensation of the sacraments, it cannot act without just reasons." And since every human law, as St. Thomas teaches, receives its force from the eternal law of God which commands us to obey our superiors, we are by consequence bound to observe human laws when they are made known to us by a superior. But we are not obliged to believe with the certainty of faith the justice of every human law, but only of those in the enactment of which we know that God has promised to assist the human legislator, as he has promised

to assist the Church in laws regarding religion, although these laws may vary with the circumstances of the times.

23. Cardinal Madruccio endeavoured to prove that the Council could, and ought to grant to the emperor the use of the chalice which had been granted to the Bohemians. But he was opposed by the Patriarch of Jerusalem and by the Patriarch elect of Aquileia. They said that the intention of the emperor was good, but perhaps the motives of others who sought for the use of the chalice were different. For among some of them was circulated the error of John Wiclef, and Peter of Dresden, that communion under both species was necessary for salvation. Hence there was just reason to fear that were the use of the chalice granted to them, they would argue that it was necessary, or that the species of bread contained only the body, and the species of wine only the blood of Christ.

24. The archbishop of Otranto proposed to leave the matter to the pope: but this was opposed by the Bishop of Granada and others, who said that to change the rites of the Eucharist in such disturbed times would be very dangerous. He added that the Church had not abolished the use of the cup without reason: for on account of the increased number of the faithful, it would be attended with danger of spilling the blood, and might be an occasion of disgust to some. Hence, he said, the concession would tend to encourage, rather than to remove the unbelief of those who sought for the use of the cup. He added, that it was inconvenient that the Council should make particular ordinances for a single nation; he said that in order to extirpate the error which was held in Bohemia, viz. that it was a matter of divine precept to receive under the species of wine, the Council of Constance had forbidden the use of the chalice. He also said that no objection could be taken from the example of St. Leo, who had permitted the use of the cup; for he granted it in order to

abolish the error of the Manicheans who denied that Jesus Christ had a real body and real blood. He also said that the remedy which some one had proposed, viz. to give the communion as the Greeks do, with the host dipped in the consecrated chalice, was inconvenient; since it was prohibited by Pope Julius in the canon, (cum. omne dist. 2 de consecr.): and since Christ had given each species separately to the Apostles.

25. Finally, Lainez said that the Council could certainly grant the use of the chalice, and annul the decree of Con-. stance: but that the dispensation from such a law by any action belonged to the Pope. He also said that in his opinion it was not expedient either to grant the use of the chalice, or to annul the decree of the Council of Constance, that there was no force in the reason assigned for the concession, viz. to apply a remedy to the infirmity of those Catholics who asked for the chalice. And that were the dispensation granted, they would be encouraged to make other impertinent demands. For they gave no proof of their faith in the authority of the Council: but wished for the concession only that they might use it without exposing themselves to the danger of being punished by the emperor. He moreover said that the concession would excite in other nations a desire of the use of the chalice.

26. In a word, the reasons for refusing the use of the chalice were, first the deordination of introducing into the rites of the Church a variety, which is always injurious to truth: secondly, because the conditions under which the dispensation had been granted by the Council of Basil, and Paul III. were not observed: thirdly, that in Germany the same reasons existed which induced the Council of Constance to refuse the use of the cup, and particularly the danger of spilling the blood, the difficulty of preserving it, the inconveniences arising from the distribution of it to the people when the number was great, the difficulty of

carrying it to the sick in the country, the disgust which it would naturally excite in the faithful when the number of communicants would be very large; fourthly, the danger of confirming the error which had been spread through Germany that the blood of Jesus Christ was not contained under the species of bread: fifthly, the danger of giving occasion to further demands, and of inspiring other nations with the desire of asking the use of the cup.

27. I subjoin a notice of many ancient usages regarding the communion, and other uses of the Eucharist. In ancient times in the administration of the Eucharist, the deacon used to say in a loud voice *Sancta sanctis*. In giving the consecrated host, the Priest would only say, *Corpus Domini*; and in token of his faith, the communicant would answer, *Amen*. This custom lasted till the sixth century, as we learn from the author of the Apostolical constitutions (l. 8, c. 13,) and from St. Leo, (serm. 6, de jejum.) who lived about that time. But in his life of St. Gregory, John the Deacon relates that in his time, it was usual to say: *Corpus Domini nostri Jesu Christi custodiat animam tuam.* At the common mass the communion was given first to the priests, then to the deacons, to the subdeacons, ecclesiastics, and finally to the laity, to the men and women, but not to all indiscriminately. They who were to communicate were distinguished from the others: and the fragments that remained were given to innocent infants: the practice of giving the fragments to children continued till the twelfth century; it was then abolished. The communion was given only to ecclesiastics at the altar; to the others it was given at the balustrades, or in their own places.

28. In the oriental churches, even the laity received the communion standing: each person casting down his eyes and bowing down the head, stretched out his hand and took the consecrated host, as we learn from Tertullian (lib. de idol. c. 7), from St. Cyprian (ep. 56) and from St.

Ambrose, (Apud. Theodoret. hist. l. 5, c. 17). According to St. Cyril of Jerusalem, (ep. 289,) the right hand was stretched out with the fingers extended, but close to each other; the right hand was supported by the left. The men extended the naked hand; but the hands of the women were covered with a little cloth which was called *Dominicale*. This is mentioned by St. Augustine to whom Father Chalon refers in treating of the Eucharist (c. 7.): and St. John Damascene and the Venerable Bede assert that this custom continued till the eighth century. The Eucharist was brought to the sick only under the species of bread: it was thus St. Honoratus gave the communion to St. Ambrose before death. However the Eucharist was sometimes given under both species to the sick: they frequently went to the church to receive the viaticum, and when they were unable to go to the church, mass was celebrated in their chamber.

29. It is well known that the first Christians kept the Eucharist in their own houses, but only under the species of bread, and according to the words of St. Luke; " Frangentes circa domos panem," (Act ii. 46,) they there received privately the communion from their own hands. Tertullian speaks of this as an ordinary thing. (Lib. 2, ad uxor, c. 5.) And in the times of persecution the faithful provided themselves with as much of the consecrated species as would suffice for a long time, particularly in towns where there was but one mass. In a letter to Cesaria, St. Basil says that the solitaries though they had no priests, had the Eucharist with them. This practice continued in the East till the sixth century, as Anastasius the librarian relates. It did not last so long in the west, although it was followed on a few occasions.

30. With regard to the frequency of communion, there is no doubt but during the three first centuries, the priest, as the apostolical constitutions and St. Justin attest (apolog.

2, l. 8, cap. 20.), gave communion to all who had assisted at mass. St. Cyprian writes: "We receive every day the Eucharist as the food of salvation......unless on account of some grievous sin, we are obliged to abstain from it." (de orat. dom.) This custom afterwards passed into a law, according to the canon of the Apostles, which was framed about the end of the third, or in the beginning of the fourth century. That canon ordains: "It is necessary to remove from communion those Christians who after coming to the church and listening to the lessons of the sacred Scriptures, do not remain to receive the holy communion." This precept was renewed by the Council of Antioch under Pope Julius, and was observed in many places till the fifth century. Some believed, as Strabo relates (c. 22.), that they were even obliged to communicate several times in the day if they assisted at several masses. However when the fervour of the faithful grew cold, the Council of Agda in the year 506, (in the 18th canon, which afterwards became an ecclesiastical law) ordained that every Christian should communicate at least three times in the year, at Christmas, Easter, and Pentecost. But Theodore Archdeacon of Canterbury in his Spicilegium (tom. 9, c. 52.) has said of the Greeks: "The Greeks, whether ecclesiastics or laymen, communicate every sunday: and whoever does not receive the Eucharist is excommunicated. The Romans follow the same practice, but not under the penalty of excommunication." When the devotion of Christians grew still colder the Council of Lateran thought it necessary to ordain that each of the faithful who had come to the years of discretion should go to confession and communion at least once in the year, as we find in the chapter, *omnis utriusque sexus* (*de pœn. et rem.*)

31. Let us say something on the *Agape*, which was practised in the first ages of the Church. Because Jesus Christ had instituted this sacrament after the last supper in

Jerusalem, the first Christians were likewise accustomed to communicate after a simple supper, at which the bishop or a priest assisted. Such suppers were called *Agape*, or suppers of charity, for the Greek word *Agape* signifies friendship. These suppers took place in the churches: at them the rich relieved the poor; hence the Apostle reproved those who did not succour the needy: " For," he says, " every one taketh his own supper to eat. And one indeed is hungry, and another is drunk. What, have you not houses to eat and drink in? Or despise ye the church of God: and put them to shame that have not?" (1 Cor. c. xi. 21, 22.) St. Ignatius martyr (ep. ad Smyrnœs. n. 8,) and Tertullian (apol. 18, c. 59,) make mention of these *Agape*. The practice of fasting till after communion was afterwards introduced; but the period of its introduction is not known. St. Isidore speaks of it as being general in his own time.

32. With regard to the festivals in honour of this sacrament, at first there was no other celebrated than that of Holy Thursday, on which the Eucharist was instituted. But in the year 1208, our Lord revealed to St. Juliana virgin, an hospitaler nun at Liege, in her seventeenth year, that he wished that in the Church there should be a particular solemnity in honour of the great gift bestowed upon us in the sacrament of the altar. The festival was first instituted by the bishop of Liege; but afterwards in the year 1264, it was extended to the whole Church, and fixed on the Thursday after the Octave of Pentecost. It was confirmed by Clement V. in the year 1311, and was accepted by the general Council of Vienna. At first, as Monsignor Baillet says, the office of the sacrament was recited on the festival, according to the usage of the Gallican Church; this office was composed by St. Juliana herself, or as others say by a devout religious of the name of John, who was assisted by the prayers of St. Juliana. But after-

wards the office which is now recited was introduced: it was composed by St. Thomas Aquino, who in obedience to the command of Urban IV., prepared it for the use of the Roman Church.

33. With regard to the processions of the most holy sacrament, the time of their institution is not known: for Urban IV. does not mention it in his brief. Monsignor Thiers says that they were instituted by John XXII. who died in the year 1433. It is certain that during the Pontificate of Martin V., in 1433, and of his successor Eugene IV., such processions were in use; for these pontiffs granted a plenary indulgence to all who after having confessed their sins, would recite the office of the sacrament, and also to all who assisted at the procession.

34. Neither do we know the time when the custom of exposing the blessed sacrament on the altar was first introduced: we only know, as Father Crasset says in his large work, (25th of August) that during the illness of St. Lewis of France, the holy sacrament was exposed throughout the entire kingdom. This happened about the year 1248, that is 17 or 18 years before the institution of the festival of Corpus Christi. At first the remonstrances were of various forms; of the form of a cross, of the sun, of little turrets: these were in use three hundred years ago. In these the sacramental species were exposed to view; for at first the sacrament was carried under cover in the processions. Be it observed that by a decree of the sacred congregation of the Council, priests have been forbidden to bring the sacrament to the sick that they may adore it, or to carry it with them in order to prove their own innocence, or even to bring it to the door of the church in order to calm a tempest, or to extinguish a fire.

35. The ancients made use of the Eucharist for various purposes. The bishops sent it to each other as a mark of communion. In travelling it was carried for protection

from danger.   A part of the sacrifice used to be kept for the following day. (See Father Chalon c. 2.)   The Eucharist used also to be buried with the dead: the author of the life of St. Basil, says that it was buried with the Saint. St. Theodore Pope wrote the condemnation of Pyrrhus, the monothelite on the tomb of St. Peter with ink mixed with the divine blood, as Paul the deacon of Aquileia relates. Nicetas (apud. Chalon, c. 12.) in the life of St. Ignatius Patriarch of Constantinople, mentions a similar condemnation against Photius.   Father Martene (tom. 1, de rit. l. 1, c. 5, a. 4.) says that in the dedication of churches, it was usual to deposit in the altar three consecrated particles: this was done by Pope Urban in the consecration of the Church of the monastery of Marmoutiers.

36. Formerly in the oriental Churches the Eucharist was preserved in doves of gold or silver suspended on the altar. (Le Brun tom. 2, p. 171,) says that this was the custom in France.   There it was also usual to preserve the Eucharist in ciboriums of the shape of turrets: these were succeeded by pixes in the form of covered cups.   These ciboriums were made of gold, silver, of precious stones, of ivory, chrystal, of glass, and even of wood. (Chalon c. 13.) At present the orientals keep the Eucharist not on the altar, but either in the sacristy, or in a press, or in the wall on one side of the altars: they suspend it from a nail in a burse; and do not preserve it with that decency and respect with which it is preserved in our churches.

TWENTY-SECOND SESSION.

ON THE SACRIFICE OF THE MASS.

1. The bishop of Granada censured the second canon in which it was said that Jesus Christ ordained the Apostles priests by these words: "Hoc facite in meam commemorationem." He adduced the opinion of Nicholas Cabasila who held that the priesthood was conferred on them on the day of Pentecost. St. Thomas and Scotus say that it was conferred at the last supper, but on the condition that the Apostles should not be able to exercise it till after they had received the Holy Ghost on the feast of Pentecost: but Pallavicini states that these opinions had but little support.

2. A Portuguese theologian, Brother Francis, of the order of St. Dominick, said that the sacrifice of the mass is proved rather by the interpretation of the Fathers, than by the literal meaning of the words of the Gospel, "*do this for a commemoration of me*," (Luke xxii. 19.) or of the words of Malachy: "*from the rising of the sun to the going down, my name is great among the Gentiles, and in every place there is sacrifice, and there is offered to my name a clean oblation : for my name is great among the Gentiles, saith the Lord of hosts.*" (i. 11.) And therefore he said that it was proved not from the Scripture alone, but with the aid of tradition, that the power of offering sacrifice was given to priests. But he was heard with displeasure, for his doctrine was contrary to the common opinion. Melchior Cornelius, theologian of the king of Bastia, made a learned discourse, in which he showed that the words of Malachy were understood of the sacrifice

of the mass, by the second Council of Nice: and that in saying to the Apostles, *do this for a commemoration of me*, Jesus Christ commanded each of them to consecrate the bread and wine.

3. It was also discussed whether the doctrine should be laid down before the canons, and the Fathers agreed that it should: because the Council held also the office of teaching, and should illustrate its definitions by reasons, which would serve not as foundations of our faith, but as answers to the objections of the heretics. The principal question was whether Christ offered himself for us to his Father at the last supper as Salmeron held, or in the sacrifice of the cross, as was maintained by Soto.

4. Guerrero, Duinius, and others were unwilling to admit the institution of the priesthood at the last supper: they said it was doubtful, and contrary to the sentiment of some of the Fathers. Guerrero and Duinius disapproved of the assertion that Jesus Christ offered himself to the Father at the last supper. Aaila objected to the doctrine that at the last supper all the sacrifices of the law of nature, and of the Mosaic law were accomplished; because this was not demonstrated either from the Scripture or from tradition; and it appeared to derogate from the sacrifice of the cross.

5. Soave says that twenty-five Fathers objected to the decree in which the Council declared that Jesus Christ offered himself at the last supper: but Pallavicini states that there were only two, Guerrero, and Duinius, as appears from the acts of the Council. But let us come to what the Council taught and afterwards defined. In the first chapter, in treating of the institution of the mass, the Council says that since the priesthood of the Old Testament was imperfect, it was necessary that another priest according to the order of Melchisedech, our Lord Jesus Christ, should arise, who could perfect in sanctity all who were to become saints.

Hence although he was to offer himself to God once by dying on the cross for the redemption of man, still, because his priesthood was not to cease with his death, he offered himself to the Father at the last supper, thus declaring himself an eternal priest according to the order of Melchisedech, and leaving to the Church a sacrifice by which is represented the sacrifice of the cross, in order to preserve the remembrance of it, and at the same time to apply to us its salutary virtue in remitting the sins which we daily commit. " Quoniam sub priori Testamento, teste Apostolo (Hebr. vii.) propter Levitici sacerdotii imbecillitatem consummatio non erat, oportuit sacerdotem alium secundum ordinem Melchisedech surgere, D. N. Jesum Christum, qui posset omnes, quotquot sanctificandi essent, ad perfectum adducere. Is igitur Deus et Dominus noster etsi semel seipsum in ara crucis, morte intercedente, Deo Patri oblaturus erat, ut æternam illic redemptionem operaretur, quia tamen per mortem sacerdotium ejus extinguendum non erat, in cœna novissima, qua nocte tradebatur, ut dilectæ sponsæ suæ Ecclesiæ visibili...relinqueret sacrificium quo cruentum illud ...repræsentaretur ejusque memoria......permaneret, atque illius salutaris virtus in remissionem eorum quæ a nobis quotidie committuntur peccatorum applicaretur, sacerdotem secundum ordinem Melchisedech se in æternum constitutum declarans, corpus et sanguinem suum sub speciebus panis et vini Deo Patri obtulit."

6. To this first part of the first chapter the first canon appertains. Can. 1: " Si quis dixerit in missa non offerri verum et proprium sacrificium aut non sit aliud quam nobis Christum ad manducandum dari, anathema sit."

7. Thus from the words just quoted it follows that the mass is in the strict sense a true sacrifice offered by Jesus Christ, a priest according to the order of Melchisedech, as was foretold by David, in the words: " Tu es sacerdos in æternum secundum ordinem Melchisedech," and as the

Apostle says in the epistle to the Hebrews. (5, 6.) He is said to be a priest, according to the order of Melchisedech, because Melchisedech offered bread and wine in sacrifice. "Melchisedech enim......proferens panem et vinum; erat enim sacerdos Altissimi." (Gen. xiv. 18.) The particle *enim* shows clearly that Melchisedech offered in sacrifice bread and wine. Since then the Redeemer was a priest according to the order of Melchisedech, it must be admitted that at the last supper he instituted the sacrifice of the mass, offering himself to the Father under the appearance of bread and wine: for we cannot assign any other time in which he offered such sacrifice.

8. In the continuation of the first chapter, it is said that under the species of bread and wine, Jesus Christ gave the Apostles his body to eat, and his blood to drink, and that in the words: *Hoc facite in meam commemorationem,* (Luc. xvii. 19.) he constituted them priests along with all their successors in the priesthood, that thenceforward they might continue to offer that sacrifice. For, at the celebration of the ancient Pasch, which the Jews celebrated in remembrance of their going forth from Egypt, he instituted the new Pasch, that is himself, who was to be offered in sacrifice by the Church through her priests in remembrance of his passage from the world to the Father, when he redeemed us by his blood: and this is the clean oblation which cannot be defiled by the unworthiness of the offerers, and which, according to the prediction of the prophet Malachy, should be offered in all places to his name; and to which the Apostle clearly alluded in these words: "Non potestis mensæ Domini participes esse, et mensæ dæmoniorum." (1 Cor. x. 21.) By the table of the Lord, he meant the altar on which sacrifice was offered. To the preceding text the following corresponds: "Habemus altare de quo edere non habent potestatem qui tabernaculo deserviunt." (Hebr. xiii. 10.) Where there is an altar there

must be a victim and sacrifice. Hence in the above mentioned chapter, the Council adds: " Ac, sub earum rerum symbolis, Apostolis, quos tunc novi Testamenti sacerdotes constituebat ut sumerent (corpus et sanguinem suum) tradidit; et eisdem eorumque in sacerdotio successoribus, ut offerrent, præcepit per hæc verba : *hoc facite in meam commemorationem,* ut semper Catholica ecclesia intellexit et docuit; nam celebrato veteri pascha, quod in memoriam exitus de Ægypto multitudo filiorum Israel immolabat, novum instituit pascha seipsum ab Ecclesia per sacerdotes sub signis visibilibus immolandum in memoriam transitus sui ex hoc mundo ad Patrem, quando per sui sanguinis effusionem nos redemit, &c. Et hæc quidem illa munda oblatio est quæ nulla indignitate aut malitia offerentium inquinari potest; quam Dominus per Malachiam nomine suo, quod magnum futurum esset in gentibus, in omni loco offerendum prædixit; et quam non obscure innuit apostolus Paulus scribens Corinthiis i. 10, 21, cum dicit non posse eos qui participatione mensæ dæmoniorum polluti sunt, mensæ Domini participes fieri; denique illa est quæ per varias sacrificiorum naturæ et legis tempore, simultudines figurabatur; utpote quæ bona omnia per illa significata, velut illorum omnium consummatio et perfectio, complectitur."

To this part of the chapter the second canon corresponds. Can. 2: " Si quis dixerit illis verbis—*Hoc facite in meam commemorationem,* Christum non instituisse apostolos sacerdotes; aut non ordinasse ut ipsi aliique sacerdotes offerrent corpus et sanguinem suum, anathema sit."

9. It was objected by some in the Council, as has been already said, that the words, *hoc facite in meam commemorationem* did not sufficiently prove that Jesus Christ had offered a real sacrifice, so that he had not only given his body to be eaten by the Apostles, but had also offered himself to the Father for the redemption of the world. But this was rejected by the others; for there is no doubt

but Jesus Christ really offered his body in sacrifice to the
Father at the last supper: otherwise, as has been proved,
he would not have been a priest according to the order of
Melchisedech, nor a figure of the paschal lamb.   This is also
proved by the words of St. Luke: " Hoc est corpus meum,
quod pro vobis datur," (xxii. 19.) and from the words of
St. Paul, " *Quod pro vobis frangitur.*" (1 Cor. xi. 24.)
The words *datur* and *frangitur* do not mean that his
body was merely given in food, but that it was given and
broken in sacrifice: for it is not said that his body was
given and broken *to you*, but that it was given and broken
for you.   Besides, as St. Chrysostom remarks, (Hom. 24.)
the word *frangitur* could not be properly applied to the
body of Christ except under the species of bread.   And it
is certain that in using the word *frangitur* the Apostle
alluded to the species of bread: for in another place he
says: "Panem quem *frangimus*," &c. (1 Cor. x. 16.)
In the Acts we also read: " *Frangebant circa domos
panem.* (Acts ii. 46.)   Since then Christ offered himself
in sacrifice at the last supper, and afterwards said: *Do this
for a commemoration of me,* the word *this* shows that
the Apostles and their successors in the priesthood were to
do the same thing which our Lord had done, that is, that
they were to offer him in sacrifice on the altar.   Nor is
there any force in the observation of the heretics that Christ
was called the sole priest, according to the order of Melchisedech: for priests are not strictly speaking successors in
the priesthood of Christ, but only vicars: since in the oblation of the mass, he is the principal minister, although
they too offer him in sacrifice.

10. Nor can it be said that by the *clean oblation,*
Malachy meant alms and other good works which are
offered to God with a pure intention: for these have been
at all times acceptable to God, and have never been rejected
by him.   But by the mouth of Malachy the Lord says, " I

will not receive a gift from your hands." (i. 10): hence he does not speak of good works, but of the ancient sacrifices which he thenceforward rejected, on account of the clean oblation which was to be offered to him in every place: " And in every place there is sacrifice, and there is offered to my name a clean oblation." These words exclude the false exposition of the heretics, who understand them of the sacrifice of the cross, for the sacrifice of the cross is not offered in every place; but was offered only on Calvary and only once.

11. In the second chapter the Council teaches that the mass is a visible sacrifice, which is propitiatory for the living and the dead. "Et quoniam in divino hoc sacrificio," says the Council, " quod in missa peragitur, idem ille Christus continetur et incruente immolatur qui in ara crucis semel seipsum obtulit, docet S. Synodus sacrificium istud vere propitiatorium esse, per ipsumque fieri ut, si cum vero corde et recta fide... pœnitentes ad Deum accedamus, misericordiam consequamur, &c. Hujus quippe oblatione placatus Dominus gratiam et donum pœnitentiæ concedens, crimina et peccata, etiam ingentia, dimittit; una enim eademque hostia, idem nunc offerens sacerdotum ministerio, qui seipsum tunc in cruce obtulit, sola offerendi ratione diversa. Cujus quidem oblationis, cruentæ, inquam, fructus per hanc uberrime percipiuntur, tantum abest ut illi per hanc quovis modo derogetur. Quare non solum pro fidelium vivorum peccatis, pœnis, satisfactionibus et aliis necessitatibus, sed et pro defunctis in Christo nondum ad plenum purgatis, rite juxta Apostolorum traditionem offertur."

12. The Council therefore teaches that by the mass the fruit of the cross is applied to the faithful. Hence the innovators err in saying that the fruit of the cross is applied to all, that therefore the sacrifice of the cross is sufficient not only for redemption, but also for the application of its fruit, and consequently that the sacrifice of the

altar is superfluous. In answer to them I say, that according to the doctrine of the Council, the sacrifice of the mass is the same as that of the cross. The former differs from the latter only in the mode of offering; and, therefore, the sacrifice of the altar does not derogate in any way from the sacrifice of the cross. Neither has the sacrifice of the altar been instituted to supply the deficiency of the sacrifice of the cross, but only as a means by which God applies to us the merit of the sacrifice of Calvary.

13. The innovators say that the sacrifice of the altar is called a sacrifice only because it is a figure and commemoration of the sacrifice of the cross. But they err, for although the Council of Trent says that the mass has been instituted (*in memoriam et repræsentationem*) to commemorate and represent the sacrifice of the cross, still it is of faith that the mass is in itself a real sacrifice, because there is a victim present which contains the real oblation of Christ, who there offers himself under the appearance of bread and wine. Thus the mass is not only a representation of the bloody sacrifice of the cross, but also a true oblation of Christ, who is really present as he was on Calvary. Hence the Council says: " Idem ille Christus continetur qui in ara crucis semel seipsum cruente obtulit."

14. The Council declares in the words: "peccata etiam ingentia dimittit," that the sacrifice of the altar is impetratory, and obtains spiritual as well as temporal goods, not, (as theologians say) directly but indirectly, inasmuch as God, through the sacrifice of the altar, grants grace by which man is moved to contrition, and to purify his soul from sin in the sacrament of penance. As to the temporal punishment which remains due after the remission of the guilt of sin, this is relaxed, if not altogether, at least in part, by virtue of the mass, as is evident from the example of the dead who are relieved by the holy sacrifice of the altar, although they are no longer capable of merit.

15. To this chapter, the third canon corresponds. Can. 3: " Si quis dixerit missæ sacrificium tantum esse laudis et gratiarum actionis aut nudam commemorationem sacrificii in cruce peracti non autem propitiatorium: vel soli prodesse sumenti; neque pro vivis et defunc tis, pro peccatis, pœnis satisfactionibus et aliis necessitatibus offerri debere, anathema sit." The word *necessitatibus* includes the other temporal goods which God in virtue of the mass dispenses to the faithful, when he knows that they will tend to their eternal salvation.

16. That the mass is a true propitiatory sacrifice, which renders God propitious, and inclines him to pardon, not only the punishment, but also the guilt of sin, as the Council declares in this second chapter, is proved from the very institution of the Eucharist, which was intended in a special manner, for the remission of sin. " *Hic est sanguis meus, qui pro multis effindetur* (or according to the Greek version *effunditur*) *in remissionem peccatorum.* The word *effundetur* has reference to the bloody sacrifice of the cross, and the word *effunditur* refers to the present unbloody sacrifice which is offered in every mass. Both the one and the other were offered for the remission of sins: but in the sacrifice of the cross Jesus Christ paid the price of our redemption, and in the sacrifice of the altar, he applies to us the fruit of that price. Since then the mass is a propitiatory sacrifice, it is by consequence impetratory of new graces, as is taught by the generality of the Fathers, by St. Cyril, St. John Chrysostom, St. Ambrose, St. Jerome, and St. Augustine. (See Bellarmine.).

17. It is also said in the second chapter: "Non solum vivorum, sed pro defunctis, &c." This is repeated in the third canon, and is proved from the second book of Machabees (c. 12. v. 43, 46,) where we read: "And making a gathering, he sent twelve thousand drachms of silver to Jerusalem, for sacrifice, to be offered for the sins of the dead

......It is therefore a holy and wholesome thought to pray for the dead, that they may be loosed from their sins." This is also proved by the perpetual tradition of the Church, as St. Augustine attests in several places, and particularly in the work entitled *de cura pro mortuis* (c. 1, n. 3,) St. Chrysostom writes: " Non frustra ab apostolis sancitum est ut in celebratione mysteriorum memoria fiat eorum qui hinc discesserunt." (Hom. 3, in ep. ad Philip.) And in reality we find the commemoration of the dead, in the liturgy of St. James, and St. Clement, and in all the other liturgies. Calvin says, " Defunctos neque accipere neque manducare." This only shows that the dead cannot partake of the Eucharistic food, but not that they cannot partake of the fruit of the sacrifice. Speaking of the recommendation of the dead in the mass, Tertullian says: " Hunc ritum ex consuetudine retentum traditio est auctrix, consuetudo confirmatrix." (De coron mil.) He adds: " Oblationes pro defunctis, pro natalitiis annua die facimus." St. Athanasius has written: " Incruentæ hostiæ oblatio propitiatio est." (Serm. de defunct.) St. Epiphanius (hæres. 75) states that the opinion of Aerius who asserted that sacrifice could not be offered for the dead, had been condemned by the ancient church. St. Cyprian writes: " Sacrificium celebrari pro defunctis in altari." (Lib. i. ep. 9.) St. Augustine says the same. (In Euchir. c. 110.) But we shall speak more at length on this point, in treating of the 25th Session, on Purgatory.

ON THE EFFICACY OF THE SACRIFICE OF THE MASS.

18. Bellarmine says (lib. 6, c. 4,) that the sacrifice of the mass is offered by three; by Christ, by the Church, and by the priest, but not in the same manner. Christ offers it as a priest or primary minister, through the ministry of his priest: the Church offers it not as a priest and minister,

but as the people through the ministry of the priest: and the priest offers it as minister of Christ, and as intercessor for the entire people. However in the mass, Christ is always the principal minister who perpetually offers himself under the species of bread and wine by the ministry of his priests (as the Council says, " idem offerens Christus sacerdotum ministerio"), who in the oblation of the sacrifice of the mass, represent his person. Hence, the Council of Lateran has said: " Simul (Christus) est sacerdos et sacrificium." In cap. Firmiter, de sum. Trin. Thus to the dignity of this sacrifice it was suited that it should be offered principally not by sinful men, but by that high priest who is not subject to sins. " It was fitting that we should have such a high priest, holy, innocent, undefiled." (Hebr. vii. 26.) This sacrifice is offered *habitually* by some, that is by them who are absent and desire that the sacrifice be offered: it is offered *actually* by others, that is by those who assist at mass: others offer it *causally*, because they cause the mass to be celebrated.

19. The mass has efficacy *ex opere operato*, that is of itself, and independently of the merit of the priest. This arises from the promise of God: " For this is my blood of the new Testament which shall be shed for many unto the remission of sins." (Mat. xxvi. 28.) Hence, the Council has justly said: " Hujus quidem oblationis cruentæ fructus per hanc uberrime percipiuntur." It matters not that the effect be not produced suddenly, or for all: it is sufficient that it be infallible on the part of the sacrifice: for to produce its effect, the sacrifice requires dispositions on the part of man, without which he receives no fruit from it: but this arises from the defect of man, and not from the defect of the sacrifice.

20. A sacrifice may have value *ex opere operato* in two ways: first, if it be a certain instrument which produces its effect; in this manner the sacraments operate

immediately. Secondly, if it is an instrument which does not immediately produce its effect, but infallibly moves God to produce it independently of the sanctity of the minister. The mass produces its effect in this manner *ex opere operato*: for example, it does not obtain justification like the sacrament of penance, which immediately justifies a penitent whenever he is disposed for it by contrition: but it obtains justification for him mediately, as St. Thomas (in 4, sent. dist. 12, q. 2, ad 4.) and the generality of theologians teach. Hence, in the second chapter the Council said: "Per hoc sacrificium peccata etiam ingentia dimitti, quia Deus, hoc sacrificio placatus, gratiam et donum pœnitentiæ concedit." Hence, the effect does not depend on the sanctity of the minister. The mass has efficacy by way of impetration: and because the prayer is offered by Christ, the impetration is infallible, provided the persons for whom the prayer is offered do not place an obstacle to the grace obtained.

21. There is no force in the objection of Kemnitius, that if the mass remits sins, the sacraments are useless: this objection might have some force if it were said that the mass remits sins immediately: but for the remission of sins, the sacrament of penance is always necessary. The mass infallibly obtains for sinners special aid, which corresponds to their disposition: hence if a sinner resists the grace offered it is then through his fault that the sacrifice does not produce its effect. But with regard to temporal goods, God always grants them when they are conducive to salvation. Sanctity in the minister is not necessary, in order to obtain the effects of the mass; because it is offered principally by Christ: and therefore although the priest should be a sinner, the mass produces its effect of itself *ex opere operato*. However the sanctity of the priest always contributes to obtain favours *ex opere operantis*.

22. According to the more common opinion of theologians the value of the mass is finite, and therefore in conformity

with the universal practice of the Church, it is usual to offer several masses in order to obtain the same favour; in this it differs from the sacrifice of the cross, which was of infinite value, and therefore is not repeated. The principal reason why the value of the mass is finite, is because such is the will of Christ, who wishes to grant only a certain measure, by applying a part of the fruit of his passion, that thus men may frequently offer this sacrifice.

23. It is asked for whom can the mass be offered? It is certain, as we have seen, and as the Council teaches, that the mass can be offered for all Catholics who are living, even though they be sinners, and for all who are dead, as we read in the canon of the mass: "*Pro omnibus orthodoxis atque catholicæ fidei cultoribus.*" It is certain, on the other hand, that it cannot be offered for the damned: since their sins and punishment are irremissible. Neither can it be offered for heretics; for the Church (cap. A. nobis, de sent. excommun.) has forbidden priests to offer the mass directly for excommunicated persons, among whom are all heretics. However the mass is offered indirectly for them in the oblation of the chalice, in these words, "Offerimus pro totius mundi salute."

24. With regard to infidels, Bellarmine thinks that the mass may be offered for pagan princes, as St. Chrysostom has written. (Hom. 6, in ep. ad Tim.) Tertullian says: "Sacrificamus pro salute imperatoris." (lib. ad Scapulam.) In the old law sacrifices were offered for Darius (lib. 1, Esdr. c. 6,) and for Heliodorus. (2 Mac. c. 3.) Nor is this doctrine opposed to the words of St. Augustine: "Quis offerat sacrificium corporis Christi, nisi pro iis qui sunt membra Christi?" (L. 1, de orig. an. c. 9.) For Bellarmine says, that there the saint speaks not of living, but of deceased pagans, for whom it certainly is not lawful to pray in the mass. But Bellarmine says that the sacrifice may be offered for the conversion of pagans and of heretics.

2 B

25. Let us pass to the third chapter, in which the Council speaks of the celebration of the mass, in honour of the saints: " Et quamvis in honorem et memoriam sanctorum nonnullas interdum missas Ecclesia celebrare consueverit, non tamen illis sacrificium offeri docet, sed Deo soli qui illos coronavit. Unde nec sacerdos dicere solet: offero tibi sacrificium, Petre et Paule; sed Deo de illorum victoriis gratias agen, eorum patrocinia implorat, ut ipsi pro nobis intercedere dignentur in cœlis quorum memoriam facimus in terris."

To this chapter corresponds the following canon: " Si quis dixerit imposturam esse missas celebrare in honorem sanctorum et pro illorum intercessione apud Deum obtinenda, sicut Ecclesia intendit, anathema sit." The sacrifice of the mass is the supreme worship which can be offered to God alone as a mark of his supreme dominion. Hence, although in saying the mass of any saint, we offer it in honour of the saint, still we offer it directly to God alone: such is the doctrine of St. Augustine. (lib. 8, de civ. Dei. c. 27.) This is also the tradition and practice of the ancient church, as we know from the ancient liturgies. The Church justly offers the mass in honour of the saints, as well to thank God for the graces which he has bestowed upon them, as also to implore their patronage before the throne of God, and at the same time to animate ourselves to imitate their virtues by the remembrance of them.

26. In the fourth chapter the Council treats of the canon of the mass, and repels the calumnies of the heretics, who endeavoured to represent it as full of errors and absurdities. In this chapter the Council says, that the canon of the mass contains nothing which does not savour of sanctity and piety. " Et cum sancta sancte administrari conveniat, sitque hoc omnium sanctissimum sacrificium, ecclesia catholica, ut digne reverenterque offerretur ac percipereter, sacrum canonem multis ante sæculis instituit ita ab omni errore purum ut nihil in eo contineatur quod non maxime sanctitatem ac

pietatem quandam redoleat mentesque offerentium in Deum erigat; is enim constat cum ex ipsis Domini verbis, tum ex apostolorum traditionibus." To this fourth chapter the 6th canon corresponds. Can. 6: "Si quis dixerit, canonem missæ errores continere, ideoque abrogandum esse, anathema sit."

27. In the first place, the very word *canon*, which signifies a fixed rule, dipleases the innovators. They say that all should be free to use in the mass the prayers which please them most. Hence Kemnitius censures the Council of Trent for saying that the canon is composed, partly of the words of Christ, and partly of the words of the Apostles and Pontiffs. He supposes that a certain Scholastic was the author of the canon, because St. Gregory says: "Precem Scholastici recitari super oblationem." (Lib. 2. ep. 54.) But he errs; for St. Ambrose, St. Optatus, and St. Gregory himself, call the canon of the mass the order or rule; they even give it the appellation of canon. It is true that the Greek canon of the mass differs from ours; for in the Greek Church they use the liturgy of St. Basil, or of St. Chrysostom; in Milan they use that of St. Ambrose, in Toledo in Spain, they use the Mosarabic liturgy, and in Rome they use that which is common in the Latin Church. But all these canons have been allowed and approved by the sovereign Pontiffs; there is no substantial difference among them, neither do they contain any error.

28. With regard to the Scholastic whom Kemnitius infers from the words of St. Gregory, to have been the author of the canon, it is necessary to observe that it is not known whether St. Gregory used the word Scholastic as a proper name, or as a name of authority; for example, to signify a master or teacher, which is more probable: for the saint gives the title of Scholastic even to St. Matthew. Besides, Bellarmine remarks that the words of St. Gregory, "*pre-*

cem Scholastici recitari super oblationem,—did not apply to the entire canon, but probably only to the three prayers which are said before the communion: for Micrologus says (c. 18) that these prayers do not belong to the canon. Moreover, it is certain, as Bellarmine states (lib. 6, c. 19); that in the mass the apostles at first added to the words of consecration only the *Pater noster*, although they afterwards added other things, and among them the prayer for the dead: for St. Chrysostom asserts that the prayer for the dead in the mass descends from the tradition of the apostles. (Hom. 3, in ep. ad Phil.) St. Isidore attests, (l. de offic. c. 15,) that St. Peter was the first that gave to the church a certain form of celebrating mass, in which he prescribed certain prayers and rites. The sovereign Pontiffs afterwards added various prayers: St. Gregory the Great was the last who added to the canon (Walfridus de observ. Eccl. c. 22,); he inserted the words: *Diesque nostros in tua pace disponas.* And although the ancient liturgies bear the names of different authors, such as of St. Basil, of St. John Chrysostom, St. Ambrose, St. Gelasius, of St. Gregory (which is the liturgy we use in the Latin church) and of St. Isidore, these saints have not, as Bellarmine proves (loc cit.), composed new liturgies, but have only reduced to a better form those that were used in their own times.

29. In the fifth chapter the Council speaks of the solemn ceremonies of the sacrifice of the mass: and says that since the nature of man is such that he requires to be raised to the meditation of the divine mysteries, by means of external signs, the holy Church has instituted certain rites to be observed in the celebration of mass, and has specially ordained that certain prayers be said in a loud, and others in a low voice. Besides, the church has prescribed ceremonies, such as benedictions, lights, vestments, &c., in accordance with the ancient tradition, in order to preserve the majesty of the sacrifice, and to excite the faithful to the

contemplation of the great things which this sacrifice contains: "cumque natura hominum," (these are the words of the Council) "ea sit ut non facile queat sine adminiculis exterioribus ad rerum divinarum meditationem sustolli, propterea pia mater Ecclesiæ ritus quosdam, ut scilicet quædam submissa voce, alia vero elatiore, in missa pronuntiarentur, instituit. Cæremonias item adhibuit ut mysticas benedictiones, lumina, thymiamata, vestes aliaque id genus multa ex apostolica disciplina et traditione, quo et majestas tanti sacrificii commendaretur, et mentes fidelium per hæc visibilia religionis et pietatis signa ad rerum altissimarum, quæ in hoc sacrificio latent contemplationem excitarentur." To this chapter (5) corresponds the ninth canon, in which the Council pronounces an anathema against all who assert that the rite of saying in a low voice a part of the canon, and particularly the words of consecration, should be condemned.

30. Calvin acknowledges (lib. 4. inst. c. 17, S. 43.) that the ceremonies of the mass are most ancient, and not far from the age of the apostles: but still he calls them " rubiginem cœnæ Domini natam ex precacitate humanæ confirdentiæ." Luther and the Lutherans have not rejected all the ceremonies; for in their masses, they observe some of them. But Luther (lib. de capt. babil.) says that the mass should be celebrated, as it was by Jesus Christ, without vestments, without ceremonies, and without singing. He does not condemn the use of lights, of incense and the like; in this he contradicts himself. There is but little probability in the opinion of those who say that lights were used on account of the darkness of the places in which mass was formerly celebrated; and that incense was employed in order to remove the disagreeable odour of the subterraneous caverns in which the sacrifice was offered. For, these and similar ceremonies were instituted principally for spiritual ends: for example, lights were used as a mark of veneration

for the majesty of the sacrament, and as St. Jerome says, to
point out under the figure of light, the light of the Gospel;
" Per totas orientis ecclesias," says the holy Doctor " quando
legendum Evangelium, accenduntur luminaria......ut sub
typo luminis illa lux" (that is the divine light) " ostenda-
tur." (ad Vigilan. tom. 4, par. 2, 289.) Thus also St.
Thomas says that the incense was used *to represent the
effect of grace*. (3, p. q. 83, a. 5, ad 2.). Kemnitius
allows the benediction of the sacramental species, and also
the recitation of Psalms, of the symbol and other prayers,
(which are not strictly speaking ceremonies): he also allows
the use of vestments, of the sacred vessels and other orna-
ments: but he says that these things are arbitrary and not
necessary. He adds that it is superstitious and impious to
offer the mass for the living and for the dead, to invoke the
saints, to perform satisfactory works for the souls in
purgatory, or to bless water.

31. We say that these things are not of themselves
intrinsically necessary, but that the Church has been invested
with power to prescribe them, and that we are bound to
obey. The Council of Trent says that many of them have
come to us by apostolical tradition. Nor is it of any
moment that St. Paul does not make mention of them:
(1 Cor. 11.) for the Apostle only speaks of what the
Saviour did; and the tradition to which the Council alludes,
did not commence till after his Ascension. With regard to
vestments, they were prescribed in the old law for priests
offering sacrifices: and it is certain that the use of them is
most ancient, as appears from the authorities quoted by
Bellarmine. (lib. 6, c. 24.) St. Gregory, as we read in his
life by John the deacon, (lib. 2, c. 37,) sent to England
vessels and vestments for mass. St. Jerome (contra. Pelag
l. 1,) says that in the mass, priests and ecclesiastics used to
wear white vestments; and St John Chrysostom (hom. 83,)

describes the prayers which the priest should recite in putting on the sacred vestments.

32. With regard to temples and altars, the innovators allow them, but censure the consecration of them. But Bellarmine (c. 14.) proves that such consecrations were most ancient. There is no force in the objection which Calvin takes from the words of St. Ambrose: " Aurum sacramenta non quærunt." (l. 2, de offic. c. 28.) The Saint does not disapprove of golden vessels, but says that gold is not necessary for the validity of the sacraments; hence, these vessels may be sold in order to relieve the wants of the poor. The saint preserved them till such necessity existed.

33. Luther and Calvin disapprove of the obligation of fasting until after the celebration of mass: Luther says that it is sufficient not to be guilty of excess in eating or drinking; if, he adds, reverence for the sacrament requires fasting we should be forbidden even to breathe; for the air enters the body before Jesus Christ. Foolish comparison! in receiving the air there is no irreverence, but there is irreverence in taking earthly before celestial food. The practice of fasting till after communion is most ancient, as is attested by Tertullian, (in lib. 2, ad uxor.) by St. Cyprian (lib. 2, ep. 3.) by St. Chrysostom, (hom. 27, in prior. ad Corinth. et. ep. 3, ad Cyriac.) and St. Augustine who (ep. 118, c. 6.) says that the fast was instituted by the Apostles under the influence of divine inspiration, and was thenceforward observed throughout the whole church in honour of so great a sacrament. This fast is also prescribed by the most ancient Councils, by the third Council of Carthage, by the second Council of Mascon, by the first council of Bracare, and by the first Council of Toledo. Finally the general Council of Constance condemned the celebration of mass after taking meat or drink. But the adversaries say: Christ celebrated after supper. I answer that that was the paschal

supper, which was celebrated in commemoration of the going forth from Egypt: and this supper has ceased. But, they add, St. Paul permits Christians to eat before communion: "Si quis," he says "esurit, domi manducet." But the meaning of these words is not that the faithful were first to eat and then to receive communion; but as St. Chrysostom, Theophylactus and others say, that if any one is hungry and will not wait, he should go home to eat.

34. With regard to the ceremonies prescribed in the mass, such as the elevation of the hands or eyes, the inclinations, genuflexions &c., I say that of these there are several examples in the sacred Scriptures. Bellarmine (c. 15.) says that the elevation of the host and chalice, the breaking of the host and commixture of it with the blood, are most ancient: the singing and instrumental music, which were in use in the old law, are also most ancient. Peter Martyr censures music as a Jewish ceremony: but in answer Bellarmine says that the Mosaic ceremonies which have been abolished are those which were figures of things to come in the new law, and not the other ceremonies which were dictated by natural reason, such as to sing the praises of God, to make use of incense, to genuflect, to strike the breast, &c.

35. In the sixth chapter the Council treats of private masses at which the priest alone communicates. In that chapter the Council says: "Optaret quidem sacrosancta synodus ut in singulis missis fideles adstantes non solum spirituali affectu, sed sacramentali etiam Eucharistiæ perceptione communicarent, quo ad eos ss. hujus sacrificii fructus uberior proveniret. Nec tamen, si id non semper fiat, propterea missas illas in quibus solus sacerdos sacramentaliter communicat, ut privatas et illicitas damnat, sed probat atque commendat siquidem illæ quoque missæ vere communes censeri debent: partim quod in eis populus spiritualiter communicet; partim vero quod a publico

Ecclesiæ ministro non pro se tantum, sed pro omnibus
fidelibus qui ad corpus Christi pertinent, celebrentur." To
this chapter the eighth canon belongs. In that canon, the
Council says: " Si quis dixerit missas in quibus solus
sacerdos sacramentaliter communicat illicitas esse, ideoque abrogandas, anathema sit." Strictly speaking, all
masses may be called public masses: as well because the
mass is a public sacrifice, since it is offered for the entire
Church; as also because the priest is a public minister,
since according to the words of the Council, he celebrates
not only for himself but also for all the faithful: " Quod
a publico Ecclesiæ ministro non pro se tantum, sed pro
omnibus fidelibus celebrentur." This is proved also by the
ancient custom of the Church, as we know from the Council of Agatha, held in the year 514, and from the twelfth
Council of Toledo. (can. 5, &c.) Reason proves the truth
of this doctrine: for the nature of sacrifice requires the personal presence only of the minister, and not of the persons
for whom it is offered.

36. Luther made a distinction, and said that a public
mass is that which is sung, at which the ministers attend,
and at which all communicate in the Church, and that a
private mass is that which is not sung, or which is said in
a private oratory, or at which the priest alone communicates:
such private masses he condemns as unlawful, (lib. de miss.
priv.) and in this he is followed by the other Lutherans.
But as we have seen, this opinion was condemned as heretical
in the eighth canon.

37. It is a manifest error to say that the mass in which
the priest alone communicates, is unlawful: for, the dispensation of the victim to those who assist, is not at all essential to the sacrifice, as is its consecration and consumption.
Even in the old law (Lev. 6, 7.) when the sacrifice *pro
peccato* was offered the people did not taste any part of

the victim, and still that oblation was held to be a real sacrifice.

38. The adversaries object first that private masses are contrary to the institution of Christ, because he gave communion to all who were present, and afterwards said: " Quemadmodum ego feci......ita et vos faciatis." (Jo. 13, 15.) I answer that by these words our Lord did not intend to impose an obligation of celebrating with all the circumstances with which his celebration of the Eucharist was accompanied: otherwise all masses should be celebrated after supper, by night, and women should be excluded, &c. Our Lord only prescribed that the priest should always communicate, and that he should not refuse communion to any one who would ask it.

39. Kemnitius objects, that as the minister of the divine word (who is also a public minister) cannot preach if the people are not present, so the priest cannot offer sacrifice and partake of it unless in the presence of other communicants. I answer that the act of the minister offering sacrifice is very different from that of a preacher: the act of preaching is offered to men, the act of offering sacrifice, to God; for the act of sacrifice the presence of the people is the less necessary, since sacrifice is like prayer, which is profitable even to the absent.

40. The adversaries also say that private masses are contrary to the ancient practice of the Church: for in the first epistle to the Corinthians (11, 20.) the supper of the Lord is represented as opposed to private suppers: " Jam non est Dominicam cœnam manducare." Besides it appears from the ninth or tenth canon of the Apostles, and from the canon (Peracta dist. 2, de consecr.) that all who did not communicate were excluded from the mass. In answer to the first objection I say that the Apostle does not speak of the communion but of the *agape*, in which the rich, through a motive of charity, invited the poor to sup with them: and

therefore St. Paul reproves those who did not practise that
charity. "And he says, one indeed is hungry, and another
is drunk. What, have you not houses to eat and drink
in? or despise ye the Church of God; and put them to
shame that have not?" Thus the Apostle speaks of
the private suppers at which the faithful assembled in imita-
tion of the supper of our Lord with his servants on the festival
of the pasch. And although it were admitted that St. Paul
had spoken of the Eucharist, it would only follow that he
censures private suppers from which some were excluded, but
not those from which (though all are not present at them) no
one was excluded, as is the case in our masses. To the second
objection I answer that although by the ninth canon of the
Apostles, and the canon (Peracta) all that might be present,
were obliged to communicate, still priests were not commanded to abstain from celebrating, when there was no one present to communicate. In ancient times the celebration of
mass was forbidden only to priests who did not communicate, as
we learn from the fifth canon of the twelfth Council of Toledo,
in which it is said: "Quale erit sacrificium, cui nec ipse
sacrificans participasse dignoscetur?" The Council then
speaks of a mass in which no one communicated: and this
Council was held more than nine hundred years ago.

41. Secondly, there is no force in the objection against
private masses that they are celebrated in a private place:
for Jesus Christ celebrated in a private house, and of the
Apostles, it is written: "Frangebant circa domos panem."
(Act. ii. 46.) In times of persecution, the Pontiffs celebrated in private houses, in caves, and prisons: and Bellarmine states that St. Gregory Nazianzen and St. Ambrose
said mass in private houses.

42. Secondly there is no force in the objection that
masses are celebrated on days which are not festivals.
The adversaries celebrate only on Sundays: but do not

censure the daily celebration of mass. It would be wrong to censure it, for it is certain the daily celebration of mass was practised in the early Church, as St. Chrysostom (ad. Ephes. hom. 3.), St. Jerome (in c. 1 ad Tit.), and others attest.

43. Thirdly, there is no force in the objection against private masses, that they are offered for particular individuals, or for a particular object. It cannot be said that private masses are applied for particular objects, since every mass is offered for all the faithful, living and dead (except for the damned), as appears from the missal. Hence, if the mass is offered for a single individual, he will partake more abundantly of the fruit of the sacrifice; but each of the faithful will have his own share. This practice of offering sacrifice for particular persons, was most ancient, as we know from Leviticus (c. 4 and 5), where the inspired writer speaks of sacrifices for the prince and for the priest, &c. Job (c. 1.) offered sacrifice for his children. And in the new law, it is evident that mass was celebrated on the birth days of the saints. Speaking of his deceased mother, St. Augustine says: "Cum offerretur pro ea sacrificium, &c." (Lib. 9, Conf. c. 12.)

44. Fourthly, there is no force in the objection taken *from the absence of the faithful*. Melancton censures the Church of Rome, for causing mass to be said without having all the people present: but the other Lutherans have no scruple on this point. We know that St. Ambrose celebrated mass in the house of a Roman matron. St. Maris said mass in his own little cell, as Theodoret attests, and St. Gregory (lib. 4, ep. 43) even prohibited the celebration of mass in monasteries before a multitude of the people, that the recollection of the monks might not be disturbed.

45. Fifthly, there is no force in the objection against private masses, that other masses besides the conventual

masses, are said in the Church. The Lutherans censure a
multiplicity of masses; but they are wrong, for there has
been at all times a great number of priests in the Church; and
it is not credible that only one, or a few, said mass, and that
the rest abstained. This is also proved by the great number
of Churches erected in the early ages, and by the multitude
of altars in these Churches. That the number of Churches
and altars was very great, is attested by St. Ambrose,
(ep. 33,) by St. Gregory, (l. 5, ep. 50,) and by St. Leo,
(ep. 81. ad Diosc.).

45. Lastly, there is no force in the objection, that in
private masses the priest alone communicates: for, as we
have already seen, we find in such masses, the entire essence
and integrity of the sacrifice instituted by Christ. But the
adversaries say: "Christ was offered once." (Heb. ix. 28.)
But, in that passage, St. Paul speaks of the sacrifice of the
cross, which Jesus Christ wished to be commemorated in
the sacrifice of the altar, and by which the fruit of the sacrifice of the cross is applied to the faithful.

47. In the seventh chapter, the Council speaks of the
water to be mixed with the wine: "Monet deinde, s. synodus
præceptum esse ab Ecclesia sacerdotibus ut aquam vino in
calice offerendo miscerent; tum quod Christum Dominum
ita fecisse credatur, tum etiam quia e latere ejus aqua simul
cum sanguine exierit, quod sacramentum hac mixtione
recolitur: et cum aquæ in Apocalypsi B. Joannis populi
dicantur, ipsius populi fidelis cum capite Christo unio
repræsentatur.

48. In the eighth chapter, the Council says that it is not
expedient to permit the celebration of mass in the vulgar
tongue, and commands pastors to explain to the people
some part of the mass which they read. "Etsi missa
magnam contineat populi fidelis eruditionem, non tamen
expedire visum est Patribus ut vulgari passim lingua
celebraretur. Quamobrem, retento ubique cujusque ecclesiæ

antiquo et a S. Romana ecclesia, omnium ecclesiarum matre
et magistra, probato ritu, ne oves Christi esuriant, neve
parvuli panem petant, et non sit qui frangat eis, mandat
S. Synodus pastoribus et singulis curam animarum gerentibus
ut frequenter, inter missarum celebrationem, vel per se vel
per alios, ex iis quo in missa leguntur aliquod exponant:
atque inter cætera hujus SS. sacrificii mysterium aliquod
declarent, diebus præsertim dominicis et festis."

49. To this chapter, the 9th canon partly corresponds:
in that canon the Council speaks of three things: of saying
part of the mass in a low voice, of celebrating mass in the
vulgar tongue, and of mixing water with the wine in the
chalice: " Si quis dixerit ecclesia Romana ritum quo submissa voce pars canonis et verba consecrationis proferuntur
damnandum esse; aut lingua tantum vulgari missam celebrari debere; aut aquam non miscendam esse vino in calice
offerendo, eo quod sit contra Christi institutionem, anathema
sit."

50. The innovators contend that mass should be celebrated only in the vulgar tongue: Luther left this matter
to the choice of the celebrant. (lib. de form. missæ.)   But
the Catholic Church has, for several reasons, ordained the
contrary: for, Bellarmine justly observes (de missa c. 11.)
that the oblation of the mass consists more in the act which
is performed, than in the words: since, without offering
him in words, the very action by which the victim, Jesus
Christ, is presented on the altar, is a true oblation.   For
the consecration, the words are, indeed, necessary: but these
are said, not to instruct the people, but to offer the sacrifice.
And even the words of oblation are not directed to the
people, but to God, who understands every language.   Even
the Jews, in their public functions, used the Hebrew language, although it had ceased to be their vulgar tongue
after the Babylonian captivity.   Besides, it has been always
the custom in the east to celebrate in the Greek or Chaldaic,

and in the west, in the Latin language: this custom existed
after these languages ceased to be commonly understood in
the western nations.

51. The use of the Latin tongue was necessary in the
west, in order to preserve the communication among the
churches: had not this custom existed, a German could
not celebrate in France. Besides, it frequently happens
that the words of one language cannot express the full force
of certain phrases in another tongue: hence, if in different
countries, mass were celebrated in different languages, it
would be difficult to preserve the identity of sense. The
use of the common language was also necessary for the
constant uniformity in the rite prescribed by the Church in
the administration of the sacraments, and as a preventive
of schisms in the Church: great confusion would arise from
the translation of the Roman missal into the language of
various countries. Hence, the Bishops of France unani-
mously supplicated Alexander VII., in 1661, to suppress
a translation of the Roman missal into the French language,
which was published by Doctor Voisin, in 1660. On the
12th of January, in the same year, the Pope condemned it.

52. The innovators object that, in the fourth Council of
Lateran, (c. 9,) in the year 1215, every nation was permitted to recite the office in the vernacular tongue. The
Council only spoke of persons of the Greek and Latin rite,
who lived in the same city: the permission was granted
only to them. The Council even commanded them to
celebrate in the language of their own rite, whether it was
Greek or Latin.

53. Peter Soave says, that the decrees of Trent did not
leave room for animadversion, inasmuch as they were drawn
up in so obscure a style, that they could not be understood.
But this is in the first place a pure calumny: for the
decrees are so clear, that any one, however moderate his
abilities may be, can easily understand them. He also says,

that the Protestants complained but little of the prohibition
to celebrate in the vulgar tongue. If they said but little,
Soave has fiercely assailed the Church and the Pontiffs, for
the prohibition, and has gone so far as to say, that they
subjected heaven to earth. He labours to prove that all
languages were at one time common, in order to show that
mass was first celebrated in the vulgar tongue. This is not
denied by Catholics, nor condemned by the Council. In
the 9th canon the Council condemns only those who say:
"Lingua tantum vulgari missam celebrari debere." The
condemnation of those who say that mass should be celebrated only in the vulgar tongue, was most just: as well on
account of the most ancient custom of celebrating in Greek
and Latin, even ,where these languages were not spoken,
as also on account of the reasons for this custom. First,
as has been already said, it often happens that the sense of
certain words in one language, cannot be fully expressed in
another; hence, if in different countries mass were celebrated
in different languages, it would be very difficult to preserve
the identity of the sense, and by consequence the unity of the
churches; hence, many controversies and scandals would
arise. For this reason the civil laws are left in the ancient
language. Besides, if the priests of every country were to
celebrate in the vernacular language, they would not be
able to hold communication with each other in different
nations. Moreover, it is not right that the people should
hear, every day, the mysteries of our faith in the vulgar
tongue, without an explanation from the minister of religion,
accommodated to their capacity.

54. Soave brings forward two papal letters to disprove
the doctrine of the Council: the first was from John VIII.,
epist. 247, (see Baronius, anno 880.) in which the Pontiff
permitted the Sclavonians (from whom the Bohemians are
descended) to say mass and to recite the office in the Scla-
vonian language. But this concession shows, that at that

time it was not lawful to celebrate in the vernacular tongue without a special privilege, which was granted to the Sclavonians at the solicitation of St. Methodius, by whom they had been just converted. The Pope consented to grant them this privilege, because they had not a sufficient number of priests capable of celebrating in the Latin language.

55. The second papal letter was from St. Gregory VII., (lib. 7, ep. 11.) to the people of Sclavonia; it was within two hundred years after the epistle of John VIII., and when the Catholic religion and the knowledge of the Latin language were spread over the country. In that letter St. Gregory said that he could not consent to the celebration of the divine office in the vulgar tongue. The reason which he assigned was that God wished that the Scripture should be obscure in some places, because if it were within reach of all it might perhaps be exposed to the danger of contempt, or might be misunderstood by the unlearned, and might therefore lead them into error. How is this letter opposed to the doctrine of the Council? St. Gregory mentioned that the permission granted on former occasions was not sufficient to justify them in continuing to use the vulgar tongue; because the Church in former times tolerated some things which were afterwards better examined and corrected. But here Soave breaks forth with still greater fury against St. Gregory, and exclaims: "Then are good institutions proclaimed to be corruptions, and tolerated only by antiquity? And are abuses afterwards introduced, canonized as perfect corrections?" Behold how he sends forth his poison against the Church. But where has St. Gregory ever called an ancient usage, a corruption? It is true he says that the custom was *corrected*, that is, from being good it was made better, but was not made lawful from being unlawful: thus a law in the Digest is said to be corrected in the Codex, and a canon in the five books of the Decretals is said to be corrected in the sixth, without charging the

2 c 2

first law or canon with corruption. And how could Soave have the temerity to call the custom of not celebrating in the vulgar tongue an abuse, when for such custom there are so many solid reasons?

56. To the eighth chapter corresponds the ninth canon, in which it was condemned to say that the rite of saying part of the canon in a low voice, should be condemned, or to say that the mass ought to be celebrated only in the vulgar tongue, or to say that water should not be mixed with the wine to be offered in the chalice: "Si quis dixerit ecclesiæ Romanæ ritum quo submissa voce pars canonis et verba consecrationis proferuntur, damnandum esse; aut lingua tantum vulgari missam celebrari debere; aut aquam non miscendam esse vino in calice offerendo, eo quod sit contra Christi instutionem, anathema sit." With regard to the celebration of mass in the vulgar tongue, enough has been already said. (n. 50, et seq.) For mixing water with the wine in the chalice, Alexander I. assigns the reason. (Can. in sacramentorum &c., de consecr. dist. 2.) "In sacramentorum oblationibus," says the Pontiff, "quæ inter missarum solemnia Domino offeruntur, passio Domini miscenda est ut ejus, cujus corpus et sanguis conficitur, passio celebratur: ita ut, repulsis opinionibus superstitionum, panis tantum et vinum aqua permixtum in sacrificium offerantur. Non enim debet (ut a Patribus accepimus, et ipsa ratio docet) in calice Domini aut vinum solum aut aqua sola offerri, sed utrumque permixtum, quia utrumque ex latere ejus in passione sua profluxisse legitur.

57. Finally, with regard to saying in a low voice, a part of the canon, and particularly the words of consecration, the Council says in the fifth chapter, that one of the rites of the Church is: "ut scilicet quædam submissa voce, alia vero elatiore in missa pronuntiarentur." Kemnitius and the other innovators say that this is opposed to the institution of Christ: but in conformity with

ancient documents, the Council of Trent teaches the contrary. In the Liturgy of St. John Chrysostom the priest is directed in one part of the mass to pray secretly: *Sacerdos oret secreto*: the same direction is given in the liturgy of St. Basil. And in the Latin Church, Innocent I. in his first letter to the Bishop of Eugubium, expressly says that the principal part of the mass was said in secret. Nor can it be said with Kemnitius that this is contrary to the institution of Christ who pronounced in a loud tone the words of consecration: *Hoc est corpus meum, hic est calix, &c.;* for that was then necessary in order to teach the Apostles the rite of consecrating. The words of consecration are also pronounced in a loud voice, at present, by the bishop at the ordination of priests: but this reason does not hold in masses which are celebrated for the people. It is true that in the Greek Church the words of consecration are said in a loud tone: but what does this prove? We do not say that it is unlawful to pronounce these words in an audible voice, but we say that neither is it unlawful to say them in a low tone: hence, we should in this matter obey the Church in what she has prescribed for the Greeks and for the Latins. Besides even in the Greek Church, the priest is directed to say certain other words in a low voice. Cardinal Bona (lib. 2, c. 13, rerum liturg.) thinks that the custom of saying the canon in secret commenced in the tenth century. However, others say that it cannot be proved by any ancient document that it was said in a loud tone before that period. But although the custom of saying the canon in secret should have begun in the tenth century, it ought to be enough for us to know that this custom has existed through the whole of the western Church for eight centuries, and that it has been approved by the Council of Trent for just reasons.

58. I here subjoin a brief statement of certain ancient usages of the eastern Churches regarding the celebration of

mass and the oblations. At first, the Greek Churches contained three parts: the porch, the nave, and the sanctuary. At present on account of the poverty of the Greeks, their Churches contain only the nave and sanctuary, which is divided by a large balustrade, in which there are three parts: only bishops, priests, and deacons, enter the sanctuary. The altar stands by itself in the middle. At the entrance on the left hand there is a small altar called *protesis*, or *proposition*, on which the bread and wine are prepared for mass. On the right hand there is another small altar for the sacred vestments, and another which serves for the sacrifice. The deacon in vestments places the host on the paten which is a large basin. The host is either round or square, or of the form of a cross, and on the upper side a cross is always imprinted. The priest then punctures the host with a small knife, and at each incision the deacon says: *let us pray to God.* Then the priest cuts a piece of the host, saying: *because his life was taken away by men.* The deacon answers: *sacrifice to the Lord.* The priest then deposits the host on the paten and makes a new incision, saying: *One of the soldiers opened his side and blood and water instantly came forth.* The deacon says: *Bless, O Lord,* and puts wine and water into the chalice. The priest then cuts a great number of particles off the host, and afterwards incenses the gifts and the veil which is to cover them.

59. Let us now say something of the oblations. After having sent out of the Church the catechumens and public sinners, who were not allowed to assist at the mass of the faithful, the doors were locked; and whilst the offertory and other verses were sung the bishop took the oblations. At first, gifts of various kinds were offered, but it was afterwards ordered that in these oblations only bread and wine should be received: a portion of the bread and wine was laid aside for the sacrifice, and for those who received the communion;

the remainder was preserved. This is stated by Father le Brun in his work on the liturgies. (t. 1, p. 286.) This practice continued till the ninth century. Formerly the corporal was turned over the *oblata,* and was therefore called *pallium ;* hence, the pieces of linen with which the chalice is covered have got the name of *Palla :* it was also called *animetta.* The Carthusians still use these large corporals for covering the chalice.

60. The words of consecration have been always said in secret. Father Chalon also states in his history of the sacraments that the words of consecration were not written in the liturgy, but were transmitted by word of mouth to the priests. This was done from the time of the Apostles till the fourth century, in which the canon was made similar to ours. The euchology of the Greeks for the mass, differs from our canon only in this that the prayer *fiat corpus et sanguis D. N. Jesus Christi,* is said after the words of consecration, *hoc est corpus meum.* But in our canon that prayer is recited immediately after the words, *quam oblationem, &c.* Be it here observed that in another place we have stated that if some of the Fathers said that transubstantiation is effected by the prayer of the priest, *fiat corpus, &c.,* they meant to say so because the words of Jesus Christ, *hoc est corpus meum,* were comprehended and recorded along with that prayer, as we find in all the liturgies. Be it also observed that Cardinal Bessarion in the Council of Florence (anno 1438,) stated that according to the doctrine of St. Chrysostom, the Greeks held as we do, that by the words, *hoc est corpus meum,* and *hic est calix, &c.,* the substance of the bread and wine is changed into that of the body and blood of Jesus Christ. The rite of the Cofts (which has been embraced by other orientals), regarding the consecration is somewhat different from ours: the priest says: *he blessed it,* and the people answer,

*amen : and gave it to his disciples saying : This is
the body which is broken, and given for the remission
of sins :* the people answer: *amen, we believe that it is.*

61. Be it also observed, that St. Gregory (c. 22, de reb.
eccl.) has said: " Fuit mos apostolorum solummodo ad orationem dominicalem hostiam oblationis consecrare." From
this passage Strabo erroneously inferred, that the apostles
celebrated, as we do on Good Friday, without pronouncing
the words of Christ; " *hoc est corpus meum.* But St.
Gregory has not said that the apostles consecrated by merely
saying the Lord's prayer, but *solummodo ad orationem
dominicalem*, that is, at the time the *Pater noster* is said,
without excluding the preceding words of Christ. St. Chrysostom, and his successor, Procolus, say that in the mass
the apostles added hymns and other prayers along with the
Pater noster.

TWENTY-THIRD SESSION.

ON THE SACRAMENT OF ORDER.

1. The modern heretics have laboured hard to remove Order from the number of the sacraments; hence the Council wished that this subject should be examined with great care and exactness in several sessions, by the major as well as by the minor theologians. And, first of all, seven articles were drawn up, in which were contained the errors of the adversaries on the sacrament of Order.

2. Article 1. That Order is not a sacrament, but only a certain rite of electing the ministers of the Word of God, and of the sacraments. Art. 2. That Order is an invention of men unacquainted with ecclesiastical matters. Art. 3. That Order is not one Sacrament only, and that the inferior orders do not tend as steps to the priesthood. Art. 4. That there is no ecclesiastical hierarchy, but that all christians are priests: and that for the election to the priesthood, the call of the magistrate, and the consent of the people are required: and that a person who had been once a priest, can again become a layman. Art. 5. That in the New Testament there is no visible priesthood, nor power to consecrate and to offer the body of Jesus Christ, or to absolve from sins, but only to preach the gospel: and that they who do not preach, cease to be priests. Art 6. That in the collation of orders, the unction and other ceremonies are not necessary; that they are even useless and injurious: and that the Holy Ghost is not given by the sacrament of Order. Art. 7. That bishops are not superior to priests, and that they have not power to

ordain priests: and that if they have, it is common to
priests: and that ordinations by bishops without the
consent of the people, are invalid.

3. In the first congregation which was held, Salmeron
spoke: he said, first that the sacrifice and the priesthood
are not only united, but inseparable; hence, the teaching
of the one necessarily followed from that of the other.
Secondly, he said, that St. Augustine (l. 19, de civ. Dei)
made a distinction between the order by which things are
arranged, and the ecclesiastical order, which distinguishes
deaconship from the priesthood, and priesthood from the episcopal order.   Order, as the Master of the Sentences has
written, is also taken for the sacred ceremony, by which a
person receives power in the church: Salmeron said, that
Order taken in this last sense is a true sacrament, as he
proved by the words of St. Paul, " *Noli negligere*," &c.
Resuscites, &c., from the Council of Florence, and from the
fourth Council of Carthage.   Thirdly, he said that, according to the doctrine of the Fathers, and of the Council itself,
in the preceding session, this sacrament was instituted by
Christ, when he said: " *Hoc facite in meam commemorationem*," (Luc. xxii. 19,) and, *Accipite Spiritum
Sanctum: quorum remiseritis peccata*," &c. (Jo.
xx. 22.)   In these last words our Lord, by breathing
the Holy Ghost *(insufflavit in eos)*, gave his disciples
power over his mystic body, that is, the power of absolving
from sin.   Fourthly, he said that, as we read in the last
chapter of St. Mark, when Jesus Christ brought out the
Apostles and blessed them, he then, according to the
doctrine of St. Augustine and St. Clement of Rome, (lib.
8. Constitut. apostol.) constituted them bishops.   This
was very congruous, for in sending them to preach and to
found his Church, it was necessary to give them the power
of ordaining new priests and bishops.   Fifthly, he added,
that deaconship is a real sacrament, as appears from the

Acts of the Apostles (vi. 6), where St. Luke says: "Orantes imposuerunt eis manus." By the imposition of hands, the grace of the Holy Ghost was given to them, as we read of St. Stephen, who was then ordained deacon: "Erat plenus Spiritu Sancto, et prædicabat." It is not true that the deacons were ordained for the purpose of assisting at the ordinary tables of the faithful, but at the holy tables of the sacrament of the altar; for as Clement, Evaristus, Ignatius Martyr, Cyprian, Jerome, the Council of Neocesarea and Bede attest, the deacons received, at their ordination, power to distribute the eucharist. And, said Salmeron, although in some canons of the sixth Council, their institution is referred to the care of the tables of the widows, these canons were not accepted by the church: besides, it may be said, that deacons were then entrusted with the care of the temporal and spiritual tables.

4. The same is said of St. Paul and St. Barnabas, when they were told to go and preach: *Ite et prædicate :* hands were imposed upon them, and they were afterwards commanded to go and preach. This could not be understood of the priesthood which they had already received, and, therefore, must be understood of episcopal ordination. It is afterwards said of them, that they appointed priests in the cities and towns; such appointments can be made only by bishops. Lastly, he said that, by ordination, a spiritual character is impressed: hence, he concluded that Order is not a mere election to preach the divine word, but that it is a true sacrament and character, through the divine power conferred on the Church. He also impugned the assertion, that priests and deacons can be appointed by the lay magistrate, because they have supernatural power to feed the sheep of Christ, according to the words of our Lord to St. Peter—the first pastor. The people were forbidden to make such appointments, by the eighth Council of Lateran, and by the Council of Florence. He said that, if the people had sometimes chosen

2 D

priests or deacons, the election was made by the concession of the Holy See: but the right of confirming it, and of giving spiritual power, belonged exclusively to the Church.

5. In the second meeting, Peter Soto, of the Order of St. Dominick, spoke against the fourth article, and said that there was an ecclesiastical hierarchy, or a pre-eminence in church government which bishops possessed over priests, according to the words of St. Paul: " The Holy Ghost hath placed you bishops, to rule the church of God." (Acts xx. 28.) He also adduced the text of the Apostle: " Obey your prelates, and be subject to them." (Heb. xiii. 17.)Hence, there are in the church superiors whom we must obey. Nor are the words of St. Peter: "you are a chosen generation, a kingly priesthood," (1 ep. ii. 9.) opposed to this doctrine. For, this passage should be understood of the corporal, and not of the spiritual priesthood. He afterwards spoke of the fifth article, and proved that in the church there is a true priesthood. He then contended against Salmeron that at first the election of ministers was given to the people, and proved his assertion by the following words: " Then it pleased the apostles and ancients with the whole church, to choose men of their own company, and to send to Antioch," &c. (Act. xv. 22.) He maintained that this was a true apostolical tradition: but he was opposed by Melchior Cornelius who had been sent to the Council by the King of Portugal, and maintained that the people assisted at the election only to give the necessary testimony, but that they did not elect.

6. In the next meeting, Melchior Cornelius spoke, and said that Pope Fabian, St. Denis, and Innocent III. (c. 1, de sacr. unct.) make mention of the anointing of priests, which the heretics have despised. He proved that bishops are superior to priests, and that no objection could be taken from the words of St. Jerome, in which the holy doctor appeared to place priests on equality with bishops. He

showed that in many other parts of his writings, the saint spoke of the pre-eminence of bishops, and that in the passage from which the adversaries object, the saint intended to speak only of the power which priests have, equally with bishops. Finally, after the above mentioned seven articles were fully discussed in the preceding and other meetings, the Council drew up four chapters, and eight canons on the sacrament of Order.

CHAPTER 1.—ON THE INSTITUTION OF THE PRIESTHOOD OF THE NEW LAW.

7. In the first chapter, the Council says that the sacrifice and the priesthood are so united that in every law both have always existed together. Since by the institution of Christ, the sacrifice of the Eucharist is external and visible, it must be admitted that he has also instituted an external visible priesthood in which he gave to the apostles and their successors power to consecrate and to absolve, as is demonstrated by the sacred Scripture, and taught by tradition: " Sacrificium et sacerdotium ita Dei ordinatione conjuncta sunt ut utrumque in omni lege extiterit. Cum igitur in novo Testamento sanctum Eucharistiæ sacrificium visibile ex Domini institutione catholica ecclesia acceperit, fateri etiam oportet in ea novum esse visibile et externum sacerdotium, in quod vetus translatum est. Hoc autem ab eodem Domino Salvatore nostro institutum esse, atque apostolis eorumque successoribus in sacerdotio potestatem traditam consecrandi, offerendi et ministrandi corpus et sanguinem ejus, necnon et peccata dimittendi et retinendi, sacræ litteræ ostendunt et catholicæ ecclesiæ traditio semper docuit."

8. To this chapter the first canon corresponds. Can. 1. " Si quis dixerit non esse in novo Testamento sacerdotium visibile et externum, vel non esse potestatem aliquam consecrandi et offerendi verum corpus et sanguinem Domini et

peccata remittendi, et retinendi, sed officium tantum, et nudum ministerium prædicandi Evangelium; vel eos qui non
prædicant prorsus non esse sacerdotes, anathema sit."

9. To this chapter the eighth canon also has reference.
Can. 8. " Si quis dixerit episcopos qui auctoritate romani
pontificis assumuntur, non esse legitimos et veros episcopos
sed figmentum humanum, anathema sit."

10. Thus Jesus Christ really instituted the sacrament of
Order, and afterwards gave to the apostles and their successors, power to exercise their order: he gave them power
to consecrate, and to offer the sacrifice of the altar, saying: " Do this for a commemoration of me," (Luc. xxii.
19;) and to absolve from sins, saying, " Receive ye the
Holy Ghost, whose sins you shall forgive, they are forgiven
them, and whose sins you shall retain, they are retained."
(John xx. 22, 23.)

SECOND CHAPTER.—ON THE SEVEN ORDERS.

11. In the second chapter the Council says, that since
the ministry of the holy priesthood is divine, it was conve-
nient that in the church there should be several orders of
ministers to serve priests; some in tonsure, some in minor
orders, and some in holy orders; of deacons the scriptures
make mention. And it is well known, continues the Council, that from the commencement of christianity there were,
as is frequently mentioned by the Fathers, and by the sacred Council itself, in the church sub-deacons, acolytes, exorcists, lectors, and doorkeepers, each of whom performed
the ministerial functions peculiar to his order: but all these
are not of equal dignity; for subdeaconship is numbered
among the holy orders by the Fathers and Councils, and
both make very frequent mention of the other inferior
orders. " Cum antem divina res sit tam sancti sacerdotii
ministerium, consentaneum fuit, quo dignius et majori cum
veneratione exerceri posset, ut in Ecclesia ordinatissima

dispositione plures et diversi essent ministrorum ordines qui sacerdotio ex officio deservirent; ita distributi ut qui jam clericali tonsura insigniti esse per minores ad majores ascenderent: nam non solum de sacerdotibus, sed et de diaconis sacræ litteræ apertam mentionem faciunt, et quæ maxime in illorum ordinatione attendenda sunt, gravissimis verbis docent, et ab ipsa Ecclesiæ initio sequentium ordinum nomina atque uniuscujusque eorum propria ministeria subdiaconi scilicet, acolithi, exorcistæ, lectoris et ostiarii, in usu fuisse cognoscuntur, quamvis non pari gradu; nam subdiaconus ad majores ordines Patribus et sacris conciliis refertur, in quibus et de aliis inferioribus frequentissime legimus."

12. To this chapter the second canon corresponds. Can. 2. Si quis dixerit, præter sacerdotium, non esse in ecclesia catholica alios ordines, et majores et minores, per quos, velut, per gradus quosdam, in sacerdotium tenditur, anathema sit."

13. All the ecclesiastical orders, the higher as well as the inferior orders, are referred to the consecration, administration, and veneration of the most holy Eucharist: and for this end, as St. Thomas teaches, they have been all instituted; hence, Order is thus defined: Ordo est ritus sacer quo spiritualis potestas confertur ad ea quæ ad Eucharistiæ confectionem et dispensationem pertinent."

Peter Soave says, that many have been surprised at the definition of the Council, that the inferior orders are only steps to the superior orders, and that all are steps to the priesthood: because in ancient times many remained in these orders, and never ascended to the priesthood. I answer, that the Council has not said that the inferior orders are mere steps to the priesthood: but said that in the Church there were minor and sacred orders, through which, as by certain steps, ecclesiastics ascended to the priesthood. Hence, from the doctrine of the Council it does not follow that many may not remain in the inferior orders.

IN THE THIRD CHAPTER THE COUNCIL TEACHES THAT ORDER IS A REAL SACRAMENT.

14. In the third chapter, the Council declared that Order is a true sacrament, as is evident from the Scriptures, from tradition, and from the uniform consent of the Fathers. In that chapter it is also said that ordination which is conferred by words and external signs, gives grace to those who are ordained: and that therefore no one can doubt but Order is one of the seven sacraments, since of this the Apostle assures us in the second epistle to Timothy. "I admonish thee, that thou stir up the grace which is in thee by the imposition of my hands, &c." (2 Tim. i. 6.): "Cum Scripturæ testimonio, apostolica traditione et Patrum unanimi consensu perspicuum sit per sacram ordinationem, quæ verbis et signis exterioribus perficitur, gratiam conferri, dubitare nemo debet ordinem esse vere et proprie unum ex septem S. Ecclesiæ sacramentis; inquit enim Apostolus: *Admoneo te ut resuscites gratiam Dei, quæ est in te per impositionem manuum mearum ; non enim dedit nobis Deus spiritum timoris, sed virtutis et dilectionis et sobrietatis.*"

15. To this chapter the third and fifth canons correspond. In the third canon, the Council declared: "Si quis dixerit Ordinem sive sacram ordinationem non esse vere et proprie sacramentum a Christo Domino institutum, vel esse figmentum quoddam humanum excogitatum a viris rerum ecclesiasticarum imperitis; aut esse tantum ritum quemdam eligendi ministros verbi Dei et sacramentorum, anathema sit."

16. In the fifth canon, the Council says: "Si quis dixerit sacram unctionem quæ Ecclesia in sacra ordinatione utitur non tantum non requiri, sed contemnendam et perniciosam esse, similiter et alias cæremonias, anathema sit."

17. That Order is a true sacrament cannot be doubted, since it wants none of the requisites for a sacrament. First, it is a sensible sign which consists in the imposition of hands (and also in the delivery of the instruments which some require), along with the form, which is the prayer recited by the bishop, as we read in the Acts regarding the ordination of deacons: "And they, praying, imposed hands upon them." (Act. vi. 6.) The same is said of the ordination of Paul and Barnabas. (Act. xiii. 3.) Secondly, there is a promise of grace, as we learn from St. Paul, who in his epistle to Timothy says: "Neglect not the grace that is in thee, which was given thee by prophecy, with the imposition of the hands of the priesthood," (1 Tim. iv. 14.); and from St. John, who has committed to writing the words of the Lord: "Receive ye the Holy Ghost, whose sins you shall forgive," &c. Thirdly, Order is of divine institution, as we read in the Acts: "And as they were ministering to the Lord, and fasting, the Holy Ghost said to them: Separate me Saul and Barnabas, for the work whereunto I have taken them. Then they, fasting and praying, and imposing their hands upon them, sent them away." (xiii. 2, 3.)

18. With regard to the matter of this sacrament, the Greeks have always held that it consists solely in the imposition of hands: but among the Latins there are various opinions: some say that it consists solely in the delivery of the instruments, that the accompanying words of the bishop are the form, and that the imposition of hands is accidental matter. Others hold that the essential matter consists solely in the imposition of hands with the accompanying prayer of the bishop, which is the form: and that the delivery of the instruments and the accompanying prayer of the bishop are adventitious, accidental, or integral, matter and form to express more clearly the effects of the power conferred. The third opinion is held by those who for the matter of the sacrament, require both the imposition of hands and the

delivery of the instruments as essential parts of the sacrament, along with the accompanying words as the form: this opinion should be followed in practice. But the second opinion, viz., that the imposition of hands is the only essential matter, appears to me to be the most probable: it is proved by the passages of scripture which have been just quoted: " Then they, fasting and praying, and imposing their hands upon them, (that is, on Paul and Barnabas,) sent them away." (Acts. xiii. 3.) " Neglect not the grace that is in thee, which was given thee by prophecy, with the imposition of the hands of the priesthood." (1 Tim. iv. 14.) " I admonish thee, that thou stir up the grace of God which is in thee by the imposition of my hands. (2 Tim. i. 6.) St. Ambrose writes, " Homo imponit manum, Deus largitur gratiam." (De dign. Sacerdot.) Tournely (tom. 2, de sacram. p. 350, et seq.) collects a great number of passages of the holy Fathers on this point, and says that even in the Latin Church, before the tenth century, the imposition of hands was the only matter used. Bellarmine holds the same opinion, and Maldonatus (de ord. p. 1, q. 3.) goes so far as to say that it appertains to faith: and Estius (in 4, sent. dist. 24.) says that it is an error to confound this imposition of hands with the delivery of the instruments. Thus, according to our opinion, the imposition of hands is the sole matter of Order, and the form consists in the prayer of the bishop, in which the Holy Ghost is invoked. The adversaries say: does not the form then consist in the words of the bishop, " *Accipe potestatem offerere sacrificium*," &c., by which is given the power of offering sacrifice, and in the words, " *Accipe Spiritum Sanctum*," quorum remiseritis peccata remittuntur eis, &c. ? We answer, no; but they are declarations made by the bishop of the twofold power conferred by the imposition of hands and the annexed prayer.

19. However, the third opinion, that in the ordination of priests and deacons the imposition of hands as well as the

delivery of the instruments, is necessary, should certainly be followed in practice. To this opinion the words of the decree of Eugene IV. are favourable: " Sextum (sacramentum) est ordinis, cujus materia, est illud per cujus traditionem confertur Ordo." In the Latin church the delivery of the instruments has been in use at least for seven centuries, as we learn from the Roman order, and the other rituals. " Si conjecturis locus est," says Morinus, " anni sunt septingenti circiter cum initium huic additamento factum est." (De Ord. p. 3, exerc. 7, c. 1.) And Father Martene writes: " Hanc instrumentorum traditionem præscriptam reperi in pontificali Radbodi Noviomensis episcopi ab annis octingentis." (De antiq. eccl. rit. c. 8, art. 6, n. 17.) But this proves that the delivery of the instruments is not essential; since, for the space of so many antecedent centuries, we do not find any mention made of it, nor do we find that for want of it, any ordination had ever been declared invalid. To this opinion the Council of Trent appears certainly to adhere; for in the 14th session (c. 3.), speaking of the ministers of extreme unction, it says that they are " sacerdotes ab ipsis (episcopis) rite ordinati per impositionem manuum presbyterii:" that is, the second imposition of hands by the bishop, in the mass of ordination, when, along with three other priests, he extends the hands over the persons to be ordained.

20. We read in the Acts, that the deacons were ordained in the same manner by the Apostles: " And they, praying, imposed hands upon them." (vi. 6.) Hence, we say, that subdeaconship is not a sacrament; because, in the ordination of subdeacons, there is no imposition of hands, as Urban II. appears to have sufficiently declared in the Council of Benevento, in the following words: " Super his solis (scil. sacerdotibus et diaconis) præceptum apostolicum habemus." And Juenin says (de sacr. ord. q. 1, concl. 3, p. 438.), that for twelve centuries, subdeaconship was not

reckoned, in the Latin Church, among the holy orders; nor is it at present considered a holy order by the Greeks.

21. Kemnitius says, that the Apostles imposed hands on those who were ordained, not because they conferred a sacrament on them, but as a sign of recommending them to God. But Bellarmine answers, that, in the sixth chapter of the Acts of the Apostles, the prayer is clearly distinguished from the imposition of hands: this is made still more clear by the following words of the Apostle, in the first epistle to Timothy: " Impose not hands lightly on any man, neither be partaker of other men's sins." (v. 22.) It is he alone who ordains an unworthy person, and not he who prays for another, though most unworthy, that can *be partaker of other men's sins.* Kemnitius also says, that in the scriptures there is a promise of grace to those who are ordained: but not of sanctifying grace, as is required for every sacrament. Bellarmine answers that when Jesus Christ gave the Apostles power to remit sins, which is a part of the priesthood, he said to them: *Receive ye the Holy Ghost.* It is certain, that in the scriptures, a gift to which sanctifying grace is not annexed, and which may exist with sin, is never absolutely called the Holy Ghost.

22. On the other hand, that episcopal order is a real sacrament, we may well hold with Bellarmine, and Juenin, (loc. cit. concl. 6.) against some who say that it is only an extension of the priesthood. For, in the first place, we know from the words of St. Paul: *Posuit episcopos regere ecclesiam Dei*, that the episcopal order is of divine institution. Secondly, we find in episcopal ordination a sensible rite, as appears from the words of the Apostle to Timothy. " I admonish thee to stir up the grace of God, which is in thee, by the imposition of my hands." (2 Tim. i. 6.) In these words we find also a promise of grace.

FOURTH CHAPTER.—ON THE ECCLESIASTICAL HIERARCHY, AND ON ORDINATION.

23. In this fourth chapter the Fathers say that since in the sacrament of Order, a character is impressed, they condemn all who assert that the priests of the New Testament have only a temporary power, so that they who do not exercise the ministry of preaching return to the state of laymen. The Council also condemns those who assert that all Christians are priests, and that all priests have equal power, thus confounding the ecclesiastical hierarchy, in opposition to the words of St Paul: " Non omnes apostoli," &c. The Council also declares that besides the ecclesiastical degrees, the bishops as successors of the Apostles, principally belong to the hierarchical order, since they are placed by the Holy Ghost to rule the Church of God. Hence, they are superior to priests, and can confer the sacrament of Confirmation and of Order, and can do several other things which persons in inferior orders cannot do. The Council moreover declares that in the ordination both of bishops and of those who are promoted to the other orders, the authority of the people, or of any secular power is not essentially required: and that all who ascend to orders by their own authority, are robbers because they do not enter by the door. Behold the words of the council: " Quoniam vero in sacramento Ordinis, sicut et in Baptismo et Confirmatione, character imprimitur qui nec deleri neque auferri potest, merito S. Synodus damnat eorum sententiam qui asserunt novi Testamenti sacerdotes temporariam tantummodo potestam habere et semel rite ordinatos, iterum laicos effici posse, si verbi Dei ministerium non exerceant. Quod si quis omnes christianos promiscue novi Testamenti sacerdotes esse aut omnes pari inter se potestate spirituali præditos affirment, nihil aliud facere videntur quam ecclesi-

asticam hierarchiam, quæ est ut castrorum acies ordinata, confundere, perinde ac si, contra B. Pauli doctrinam, omnes apostoli, omnes prophetæ, omnes Evangelistæ, omnes pastores, omnes sint doctores. Proinde sacrosancta synodus declarat, præter cæteros ecclesiasticos gradus, episcopos, qui in apostolorum locum successerunt, ad hunc hierarchicum ordinem præcipue pertinere et positos, sicut idem Apostolus ait, a Spiritu Sancto, regere Ecclesiam Dei: eosque presbyteris superiores esse ac sacramentum confirmationis conferre, ministros Ecclesiæ ordinare, atque illa pleraque peragere ipsos posse, quarum functionum potestatem reliqui inferioris ordinis nullam habent. Docet insuper sacrosancta synodus in ordinatione episcoporum, sacerdotum et cæterorum ordinum, nec populi nec cujusvis sæcularis potestatis et magistratus consensum sive vocationem sive auctoritatem ita requiri ut sine ea irrita sit ordinatio: quin potius decernit eos qui tantummodo a populo aut sæculari potestate ac magistrati vocati et instituti ad hoc ministeria exercenda ascendunt, et qui ea propria temeritate, sibi sumunt, omnes non Ecclesiæ ministros, sed fures et latrones per ostium non ingressos, habendos esse."

24. To this fourth chapter the 4th, 6th, and 7th canons correspond. Can. 4. " Si quis dixerit per sacram ordinationem non dari Spiritum Sanctum, ac proinde frustra episcopos dicere: *Accipite Spiritum Sanctum:* aut per eam non imprimi characterem; vel eum qui sacerdos semel fuit laicum rursus fieri posse, anathema sit."

25. Can. 6. Si quis dixerit in ecclesia catholica non esse hierarchiam divina ordinatione institutam quæ constat ex episcopis, presbyteris et ministris, anathema sit."

25. Can. 7. " Si quis dixerit episcopis non esse presbyteris superiores, vel non habere potestatem confirmandi et ordinandi, vel eam quam habent illis esse cum presbyteris communem; vel eam vel ordines ab ipsis collatos sine populi vel potestatis sæcularis consensu aut vocatione,

irritos esse; aut eos qui nec ab ecclesiastica et canonica potestate rite ordinati nec missi sunt, sed aliunde veniunt, legitimos esse verbi et sacramentorum ministros, anathema sit."

27. Peter Soave disapproves of the word hierarchy; in which the Council included all the ecclesiastical orders and degrees. "The word *hierarchy*," he says, "is unknown, not to say, contrary, to the sacred Scriptures, and was not in use in the ancient Church: it was invented by an individual (he meant St. Denis, the Areopagite,) who, though an author of some antiquity, is not well known; neither can the age in which he lived be ascertained. But he is an hyperbolical writer, and is not imitated by any ancient author in the use of that or of the other words which he invented. For, the word *hierodiaconia* or *hierodulia*, and not *hierarchia*, was suited to the language of Christ, of the Apostles, and of the ancient Church." He adds: "Peter Paul Vergerius, in Valtellina, made these and other objections against the doctrine of the Council, the subject of his sermons."

28. He quotes Vergerius, a heretic, a man with scarcely a tincture of learning, but full of audacity, as appears from his writings, which excite universal disgust. The word *hierarchy* was used by St. Denis, and was the title of one of his principal works: this book has been generally praised by the learned. Some have doubted whether he was the author of the work, but we have many strong proofs from the Holy Fathers and Councils that it is the genuine production of St. Denis. St. Gregory, in the 34th Homily, calls him *an ancient and venerable Father*, and quotes his book on the Hierarchy. St. Martin, Pope, did the same in the Council of Rome, as also St. Agatho, in his epistle to the Emperor Constantine IV. It has been likewise quoted by Nicholas I., in his epistle to the Emperor Michael, by the sixth General Council in the fourth action, and by

2 E

the seventh Council in the second action. Besides, St.
Maximus, a monk, and St. Thomas, have written a Commentary on this work of St. Denis. But though the book
had not been written by the Saint, the veneration in which
it was held by the Church, for so many centuries, was sufficient reason for the Fathers of Trent not to reject, but to
adopt a word so appropriate, and so well calculated to express their meaning. St. Maximus, in his Commentaries on
St. Denis, wrote on the Hierarchy nine hundred years before
the Council; St. Bonaventure, three hundred years before
the Council, composed a Treatise on the *Hierarchy*, and
John Scotus had taken his definition of Order from the word
Hierarchy. Order, he says, is *a special power to exercise some spiritual act in the Ecclesiastical Hierarchy*.

29. Soave maintains that the word *hierodiaconia*,
which signifies the body of the Deacons of the Church, was
applied, in common, to the whole Ecclesiastical Order;
and says, that this would be more in accordance with the
language and humility of Christ and his Church. But we
know that, in the Scriptures, the order of Deacons is placed
after that of Priests and Bishops. How, then, could the
Council employ the word *hierodiaconia* in describing the
Ecclesiastical Order, which is composed of Bishops, Priests,
and Deacons, without confounding the lowest with the two
highest portions? But Soave unjustly assails the Council
for having used the word *hierarchia* (which signifies *prin-
cipality*), as being opposed to the language of Christ and
the Scripture. In condemning the use of the word *princi-
pality*, he, at the same time, condemns so many of the
Holy Fathers, St. Cyril of Alexandria, St. Jerome, St. Hilary, St. Augustin, St. Gregory, Bede, and others, who call
the Pontiffs and Bishops, Princes of the Church. Soave
rejoins, and says, that the Council ought not to use a
word, which had not been used by any preceding Council.
But, omitting the other answers, I say that he ought to

know that this word was used twice in the eighth Council, (in the sixth and tenth action). In the sixth action, Nectarius, Ambrose, and Nicephorus were called *memorable hierarchs*; and in the tenth action (c. 14), the term hierarchical, which is applied to the Angels, is applied also to the Bishops of the Church.

30. But let us take leave of the silly remarks of Soave, and come to the objections which the heretics urge against the points of doctrine taught by the Council in this fourth chapter. In the first place they say, as has been already observed, that, according to the words of St. Peter, " you are a chosen generation, a kingly priesthood, a holy nation, &c." (1 Peter ii. 9,) all Christians are priests. But, in answer, I say that in this passage laymen are not called priests in the strict sense; for it cannot be strictly said, that by the oblation of their praises, prayers, and other good works, they offer sacrifice in the strict sense. Behold how St. Augustin clearly explains the words of the Apostle : Episcopi et presbyteri proprie vocantur sacerdotes: sed sicut omnes christiani dicuntur propter mysticum chrisma, sic omnes sacerdotes, quoniam membra sunt unius sacerdotis, de quibus Apostolus dixit: *regale sacerdotium*. (Lib. 20, de civ. Dei. c. 10). This is also proved from the words which our Lord addressed exclusively to the Apostles: " Do this for a commemoration of me." (Luc. xxii. 19.) All then are not priests; besides we know that after they had been ordained bishops by the Apostles in Antioch, St. Paul and St. Barnabas ordained many priests: " And when they had ordained to them priests in every Church, and had prayed, with fasting, they commended them to the Lord, in whom they believed." (Acts xiv. 22.) Hence all the faithful are not priests.

31. Secondly, the heretics say that all bishops and priests are equal. But they err; for bishops, as the successors of the Apostles, as well in the power of ordaining as in juris-

diction, are, by the divine law, superior to priests. This we
know from apostolical tradition, from St. Leo, and St. Gregory ; St. Jerome says : " Quid facit episcopus, excepta
ordinatione, quod non facit presbyter?" Behold how
bishops are superior in the power of conferring holy orders.
With regard to jurisdiction, we have the words of St. Paul
to Timothy: " Against a priest receive not an accusation,
but under two or three witnesses." (1 Tim. v. 19.)
Aetius was the first that spread abroad the error that
priests are equal to bishops; and, therefore, he is reckoned
among the heretics by St. Augustine. This doctrine
has been taught by St. Ignatius Martyr, St. Cyprian, and
St. Jerome. Before them, St. Clement said: " Episcopos
vicem apostolorum gerere, discipulorum presbyteros."
(ep. 1. ad fratrem Dom.) St. Epiphanius writes: " Episcopum et presbyterum æqualem esse quomodo erit possi-
bile?" (hæres. 75.) St. Ambrose says: "Post episcopum
diaconi ordinationem subjicit, quare? nisi quia episcopi et
presbyteri una ordinatio est, sed episcopios primus est, ut
omnis episcopus presbyter sit, non tamen omnes presbyteri episcopi. (c. 3, in ep. 1, ad Tim.) The Council of
Trent, as has been observed on the seventh canon, pronounces an anathema against all who say, " episcopos
non esse presbyteris superiores, vel eam (potestatem) quam
habent, illis esse cum presbyteris communem." And in
the fourth chapter, it appears to be clearly defined that
bishops are, by the divine law, superior to priests.

32. Against this doctrine the adversaries object, first:
that in the Scriptures we find bishops confounded with
priests; hence it appears that they are equal. We do not
deny that, with regard to the oblation of the Eucharistic
sacrifice, and some other ministerial functions, priests are
equal to bishops; and, therefore, with regard to these things,
they are confounded with bishops in the Scriptures, but not
with regard to the power of order or jurisdiction. They

object, secondly; that St. Jerome has expressly said, that priests and bishops are the same: " Idem presbyter qui episcopus." I answer, first, that we do not find these words in the editions of the works of the Saint, published in Rome or Cologne, but only in the edition of Basil, which was corrupted several times by Erasmus of Rotterdam. I answer, secondly, with Juenin (de sacram. ord.) that in the ancient Church priests were frequently permitted to exercise episcopal jurisdiction : but *in actu primo* it remained entirely in the bishop. Even the Lutherans do not give all their priests or ministers the power of ordaining, but only to those whom they call *superintendents*. One of the Lutherans, Lomero, says, that they have no priests, and justly: for it cannot be said that they have in their body bishops legitimately ordained.

33. It is disputed whether simple priests can, by dispensation, confer minor orders; some abbots are said to have this privilege. But it is certain, as we have already seen in the fourth chapter, and seventh canon, that the Council teaches, that the minister of the sacrament of Order is exclusively a bishop; and this we know from uninterrupted tradition. Hence, Juenin holds as certain, (de sacr. ord. quo 4 in fin. concl. 2, p. 442,) and not without just reason, that a simple priest cannot be even the extraordinary minister of Order.

34. The adversaries object, first: that in the first Council of Nice, and, particularly, in the epistle to the Church of Alexandria, it is said, that the power of *ordaining and nominating those who were worthy among the clergy*, was granted to the priests who did not adhere to the schism of Meletius. Tournely says, (p. 363.) in answer, that the power of ordaining ministers of the Church, was not given to them, but only the power of approving by their vote, and confirming the choice made by the people, without waiting for the approbation of the rest of the clergy. He adds, that

the thirteenth canon of the Council of Ancyra is adul-
terated, or not genuine. In that canon it is said: " Non licere nec presbyteris civitatis ordinare sine litteris episcopi
in unaquaque parochia." The words of the canon should
be: ": sed nec presbyteris civitatis sine litteris episcopi in
unaquaque parochia aliquid agere." This interpretation is
conformable to the ancient discipline, by which priests were
forbidden to exercise their ministry in the presence of the
bishop, except at his command.

35. Secondly, they object, that Eugene IV., in his decree
to the Armenians, says, that a bishop is the ordinary minister of the sacrament of Order; hence priests, they say, may
be extraordinary ministers. I answer, that, in his decree,
the Pontiff did not intend to affirm that a priest can be an
extraordinary minister of Order.

36. Thirdly, they object that, in 1489, Innocent VIII.
gave power to the Cistercian Abbot to confer deaconship
and sub-deaconship on his monks; and Vasquez says (in 3
p. S. Thom. disp. 243, c. 4.) that he read the Bull of Innocent, which is preserved in the Cistercian college of Com-
plutum. But the existence of this Bull is questioned by
St. Thomas, Silvius, Navarre, and others; and Tournely
says (p. 368), that there is no other copy of this Bull, neither
is it found in the Bullarium. Besides, in his petition, the
Abbot only asks for a renewal of the privilege or power to
confer tonsure and minor orders on his own monks.
From this it is inferred that all the rest is false, particularly
since the Council of Trent (Sess. 23, c. 10, de reform.)
has forbidden the abbots to give tonsure and minor orders
to any one except their own monks.

37. Fourthly, they argue from the axiom, " *Qui potest
majus, potest minus;*" priests can consecrate the Eucharist
and remit sins: these are greater than the collation of Orders: why, then, cannot priests give ordination? It is necessary to make a distinction; he who can do what is

greater, can do what is less in the same order; for example; he who can absolve from grievous sins, can absolve from lesser sins; but the axiom does not hold when things are in a different order. Is it surely a greater work to remit sins than to raise the dead to life? but still the power of giving life to the dead has not been granted to priests. With regard to things of the same order, an ordinary confessor may absolve from sins, but he cannot absolve from reserved sins.

38. In the end of the fourth chapter, the Council says that in the ordination of the sacred ministers, "nec populi nec cujusvis sæcularis potestatis et magistratus consensum sive vocationem sive auctoritatem ita requiri, ut sine ea irrita sit ordinatio; quia potius decernit eos qui, tantummodo a populo aut sæculari potestate ac magistratu vocati et instituti, ad hæc ministeria exercenda ascendunt, et qui ea propria temeritate sibi sumunt, omnes non Ecclesiæ ministros, sed fures et latrones, per ostium non ingressos, habendos esse." It is certain that without a divine vocation it is not lawful for any one to take upon himself the exercise of the ministry of the Church. This vocation may be ordinary, or extraordinary. It is extraordinary when it comes immediately from God, as was that of St. Paul. It is ordinary when it comes from the superiors who rule the Church, such as the Pope or the Bishops. Hence, it follows that the religion of Luther and Calvin is a false one; for they have promulgated their doctrine without any vocation, either ordinary or extraordinary. The Lutherans say that the vocation of the sacred ministers should come from the people, or from the secular power. But they err: for the ministers of religion should be called in the manner in which Christ called his disciples and sent them to found the Church, without waiting for any consent from the people, or from the secular authorities. We do not find in any part of ecclesiastical history that any priest was ever ordained by a person who was not a bishop. St. Clement writes:

"Presbyter ab uno episcopo ordinetur." (Can. 1.) And
St. Ambrose says: "Neque enim fas erat ut inferior ordi-
net majorem, nemo enim tribuit quod non habet." (in cap.
3, ep. 1, ad Tim.) Hence, when our Lord sent the Apostles to propagate the faith, giving them power to consecrate bishops and priests, he said to them: "As the
Father hath sent me, I also send you." (John xx. 21.)

39. It is true that in the first ages of the Church, the
people assisted at the election of the ministers of religion:
but this was a mere gratuitous concession, like the right of
nominating, or of presenting to certain offices or ecclesiastical benefices, which is at present granted to laymen. But
they never had power to appoint, or ordain; when the people assisted at the election of the minister, it was generally
to give testimony to the good conduct of the persons who
were to be ordained. This was in accordance with the
words of the Apostle: "Oportet......illum et testimonium
habere bonum ab iis qui foris sunt." (1 Tim. iii. 7.) In
reality it would be a great deordination that the sheep
should appoint their own pastor.

SECTION I.—ON THE CELIBACY REQUIRED BY THE CHURCH FOR THOSE WHO RECEIVE HOLY ORDERS.

48. Luther and all the innovators censure the Church
for obliging persons promoted to holy orders to lead a life
of celibacy. They say that for persons in sound health,
the practice of celibacy is impossible without a miracle: and
therefore they hold that marriage is necessary for all, and
that the obligation of continence imposed on ecclesiastics is
the cause of a thousand disorders and sins. But however
great the clamour of these new teachers of the faith, it is
certain that celibacy is a more perfect state than matrimony.
Picenino the Calvinist asks: *how it is proved that the*

state of celibacy is the more perfect ? It is proved first from the words of St. Paul, in which he counsels all who practise continence to make choice of the state of celibacy as he had chosen it for himself. "For I would that all men were even as myself. But I say to the unmarried, and to the widows; it is good for them if they so continue, even as I. But if they do not contain themselves, let them marry. (1 Cor. vii. 7, 8, 9.) He afterwards adds: "Art thou loosed from a wife? seek not a wife." And in the thirty-eighth verse, he says that the conjugal state is good, but that celibacy is better. "Therefore both he that giveth his virgin in marriage doth well; and he that giveth her not doth better."

41. Reason also shows that celibacy is more perfect than the matrimonial state. The same Apostle says that he who has a wife cannot but attend to the things of the world, and must seek to please her, and therefore his heart is divided between the world and God: but he who is unmarried thinks only of pleasing God, and thus his heart is not divided but belongs entirely to God: "He that is without a wife is solicitous for the things that belong to the Lord how he may please God. But he that is with a wife is solicitous for the things of the world how he may please his wife: and he is divided." (Ib. v. 32. 33.) Finally the Apostle says that he does not intend to oblige any one to a life of celibacy; but only counsels it to those who desire to serve God without impediment; observing at the same time that there are a thousand obstacles to hinder married persons from serving God as they would wish.

42. If then celibacy befits every secular who wishes to belong entirely to God, and to serve him without impediment, how much more is it suited to priests, who by the obligation of their state should belong entirely to God, and should be wholly occupied in the things that appertain to his divine glory! In the old law, the priests and Levites

should live apart from their wives during the year they were
to serve in the temple: and for the neglect of this duty the
sons of Heli were punished.   How much more just is it that
the priests of the new law whose duty it is to offer in sacrifice the divine Lamb, should be without wives?   St. Paul
wished that even married persons should abstain for a time
from the use of marriage in order to attend to prayer:
" Defraud not one another, except, perhaps by consent, for
a time, that you may give yourselves to prayer." (1 Cor. vii.
5.)   How much more then should the priest be free from
the care of the things of the world, who has to serve at the
altar of the divine majesty, and to promote the common
good of his neighbour, by preaching, hearing confessions, at-
tending the dying:—duties which can scarcely be discharged
with success without continual study and continual prayer?
St. Francis de Sales had once to convert a heretic: after
having importuned him with a thousand difficulties and
questions, she went one day to propose her greatest objection, which was that she could not conceive why the Church
had prohibited the clergy to marry.   The Saint answered:
" My sister, had I been married, and burdened with a wife
and children, could I have found time to listen to you so
often and to solve so many doubts which you have proposed?   Certainly not."   Thus the saint made her understand the reasonableness of the prohibition, and all her
doubts were removed.   Hence, the Apostle required that
bishops, priests, and deacons, should practise continence.
Hence, in the first epistle to Timothy, he writes: " It
behoveth therefore a bishop to be blameless, the husband
of one wife, sober, prudent, of good behaviour, chaste," &c.
(1 Tim. iii. 2.)   And with regard to Deacons, he says:
" Deacons in like manner chaste," &c.   (Ibid. v. 8.)

43. With regard to the Greek Church, the practice has
been that bishops should abstain absolutely, not only from
contracting marriage, but also from the use of marriage

previously contracted. To priests who had been married before they received holy orders, the use of marriage was permitted; but they were never allowed to contract marriage after they had taken orders. So much for the Greek Church: in the Latin Church even the use of marriage already contracted, has never been allowed to priests or deacons. Behold the words of St. Clement, in the 27th of the apostolic canons: "Innuptis qui ad clerum provecti sunt præcipimus ut solis lectoribus et cantoribus liceat, si voluerint uxores ducere." Hence the assertion of Piceninus that all the apostles were married, and retained their wives, is utterly false: for St. Peter was the only one of them whose marriage we know from the Gospel; we find mention made of his mother-in-law: but after he became an apostle, he left his wife, as Tertullian attests. "Petrum solum invenio maritum per socrum: cæteros, cum maritos non invenio, aut spadones intelligam necesse est aut continentes." (Tert. Monogam, c. 8.) St. Jerome grants to Jovinian *(ex superfluo)* that the other apostles had been married, but says that when they embraced the Gospel, and were called to the apostleship, they all left their wives: "Petrus et cæteri apostoli, ut ei ex superfluo interim concedam, habuerunt quidem uxores, sed quas eo tempore acceperant quo evangelium nesciebant. Qui assumpti postea in apostolatum relinquunt officium conjugale." St. Jerome attests that the perpetual practice of the Latin Church has been, that not only the apostles, but also bishops, priests, and deacons, were chosen virgins, or were obliged to lead a life of continence after their election. "Apostoli vel virgines fuerunt, vel post nuptias continentes; episcopi, presbyteri, diaconi aut virgines eliguntur aut vidui aut certe post sacerdotium in æternum pudici." (Ap. pro libris contra Jovin. ad Pammach. in fin.) Besides we know that bishops, priests, and deacons were commanded by the second Council of Carthage to practise

336 A DOGMATIC WORK, ETC.

continence : " Omnibus placet ut episcopi, presbyteri, diaconi vel qui sacramenta contrectant, pudicitiæ custodes, etiam ab uxoribus se abstineant. Et præmittitur ut quod apostoli docuerunt et ipsa servarit antiquitas, nos quoque custodiamus." (Can. 2.) The same was clearly ordained by the Council of Nice, in the 13th canon, which forbade ecclesiastics to admit into their houses any female, præter matrem, sororem, amitam: hence wives were excluded. A similar law was passed in the Councils of Aquisgrana, of Magunza, and Worms. Hence the centuriators have asserted what is false, in saying that celibacy was introduced into Germany a little before the year 400, after great resistance on the part of the clergy, among whom many refused to obey.

44. Besides we find the celibacy of the clergy confirmed by Pope Siricius (ep. ad Himer. Tarracon), by Innocent I., (ep. 1, ad Victric.), by St. Leo (ep. ad Anast.), and also by the Councils of Turin, Carthage, Tours, Toledo, and by many other Councils quoted by Cardinal Gotti in his work entitled *The True Church, &c.* (tom. 2, art. 5 & 4, n. 14), in which continence was prescribed for bishops, priests, and deacons. It was only in the twelfth century that the first Council of Lateran in 1123, (Can. 21.), and the second of Lateran, (Can. 7,) in 1139, declared that sub-deaconship is an impediment which annuls any subsequent marriage. Piceninus says, that Virgilius Polidorus states (lib. 5, de rer. invent. c. 4.), that priests were accustomed to marry till the time of Pope Gregory VII; but Polidorus speaks only of the Jewish priests; St. Gregory made no change in the law of celibacy, but only endeavoured to enforce the observance of the ancient precept of the Church, as Lambert attests in his annals, where, speaking of St. Gregory, he says: " Hildebrandus decreverat ut, secundum instituta antiquorum canonum, presbyteri uxores non habeant." At first celibacy in ecclesiastics was of counsel, but was afterwards imposed as a precept.

45. Piceninus asserts that many of the ancient bishops were married, and lived with their wives; but he only mentions two, Gregory Nazianen and Demetrian. He says that the younger Gregory was begotten during the episcopacy of his father, the elder Gregory; but Cardinal Gotti (tom. 3, de vera ecclesia, &c. art. 5, sec. 3, p. 220,) proves, by sufficient documents, that St. Gregory could not have been born after his father had been raised to the episcopacy; and Piceninus does not prove, as he should have done, that the elder St. Gregory had a son after his consecration, neither does he prove this with regard to Demetrian. It is certain that if, in these times, married persons were sometimes chosen bishops, it was on the condition that they should separate from their wives after their consecration. Of this St. Jerome assures us in his book against Vigilantius: " Orientis ecclesiæ Ægypti aut sedis apostolicæ aut virgines clericos accipiunt aut continentes." It is true that, in the reign of Elizabeth, the Church with great grief saw many bishops in England, who were married and lived with their wives, after their elevation to the episcopacy. But as Saunders (lib. 3, de schism. Anglic. pp. 403, 404) writes, no man of rank was found to give his daughter in marriage to a bishop: for such nuptials were regarded as concubinage rather than marriage. Elizabeth herself, although she encouraged the marriage of her bishops, would not permit their wives to live in the court.

46. But let us come to the other objections of the adversaries: They object, first, from the words of Genesis, " Increase and multiply." (i. 28.) All then, they say, are commanded to marry. I answer, that this was not a precept, but a benediction for the propagation of the human race, and of animals, for to these also this benediction was given. And if it ever were a precept, it was only in the beginning, but afterwards it was not obligatory on any person in particular, but on the human race in general; otherwise Elias,

2 F

Jeremias, the Baptist, and so many others, who refused to marry, would have been guilty of sin, which no one will dare to say.

47. They object, secondly, that the patriarchs, who had attained such a high degree of sanctity, and the priests of the old law, entered into the married state. Were this argument a valid one, it might be said, with the impious Bernardine Ochin, that it would be as lawful for our priests as it was for the patriarchs and ancient priests, to have several wives. When Ochin attempted to propagate this error in Geneva, the people banished him as a blasphemer. God chose Abraham, Isaac, Jacob, and the other descendants of Abraham, to propagate the race from which the Divine Word was to take human flesh: " In thy seed," said the Lord to Abraham, " shall all the nations of the earth be blessed." (Gen. xxii. 18.) On the other hand, Jesus Christ chose the Apostles, not to propagate a race, but that, by their preaching, they might spread the faith through all nations: " Going...teach ye all nations." (Matt. xxviii. 19.) Hence, wives were necessary only for the patriarchs, but not for the Apostles. Likewise, God permitted Aaron and the Levites to have wives, because he wished the priesthood to be confined to the tribe of Levi. Hence, to prevent the failure of the ancient priesthood, it was necessary for the Jewish priests to enter the married state. But the priesthood of the new law is not confined to a single tribe or people: it is obtained, not by inheritance, but by a divine vocation.

48. Thirdly, they object, from the words of St. Paul to Timothy: " It behoveth a bishop to be the husband of one wife." (1 Tim. iii. 2): " Let deacons be the husband of one wife." (Ibid. v. 12.) These texts of the Apostle do not impose an obligation on bishops and deacons to be once married, but only command that no one who had several wives, or had been a bigamist, should be chosen a bishop or dea-

con. Behold the explanation of St. John Chrysostom (hom. 10, 1 ad. Tim.): when St. Paul said that a bishop should be the husband only of one wife, he did not ordain that a bishop should be married. " Non hoc veluti sanciens dicit, quasi non liceat absque uxore episcopum fieri." Otherwise many ancient bishops and saints, who had always lived in the practice of continence, either did not understand the words of the Apostle, or they committed sin by their disobedience. St. Jerome gives the same exposition of the words of St. Paul, in answer to Jovinian's objection from them. The Saint observes that the Apostle did not say: " Eligatur episcopus qui unam ducat uxorem et filios faciat; sed qui unam habuerit uxorem......unius uxoris virum; qui unam uxorem habuerit, non habeat. (lib. 1, adv. Jovinian, in c. 3). Mark the words *non habeat.* St. John Chrysostom makes the same observation (in 1 Tim. iii. et in c. 1, ad. Tit.) He says that bishops and deacons, though they had but one wife, should separate from her after their ordination.

49. Fourthly, the adversaries object, from another text of St. Paul, in which he calls the doctrine of certain persons who forbid marriage, the doctrine of devils: " Doctrinam dæmoniorum......prohibentium nubere." (1 Tim. iv. 1, 3.) But this passage is to be understood of those who wish to compel by force seculars to observe celibacy; hence, it cannot be applied to those who have spontaneously chosen the ecclesiastical state. But Piceninus asks: since the Apostle says that *marriage is honourable in all,* (Heb. xiii. 4.) how can it be dishonourable in a bishop, a priest, or a deacon? I answer, that since bishops, priests, and deacons must be entirely occupied, in thought and heart, with the things of God and of the Church, whose consecrated ministers they are, the married state would not be suited to them, on account of the distractions caused by affection for their wives, by the care of their children, and the maintenance of their

families. Hence, the Church wisely prohibits the marriage of her clergy who have voluntarily chosen the ecclesiastical state.

50. Fifthly, they object from another text in which St. Paul has said: "Have we not power to carry about a woman, or a sister, as well as the rest of the Apostles, and the brethren of the Lord, and Cephas?" (1 Cor. ix. 5.) Behold, say the adversaries, how St. Peter and the other Apostles brought about their wives with them. But the Apostle does not say *a woman, a wife, or sister*, but *a woman, a sister*. These women sisters were pious females who went about with the Apostles, to prepare their food, as may be inferred from the preceding verse in which St. Paul says: "Have we not power to eat and drink?" The words of the Apostle are thus explained by St. Chrysostom, Theodoret, Theophylactus, St. Augustine, (de op. monach. c. 4, 5.) and before them by Tertullian, who says: "Non uxores demonstrat ab apostolos circumductas......sed simpliciter mulieres qui illis, eodem instituto quo et Dominum comitantes, ministrabant." (De monogamia c. 8.) Clement of Alexandria has said the same: "Non ut uxores, sed ut sorores circumducebant mulieres." (l. 3, strom.) The same exposition is given by St. Jerome: " Perspicuum est," writes the holy Doctor, " non uxores intelligi, sed eas quæ de sua substantia ministrabant." (lib. 1, contra Jovin.) And in answer to Jovinian, who objected from this text of St. Paul, the saint says: " Et ostendit eas germanas in spiritu, non conjuges." (Ibid.) In support of this objection Piceninus adduces the canon *Omnino* (dist. 31.) in which Leo IX. has said: " Non licere episcopo, presbytero, diacono, subdiacono propriam uxorem causa religionis abjicere a cura sua." But these words are in no way favourable to the cause of Piceninus, for the Pontiff immediately adds: " Scilicet ut ei victum et vestitum largiatur, non ut cum illa, ex more, carnaliter jaceat." In conclusion the Pontiff,

speaking of the text of St. Paul, says: " Vide inspiciens quia non dixit; Numquid non habemus potestatem sororem mulierem amplectendi sed circumducendi? scilicet ut de mercede prædicationis sustentarentur ab eis, nec tamen foret deinceps inter eos carnale conjugium.

51. Sixthly, they object that the Council of Nice in the third canon, declared that no one should separate from his wife; that it gave permission to Pannutius to marry, and forbade only the abuse of admitting strange women: "Nolite et episcopo, presbytero, diacono subintroductam habere mulierem." But Cardinal Gotti says (§ 4, p. 222, n. 10.) that Socrates and Sozomen state that the Fathers of Nice permitted bishops, priests, and deacons, (as is allowed in the Greek Church,) to retain the wife to whom they had been married before ordination; but not, as the adversaries infer from the example of Pannutius, to contract marriage after they had received the sacrament of order. Cardinal Baronius doubts the truth of the story of Pannutius; and justly, for in the abovementioned canon we find nothing in favour of the marriage of bishops. And in the same Council of Nice ecclesiastics were forbidden to keep in their houses, any woman except their mother, or sister, or aunt: "Interdixit per omnia magna synodus non episcopo, non presbytero, non diacono, nec alicui omnino qui in clero est licere subintroductam habere mulierem, nisi forte aut matrem aut sororem aut amitam vel eas tantum personas quæ suspicionem effugiunt."

ON THE VOW OF CHASTITY MADE BY ECCLESIASTICS.

52. Luther condemns this vow as rash, because, he says, men are not able to observe it: thus he censures the entire Church which, in all ages, if it has not always commanded, has at least approved of continence in her ministers, and has ex-

horted them to the practice of it. The greatest saints that
have adorned the Church were those who have observed
in the ecclesiastical state or in the cloister, the vow of
chastity which they had voluntarily made. Piceninus says
that nature calls men to matrimony: he is right, if he means
carnal and animal nature, but not if he speaks of rational
and prudent nature. It would certainly be rash in any one
to presume to make a vow of chastity, with the hope of
observing it by his own strength: but such a vow is not
rash in those who place their trust in God and say with the
Apostle: "I can do all things in him who strengtheneth
me." (Phil. iv. 13.)

53. Our ecclesiastics and religious make a vow of chastity,
but do not presume on their own strength for its observance.
On the contrary, with humility and confidence they constantly implore God, who in his goodness has called them
to a state of continence, to give them aid to persevere in the
practice of chastity; and God does not fail to strengthen
them and to be faithful to them. The Council condemns (Sess.
24, can. 9.) all who say: " posse omnes contrahere matrimonium qui non sentiunt se castitatis, etiamsi eam voverint,
habere donum......cum Deus id recte petentibus non deneget, nec patiatur nos, supra id quod possumus, tentari."
Since then the Lord is ready to give perseverance to all who
ask it, as they ought, if any ecclesiastic violates the vow he
has made, the fault is altogether his own. The innovators
speak of the observance of this vow as an impossibility, and
say that it is contrary to the order of heaven. Have then all
the great saints whom we venerate on the altar, and who have
made such a vow, have they, I ask, transgressed the order
of heaven? But if not to marry be contrary to the order
of heaven, how could St. Paul say that celibacy is better
than matrimony? " Therefore both he that giveth his
virgin in marriage, doth well: and he that giveth her not,
doth better." (1 Cor. vii. 38.) How could he counsel widows

not to marry again, and at the same time say that he spoke with the spirit of God? "But more blessed shall she be, if she so remain, according to my counsel, and I think that I also have the spirit of God?" (Ibid. v. 40.) It is not temerity to make a vow of chastity, trusting in God, and following the counsel of the Apostle: but it is temerity and great temerity to censure those who practise a counsel which has been praised not only by St. Paul, but also by the Saviour himself, when he said: "And there are eunuchs who have made themselves eunuchs for the kingdom of heaven." (Mat. xix. 12.)

54. But how can the Church forbid matrimony? The Church does not prohibit it to those who are free; with the Apostle, she says: "Let her marry to whom she will; only in the Lord." (1 Cor. vii. 39.) But those who, when free, have voluntarily imposed on themselves the obligation of chastity, the Church justly commands to fulfil their obligation, and justly chastises them if they violate it. No one is bound to make vows: but if a person promise anything to God by vow, the Lord requires the fulfilment of his promise. "If thou hast vowed anything to God, defer not to pay it: for an unfaithful and foolish promise displeaseth him; but whatsoever thou hast vowed, pay it." (Eccl. v. 3.)

SECTION III.—ANCIENT PRACTICES REGARD-ING THE SACRAMENT OF ORDER.

55. In the first ages of the Church there were only bishops, priests, and deacons. In a Council held in Rome under Pope Slyvester, we find mention made of subdeacons, acolytes, exorcists, readers, door keepers, and guardians of the martyrs. In Africa, instead of the guardians, there was an order of psalmists or chanters. The number of these orders was greater or less according to the times and places.

The Greeks, as we read in St. Denis, (c. 5.) have only the orders of bishop, priest, deacon, subdeacon, and reader. However, it may be justly said that all the minor orders are of divine institution: for in giving to the Apostles power to establish the Church, Christ at the same time empowered them to appoint the ministers that appeared necessary for the celebration and decorum of the sacred mysteries. Before the twelfth century, subdeaconship was not a holy order: for in the Council of Beneventum held in 1091, it was declared that only priesthood and deaconship were holy orders, and Peter Cantor (l. de verb. mir.) who died in 1197 has written that sub-deaconship had been recently declared to be a holy order. The Greeks impose hands in giving the order of sub-deaconship and readership. Luther and Calvin admit no distinction between ecclesiastics and laymen except that which arises from the will of their superiors.

56. In ancient times, only as many were ordained as were necessary for the service of the churches, or of the bishops: hence, as soon as a person was ordained, he was immediately sent to his charge; vague ordinations were forbidden by the Council of Chalcedon. This discipline lasted till the eleventh century. And because it became relaxed, the Council of Trent (Sess. 23, de ref. cap. 16.) commanded that no one should be ordained without a benefice, and that persons having a patrimony should be ordained only in case of necessity, or utility to the church. Formerly it was necessary for taking priesthood that according to the Apostolical Constitutions, (l. 2, c. 1,) a person should be thirty years of age for priesthood, twenty-five for deaconship, and fifty for episcopal ordination: but afterwards the age for bishops was reduced to thirty years.

57. With regard to the interstices, Pope Zosimus, as Father Martene relates, (lib. 1, c. 8, art. 3.) ordained that if any one had attended to the service of the church from his

infancy, he should remain in the order of reader at least till his twentieth year: that they who, after having grown up had entered into the service of the church, should continue for five years as readers or exorcists, that they should then serve four years as acolytes or sub-deacons, that then they might receive the order of deaconship in which they should remain five years more, and that after that period they might ascend to the priesthood, if the bishop deemed them fit for it. However, even in ancient times, the time of preparation for Order was, as Pope Gelasius says, (ep. 9, c. 1,) sometimes abridged on account of the necessity of the church, and particularly when a person entered among the clergy from the monastic state. Formerly, persons of great merit, who had not been before in the order of deacon, were without much difficulty promoted to the priesthood, because the superior were supposed to contain the inferior orders in an eminent degree: it was thus that St. Cyprian and St. Augustine were ordained priests. With regard to the time of ordination, Pope Gelasius has written (ep. 9. c. 11,) that priests and deacons could be ordained only on the fast days of the fourth, seventh, and tenth month; also in the beginning of Lent, and on Saturday evening in the middle week. The same was declared in the Council of Rome, under Pope Zachary.

58. The delivery of the instruments, with the formula, *Accipe potestatem, &c.*, has not, according to Father Morino, (de ordin. exerc. 6, c. 2,) been in use for more than about the space of five hundred years. The same author says, (ex. 7, c. 2,) that the imposition of hands after the communion at mass, accompanied with the formula, *Accipe Spiritum Sanctum, &c.*, is more recent than the delivery of the instruments. Morino also states, (ex. 3, c. 1,) that before the ninth century, there is no mention made in any ritual of the instruments used in the ordination of priests and deacons, but only of the imposition of hands.

TWENTY-FOURTH SESSION.

ON THE SACRAMENT OF MATRIMONY.

1. Before coming to the canons passed regarding this sacrament, the Council resolved to state briefly the doctrine on it in the following manner: the first father of men, by the instinct of the Holy Ghost, declared the perpetual and indissoluble bond of marriage, when he said: " This is now bone of my bones, and flesh of my flesh......Wherefore a man shall leave father and mother, and shall cleave to his wife: and they shall be two in one flesh." (Gen. ii., 23, 24.) In like manner, our Saviour afterwards openly taught that, in marriage two persons are united and become one flesh: for, quoting the last words as pronounced by God himself, he said: " Therefore, now, they are not two, but one flesh." (Matt. xix. Mark x.) And immediately after, he confirmed, in the following words, the indissolubility of the bond which Adam had declared: " What, therefore, God hath joined together, let no man put asunder." (Matt. xix. 6.)

2. Christ himself, by whom the sacraments were instituted, has merited by his passion, the grace which sanctifies spouses, and confirms the indissoluble union between them. This the Apostle insinuated in the following words: " Husbands love your wives, as Christ also loved the Church, and delivered himself up for it......This is a great sacrament: but I speak in Christ, and in the Church." (Eph. v. 25, 32.)

3. Since, in the evangelical law, matrimony is superior to the ancient marriages, in grace through Jesus Christ, the holy Fathers, the Councils and the tradition of the whole Church have always taught that it should be reckoned among the sacraments of the new law. This is contrary

to the doctrine of the innovators, who have not only erred regarding this sacrament, but according to their custom have, under the pretext of the Gospel, introduced the liberty of the flesh, to the great detriment of the faithful, and have asserted many things opposed to the sentiments of the Catholic Church, and to the approved custom of the Apostles. Hence, the Council wishing to crush their errors, has thought proper to condemn them with the following anathemas:

4. Canon 1. "Si quis dixerit Matrimonium non esse verum et proprie unum ex septem legis evangelicæ sacramentis a Christo Domino institutum, sed ab hominibus in Ecclesia inventum, neque gratiam conferre, anathema sit."

5. The ancient heretics condemned marriage as bad and censurable: but from the beginning of the world, God declared it to be good and laudable: "And the Lord God said: It is not good for man to be alone: let us make a help like unto himself." (Gen. ii. 28.) This the Apostle confirmed in the epistle to the Corinthians: "Therefore both he that giveth his virgin in marriage, doth well." (1. Cor. vii. 38.) Luther and Calvin, along with their followers admit that matrimony has been instituted by God, but they deny that it is a sacrament. Lauonius, on the other hand, in his treatise (de regia in matr. potest. par, 1. a. 2. c. 11,) goes to another extreme, by labouring to prove that even before the coming of the Redeemer, marriage was a sacrament in the law of nature. Lauonius errs: for although the ancients called marriage a sacrament, they did not mean to call it a sacrament in the strict sense, but in as much as it signifies of itself something spiritual or conducive to the spiritual good of married persons. There is no doubt but the indissolubility of marriage, in as much as it is a natural contract, takes its origin from the law of nature: since by marriage the human race is better preserved, and the education of children is provided for. Hence fornication is repugnant

to nature itself: all that belongs to nature is referred to God, the author of nature and of marriage. " A man," said Adam, " shall leave father and mother and shall cleav e to h s wife; and they shall be two in one flesh." (Gen. ii. 24.)   Hence the Council of Trent has said: " Quibus verbis perpetuum et indissolubilem esse matrimonii nexum primus parens, divini spiritus instinctu, pronuntiavit." (Sess. 24.)   Hence Christ reproved the Pharisees when they asked if it were lawful for a man to leave his wife: " Have ye not read...For this cause shall a man leave father and mother and shall cleave to his wife.......What therefore God hath joined together, let no man put asunder." (Mat. xix. 6.)   But all this does not show, as Lauonius supposes, that matrimony was a sacrament before the promulgation of the Gospel.

6. On the other hand, the innovators, as has been already said, err in denying that matrimony is a sacrament. To prove that marriage is a sacrament it is enough to show that it has all the requisites for a sacrament: that is, first, that it is a sensible sign of something sacred: secondly, that it has been instituted by Christ: thirdly, that a promise of grace has been annexed to it.   First, that in matrimony there is a sensible sign which is the mutual expressed consent of the parties, and that it is a symbol of something sacred, we learn from the words of St. Paul: " This is a great sacrament, but I speak in Christ and in the Church." (Eph. v. 32.)   Luther and Calvin object that in the Greek, the word sacrament only signifies something mysterious or hidden.   But Bellarmine justly answers (de matr. c. 1. Controv. 1.) that in the passage which has been quoted, matrimony is proved to be a sacrament, not only from the word sacrament, but from the entire context, from which it appears that marriage is a sign, not only of a natural contract, but also of something sacred: for the Apostle immediately adds: " but I speak in Christ and in the Church." These words plainly show that matrimony is not a mere

hidden mystery, but a real symbol of something sacred. Bellarmine justly remarks, that after the words: " For this cause shall a man leave his father and mother, and shall cleave to his wife, and they shall be two in one flesh," the Apostle immediately adds, " This is a great sacrament: but I speak in Christ and in the Church." (Eph. v. 31, 32.) The pronoun *this*, necessarily refers to the antecedent words, " For this cause shall a man leave his father and mother, &c." St. Paul says that it *is a great sacrament* that a man should leave his father and mother, and should cleave to his wife; and why is it great? Because this sacrament represents the union of Christ with his Church. But, says Erasmus, what great mystery is there in saying that a man is joined to a woman? In answer, Bellarmine says, that the mystery does not consist in the carnal union between married persons, but in the indissolubility of this union, on account of its representing the perpetual union of Christ with his Church.

7. All this has been taught by the Holy Fathers. In the Commentary attributed to St. Ambrose, we read: " Mysterii sacramentum grande, in unitate viri, ac fœminæ esse significat. On the above-mentioned words of St. Paul, St. Jerome writes: " Idipsum per allegoriam in Christo interpretatur et in Ecclesia, ut Adam Christum et Eva præ figuraret Ecclesiam." There the Holy Doctor quotes the words of St. Gregory Nazianzen. " Scio quia locus iste ineffabilibus plenus sit sacramentis et divinum cor quærat interpretis; ego autem pro pusillitate sensus mei in Christo interim illud, et in Ecclesia intelligendum puto." " Proinde" adds Bellarmine, "magnum mysterium de quo Paulus loquitur, in ipso conjugio ponit, quatenus Christi et Ecclesiæ conjunctionem repræsentat." St. John Chrysostom also says, that in matrimony there is a great mystery. (hom. 20, in ep. ad Eph.) Pope Lucius the Third also, who lived before the year 400, said, that the opinion of those who deny that matrimony is a sacrament, is contrary to the

2 G

doctrine of the Church. The same is taught by St. Justin, (dial, cum Tryphone,) by Clement of Alexandria, (lib. 3 Strom.) by St. Ambrose, (lib. 1, Abrah. c. 7,) and by St. Augustine, who says: " Sacramentum nuptiarum commendatur fidelibus conjugatis; unde dicit Apostolus: Viri, diligite uxores vestris (lib. 1, de nupt. et concup., c. 10). In another place the Saint writes: "In Ecclesia nuptiarum non solum vinculum, sed etiam sacramentum commendatur." (De fid. et op. c. 7.)

8. Kemnitius objects, that before St. Augustine none of the Fathers called matrimony a sacrament. But he errs, for St. Leo I., who lived 150 years before St. Augustine, called marriage a sacrament; and St. Chrysostom, who lived before St. Augustine, says: " Mysterium magnum esse in conjugio insolubili viri et fœminæ." (Hom. 20 in ep. ad Eph.) St. Ambrose, who was anterior to St. Augustine and St. Chrysostom, writes: " Qui sic egerit, peccat in Deum, cujus legem violat et gratiam solvit; et ideo qui in Deum peccat, sacramenti cœlestis amittit consortium." (in c. 5, ad Eph. l. 1, de Abr. c. 7.) Pope Siricius has said the same. (ep. c. 4). He calls it a sacrilege to contract marriage during the life of a former husband or wife; such is also the doctrine of Innocent I. (ep. 9, ad Prob.) and of St. Cyril (lib. 2 in Jo. c. 22). Hence matrimony has been declared to be a sacrament by the Council of Constance (sess. 15), by the Council of Florence, in the decree of Eugene IV. to the Armenians, and by the Council of Trent, in these words: " Merito inter novæ legis sacramenta annumerandum, SS. Patres nostri, concilia et universalis Ecclesiæ traditio semper docuerunt." (Sess. 24, sub initio.) The strongest proof that matrimony is a sacrament, is taken from the consent and authority of the universal Church, of the Greek as well as of the Latin Church.

9. Thus there can be no doubt but that, in matrimony, there is, first, a sensible sign of something sacred; secondly, it cannot be doubted that matrimony was instituted by Christ, and was raised to the dignity of a sacrament, either

when the Saviour assisted and blessed the marriage of Cana,
or when he restored matrimony to its original state, saying: " For this cause shall a man leave father and mother,
and shall cleave to his wife, and they shall be two in one
flesh......What therefore God hath joined together, let no
man put asunder." (Matt. xix. 5, 6.)

10. Thirdly, there can be no doubt but that, in matrimony, there is a promise of grace. This may be inferred
from the words of the Apostle: " She shall be saved through
childbearing, if she continue in faith and sanctification, with
sobriety." (1 Tim. ii. 15.) All these are gifts received with
the grace of the sacrament; besides the promise of grace
follows from the declaration of our Lord that marriage is
indissoluble: " I say to you that whosoever shall put away
his wife, except for fornication, and shall marry another,
committeth adultery." (Mat. xix. 9.) We cannot believe
that our Lord had made marriage indissoluble without annexing grace to it: since, without the divine aid, men
with their own natural strength could not observe such a
perpetual obligation. Besides, without grace, matrimony
would not be a sufficient remedy for concupiscence; for, in the
married state, concupiscence is excited rather than extin-
guished. Hence the Council of Trent (sess. 24, sub initio) says, that by his Passion, Christ, who is the author of
the sacraments, has merited for us the grace " quæ naturalem illum amorem perficeret, et indissolubilem unitatem
confirmaret," to which the Apostle exhorts in these words:
" Husbands love your wives, as Christ also loved the
Church." (Eph. v. 25.) The Council then adds: " Cum
igitur matrimonium in lege evangelica veteribus connubiis
per Christum gratia præstet; merito inter novæ legis sacramenta annumerandum, &c."

11. In the second canon, the Council says: " Si quis
dixerit licere christianis plures simul habere uxores et hoc
nulla lege divina prohibitum esse, anathema sit." There

are two kinds of polygamy: successive and simultaneous. Successive polygamy is lawful, as the Apostle has declared: " But I say to the unmarried and to the widows: it is good for them if they so continue, even as I. But if they do not contain themselves, let them marry. For it is better to marry than to be burnt." (1. Cor. vii. 8, 9.) Here we see that St. Paul counsels, but does not command the unmarried not to enter into the married state. Simultaneous polygamy, which consists in having two wives or two husbands at the same time, is altogether forbidden in the evangelical law, as being contrary to the law of nature. In his exposition of the 16th chapter of Genesis, Luther says, and his doctrine is adopted by the Anabaptists, that, after the example of the patriarchs, the Church cannot condemn a multiplicity of wives. But Christ has said: " And I say to you that whosoever shall put away his wife, except it be for fornication, and shall marry another, committeth adultery." (Mat. xix. 9.) And, in the same chapter, when the Pharisees asked: " Is it lawful for a man to put away his wife for every cause?" (Mat. xix. 3.) the Redeemer answered: " Have ye not read that he who made man from the beginning, made them male and female? And he said: For this cause shall a man leave father and mother, and shall cleave to his wife. Therefore, now they are not two, but one flesh. What therefore God hath joined together, let no man put asunder." (Ibid.) If a man had several wives, there would not be one flesh, as there ought to be, according to the unanimous interpretation of the Holy Fathers. (See Bellarmine, cap. 10, de Matrim.) It is not denied that it was lawful (as we find in Deutoronomy xxi. 15.) for the patriarchs and the other Jews to have two wives. But as St. Augustin says, (l. 3, de Doct. Christ. c. 17,) this was permitted by God, on account of the circumstances of the times. Hence we find that God himself told Abraham to attend to the words of Sara his wife: " Audi vocem ejus." (Gen. xxi. 12.) And Sara persuaded him to take for his wife even his own servant Agar. But it may be asked; if simultaneous polygamy is contrary to the law of nature, how could it be permitted to the patriarchs? I answer, that polygamy is opposed to the secondary ends of matrimony, but not to the primary end, which is, to beget children. In the time of the Jews, it was congruous, as I have said, on the authority of St. Augustine, that special regard should be had to this end.

12. It is not true that the patriarchs had but one wife, and that the others were concubines, for the propagation of children; for Tournely justly says (de Matr. qu. 5, p. 528, in fin.) that had that been the case, the holy patriarchs would have been guilty of a violation of the marriage-bed. They had wives of the first and of the second order; there was only one wife of the first order; she was espoused in a solemn manner, and her children succeeded to the paternal inheritance. The wives of the second order were married privately; their children had no share in the inheritance, but only received certain gifts from the father. Thus of Abraham we read: " And Abraham gave all his possessions to Isaac: and to the children of the concubines he gave gifts." (Gen. xxv. 5, 6.) These second wives were sometimes called concubines, and sometimes wives, as we read of Agar and Cetura, the second wives of Abraham, and of Bala and Zelpha the second wives of Jacob. And the Lord said to David: " I gave thee...thy master's wives into thy bosom." (2 Kings xii. 8.) But as has been already said, in the evangelical law it is forbidden to have two wives. But, notwithstanding this prohibition, Luther, who was afterwards joined by Melancton, had the temerity to give a solemn license, in a formal rescript, (quoted by Bossuet in his Variations) to the Landgrave Philip, to marry a second wife, during the lifetime of his first wife. This was certainly contrary to the divine positive law, and in our opinion, to the natural law; although Juenin thinks

2 G 2

the latter doubtful. (Tom. 7, de Matr. p. 459, in fin. v. Quæres.)

13. In the third canon, the Council says: " Si quis dixerit eos tantum consanguitatis et affinitatis gradus qui Levitico exprimuntur posse impedire Matrimonium contrahendum et dirimere contractum; nec posse Ecclesiam in nonnullis eorum dispensare aut constituere, ut plures impediat et dirimat, anathema sit."

14. And in the fourth canon the Council has declared: " Si quis dixerit Ecclesiam non potuisse constituere impedimenta Matrimoninm dirimentia, vel in iis constituendis errasse, anathema sit."

15. Against these two canons Peter Soave objects that the marriage contract was a real sacrament before the promulgation of the Gospel, and the establishment of our Church, and that therefore as the Church cannot change the sacrament, so neither can it alter the contract.

16. In answer to this objection I say that it is not true that before the promulgation of the Gospel, matrimony was a sacrament: Christ has instituted all the sacraments, and among them the sacrament of matrimony. It is certain that in matrimony the contract is of its own nature distinct from the sacrament: hence, the former could absolutely exist without the latter.   But this the Church does not permit, and has never permitted. It is true that no ecclesiastical power can change the sacrament: but it can change the contract, by annexing conditions, or limitations, and thus it can prevent the contract from being a sacrament, as it would be if these conditions were not annexed. And in such cases, the Church does not change the matter of the consent, but renders the spouses incapable of contracting marriage. Thus the Church can make laws, and determine what is the legitimate contract for matrimony. Hence, it follows that as it can establish impediments which render marriage unlawful and even null, not, as the Council says, *de jure divino,* but only *de jure humano,* so

in these impediments it can also dispense. (See Juenin, de Matrim. p. 469, in princ. &c., p. 471, vers. Quæres.)

17. In the fifth canon the Council has declared: " Si quis dixerit propter hæresim aut molestam cohabitationem aut affectatam absentiam a conjuge dissolvi posse Matrimonium, anathema sit."

18. The bond of matrimony is by the law of nature indissoluble, as well between infidels, as between Christians, as God declared to Adam in the following words: " A man shall leave father and mother, and shall cleave to his wife, and they shall be two in one flesh." (Gen. ii. 24.) As has been already said, a man who has two wives, carnem non facit unam sed dividit. The only difference between the marriage of infidels and that of Christians is, that the former may be dissolved when one of the parties is converted, and the other refuses to remain, or will not remain *without blaspheming the name of God*, or endeavours to bring the converted party into sin. In these three cases (which are expressly mentioned in the chapter *Quanto* 7, *de divort.*) the person converted to the faith can contract marriage with a Christian: this may be inferred from the words of the Apostle: " And if any woman have a husband that believeth not, and he consent to dwell with her, let her not put away her husband......But if the unbeliever depart, let him depart. For a brother or sister is not under servitude in such *cases*." (1 Cor. vii. 13, 15.) But the marriage is not dissolved by the conversion of both parties, as was declared by Innocent III. in the following words: " Per baptismum non solvuntur conjugia, sed dimittuntur crimina" (Cap. Gaudemus 8, eodem tit. de divort.) The marriage of christians is never dissolved, even though one of them should embrace heresy or infidelity, as appears from the fifth canon of the Council: for besides the natural law which God promulgated to Adam, there is a positive divine law announced by Christ, in the words: " What therefore

God hath joined together, let not man put asunder;" (Mark
x. 9.) and afterwards by St. Paul in the first epistle to
the Corinthians. (vii. 39.) The marriage of a Catholic with
a heretic is valid, but is at present unlawful, unless the pope
for the public good grants a dispensation as he has sometimes done. (See Tournely de matr. p. 500.) The question of the dissolubility of the *Matrimonium ratum et
non consummatum* shall be discussed in treating of the
next canon.

19. The Jews were permitted by a divine dispensation
to give a bill of divorce, which implied a dissolution of the
marriage bond, and differs from simple divorce, which implies only a separation of the parties. This we know from
Deuteronomy, (xxiv. 1.) where we find that by giving her
a bill of divorce, a person could send away his first wife, and
take another. " If a man take a wife, and have her, and she
find not favour in his eyes for some uncleanness: he shall
write a bill or divorce, and shall give it in her hand, and
send her out of his house." (xxiv. 1.) The woman who
was thus dismissed could also marry another husband. (See
Tournely de Matrim. compend. p. 436, Prob. 2.) Besides,
Juenin says (de Matrim. art. 2, concl. 1, p. 461.) that the
Jews, though permitted to take another wife, would be guilty
of sin *si ductas uxores dimitterent a domo et thoro.*
In the new law Christ abolished this bill of divorce. The
Pharisees asked two questions of our Lord: first, whether a
man could separate from his wife, and secondly, whether he
could marry another woman. In answer to the first question Jesus Christ said that it was lawful for a man to separate
from his wife if she were guilty of fornication: in answer
to the second, he said that it is never lawful to take another
wife during the lifetime of the first wife. " And I say to
you that whoever shall put away his wife, except it be for
fornication, and shall marry another committeth adultery."
(Mat. xix. 9.) It is necessary to remark that the words:

" *except it be for fornication,*" should be joined to the
preceding member, " *whosoever shall put away his wife,*"
that is he is guilty of sin if he separate from his wife except it be for fornication; but should not be connected with
the subsequent member, " *and shall marry another,*"
that is, it is not lawful on account of fornication to take
another wife: for if he take another, he *committeth adultery.* But the Pharisees said: " Why then did Moyses
command to give a bill of divorce, and to put away?"
The Saviour answered: " Because Moses by reason of the
hardness of your heart permitted you to put away your
wives: but from the beginning it was not so." (Mat. xix. 7,
8.) Hence, in the new law which is more perfect than the
old, Jesus Christ has forbidden the bill of divorce, and has
restored matrimony to its original state.

20. Canon 6: " Si quis dixerit Matrimonium ratum, non
consummatum, per solemnem religionis professionem alterius
conjugum non dirimi, anathema sit." A marriage *merely*
contracted between two infidels, may be dissolved at their
discretion: but such a marriage between Christians, because
Baptism confirms and renders it indissoluble, can be dissolved only when one of the parties makes a religious profession: the marriage is then rendered null. But how can
it be dissolved since the marriages of Christians are indissoluble? I answer, that it is dissolved not by the
human power, but by the ordination of God, who, in
that case, grants a dispensation on account of the perfection of the religious state. However, the Church allows
the parties two months to deliberate whether they will enter
the religious state: and in these two months they are not
obliged to use marriage. With regard to the power of the
Pope to dissolve by dispensation a marriage which has not
been consummated, some deny, but several grave authors,
such as Bellarmine, Cajetan, Navarre, Sanchez, the Salamanca theologians and others, hold that he has that power;

they say that, as vicar of Christ, he can, for reasons of very great moment, dispense in those things which, although they appertain to the divine law, have nevertheless had their origin in the will of man. For, as Father Pickler wisely says, although the marriage contract gives a right to the matrimonial acts, the marriage consists in the union of the wills, and in the perpetual bond of the minds, and not in the use of matrimony, which is only a certain consequence of the contract. " Matrimonium consistit in consensu mutuo, dato jure ad actus conjugales; unde copula actualis est tantum aliquid consequens et usus dati juris." This is confirmed by St. Thomas: " Conjunctio illa," says the holy Doctor, " vinculum est quo conjuges ligantur formaliter, non effective." (Sup. q. 44, a. 1, ad. 4.) Hence, the Blessed Virgin was always a virgin, and was truly the spouse of St. Joseph: " Joseph, son of David, fear not to take unto thee Mary thy wife." (Mat. i. 20.) Hence, on these words St. Augustine has written: Conjux vocatur ex prima fide desponsationis, quam concubitu nec cognoverat nec fuerat cogniturus." (l. 5. c. 16, n. 62 et l. 1. de nupt., c. 11.) However, Juenin says, (tom. 7, de matr. p. 458 qu. 3,) that the marriage contract ought to have, at least, for its object the procreation of children: since each of the contracting parties gives a right to the other over his or her body, and thus consents that the other should use it for the purpose of procreation. He says that most Holy Mary contracted marriage with St. Joseph, inasmuch as she knew, by a divine revelation, that the saint would never use this right: hence, St. Thomas thinks that the Blessed Virgin made the vow of chastity, not before, but after her marriage.

21. But let us return to the sixth canon, which has been already quoted. Peter Soave asssserts, that many were surprised at finding that the Council defined as an article of faith, that a marriage which has been *merely* contracted *(ratum et non consummatum)* is dissolved by a solemn

profession, which, he says, is, according to Boniface VIII., only of ecclesiastical institution. But, in answer to this objection, St. Thomas and other very grave theologians say, that the rites of the solemn profession are of ecclesiastical origin: but that the object of the vow is of divine institution, because it immutably consecrates a man to God, and therefore the solemn vow dissolves the bond of marriage which has been *merely* contracted (ratum et non consummatum). Cardinal Bellarmine justly distinguishes between a simple vow of chastity and the solemn vow which dissolves the *matrimonium ratum.* A simple promise imposes a strict obligation, but does not transfer the dominion of the thing promised to the person to whom the promise was made: thus, if a person promises anything to a friend, and afterwards gives it to another, he is guilty of sin, but the dominion of the thing belongs to the person to whom it has been given. Thus is refuted the error of Luther, who said, that a marriage would be null if one of the parties had been before betrothed to another person: for by espousals (sponsalia) the right over a person's body is promised, but not transferred. In the solemn vow the religious changes his state, consecrating himself to God and to the Church, which can oblige him, even by judicial process, to observe his vow: this does not happen in the simple vow. This doctrine has been taught by Alexander III. in the third Council of Lateran: " Post consensum illum legitimum de præsenti datum, licitum est alteri monasterium eligere...... dummodo inter eos carnis commixtio non intervenerit: et alteri, si servare noluerit continentiam, licitum esse videtur ut ad secunda vota transire possit." (In append. p. 5, c. 1.) The same doctrine has been taught by Innocent III. (cap. Ex. parte, de convers. conjug.), by Gregory the Great (causa 26, q. 2, can. Decreta), and more diffusely by Boniface VIII. in the chapter (un. de voto, in sexto). Although in that chapter he says: " Quod voti solemnitas ex sola constitutione Ecclesia est inventa," the pontiff means, as has been already said, after St. Thomas and others, that the Church has instituted the rites, but not the essence and effect of the solemn vow which immutably consecrates a person to God: this doctrine is confirmed by the example of many saints. See Tournely, (p. 545, *vers.* 2, *Probatur.*) who asks (p. 546, Quæres), *by what law* does the solemn vow annul a marriage which has been *merely* contracted? He answers, that the religious profession does not dissolve the marriage by the natural law, nor solely by the ecclesisatical law, for no time can be assigned in which the Church has made such a law: but by a divine positive law in favour of the religious profession: the existence of this law is established by tradition, according to the rule of St. Augustine, which has been generally received: " Quod universa tenet Ecclesia, nec conciliis institutum, sed semper retentum est, nonnisi auctoritate apostolica traditum rectissime creditur." (l. 4, de Bapt. c. 26.)

22. Canon 7: " Si quis dixerit Ecclesiam errare cum docuit et docet, juxta evangelicam et apostolicam doctrinam, propter adulterium alterius conjugum matrimonii vinculum non posse dissolvi et utrumque, vel etiam innocentem qui causam adulterio non dedit, non posse, altero conjuge vivente aliud matrimonium contrahere: mœchariquæ eum qui, dimissa adultera, aliam duxerit; et eam quæ dimisso adultero alii nupserit, anathema sit."

23. Some have erroneously asserted that the commission of the crime of adultery by one of the spouses, dissolves the marriage bond: this they infer from the words of Jesus Christ: " Whosoever shall put away his wife, except it be for fornication, and shall marry another, committeth adultery." (Mat. xix. 9.) Launoius (tr. de reg. in matr. pot., p. 452,) rashly endeavours to prove that until the Council of Trent, the authors had defended that, on account of the words, *except it be for fornication,* the marriage bond

was dissolved by adultery. But Tournely (de matr. p. 541) says that in this as well as in many of his propositions, Launoius deserves castigation and censure: " profecto casti-gandus et censura notandus est." In the Gospel of St. Mark we read: " Whosoever shall put away his wife and marry another, committeth adultery," (x. 11.); and in St. Luke: " Every one that putteth away his wife, and marrieth another, committeth adultery." (xvi. 18). These propo-sitions are, as St. Augustine says, (lib. 1, de adult., c. 9,) general, and admit no exception. They clearly show that the words in St. Matthew, *except it be for fornication*, should, as has been already said, be referred to the pre-ceding member, *whosoever shall put away his wife*, and not to the following member, *and shall marry another*: that is, that the husband for the crime of adul-tery committed by his wife, can separate from her, but cannot dissolve the marriage bond, nor take another wife. Thus we find also in the first epistle of St. Paul to the Corinthians: " But to them that are married, not I, but the Lord commandeth, that the wife depart not from her husband." (vii. 10.) And in the thirty-ninth verse, he says: " A woman is bound by the law as long as her husband liveth." Hence, St. Augustine has written: Nullius viri posterioris mulier esse incipit, nisi prioris esse desierit." (L. 2 de adult., c. 5.) And in the abovementioned 7th cannon, the Council of Trent condemns all who assert that the marriage bond can be dissolved on account of adultery: "propter adulterium vinculum posse dissolvi." Launoius asserts that this canon regards discipline, and not faith. But Tournely (p. 541,) says in answer that in the canon the Council declares that the church " docuit et docet, juxta evangelicam et apostolicam doctrinam propter adulterium, vinculum non posse dissolvi." Error is opposed to faith, and abuse to discipline; since then the Council

H

says that the Church does not err in teaching this doctrine, it is clear that the doctrine belongs to faith.

24. Canon 8: " Si 'quis dixerit Ecclesiam errare cum ob multas causas separationem inter conjuges quoad thorum seu quoad habitationem ad certum incertumve tempus fieri posse decernit, anathema sit."

25. There are four just causes, for which a husband may separate from his wife; or a wife from her husband. The first is apostacy from the faith, according to the words of the Apostle: " A man that is a heretic, after the first and second admonition, avoid." (Tit. iii. 1 0.) The second is, if the husband or wife nolet cohabitare sine injuria creatoris, vel pervertendo ad peccatum, as we find in the chapter *Quanto divort.* The third is adultery, committed by one of the spouses, as appears from the Gospel of St. Matthew: " Whosoever shall put away his wife, except it be for fornication...committeth adultery." (xix. 9.)   The fourth is, the ferocious disposition of one of the parties, accompanied with danger to the life of the other.   Kemnitius condemns the separation of husband and wife, for any cause, however just. But for this there are no grounds; for the Scripture, the Holy Fathers, and all theologians are opposed to him.

26. Canon 9: " Si quis dixerit clericos in sacris ordinibus constitutos, vel regulares castitatem solemniter professos, posse matrimonium contrahere, contractumque validum esse, non obstante lege ecclesiastica vel voto; et oppositum nihil aliud esse quam damnare matrimonium, posseque omnes contrahere matrimonium qui non sentiunt se castitatis, etiamsi voverint, habere donum, anathema sit; cum Deus id recte petentibus non deneget, nec patiatur nos supra id quod possumus tentari."

27. Soave censures the last words: " Cum Deus id recte petentibus non deneget."   He rashly asserts that we

read in the Gospel that God does not grant to all the gift of chastity, and that St. Paul exhorts those who have not obtained it to enter the married state, and not to ask it, although to pray for it would have been the most easy remedy, if it could be infallibly obtained by asking it with the requisite dispositions. What a collection of falsehoods in a few words! In the first place, the Council does not speak of seculars, who, when they do not feel themselves called to celibacy, have been justly exhorted by St. Paul to enter the married state, in order to escape the danger of damnation: "But," he says, " if they do not contain themselves, let them marry, for it is better to marry than to be burnt." (1 Cor. vii. 9.) The Council speaks of persons in holy orders, or of religious who have voluntarily obliged themselves to practise continence. Secondly, the Fathers do not say, in this canon, that the gift of chastity is actually given to any one, by an efficacious grace which is certainly not given to all; but in opposition to the doctrine of Luther, who excused those who, because they did not feel that they had the gift of chastity, violated the vow they had made, they teach that, by prayer, the grace to observe the vow is obtained: and, therefore, they tell all who are tempted to sin against chastity, to ask it of God, who will not permit them to be tempted above their strength. The doctrine of Soave is opposed to all the Holy Fathers and to the sacred Scriptures, which, in a thousand passages of the New and Old Testament, exhort us to have recourse to God in our necessities, and promise that he will certainly hear humble and persevering prayer. What the Council teaches, in this canon, is in accordance with what we find in the 11th chapter of the 6th session: " Deus impossibilia non jubet, sed jubendo monet et facere quod possis, et petere quod non possis et adjuvat ut possis."

28. That great inconveniences would arise from a married priesthood in the Church, and that the Church had just

reasons to oblige persons in holy orders to practise chastity, has been shown at the end of the exposition of the preceding session (xxiii.), in treating of the sacrament of Order.

29. Canon 10: " Si quis dixerit statum conjugalem anteponendum esse statui virginitatis vel cœlibatus; et non esse melius ac beatius manere in virginitate aut cœlibatu quam jungi matrimonio, anathema sit."

30. They who assert what is condemned in this canon speak in direct opposition to the words of the Apostle: " Therefore, both he that giveth his virgin in marriage, doth well, and he that giveth her not doth better......But more blessed shall she be, if she so remain, according to my counsel." (1 Cor. vii. 38, 40.) Their assertion is also opposed to the words of the Saviour himself: " There are eunuchs, who have made themselves eunuchs for the kingdom of heaven. He that can take it, let him take it." (Matt. xix. 12.)

31. Canon 11. Si quis dixerit prohibitionem solemnitatis nuptiarum certis anni temporibus superstitionem esse tyrannicam ab ethnicorum superstitione profectam; aut benedictiones et alias cæremonias quibus Ecclesia in illis utitur, damnaverit, anathema sit."

32. Canon 12. " Si quis dixerit causas matrimoniales non spectare ad judices ecclesiasticos, anathema sit." Cardinal Bellarmine says, that all matrimonial causes, which are purely civil, or in which there is question only of succession to property, of dowries, or inheritance, belong to the civil tribunals; but the causes which regard the marriage contract, such as the causes which regard its validity, or the impediments, or the degrees of consanguinity or affinity, belong to the ecclesiastical courts: because, since the contract is not separated from the sacrament, but is the foundation of it, all such causes are spiritual: for to pronounce on the validity of the contract is the same as to pronounce on the validity of the sacrament.

33. The Council next passes to the decree of reformation regarding matrimony. This decree contains ten chapters. In the first chapter, the Council declares that clandestine marriages, that is, marriages which had been contracted before the Council, with the consent of the parties, but without the presence of the parish priest and other witnesses, as also marriages contracted by children without the consent of their parents, are valid, and true marriages. The Council then orders that, for the future, every marriage, before it is contracted, should be published three times, in order to ascertain whether there are any impediments to it; that it be afterwards contracted before the parish priest and two or three witnesses: and that, after having obtained the consent of the parties, the parish priest should say: *Ego vos in matrimonium conjungo in nomine Patris et Filii, et Spiritus Sancti,* or that he should use other words, according to the rite of the province. The ordinaries are empowered, when there is a just cause, to dispense with the three publications. But, with regard to those who shall attempt to contract marriage without the presence of the parish priest and two or three witnesses, the Council declares that the contract is null and void, and renders them incapable of contracting marriage. In this chapter the Council prescribes several other things of less importance, which are found in the following chapter:

34. Chapter 1: " Tametsi dubitandum non est clandestina matrimonia, libero contrahentium consensu facta, rata et vera esse matrimonia, quamdiu Ecclesia ea irrita non fecit, et proinde jure damnandi sunt illi, ut eos Sancta Synodus anathemate damnat, qui ea vera ac rata esse negant quique falso affirmant matrimonia a filiisfamilias sine consensu parentum contracta, irrita esse, et parentes ea rata vel irrita facere posse: nihilominus sancta Dei ecclesia ex justissimis causis illa semper detestata est atque prohibuit. Verum, cum sancta synodus animadvertat prohibi-

tiones illas, propter hominum inobedientiam jam non prodesse; et gravia peccata perpendat quæ ex iisdem clandes-
tinis conjugiis ortum habent; præsertim vero eorum qui in
statu damnationis permanent, dum priore uxore, cum qua
jam contraxerant, relicta, cum alia palam contrahunt et cum
ea in perpetuo adulterio vivunt, cui malo cum ab Ecclesia,
quæ de occultis non judicat, succurri non possit nisi effica-
cius aliquod remedium adhibeatur; idcirco sacri Latera-
nensis concilii, sub Innocenti III. celebrati, vestigiis inhæ-
rendo, præcipit ut in posterum, antequam matrimonium
contrahatur, ter a proprio contrahentium parocho tribus
continuis diebus festivis in ecclesia inter missarum solemnia
publice denuntietur inter quos matrimonium sit contrahendum: quibus denuntiationibus factis, si nullum legitimum apponatur impedimentum ad celebrationem matrimonii in facie ecclesiæ procedatur; ubi parochus, viro
et muliere interrogatis et eorum mutuo consensu intel-
lecto vel dicat: *Ego vos in matrimonium conjungo,
in nomine Patris et Spiritus Sancti*, vel aliis utatur
verbis juxta receptum uniuscujusque provinciæ ritum.
Quod si aliquando probabilis fuerit suspicio matrimonium
malitiose impediri posse, si tot præcesserint denuntiationes;
tunc vel una tantum denuntatio fiat vel saltem, parocho
vel duobus vel tribus testibus præsentibus, Matrimonium
celebretur.   Deinde ante illius consummationem denuntationes in ecclesia fiant, ut si aliqua subsunt impedimenta,
facilius detegantur; nisi ordinarius ipse expedire judicaverit
ut prædictæ denuntationes remittantur: quod illius pru-
dentiæ et judicio sancta synodus relinquit.   Qui aliter quam
præsente parocho vel alio sacerdote de ipsius parochi seu
ordinarii licentia, et duobus vel tribus testibus, matrimonium contrahere attentabunt, eos sancta synodus ad sic
contrahendum omnino inhabiles reddit, et hujusmodi contractus irritos et nullos esse decernit, prout eos præsenti
decreto irritos facit et annullat.   Insuper parochum vel

alium sacerdotem qui cum minore testium numero, et testes
qui sine parocho vel sacerdote hujusmodi contractui inter-
fuerint, necnon ipsos contrahentes graviter arbitrio ordinarii
puniri præcipit. Præterea eadem sancta synodus hortatur
ut conjuges ante benedictionem sacerdotalem, in templo
suscipiendam, in eadem domo non cohabitent: statuitque
benedictionem a proprio parocho fieri, neque a quoquam,
nisi ab ipso parocho vel ab ordinario, licentiam ad prædic-
tam benedictionem faciendam alii sacerdoti concedi posse,
quacumque consuetudine, etiam immemorabili quæ potius
corruptelia dicenda est, vel priviliegio non obstante. Quod
si quis parochus vel alius sacerdos, sive regularis sive sæcularis sit, etiamsi id ex privilegio vel immemorabili consuetudine licere contendat, alterius parochiæ sponsos, sine
illorum parochi licentia, Matrimonio conjungere aut bene-
dicere ausus fuerit; ipso jure suspensus maneat quamdiu
ab ordinario ejus parochi qui Matrimonio interesse debebat
seu a quo benedictio suscipienda erat absolvatur. Habeat
parochus librum in quo conjugum et testium nomina diem-
que et locum contracti matrimonii describat; quem diligenter
apud se custodiat. Postremo sancta synodus conjuges hortatur ut, antequam contrahant, vel saltem triduo ante matrimonii consummationem, sua peccata diligenter confiteantur
et ad SS. Eucharistiæ sacramentum pie accedant. Si quæ
provinciæ aliis, præter prædictas, laudabilibus consuetu-
dinibus et cæremoniis hac in re utantur, eas omnino retineri
sancta synodus vehementer optat. Ne vero hæc tam salubria præcepta quemquam lateant, ordinariis omnibus præcipit ut, cum primum potuerint curent hoc decretum populo
publicari et explicari in singulis suarum diocesum paro-
chialibus ecclesiis; idque primo anno quam sæpissime fiat;
deinde vero quoties expedire viderint. Decernit insuper
ut hujusmodi decretum in unaquaque parochia suum robur
post triginta dies habere incipiat, a die primæ publicationis
in eadem parochia factæ numerandos.''

35. Thus in the first place, with regard to clandestine marriages the Fathers declare that although detested and forbidden by the Church, they were before the Council, true and valid marriages, that is true sacraments: and condemn under pain of excommunication all who assert the contrary. Here Peter Soave expresses his astonishment, and says that many (that is he alone) did not understand how it could be defined that clandestine marriages, though an object of detestation to the Church, were sacraments. I answer that as a person who has made a simple vow of chastity, or had contracted espousals with a female, would receive a sacrament by marrying another, although he would be guilty of sin, so before the Council clandestine marriages though unlawful, were sacraments. Soave says: if the clandestine marriages were real sacraments, how could the Church change the substance of the sacrament by making the mutual consent in which the substance of the sacrament consists, cease to be sufficient matter? I answer that the Council did not change the matter, but rendered the parties incapable of contracting marriage against the law of the Church; since, as has been already said, the Church can annex certain conditions, not to the sacrament, but to the matrimonial contract, without which it will be null, and then the consent is not sufficient matter for the contract, nor by consequence for the sacrament. The Council then declared: " Qui aliter quam præsente parocho vel alio sacerdote, de ipsius parochi seu ordinarii licentia, et duobus vel tribus testibus, matrimonium contrahere attentabunt, eos S. Synodus ad sic contrahendum omnino inhabiles reddit, et hujusmodi contractus nullos, esse decernit." Let it be observed that this declaration does not extend to the places in which the Council of Trent has not been received.

36. Secondly, with regard to marriages contracted by children, without the consent of their parents, although

the Council says that they have been always detested and forbidden by the Church, still it declares that they are valid, and excommunicates all who assert that they are null. This had been before declared by Pope Nicholas I., (ad cons. Bulgar. c. 3,) and by Innocent III. (c. Tuæ fratern., de sponsal.) However, such marriages are, as St. Leo and Clement III. have taught, ordinarily speaking, unlawful, as well on account of the public evil which they do, as on account of the irreverence which children are, in such marriages, guilty of towards their parents. I have said *ordinarily :* for when parents unjustly refuse their consent, the marriages are lawful. The innovators, and especially Kemnitius, say that no marriage can ever be lawful, which has not God for its author. I answer, that God may be the author of matrimony in two ways, inasmuch as it is a sacrament, and inasmuch as it is a legitimate contract. In order to be a sacrament, it is sufficient that the marriage have all the requisites which God has prescribed for the validity of the sacrament. With regard to its being legitimate, I say, that when children unjustly contract marriage without the consent of their parents, God is not the author of their sin: and therefore the marriage is valid, but not lawful. In the Council, the French said that these marriages were unlawful, according to the discipline of the Church, and not according to faith, (as the innovators contend) and therefore that they should be declared null and void. But the Council declared that they were valid: and Tournely (de Matr. p. 553,) attests, that even the edicts of France, did not annul the marriages of children which were contracted against the will of their parents. And the Gallican clergy afterwards stated, that the edicts only regarded the civil contract, and prescinded from the validity of the marriage. Cardinal Pallivicini relates, that at first it was said in the Council, that children could not contract marriage, if males, before the age of 18, or if females, before

the age of 16, without the consent of their father, or
paternal uncle, unless these were absent, or unjustly refused
their assent: but the Council afterwards changed this
arrangement, and adopted the abovementioned decree.

37. Thirdly, the Council ordained that, in order to be
valid, marriages should, for the future, be contracted in the
presence of the parish priest, or of another priest with his
permission, who should pronounce the words: *Ego vos
conjungo, &c. :* the Council also declared, that the parties
who should attempt to contract marriage without having
the parish priest, and two or three witnesses present, were
incapable of contracting marriage with each other. Hence,
it follows, that such marriages have not even the force of
espousals. Be it observed, that the Council of France
ordered the deputies of the king to supplicate the Council,
in his name, to annul marriages contracted without having
the priest and three other witnesses present: the deputies
presented the petition in the general congregation: it was
supported by Cardinal de Lorraine. The Council afterwards
acceded to it, and, as has been already said, declared
that marriages contracted without the presence of the parish
priest and the witnesses, are altogether null. Hence, if while
the parties give their mutual consent, the parish priest is
asleep, or does not understand what they are doing, the
marriage is invalid. If the parish priest is present, and
only refuses his ministry, the marriage is invalid in the
opinion of those who hold that the priest is the minister of
the sacrament: but in our opinion, according to which the
contracting parties are the ministers of Matrimony, the
marriage is valid. This is conformable to a decree of the
sacred congregation of the Council. (Apud Fagnan. in cap.
Quod nobis, de clandest. n. 54.). Peter Soave asserts that
some ridiculed the Council for having ordered the parish
priest to recite the words: *Ego vos conjungo in Matrimonium, &c.,* thus making it a dogma of faith that these

words are the form of the sacrament. I answer that the Church never intended to declare that it is of faith that these words are the form of the sacrament of Matrimony: for the opinion that the contracting parties and not the priest are the sole ministers of Matrimony is far the more common opinion of divines, as we shall see in the next paragraph: many authors have censured the opposite opinion.

38. We shall now speak of the question whether the assisting priest, or the contracting parties, are the ministers of Matrimony. Some hold that the priest is the minister, and that the form consists in the words: *Ego vos in Matrimonium conjugo, &c.* This opinion is held by Tournely (de Matr. q. 3, concl. 2, p. 502.) by Melchior Cano, (de loc. theol. l. 8, c. 5.) by Estius, Peter de Marca, Silvius, Maldonatus, and others, along with Pope Siricius, (ep. ad Himer.) who has said that without the benediction of the priest, "nuptiæ non carent suspicione fornicariæ aut adulteræ conjunctionis; and with Tertullian, who (lib. 2, ad uxor. c. ult.) says, that the benediction, " aut signat aut sanctificat Matrimonium." Tournely adds, that in all the sacraments the minister is a priest; but if the contracting parties were the ministers, a woman would administer the sacrament, which is entirely repugnant to the nature of a sacrament.

39. Our opinion is, that the contracting parties themselves, are the ministers of matrimony: that the matter of the sacrament consists in the transfer which they mutually make to each other of their bodies, and that the form consists in their acceptation of it.* This opinion,

* Although St. Alphonsus maintains that the contracting parties are the ministers of the sacrament of marriage, he, and all Catholics, teach, as certain, that every marriage contracted in any place in which the decree of the Council of Trent is received, as it is in every diocess in Ireland, at which the parish priest, or another priest with the permission of the parish priest, or of the bishop of the diocess, and two or three witnesses, are not present, is null and void.

on which I have written at length in my Moral Theology,
(lib. 5. c. 2. n. 897) is admitted by Melchior Cano himself,
to be the common opinion. Bellarmine also says, that it
is commonly held by divines, and that the opposite is new
and false. Merbesius asserts that, before Cano, the opposite
opinion had never been considered probable by theologians,
and that Vasquez and Ledesma hold, that it cannot be
safely defended: Sotus, Wigandt, Vega, Lopez, Henriquez,
and Manuel, assert that it is rash. Our opinion is held
by Juenin, (tom. 7, de matr., p. 458, concl. 4,) who says,
that the form consists in the words and signs by which the
parties express their consent: it is also held by Cabassutius,
Frassen, Gonet, Suarez, Holzman, Cardinal Gotti, Benedict
XIV., (de synod., l. 7, c. 18,) and by an immense
number of other theologians, and particularly by St. Thomas.
" Verba," says the holy Doctor, " quibus consensus matri-
monialis exprimitur sunt forma hujus sacramenti, non autem
benedictio sacerdotis, quæ est quoddam sacramentale," (in
4 sent. d. 26, q. 2, a. 1, ad 1.) that is, a sacred ceremony
commanded by the Church: and this is what the Holy
Fathers mean when they say, that the benediction of
the priest is necessary. In answer to Tournely, we say,
that God has appointed the ministers according to the
nature of each sacrament: and because matrimony consists
in a contract elevated to the dignity of a sacrament, the
Lord wished that the parties themselves, who are to make
the contract, should be the ministers of the sacrament.

40. Our opinion is proved first from the chapter (Quanto,
de divort.) where Innocent III. says: " Etsi matrimonium
infidelium verum existat, non tamen est ratum. Inter fideles
autem verum et ratum existit, quia sacramentum fidei,
quod semel est admissum, nunquam amittitur, sed ratum
efficit conjugii sacramentum (mark) ut ipsum in conjugibus
illo durante perduret." Thus in ancient times clandestine
marriages between Christians were real and *rata*, (that is

indissoluble) inasmuch as they were sacraments: *ratum efficit conjungii sacramentum.* If then before the Council of Trent, marriages contracted without the presence of a priest, were sacraments, it must necessarily be said that the contracting parties were the ministers. Nor can it be said with the adversaries that the *sacramentum fidei* was not the sacrament of marriage, but the sacrament of Baptism, which rendered marriage indissoluble: for it is not true that marriage contracted between two infidels becomes indissoluble by baptism. Cardenas and others, and particularly Benedict XIV. (de synod. l. 6, c. 4, n. 5,) mention many examples of persons whose marriage, after their conversion from infidelity, was, for just reasons, declared to be dissolved by several pontiffs; such as Urban VIII., St. Pius V., and Gregory XIII. This the pontiffs could not have done if these marriages had been made indissoluble by baptism. Hence they were rendered indissoluble solely by the sacrament of marriage.

41. It is proved, secondly, from the Council of Florence, which declared: " Causa efficiens matrimonii regulariter est mutuus consensus per verba de præsenti expressus." Since then the contracting parties are the *efficient cause* of matrimony, they are the ministers not only of the contract (as the adversaries say) but also of the sacrament; for the Council intended there to speak not of the contract but of the sacrament, as appears from the words: " Septimum est sacramentum Matrimonii," &c.

42. It is proved, thirdly, from the words of the Council of Trent: " Qui aliter quam præsente parocho, &c., matrimonium contrahere attentabunt, eos S. Synodus omnino inhabiles reddit, et hujusmodi contractus nullos esse decernit." According to these words, it is sufficient for the validity of the marriage that the parties contract *præsente parocho,* although he should not speak, and even though he should positively refuse his ministry. And according to

2 I

the present practice of the Church, such marriages are
held to be valid and real sacraments.

43. It is proved, fourthly, from the words which the
Council commands the parish priest to recite at the time
the marriage is contracted: "*Ego vos in matrimonium
conjungo, &c.*, the Council then adds, "*vel aliis utatur
verbis juxta receptum uniuscujusque provinciæ
ritum.* This the Council could not have said if it had
believed that the words, *ego vos, &c.*, were the form of
the sacrament: for it cannot be supposed that the Council
would have admitted as true forms all those that were in
use in each province. Pallavicini (l. 23, c. 14,) thinks
that this argument proves conclusively that the contracting
parties are the ministers of Matrimony. Benedict XIV.
(de Syn. l. 8, c. 13, n. 8.) reasons thus: It often happens
that the parties contract *reluctante parocho, ac testibus fortuito adstantibus:* now, according to Cano, such
marriages would be mere contracts and not sacraments.
But, says the Pontiff, the Church regards them as true
sacraments; and does not require that they be renewed
præsente parocho. Hence, when the sacred Penitentiary
grants a dispensation to render valid a marriage which had
been null on account of some occult impediment, it annexes
the clause: *Secreto et sine assistentia parochi et testium reconvalidetur.* That the marriage should be
renewed in this manner, the same Benedict XIV., Van
Espen, Habert, Pontas, and Tournely hold, and was several
times declared by the sacred congregation of the Council.
I admit that although he holds our opinion, Benedict XIV.
(de syn.) speaking as a private doctor, grants that the
opposite opinion is probable: but in his epistle to the Archbishop of Goa, (Bull. tom. 4, p. 27.) where he speaks as
Pope, he says expressly that the matter of the sacrament
of marriage is the mutual transfer of the bodies expressed
by words or signs; and that the form consists in the

mutual acceptation: "Materia est mutua corporum traditio verbis assensum exprimentibus: et mutua corporum acceptatio, forma." For the answer to the arguments of our opponents I refer to my Moral Theology.

44. The priest who ought to assist at the marriage, is the parish priest of the dwelling-place of the husband or wife: but the custom is, that he should be the parish priest of the female, with the permission of the parish priest of the man. (See Tournely de matr. p. 580, quær. 2.) A parish priest of a different parish, would sin grievously by assisting at a marriage without the testimonial letters of the parish priest of one of the parties, and the marriage would be null. But a marriage contracted before the parish priest of the persons to be married, though celebrated in another parish, would, according to the Council of Trent, (c. 1,) be valid: for the celebration of marriage is an act of voluntary jurisdiction, which may be exercised in every place.

45. Let us pass to the other chapters of the Council. In the second chapter, the Council treats of spiritual relationship, and mentions the persons who contract this impediment: "Docet experientia, propter multitudinem prohibitionum, multoties in casibus prohibitis ignoranter contrahi Matrimonia; in quibus vel non sine magno peccato perseveratur, vel ea non sine magno scandalo dirimuntur. Volens igitur sancta synodus huic incommodo providere et a cognationis spiritualis impedimento incipiens, statuit ut unus tantum, sive vir sive mulier, juxta sacrorum canonum instituta, vel ad summum unus et una baptizatum a Baptismo suscipiant; inter quos ac baptizatum ipsum et illius patrem et matrem, necnon inter baptizantem et baptizatem, baptizatique patrem ac matrem tantum spiritualis cognatio contrahatur. Parochus, antequam ad Baptismum conferendum accedat, diligenter ab iis ad quos spectabit sciscitetur quem vel quos elegerint ut baptizatum de sacro fonte suscipiant; et eum vel eos tantum ad illum suscipiendum admittat, et in libro

eorum nomina describat, doceatque eos quam cognationem contraxerint, ne ignorantia ulla excusari valeant. Quod si alii ultra designatos baptizatum tetigerint, cognationem spiritualem nullo pacto contrahunt; constitutionibus in contrarium facientibus non obstantibus. Si parochi culpa vel negligentia secus factum fuerit, arbitrio ordinarii puniatur. Ea quoque cognatio quæ ex confirmatione contrahitur confirmantem et confirmatum illiusque patrem et matrem ac tenentem non egrediatur: omnibus inter alias personas hujus spiritualis cognationis impedimentis omnino sublatis."

46. In the third chapter, the Council speaks of the impediment "publicæ honestatis," and restrains it within the following limits: "Justitiæ publicæ honestatis impedimentum, ubi sponsalia quacunque ratione valida non erunt, sancta synodus prorsus tollit; ubi valida fuerint, primum gradum non excedant, quoniam in ulterioribus gradibus jam non potest hujusmodi prohibitio absque dispendio observari."

47. In the fourth chapter, the Council says, that affinity, arising from fornication, is limited to the second degree: "Præterea sancta synodus, eisdem et aliis gravissimis de causis adducta, impedimentum quod propter affinitatem ex fornicatione contractam inducitur et Matrimonium postea factum dirimit ad eos tantum qui in primo et secundo gradu conjunguntur restringit: in ulterioribus vero gradibus statuit hujusmodi affinitatem Matrimonium postea contractum non dirimere."

48. In the fifth chapter, the Council forbids the faithful to contract marriage within the prohibited degrees: and directs when a dispensation is to be given in these degrees. "Si quis intra gradus prohibitos scienter Matrimonium contrahere præsumpserit, separetur et spe dispensationis consequendæ careat; idque in eo multo magis locum habeat qui non tantum Matrimonium contrahere, sed etiam consummare ausus fuerit. Quod si ignoranter id fecerit, si quidem solemnitates requisitas in contrahendo Matrimonio neglexerit,

eisdem subjiciatur pœnis; non enim dignus est qui Ecclesiæ benignitatem facile experiatur, cujus salubria præcepta temere contempsit. Si vero, solemnitatibus adhibitis, impedimentum aliquod postea subesse cognoscatur cujus ille probabilem ignorantiam habuit, tunc facilius cum eo et gratis dispensari poterit. In contrahendis matrimoniis vel nulla omnino detur dispensatio vel raro; idque ex causa et gratis concedatur. In secundo gradu nunquam dispensetur, nisi inter magnos principes et ob publicam causam." ·

49. In the sixth chapter, several enactments were made contra raptores: "Decernit sancta synodus inter raptorem et raptam, quamdiu ipsa in potestate raptoris manserit, nullum posse consistere matrimonium. Quod si rapta a raptore separata et in loco tuto et libero constituta, illum in virum habere consenserit, eam raptor in uxorem habeat; et nihilominus raptor ipse ac omnes illi consilium, auxilium et favorem præbentes sint ipso jure excommunicati ac perpetuo infames omniumque dignitatum incapaces: et si clerici fuerint, de proprio gradu decidant. Teneatur propterea raptor mulierem raptem, sive eam uxorem duxerit, sive non duxerit, decenter arbitrio judicis dotare."

50. In the seventh chapter, the Council says, that in marrying persons who have no fixed dwelling, caution is necessary: "Multi sunt qui vagantur et incertas habent sedes; et ut improbi sunt ingenii, prima uxore relicta, aliam et plerumque plures, illa vivente, diversis in locis ducunt. Cui morbo cupiens santa synodus occurrere, omnes ad quos spectat, paterne monet ne hoc genus hominum vagantium ad Matrimonium facile recipiant: magistratus etiam seculares hortatur ut eos severe coerceant. Parochis autem præcipit ne illorum Matrimonium intersint, nisi prius diligentem inquisitionem fecerint et, re ad ordinarium delata, ab eo licentiam id faciendi obtinuerint."

51. In the eighth chapter, the Council enacted the

severest penalties against concubinage. "Grave peccatum
est homines solutos concubinas habere: gravissimum vero
et in hujus magni sacramenti singularem contemptum
admissum uxoratos quoque in hoc damnationis statu vivere
ac audere eos quandoque domi etiam cum uxoribus alere et
retinere. Quare ut huic tanto malo sancta synodus oppor-
tunis remediis provideat, statuit hujusmodi concubinarios,
tam solutos quam uxoratos, cujuscumque status et dignitatis
et conditionis existant, si postquam ab ordinario, etiam ex
officio, ter admoniti ea de re fuerint, concubinas non
ejecerint, seque ab earum consuetudine non sejunxerint,
excommunicatione feriendos esse; a qua non absolvantur
donec reipsa admonitioni factæ paruerint. Quod si in con-
cubinatu per annum, censuris neglectis, permanserint, contra
eos per ordinarium severe pro qualitate criminis procedatur.
Mulieres sive conjugatæ sive solutæ quæ cum adulteris seu
concubinariis publice vivunt si ter admonitæ non paruerint,
ab ordinariis locorum, etiam nemine requirente, ex officio
graviter pro modo culpæ puniantur, et extra oppidum vel
diœcesim, si id iisdem ordinariis videbitur, invocato (si
opus fuerit) brachio sæculari, ejiciantur; aliis pœnis contra
adulteros et concubinarios inflictis in suo robore per-
manentibus."

52. In the ninth chapter temporal lords and magistrates
are forbidden to interfere with the liberty of marriage.
"Ita plerumque temporalium dominorum ac magistratuum
mentis oculos terreni affectus atque cupiditates excæcant ut
viros et mulieres sub eorum jurisdictione degentes, maxime
divites vel spem magnæ hæreditatis habentis, minis et pœnis
adigant cum iis Matrimonium invitos contrahere quos ipsi
domini vel magistratus illis præscripserint. Quare, cum
maxime nefarium sit, Matrimonii libertatem violare et
ab eis injurias nasci a quibus jura expectantur, præcipit
sancta synodus omnibus, cujuscumque gradus, dignitatis et
conditionis existant, sub anathematis pœna, quam ipso

facto incurrant, ne quovis modo, directe vel indirecte subditos suos vel quoscumque alios cogant quo minus libere
Matrimonium contrahunt."

53. In the tenth chapter the Council prohibits the solem-
nization of marriage at certain times: " Ab adventu Domini
Nostri Jesu Christi usque in diem epiphaniæ et a feria
quarta cinerum usque in octavam paschatis inclusive anti-
quas solemnium nuptiarum prohibitionis diligenter ab omnibus observari sancta synodus præcipit: in aliis vero temporibus nuptias solemniter celebrari permittit; quas episcopi,
ut ea qua decet modestia et honestate fiant, curabunt,
sancta enim res est Matrimonium, et sancte tractandum.

TWENTY-FOURTH SESSION.

DECREE ON PURGATORY.

1. In the sixth Session (canon 30,) the Council had already taught that there is a purgatory, and had pronounced an anathema against all who should assert that after justification and the remission of the eternal punishment, no debt of temporal punishment remains to be satisfied by the sinner in this life, or hereafter in purgatory before he could enter heaven: " Si quis post acceptam justificationis gratiam, cuilibet peccatori pœnitenti ita culpam remitti et reatum æternæ pœnæ deleri dixerit ut nullus remaneat reatus pœnæ temporalis exsolvendæ vel in hoc sæculo vel in futuro in purgatorio, antequam ad regna cœlorum aditus patere possit, anathema sit." Hence in the present decree the Council says that the Catholic Church, instructed by the Holy Ghost, by the Sacred Scriptures, by the tradition of the Fathers, by the Councils, and lastly, by the holy synod itself, having taught that there is a purgatory (sess. 6, can. 30.) and that the souls therein detained are greatly assisted by the suffrages of the faithful, and particularly by the sacrifice of the mass, she commands bishops to teach the people the sound doctrine regarding purgatory, to abstain from speaking on the more subtle questions, and not to permit the promulgation of doctrines which are uncertain, or which have the appearance of falsehood. The Council also commands bishops to prohibit all practices which are superstitious, and which savour of worldly gain: and to take care that priests satisfy with diligence and devotion the obligations arising from

donations made by the people for the benefit of the faithful departed.

2. Behold the words of the Council: " Cum catholica ecclesia, Spiritu Sancto edocta, ex sacris litteris et antiqua Patrum traditione, in sacris conciliis et novissime in hac œcumenica synodo docuerit purgatorium esse, animasque ibi detentas fidelium suffragiis, potissimum vero acceptabili altaris sacrificio juvari; præcipit sancta synodus episcopis ut sanam de purgatorio doctrinam, a sanctis Patribus et sacris conciliis, traditam, a Christi fidelibus credi, teneri, doceri et ubique prædicari diligenter studeant. Apud rudem vero plebem difficiliores ac sublimiores quæstiones quæque ad ædificationem non faciunt et ex quibus plerumque nulla fit pietatis accessio a popularibus concionibus secludantur. Incerta item, vel quæ specie falsi laborant evulgari tractari non permittant. Ea vero quæ ad curiositatem quamdam aut superstitionem spectant vel turpe lucrum sapiunt, tanquam scandala et fidelium offendicula, prohibeant. Curent autem episcopi, ut fidelium vivorum suffragia, missarum scilicet sacrificia, orationes, eleemosynæ aliaque pietatis opera quæ a fidelibus pro aliis fidelibus defunctis fieri consueverunt, secundum Ecclesiæ instituta, pie et devote fiant; et quæ pro illis ex testatorum fundationibus vel alia ratione debentur, non perfunctorie, sed a sacerdotibus et Ecclesiæ ministris et aliis qui hoc præstare tenentur, diligenter et accurate persolvantur."

3. That there is a purgatory, Catholics hold as a certain dogma of faith, against the ancient Albigenses and Waldenses, and against the modern innovators, who reject it as an invention of our priests to derive from it temporal gain by means of masses and funerals. However Luther at one time admitted purgatory; that is in a controversy held in Lipsia on the 6th of July, 1519. It is not true that the existence of purgatory is denied by the Greek schismatics: they only deny that the suffering souls are purified by fire.

Even the Jewish Rabbi, according to Cardinal Gotti, (in his True Church, t. 2, par. 1, p. 519,) admit that there is a purgatory.

4. The existence of Purgatory is proved by the text of St. Matthew: " Be at agreement with thy adversary whilst thou art in the way with him; lest perhaps....thou be cast into prison. Amen, I say to thee, thou shalt not go out from thence till thou repay the last farthing." (Matt. v. 25, &c.) In the next life, then, there is a prison from which persons are finally delivered, after having suffered the punishment due to all venial sins: for it is certain that there are sins which are of their own nature venial, on account of which, if a person die without repenting of them, he cannot be condemned to hell, because he is the friend of God; neither can he enter heaven, " which nothing defiled shall enter:" " non intrabit aliquid coinquinatum." (Apoc. 21.) Such a person then goes to purgatory, in which he is purified from every stain. The same is to be said of grievous sins, the guilt of which has been remitted, though the entire satisfaction for the punishment due to them has not been made. On the text quoted from St. Matthew, Tertullian says: " In summa cum carcerem illum quem Evangelium demonstrat, inferos intelligimus, et novissimum quadrantem modicum quoque delictum mora resurrectionis illic luendum interpretemur, nemo dubitabit animam aliquid pensare penes inferos. (De anima, c. ult.) This doctrine is confirmed by the words which we read in the twelfth chapter of St. Luke: " And when thou goest with thy adversary to the prince, whilst thou art in the way endeavour to be delivered from him, lest perhaps he draw thee to the judge, and the judge deliver thee to the exacter, and the exacter cast thee into prison. I say to thee, thou shalt not go out thence, until thou pay the very last mite." (Luc. xii. 58, 59.)

5. Secondly, this doctrine is proved from the words of the Redeemer: " But he that shall speak (a word) against

the Holy Ghost, it shall not be forgiven him neither in this world, nor in the world to come." (Matt. xii. 32.) The doctrine of purgatory is certainly contained in these words, as is taught by St. Augustine, (l. 21, de civ. Dei, c. 24, and l. 6, ad Julian.) by St. Gregory, (l. 4, dial. c. 39), by Bede (in c. 3, Marci) and by St. Bernard. (hom. 66. in cant.). But the impious Peter Martyr asserts that this was said by way of exaggeration. Thus we may say that what we read in St. Matthew, "these shall go into everlasting punishment," (xxv. 46.) is also an exaggeration, and therefore that there is no hell. The adversaries also object that in the text just quoted, the Saviour speaks of sins against the Holy Ghost which are most grievous; shall these also, they say, be remitted in purgatory? I answer that with regard to grievous sins their guilt is remitted only in this life, and is not remitted without sorrow and hatred for them: but in the next life venial sins only are forgiven, and their guilt is remitted not by means of the pains of purgatory, but by means of the first act of charity towards God which the soul will make at her departure from this life: this act of charity being very intense, includes a detestation of such venial faults. With regard to mortal sins they are not remitted in the next world: but if they have been pardoned in this life, the temporal punishment which remains will be remitted in purgatory.

6. Thirdly, the doctrine of purgatory is proved by the following words, which we find in the Acts of the Apostle: "Whom God hath raised up, having loosed the sorrows of hell." (ii. 24.) This cannot be understood of the Fathers who were in Limbo, for they suffered no sorrow: the meaning then must be that our Lord delivered certain persons from sorrow from which souls can be delivered, or from the pains of purgatory: for no one can be delivered from the sorrows of the hell of the damned.

7. Fourthly, the existence of purgatory is proved from

the words of St. Paul: "Now if any man build upon this foundation, gold, silver, precious stones, wood, hay, stubble, every man's work shall be manifested: for the day of the Lord shall declare it, because it shall be revealed in fire: and the fire shall try every man's work of what sort it is. If any man's work abide which he hath built thereupon; he shall receive a reward. If any man's work burn, he shall suffer loss; but he himself shall be saved, yet so as by fire." (1 Cor. iii. 12.) &c.　St. Augustine teaches (l. de fide. et op. c. 16, Enchir. c. 68.) that here St. Paul speaks of Christians who build on a solid foundation, such as gold, silver, and precious stones, which signify holy works: and says that they who build on wood and hay, in which fire can find matter to burn, and which signify venial sins, or mortal sins not fully expiated as to the temporal punishment, shall be purified by fire, and will be one day saved by means of fire: "He shall be saved, yet as by fire."　St. Ambrose says: "Sed cum Paulus dixit: Sic tamen quasi per ignem, ostendit quidem illum salvum futurum, sed pœnam ignis passurum, ut per ignem purgatus fiat salvus, et non sicut, perfidi, æterno igne in perpetuum torqueatur." (Serm. 20, in ps. 118.)　On this text St. Augustine writes: "Ita plane quamvis salvi per ignem, gravior tamen est ille ignis quam quidquid potest homo pati in hac vita." (In ps. 37.)　This text of the Apostle is explained in the same way by St. Jerome, (in 4, c. Amos.) by St. Bonaventure, St. Anselm, St. Thomas, and other Fathers.

8. Fifthly, the doctrine of purgatory is proved from the second book of Macchabees in which it is related that Judas Macchabeus, sent to Jerusalem twelve thousand drachms of silver to be employed in offering sacrifice for the soldiers that had been killed in the war: "And making a gathering, he sent twelve thousand drachms of silver to Jerusalem for sacrifice to be offered for the sins of the dead, thinking well and religiously concerning the resurrection......And because

he considered that they who had fallen asleep with godliness, had great grace laid up for them. It is therefore a holy and wholesome thought to pray for the dead, that they may be loosed from their sins." (2 Mac. xii. 43.)

9. The innovators object that this book of Macchabees is not canonical, because it is not found in the Jewish canon. I answer that although the Jews did not admit this book as canonical, it is regarded as such by the Catholic Church. For it is reckoned among the inspired writings by the Council of Carthage, (can. 47,) by Innocent I. (ep. ad Exuper, c. ult.), by Pope Gelasius in the decree regarding the canonical books, which he published in a Council of seventy bishops, by St. Augustine, (l. 18, de civ. Dei, c. 36,) and by St. Isidore. (l. 6, etymol., c. 1, de verb. Dei, c. 1, 15.).

10. Secondly, they say that Judas did not speak of purgatory, but only of the resurrection, as appears from the words: "thinking well and religiously concerning the resurrection." I answer that although he does not mention purgatory, it is sufficiently plain from the context that he alluded to it: for he wished that prayers should be offered expressly for the souls of the dead that they might be loosed from their sins, as we read in the end of the chapter: " It is therefore a holy and wholesome thought to pray for the dead, that they may be loosed from their sins."

11. Thirdly, they object that the inspired writer does not speak of any law, but only of the example of Judas, who caused prayers to be offered for the dead; and we are not obliged to follow the example of one man because we find it recorded in the scripture. In answer to this objection, Cardinal Bellarmine says, (lib. 1 de Purgat.) that our argument is taken, not only from the example of Judas, but from the ancient custom, and solemn rite of the Old Testament. For, in the chapter quoted, we find, that all who were with Judas, " betaking themselves to prayers, besought

2 K

him" (the Lord), &c.: and then it is added: "And making
a gathering, he (Judas) sent," &c. The rest of the people,
therefore, concurred with Judas in this offering for the dead.
To this may be added the testimony of the sacred scripture
itself, which calls the prayer that is said for the dead, that
they may be loosed from their sins, holy and salutary.

12. Lastly, the existence of Purgatory is proved from
the decree of the Council, in which it teaches that the souls
there detained, receive great relief from the suffrages of the
faithful, and particularly from the sacrifice of the mass:
"Animasque ibi detentas fidelium suffragiis, potissimum
vero acceptabili altaris sacrificio juvari." All this is confirmed
by the common tradition of the Holy Fathers, and by the
universal practice of the Church. Speaking of the relief
which the dead receive from the suffrages of the faithful,
St. Augustine says: "Orationibus s. Ecclesiæ et sacrificio
salutari ex eleemosynis quæ pro defunctorum spiritibus
erogantur, non est dubitandum mortuos adjuvari. Hoc non
est negandum, non est dubium, non est dubitandum: hoc
enim a Patribus traditum universa observat Ecclesia."
(Serm. 32, de verb. Ap.) And in another place he says:
"Si nusquam in scripturis veteribus omnino legeretur, non
pauca tamen est universæ ecclesiæ, quæ in hac consuetudine
claret, auctoritas; ubi in precibus sacerdotis quæ Domino
Deo ad ejus altare funduntur locum suum habet etiam
commendatio mortuorum." (lib. de cura pro mort. c. 1.)
Tertullian says, that the wife prays for the soul of the
deceased husband, implores relief, and makes an annual
oblation for him on the day of his death. "Enim
vero et pro anima ejus orat, et refrigerium interim
adpostulat ei......et offert annuis diebus dormitionis ejus."
(De monog. c. 10.) In another place, speaking of the
practices of the Church, he says: "Harum et aliarum
disciplinarum si legem expostules, Scripturarum nullam
invenies (because, perhaps, in the scripture we find no law

or precept commanding these practices). Traditio tibi
prætenditur auctrix, consuetudo confirmatrix, fides obser-
vatrix:" among these customs he reckons "*oblations for
the dead.*" Addressing a man whose first wife was dead,
and whose second wife was living, the same author says:
" Stabis ergo ad Deum cum tot uxoribus quot illas oratione
commemoras, et offeres pro duabus et commemorabis illas
duas per sacerdotem...et ascendet sacrificium tuum libera
fronte." (de exhort. ad castit. c. 11.)

13. Speaking of a deceased person, St. Cyprian writes:
" Neque enim ad altare Dei meretur nominari in sacerdotum
prece qui ab altari sacerdotes avocare voluit." (l. 1, ep. 9.)
Hence, in his time it was usual to pray for the dead on the
altar. St. John Chrysostom says: " Non frustra ab apostolis
sancitum est ut in venerabilium mysteriorum memoria fiat
eorum qui discesserunt." (Hom. 3 in ep. Philip.) In another place the saint writes: "Non frustra oblationes pro
defunctis fiunt, non frustra preces, non frustra eleemosynæ,
ut nos mutuum juvemus." (Hom. 21, in Acta). And
again: " Non est temere hoc excogitatum, nec frustra in
memoriam mortuorum sacra mysteria celebramus. Nam...
si Jobi illius liberos patris victima purgavit quid dubites e
nobis quoque, si pro dormientibus offeramus, solatii quiddam
illis accessurum?" (Hom. 41, in 1 ad Cor.) In his commentary on the book of Proverbs, (c. 11,) St. Jerome says:
" Mortuo homine impio, non erit ultra spes: Notandum autem
quod etsi impiis post mortem spes veniæ non est, sunt
tamen qui de levioribus peccatis post mortem poterunt
absolvi, vel pœnis castigati vel suorum precibus et eleemosynis missarumque celebrationibus." This commentary
was written by Saint Jerome, or by Venerable Bede.

14. Speaking of men who lead a life of virtue, St.
Gregory, of Nyssa, says: " In præsenti vita sapientiæ studio
vel precibus purgatos, vel post obitum per expurgantis ignis
fornacem expiatos, ad sempiternam felicitatem pervenire."

(orat. de mortuis.)   Piceninus rashly says, that this passage
is of little use to prove the doctrine of purgatory; since,
St. Gregory held with the other Greeks, that even the souls
of the damned will one day escape from hell.   But the
saint was far from deserving this foul charge of Origenism:
for in another place, he says: "Absurdum enim est...eos
qui animi curam gerunt incertam mortis diem non advertere
et ardorem excruciantis illius ignis qui in æternum comburit
(mark these words) et nullum unquam refrigerium admittit."
(Orat. de M. Magd.)   Speaking of the death of Valentinian,
St. Ambrose has said: "Date manibus sacra mysteria, pio
requiem ejus poscentis affectu: animam piam nostris oblationibus prosequamur."   Calvin admits that, according to
the Holy Fathers, there is a divine tradition teaching the
existence of a purgatory, in which souls are purified.   But
he audaciously says, that the Fathers *aliquid humani
passi sunt :* he meant to say, that they have given credit
to things which are not true, and which are superstitious.
But let us come to the objections of the innovators against
the existence of purgatory.

15. The innovators object, first, that in the Scripture
we find mention made only of two places in the next life;
of heaven and hell, but not of purgatory.   "If the tree
fall to the south, or to the north, in what place soever it
shall fall, there shall it be." (Eccl. xi. 3.)   I answer that
there the Scripture speaks of the two eternal receptacles in
which souls shall be placed after judgment, when purgatory
shall no longer exist.   Besides Bellarmine rightly says, that
they who at death only owe the debt of temporal punishment are justly said to fall to the south, or to obtain eternal
salvation, and not to the north, or the place of eternal
death, since they have only to satisfy for the temporal
punishment due to their sins.

16. Secondly, they object from the words of the Apocalypse: "Blessed are the dead who die in the Lord.

From henceforth now, saith the spirit, that they may rest from their labours." (xiv. 13.) This objection may be answered by saying with St. Anselm, that the words of St. John are to be understood not of the time of death but of the time of the last judgment, of which St. John speaks, and to which the holy Doctor says the words *from henceforth* should be referred. But the best answer to the objection is that the text is not to be understood of all who die in the state of grace, but only of the perfect who leave this world, purified from all stain by patience and holy works.

17. Thirdly, they object that in the next life no sin is forgiven: as well because they who enter the next life are out of the way, as because in the other world there is no room for repentance, without which no sin is remitted. I answer with some, that after death the soul, though no longer in the way, is pardoned all venial faults on account of her perfect love for God, and the detestation which she at the same time conceives for sin. Or the objection may be answered by saying with other divines, that the souls in purgatory are in a certain manner in the way *(in via)*, since they have not reached their term which is the possession of eternal glory; and therefore they can repent so as to obtain the remission of venial sins. But the first appears to be a more adequate answer to the objection.

18. They object, fourthly, that since the guilt of sin is remitted through the merits of Jesus Christ, which are of infinite value, there is no obligation of making satisfaction for the punishment due to sin. I answer that although sins are remitted through the merits of Christ, still justice requires that the debt of temporal punishment which has not been as yet satisfied, should be paid. They rejoin and say: if the remission of punishment is obtained by means of our satisfactory works, it must be said either that the punishment of sin is remitted, not through the satisfaction

2 K 2

of Christ, but through our satisfactory works, or that every sin is remitted by two kinds of satisfaction, by the satisfaction of Christ, and by satisfaction on our part. I answer that the satisfaction of Christ would be certainly sufficient to deliver us from all obligation of making satisfaction, but the Lord wishes that we also make satisfaction, which is capable of delivering us from the punishment due to our sins, inasmuch as it derives efficacy from the satisfaction of Jesus Christ.

19. They object, fifthly, that punishment is due on account of guilt; and therefore when there is no guilt there can be no debt of punishment. I answer that by sin two debts, the debt of guilt and the debt of punishment, are contracted. God remits the debt of guilt to every contrite sinner, and admits him again to his friendship, and at the same time remits the eternal punishment: but he justly wishes that the sinner should make satisfaction for the temporal punishment, just as a prince receives a criminal into favour, but obliges him to pay a certain penalty.

20. They object, sixthly, that the same conditions are required for merit and for satisfaction; but in purgatory there can be no merit, and therefore there can be no satisfaction. I answer that though in purgatory there can be no merit, because for merit a person must have liberty, and must be in the way, still a soul may pay the debt of punishment by sufferings which are not meritorious but are satisfactory. It is true that in this life the Lord rewards satisfactory works, because they are voluntary and therefore meritorious; but in the next life where the soul is out of the way, she makes satisfaction not by her own choice, but constrained by necessity, and therefore does not merit.

21. They object, seventhly, from the words of Ezechiel: " But if the wicked do penance......I will not remember all his iniquities which he hath done." (xviii. 21, &c.). Since the Lord says that he forgets all the iniquities of penitent

sinners, he will not then think of requiring any penalty. I answer with Bellarmine, that not to remember iniquities implies that the Lord no longer entertains enmity towards the sinner, but not that he remits all the punishment which is due.

22. Eighthly, they object from another text of St. Paul: "We know if our earthly house of this habitation be dissolved, that we have a building of God, a house not made with hands, eternal in heaven." (2 Cor. v. 1.) Hence, after death souls do not go to purgatory, but to heaven. I answer with Bellarmine, that here the Apostle meant to say that heaven is opened not before but after death, as appears from the following words: "Yet so that we be found clothed, not naked." (verse 3.) But they who after death are found without the nuptial garment, that is not perfectly purified, *are saved by fire*, as the Apostle says in another place. (See Num. vii.)

23. Ninthly, they object from the words of St. Ambrose: "Qui......hic non acceperit remissionem peccatorum, illic non erit, nimirum in patria beatorum." (lib. de bono mort. c. 2.) From these words they infer that in the next life sins are never remitted to those who have not obtained pardon in this life: hence, (they say,) according to St. Ambrose, the purgatory in which Catholics believe, does not exist. I answer that the holy Doctor spoke of sinners who leave this world in the state of mortal sin, as is clear from the following words of the saint: "Non erit autem, quia ad vitam æternam non potuerit pervenire: vita æterna remissio peccatorum est." The remission of sins is called *inchoate* eternal life.

24. It is asked in what place are souls purified in the next life? On this point there are three opinions: some hold that each person will make satisfaction for his sins in the very place in which they were committed. This is very probable, if not for all, at least for some, according to the

divine judgments; of this several examples are related by the authors, and particularly by St. Gregory. Others say that purgatory is in the same place as hell: this opinion is also probable. Nor can it be objected that in hell sinners are condemned to everlasting torments: for, persons condemned to perpetual imprisonment may be confined in the same prison with those who are detained only for a time. Finally, others maintain, (and this is the more common opinion) that purgatory is a place under the earth but not so deep as hell; it is called by the Church the deep lake: "*Libera animas defunctorum de pœnis inferni, et de profundo lacu.*" Some also think that for certain souls stained with the guilt of venial sins, purgatory consists in the privation of the vision of God. Venerable Bede relates that a soul was once seen in a place of pleasure, but not in heaven. Denis the Carthusian mentions several other examples: and Bellarmine also says that this opinion is not improbable.

25. Secondly, it may be asked how long do the pains of purgatory last? Origen (tom. 14, in Luc.) says that after the general resurrection souls require a sacrament to purify them perfectly before they enter heaven: but this opinion has been justly refuted by St. Augustine: (l. 21, de civ. Dei c. 16.) there the saint says that the elect have to suffer no satisfactory pains except before the last judgment. On the other hand, Dominicus Soto, says that the pains of purgatory are so severe that they do not last longer than ten years: but this opinion does not appear to be probable. For although God can, by increasing the intensity of her pain, purify a soul from sin, as he has perhaps done with regard to several, still great sinners shall have to suffer in purgatory for more than ten or twenty years, as appears from many visions which we find in the writings of Bede, (l. 5, histor.) and in which it is related that several souls were condemned to suffer till the day of judgment. This is confirmed by the

practice of the Church, which requires that masses to be said, and pious works to be performed on account of donations made for the benefit of the faithful departed, be not omitted though they should be for persons who are dead for a hundred or two hundred years.

26. Thirdly, it may be asked with what torments are souls punished in purgatory? Luther was of opinion that they were tortured with despair: but this is false. Some Catholics think that the punishment of certain souls consists entirely in an uncertainty whether they shall be saved or damned. But Bellarmine and the generality of theologians hold that all the souls in purgatory are certain of their salvation. Because every individual at the particular judgment is assured of his salvation or eternal perdition: according to St. Bonaventure, the certainty of salvation greatly alleviates the sufferings of the souls in purgatory: the very love of God with which they are filled, makes them certain that they belong to the number of the elect. Besides it is certain that their greatest pain consists in the privation of the vision of God. It is also certain that they shall suffer the pain of sense: for since in every sin there is a turning to creatures, it is just that these souls be punished by creatures. With regard to the question, whether the fire of purgatory is corporeal or metaphorical, such as fears, anguish, or remorses of conscience, as some hold, the Church has defined nothing: but, as Bellarmine says, the more common opinion of theologians is, that the fire of purgatory is material. St. Gregory, (l. 4, dial. c. 29.) expressly says that this fire is corporeal: this is also the opinion of St. Augustine. (de civ. Dei l. 2, c. 20.). It may be added that in the Scripture the pains of sinners in the other world are called fire: and it is a rule well known to all, that the words of Scripture should be understood literally, whenever they can be explained in the literal sense.

27. It is also asked whether the souls in purgatory are

tormented by the devils? St. Thomas (in 4, sent., dist. 20, art. 1, ad 5,) says not: because since they have overcome the devils in this life it is not congruous that they should be any longer tormented by them. However, we find many revelations in the writings of the Carthusian, of Venerable Bede and St. Bernard in which it is stated that the souls in purgatory are tormented by demons.

28. With regard to the severity of the pains of purgatory, St. Augustine (in ps. 37,) speaking of the pain of fire, says: "Gravior tamen ille ignis quam quidquid potest homo pati in hac vita." St. Gregory says the same: this is also confirmed by the revelations of Bede and St. Brigid. And St. Thomas (in 4, dist. 20, q. 2, a. 2,) says that the smallest pain of sense suffered in purgatory exceeds the greatest pain of this life: besides the souls in purgatory as well as in hell suffer the pain of loss which surpasses immensely all the pains of sense. However, St. Bonaventure holds (in 4, dist. 20, a. 1, q. 2,) that every pain suffered in purgatory is not greater than the pains of this life. This opinion pleases Bellarmine, because although the privation of the vision of God is a great pain, it is greatly mitigated by the certainty of having one day to enjoy him: he adds that the pains of each soul are lightened as she approaches the end of her purgation. And St. Augustine says that "the smallest pain of loss if it be eternal is greater than all the pains of this life." (Enchir. c. 112.) Mark the words *if it be eternal :* from this passage it may be inferred that the pain of loss in purgatory will not exceed all the pains of this life.

ON THE SUFFRAGES OF THE FAITHFUL FOR THE SOULS IN PURGATORY.

29. On this subject a good deal has already been said in the preceding paragraphs. It remains to treat briefly a few

more important points. Aerius was the first to deny that
suffrages for the dead were useful; but, as St. Epiphanius
attests, (hæres. 75) he was regarded as a heretic. The
Protestants adopt the doctrine of Aerius; but the church
has declared "ex sacris litteris et antiqua Patrum traditione,
in sacris conciliis et novissime in hac œcumenica synodo
purgatorium esse, animasque ibi detentas fidelium suffragiis
potissimum vero acceptabili altaris sacrificio juvari." This
is also proved by the words already quoted (n. 8.) from the
second book of Macchabees: " It is therefore a holy and
wholesome thought to pray for the dead that they may be
loosed from their sins;" (2 Mac. xii. 46,) and by the
authority of the generality of the Fathers who attest that
the oblation of prayers for the dead is the universal tradition and practice of the Church. Speaking of the relief
which the dead receive from the suffrages of the living, St.
Augustine says: " Orationibus s. Ecclesia et sacrificio salutari et eleemosynis quæ pro defunctorum spiritibus erogantur non est dubitandum mortuos adjuvari. Hoc non est
negandum, non est dubium, non est dubitandum: hoc
enim a Patribus traditum universa observat Ecelesia."
(Serm. 32, de verb. Apos.) And, in another place, he says:
" Sed si nusquam in Scripturis veteribus omnino legeretur,
non pauca tamen est universæ Ecclesiæ, quæ in hac consuetudine claret, auctoritas: ubi in precibus sacerdotis quæ
Domino Deo ad ejus altare funduntur locum suum habet
etiam commendatio mortuorum." (Lib. de cura pro
mort. c. 1.) These two texts of St. Augustine, which
have been already quoted, would of themselves, be sufficient foundation for the doctrine of prayers for the dead.
This doctrine is confirmed by the authority of the other
Fathers, from whose writings passages have been already
quoted. (n. 12 et seq.). Besides, in all the Liturgies of the
Apostles, we find prayers for the dead.

30. The adversaries object from the prayer of the Church

for the dead: " Libera me Domine, de. morte eterna in die illa tremenda......dum veneris judicare sæculum per ignem." Can souls, then they ask, be delivered even from hell, by the prayers of the faithful? I answer, that the words of the Church refer not to the time at which they are recited, but to the hour of death, as if the soul had not as yet departed, or to the time of the last judgment.

31. They also object, that as God does not punish one for another, so he does not accept the works of one for another. In answer, I say that the argument is fallacious: for to punish one person for the sins of another would be an injustice: but to accept the good works of one for another is not unjust, but is calculated to encourage charity among men, and is conformable to the divine mercy.

32. It is asked, finally, whether the souls in purgatory can pray for us? St. Thomas has said (in 2, 2, q. 82 a. 11 ad. 3), that, being in a state in which they are making satisfaction for their own debts, by suffering, they cannot pray for us: " Non sunt," says the holy Doctor, " in statu orandi, sed magis ut oretur pro eis." But many other grave authors (such as Bellarmine, Silvius, Gotti, and others) hold that although these suffering souls are inferior to us, inasmuch as they stand in need of our prayers, still, as the beloved of God, they can pray for us, and that we should piously believe that the Lord makes known to them our prayers that they may pray for us, and that thus the communion of charity may be preserved between them and us.

33. In the abovementioned decree of the 25th session, the Council, after having spoken of Purgatory, passes to the invocation of Saints, and to the veneration which is due to their relics and to sacred images.

DE INVOCATIONE, VENERATIONE ET RELIQUIIS SANCTORUM, ET SACRIS IMAGINIBUS.

1. "Mandat sancta synodus omnibus episcopis et cæteris docendi munus curamque substinentibus ut, juxta Catholicæ et apostolicæ ecclesiæ usum, a primævis christianæ religionis temporibus receptum, sanctorumque Patrum consensionem et sacrorum conciliorum decreta, in primis de sanctorum intercessione, invocatione, reliquiarum honore et legitimo imaginum usu fideles diligenter instruant, docentes eos sanctos, una cum Christo regnantes, orationes suas pro omnibus Deo offerre, bonum atque utile esse suppliciter eos invocare, et ob beneficia impetranda a Deo per filium ejus Jesum Christum Dominum nostrum, qui solus noster Redemptor et Salvator est ad eorum orationes, opem, auxilium confugere; illos vero qui negant, sanctos, æterna felicitate in cœlo fruentes, invocandos esse; aut qui asserunt vel illos pro hominibus non orare, vel eorum ut pro nobis etiam singulis orent, invocationem esse idololatriam, vel pugnare cum verbo Dei adversarique honori unius mediatoris Dei et hominum Jesu Christi, vel stultum esse in cœlo regnantibus voce vel mente supplicare, impie sentire; sanctorum quoque martyrum et aliorum cum Christo viventium sancta corpora, quæ viva membra fuerunt Christi et templum Spiritus Sancti, ab ipso ad æternam vitam suscitanda et glorificanda, a fidelibus veneranda esse per quæ multa beneficia a Deo hominibus præstantur; ita ut affirmantes sanctorum reliquiis venerationem atque honorem non deberi, vel eas aliaque sacra monumenta a fidelibus inutiliter honorari, atque eorum opis impetrandæ causa sanctorum memorias frustra frequentari, omnino damnandos esse, prout jam pridem eos damnavit et nunc etiam damnat Ecclesia. Imagines porro Christi, Deiparæ virginis et aliorum sanctorum in templis præsertim habendas et reti-

2 L

nendas eisque debitum honorem et venerationem imper-
tiendam; non quod credatur inesse aliqua in iis divinitas
vel virtus propter quam sint colendæ, vel quod ab eis aliquid sit petendum, vel quod fiducia in imaginibus sit
figenda, veluti olim fiebat a gentibus quæ in idolis spem
suam collocabant; sed quoniam honos qui eis exhibetur
refertur ad prototypa quæ illæ repræsentant, ita ut per
imagines, quas osculamur et coram quibus caput aperimus
et procumbimus, Christum adoremus, et sanctos quorum
illæ similitudinem gerant, veneremur: id quod conciliorum,
præsertim vero secundæ Nicænæ synodi, decretis contra
imaginum oppugnatores est sancitum."

2. Illud vero diligenter doceant episcopi, per historias
mysteriorum nostræ redemptionis, picturis vel aliis similitudinibus expressas, erudiri et confirmari populum in articulis
fidei commemorandis et assidue recolendis; tum vero ex
omnibus sacris imaginibus magnum fructum percipi, non
solum quia admonetur populus beneficiorum et munerum quæ
a Christo sibi collata sunt, sed etiam quia Dei per Sanctos
miracula et salutaria exempla oculis fidelium subjiciuntur,
ut pro iis Deo gratias agant, ad sanctorum imitationem
vitam moresque suos componant, excitenturque ad adorandum ac diligendum Deum et ad pietatem colendam. Si
quis autem his decretis contraria docuerit aut senserit,
anathema sit. In has autem sanctas et salutures observa-
tiones si qui abusus irrepserint, eis prorsus aboleri sancta
synodus vehementer cupit; ita ut nullæ falsi dogmatis
imagines et rudibus periculosi erroris occasionem præbentes
statuantur. Quod si aliquando historias et narrationes
sacræ Scripturæ, cum id indoctæ plebi expediret, exprimi
et figurari contigerit, doceatur populus non propterea
divinitatem figurari, quasi corporeis oculis conspici vel
coloribus aut figuris exprimi possit. Omnis porro super-
stitio in sanctorum invocatione, reliquiarum veneratione et
maginum sacro usu tollatur; omnis turpis quæstus eliminetur

omnis denique lascivia vitetur; ita ut procaci venustate imagines non pingantur nec ornentur et sanctorum celebratione ac reliquiarum visitatione homines ad comessationes atque ebrietates non abutantur; quasi festi dies in honorem sanctorum per luxum ac lasciviam agantur. Postremo, tanta circa hæc diligentia et cura ab episcopo adhibeatur ut nihil inordinatum aut præpostere et tumultuarie accommodatum, nihil profanum nihilque inhonestum appareat; cum domum Dei deceat sanctitudo. Hæc ut fidelius observentur, statuit sancta synodus nemini licere ullo in loco vel ecclesia, etiam quomodolibet exempta ullam insolitam ponere vel ponendam curare imaginem nisi ab episcopo approbata fuerit: nulla etiam admittenda esse nova miracula, nec novas reliquias recipiendas, nisi eodem recognoscente, et approbante episcopo, qui simul atque de iis aliquid compertum habuerit, adhibitis in consilium theologis et aliis viris, ea faciat quæ veritati et pietati consentanea judicaverit. Quod si aliquis dubius aut difficilis abusus sit extirpandus, vel omnino aliqua de rebus gravior quæstio incidat, episcopus, antequam controversiam dirimat metropolitani et comprovincialium episcoporum in concilio provinciali sententiam expectet; ita tamen ut nihil, inconsulto sanctissimo romanorum pontifice, novum aut in Ecclesia hactenus inusitatum decernatur.''

3. Here we shall treat in four distinct sections, first of the worship of the saints; secondly of their invocation; thirdly of their relics; and fourthly of sacred images.

SECTION I.—ON THE WORSHIP DUE TO THE SAINTS.

4. The first who denied that religious worship is due to the saints, was Simon Magus, who obliged his disciples not to venerate the images of the saints, but to worship his own image and that of his wife Helen. Calvin and his followers say that we should not pay any honour to the saints.

Honour differs from *praise* and *worship*. Honour is shown by external signs: *praise* is offered in words, and *worship* includes both, along with internal veneration: and this is certainly due to the saints on account of their supernatural excellence. The heretics calumniate us, by saying that we give to the saints the same honour we pay to God: but we hold that to the saints on account of their supernatural virtue, is due the worship which is called *dulia*; that to the Divine Mother on account of the more sublime gifts and virtues which she possessed, should be paid the worship which is called *hyperdulia*, and that the worship of *latria* is due to God alone on account of his infinite perfections, and to Jesus Christ on account of the hypostatic union of his flesh with the divinity of the Word. These are called religious worship, and are distinguished from the civil worship or respect which is paid to men on account of their natural virtues, and from the political worship given to princes or magistrates on account of their dignity.

5. With regard to the question whether the saints can be worshipped or only venerated, I say that it is a question merely about words: it is sufficient that God be adored as our supreme Lord, with the worship of *latria*, and that the saints be honoured with the worship of *dulia*, as the servants of God, and our intercessors before his divine Majesty. In the seventh synod, or second Council of Nice, it was said:—" Sive igitur placebit salutationem sive adorationem appellare, idem illa profecto erit, modo sciamus excludi latriam; hæc enim est alia a simplici adoratione, ut alibi est ostensum." (Act. vi.)

6. Writing on the gospel for the twenty-third Sunday after Pentecost, Luther said, that all worship to the saints is diabolical; and the Centuriators say that it is idolatry. Some of the Lutherans think that the saints, and particularly the Blessed Virgin, who said of herself, " all genera-

tions shall call me blessed," merit some special worship:
but will not permit any religious worship to be paid to
them. Hence, they censure the invocation of saints, pilgrimages, and all other pious works performed in honour of the
saints. But we know, from the scripture, that Abraham
worshipped the angels (Gen. xix. 1.); that Saul worshipped
the soul of Samuel, (2 Kings, c. 28.) and that the children
of the prophets, having learned that the spirit of Elias rested
on Eliseus, worshipped him. God himself honours the
saints, as we read in the Gospel of St. John: "If any man
minister to me, him will my Father honour." (John xii. 26.)
Since God honours his servants, how can we be forbidden
to honour them? St. Ambrose writes: "Whosoever
honours the martyrs, honours Christ." (Serm. in fin.) St.
Cyprian says: "Sacrificia pro eis semper offerimus, quoties
martyrium, passiones, et dies anniversaria commemoratione
celebramus." (Lib. 4, epist. 5.) St. John Damascene has
said that "the saints are to be honoured as the servants,
friends, and children of God." (Lib. 4. orthod. fid. c. 16.)
St. Basil says: "Ecclesia, per hoc quod eos honorat qui
præcesserunt, præsentes impellit." (Orat. in S. Mam.) St.
Jerome writes: "Honoramus servos, ut honor servorum
redundet ad Dominum." (Ep. ad. Ripar.) Theodoret says:
"Atque nos Græci homines nec hostias martyribus nec
libamina ulla deferimus, sed ut sanctos homines Deique
amicissimos honoramus." (Lib. viii. de Græc.) And St.
Augustine says: "Memorias martyrum populus Christianus
religiosa solemnitate concelebrat." (Lib. 20, contra Faust.
c. 21.) The authority of so many holy Fathers ought to
convince us that it is not only lawful but a duty to pay
religious veneration to the saints, as well on account of
their supernatural excellence, as on account of the sanctifying grace with which they shall be adorned for all
eternity, and on account of the vision of God which they
enjoy and shall for ever enjoy.

2 L 2

7. The adversaries object, first from the words of St. Paul: "To the king of ages...the only God, be honour and glory." (1 Tim. i. 17.) I answer that, as has been already said, to God alone on account of his infinite and increated sanctity is due all honour: but this does not hinder us to honour the saints also on account of the sanctity which God communicates to them. Hence, appears the silliness of the assertion of the heretics that by the worship we pay the saints, we diminish that which we owe to God. For, according to St. Jerome (see paragraph 6), the honour which is given to the saints redounds to the honour of God, as the author of their sanctity. This answer was also given by St. Augustine to those who said that by honouring St. Peter, the honour due to Jesus Christ was diminished." "In Petro (says the holy Doctor) quis honoratur, nisi ille defunctus pro nobis? Sumus enim christiani, non petriani." (Ep. 232.)

8. They object secondly, that in honouring the saints we are really guilty of idolatry: because we offer them even the sacrifice of the altar. But all this is false: we offer the mass to God alone as to our supreme Lord; but we also offer it in thanksgiving for the graces and gifts which he has bestowed on his saints, imploring him, through their intercession, to grant us the graces we stand in need of: hence, though many churches and altars bear the names of certain saints, all churches and altars are, nevertheless, erected in honour of God.

9. They object, thirdly, that to the Blessed Virgin we give the honour which is due to God alone, and to Christ, by calling her co-redemptress, mediatress, and our hope. I answer that we call Mary *co-redemptress*, not because she along with Jesus Christ has redeemed mankind: but because, as St. Augustine says, (lib de Sancta virgin. c. 6.) by being the mother of our head Jesus Christ, and by co-operating by her charity to the spiritual birth of the faithful

to grace in the Church, she became the mother of us who
are members of Jesus Christ our head: "Sed plane mater
membrorum ejus (quæ nos sumus) quia co-operata est
charitate ut fideles in Ecclesia nascerentur, qua illius capitis
membra sunt." Being the carnal mother of our Saviour,
she became also the spiritual mother of all the faithful.
During her whole life, this sublime Virgin by means of her
charity towards men, co-operated to their salvation, particularly when on Mount Calvary she offered to the Eternal
Father the life of his Son for our salvation. We call Mary
a *mediatress* not of justice but of grace; for Jesus Christ
alone is the mediator of justice, who by his merits has
obtained for men reconciliation with God. Mary is a
mediatress of grace with God, as all the saints are also;
but her intercession is far more powerful than that of the
saints, whose prayers are the prayers of servants, whilst
the prayers of Mary are the prayers of a mother, which, as
St. Bernard says, are never rejected: "Let us," says the
holy Doctor, "ask grace, and ask it through Mary: for she
is a mother and cannot be disappointed." Hence, St.
Peter Damian thus addresses her: "O Lady, nothing is
impossible to thee, who art able to excite hopes of
salvation, even in those who are in despair. For thy son
honours thee by refusing nothing to thee." It is in this
sense we are to understand the following words of the same
saint, which have excited such horror in Piceninus the
Calvinist: "Accedis ad illud commune propitiatorium,
Domina, non ancilla, imperans, non rogans."*

10. They object, fourthly, that the worship of *dulia*, with
which we honour the saints, is not due to them: because
we are not servants of the saints, but fellow-servants with
them. I answer, that we are, strictly speaking, servants

* In the Glories of Mary, St. Alphonsus teaches that the
Blessed Virgin never obtains any grace for us, except by praying for it in the name, and through the merits of Jesus Christ.

only of God, our supreme Lord: but we may in a certain
sense be also called servants of the saints, on account of
their excellence, and perfect exemption from all stain; and
still more on account of the celestial kingdom which they
possess, and shall possess for eternity; whilst we on this
earth are not exempt from sins, nor certain that we shall
be among the number of the elect, and therefore, we justly
venerate the saints, and pay them the worship of *dulia*,
which is due to them.

SECTION II.—ON THE INVOCATION OF SAINTS.

11. Vigilantius, and afterwards Wickliffe asserted, that
the invocation of saints is vain and useless; but in the
decree which has been already quoted, the Council of Trent
commands bishops to teach the opposite: "Sanctos una
cum Christo regnantes, orationes suas pro hominibus Deo
offerre; bonum atque utile esse suppliciter invocare." If it
is useful to the living to recommend themselves to the
prayers of each other, it will be far more profitable to invoke the saints, that they may assist us by their prayers,
which are far more powerful than the prayers of the saints
on this earth. St. Paul recommended himself to the prayers
of his disciples: "Be instant in prayer…praying withal for
us also." (Colos. iv. 2.)   And in the Epistle to the Romans
he says: "I beseech you, therefore, brethren…that you
help me in your prayers for me to God." (xv. 30.)   God
himself exhorted the friends of Job to ask him to pray for
them, and promised to show them mercy through his
prayers: "Go to my servant Job…and my servant Job
shall pray for you: his face I will accept that folly may not
be imputed to you." (Job xlii. 8.)   If, says St. Jerome, our
prayers, while we live on this earth, can obtain for others
the divine graces, will they have less efficacy when we have
gone to reign with Christ?   "Moyses sexcentis millibus

impetrat a Deo veniam, et Stephanus pro peccatoribus veniam deprecatur: postquam cum Christo esse cœperint
minus valebunt?" (S. Hier. contra Vigil.) Lomer, a Lutheran, says, that we ask the saints not only to intercede for
us, but also to assist us. But in this objection there is no
force: for the saints assist us not by their own power, but
by their intercession, by means of which we receive the divine graces.

12. In the book of Jeremias we read: "If Moses and
Samuel shall stand before me, my soul is not towards this
people." (Jer. xv. 1.) Moses and Samuel prayed for the
people, and the Lord heard their prayers: how then can the
heretics say that we have no proof from Scripture that the
saints in the other world pray for the living? Judas Macchabeus, as we read in the second book of Macchabees, saw
in a vision the high priest Onias, and the prophet Jeremias
who were then dead, praying for the Jews, (2 Mac.) To this
argument, Calvin could give no other answer than that the
book of Macchabees is not canonical. The heretics say that
the angels and saints pray for us, but only in general.
But the contrary is evident from the twelfth chapter of
Tobias, from the tenth of Daniel, from the eighteenth of
St. Matthew, and from the eighth of the Apocalypse, in
which we read that the angels and saints have prayed for
particular individuals.

13. That the invocation of saints has been approved by
tradition, is clear from the authority of the holy Fathers.
In a work ascribed to St. Ambrose, we read: "Ut efficax mea
sit deprecatio, B. Mariæ Virginis suffragia peto; quam tanti
meriti esse fecisti &c.: apostolorum intercessionem imploro,"
&c. In prec. 2, præp. ad Miss. In his liturgy St. John Chrysostom frequently invokes the prayers of the Blessed Virgin
and the other saints. In the meditations attributed to St.
Augustine, (c. 40), we find the following prayer: "Sancta
et immaculata virgo Dei genitrix Maria, intervenire pro me

digneris. S. Michael, S. Gabriel, ss. chori angelorum
atque patriarcharum, apostolorum, martyrum, confessorum,
&c., per illum qui vos elegit, vos rogare præsumo ut pro
me supplicare dignemini, &c." We find the same doctrine
in the writings of St. Athanasius, St. Cyprian, St. Hilary,
St. Basil, St. Epiphanius, and other Fathers. Besides, the
Fathers of the Council of Chalcedon said: "Flavianus
post mortem vivit: martyr pro nobis oret." (Act. 11.)
The same was afterwards said by the Fathers of the sixth
synod: "Christianus, solo Deo creatore suo adorato, in-
vocet sanctos, ut pro se intercedere apud M. D. dignentur."
Moreover, in the Antiphonarium of St. Gregory, (t. 3, fol.
690.) we read: "Sancta Dei genitrix virgo Maria, ora pro
nobis; precibus quoque apostolorum, martyrum, &c., suppliciter petimus." Hincmar also relates that St. Remigius,
in baptizing Clodoveus, recited the litany of the saints.
Piceninus disapproves of our litanies, hymns, and prayers,
because they are directed to the saints without any
mention of Jesus Christ: but he errs, for all our litanies,
hymns, and prayers, in honour of the saints, either begin
with the name of God, or terminate by giving glory to the
most holy Trinity. Piceninus is also displeased at our
frequent repetition of the *Ave Maria*, as if we wished to
imitate the angel announcing to the virgin the mystery
of the incarnation, which has been already accomplished.
But we do not pretend to act the part of angels, or to an-
nounce the Incarnation to Mary; but only repeat this salu-
tation, so dear to her, in order to obtain her most powerful
intercession; knowing that all the praises we give to the
mother, redound to the honour of the Son, who rejoices
when we invoke her, that he may bestow favours on us for
her sake.

14. Speaking of St. Felix, St. Augustine says: "Non
solum beneficiorum effectibus, verum ipsis hominum aspec-
tibus confessorem apparuisse Felicem, cum a barbaris Nola

oppugnaretur, audivimus non incertis rumorimus, sed testibus certis." (lib. de cura pro mortuis. c. 16.) Other similar examples of saints who when invoked by their clients, have appeared to them, and have obtained the favours they asked, are related by St. Gregory of Nyssa in his life of St. Gregory of Neocesaria, by Theodoret (hist. l. 5, c. 24,) by Evodius, Lucian, and St. Ambrose, speaking of St. Gervasius and Protasius.

15. Piceninus rejoins and says: you Catholics direct your prayers, not to God, but to the saints, and you invoke them as if it depended on them to grant you the divine graces and eternal life. But we believe that God is the sole giver of graces, and we have recourse to the saints as intercessors, who obtain for us the divine graces principally through the merits of Christ. Hence, the saints are our mediators with the principal mediator, Jesus Christ, who, through his infinite merits, obtains for us whatever good we receive. Hence, the Church prays to God, not through the saints, but through Christ. " *Concede nobis, Deus, intercessione S.N. hoc beneficium per Christum Dominum nostrum.*" And when she prays through the merits of any saint, she intends to pray through them, inasmuch as the saints, because they enjoy the friendship of God, have greater power to obtain for us the divine graces. In the prayer, *sanate mentes languidas, augete nos virtutibus*, which we find in the hymn of the apostles, the Church does not mean that the saints can heal our tepidity, or increase our virtues, but only that, by their prayers, they can obtain these favours for us. Speaking of himself, St. Paul said: "If by any means I......may save some of them:" (Rom. xi. 14,) and in the first epistle to the Corinthians he says: "I became all things to all men, that I might save all." (1 Cor. ix. 22.) How could he save them? By the aid of his preaching and prayers.

16. That the invocation of saints is useful is, as we

have seen, a dogma of faith. But St. Thomas asks, whether it is not only lawful, but a duty necessary for salvation, to invoke their intercession? " Utrum debeamus sanctos orare ad interpellandum pro nobis?" He answers: " Ordo est divinitus institutus in rebus secundum Dionysium, ut per media ultima reducantur in Deum. Unde, cum sancti qui sunt in patria sint Deo propinquissimi, hoc divinæ legis ordo requirit ut nos qui, manentes in corpore peregrinamur a Domino in eum per sanctos medios reducamur; quod quidem contingit dum per eos divina bonitas suum effectum diffundit." The saint adds: " Et quia reditus noster in Deum respondere debet processui bonitatum ipsius ad nos, mediantibus sanctorum suffragiis, Dei beneficia in nos deveniunt, ita oportet nos in Deum reduci, ut iterato beneficia ejus sumamus mediantibus sanctis." (In 4, sent. dist. 45, q. 3, art. 2.) Mark the words: " Sicut mediantibus sanctorum suffragiis Dei beneficia in nos deveniunt, ita oportet nos in Deum reduci, ut iterato beneficia ejus sumamus mediantibus sanctis." Hence, according to the holy Doctor, the order of the divine law requires that we, mortals, be brought back to God, and be saved through the saints, by receiving, through them, the helps necessary for salvation. And in answer to the objection *(ad primum)* that it appears superfluous to have recourse to the saints, when God is infinitely more merciful and inclined to hear us than they are, the holy Doctor says, that the Lord has thus ordained, not through a defect of power, but to preserve the right order which he has universally established, of operating by means of second causes: " Non est propter defectum misericordiæ ipsius, sed ut ordo prædictus conservetur in rebus."

17. And in conformity with the doctrine of St. Thomas, Collet says (tom. 1, de relig. c. 2, de orat. a. 4, q. 1.) that although we ought to pray to God alone, as the author of every grace, still we are bound to have recourse also to the

intercession of the saints, in order to observe the order which God has established with regard to our salvation; which is, that inferiors should be saved by those who are of a superior order. "Quia lege naturali tenentur eum ordinem observare quem Deus instituit: at constituit Deus ut ad salutem inferiores perveniant, implorato superiorum subsidio."

18. And if it is necessary to have recourse to the prayers of the saints, how much more are we obliged to invoke the intercession of the Divine Mother, whose prayers are certainly more powerful before God than the prayers of all the other saints. For, according to St. Thomas, the saints, in proportion to their merits, can save many; but Jesus Christ, and also his mother, have merited so great a grace that they can save all men: "Magnum est in quolibet sancto, quando habet tantum de gratia quod sufficeret ad salutem multorum; sed quando haberet tantum, quod sufficeret ad salutem omnium, hoc esset maximum; et hoc est in Christo et in B. Virgine." (ep. 8.) And St. Bernard addresses Mary in the following words: "Per te accessum habemus ad Filium, inventrix gratiæ, mater salutis, ut per te nos suscipiat qui per te datus est nobis." (Serm. in Dom. infra oct. Ass.) Thus the saint insinuates that as we have access to the Father only through the Son, who is a mediator of justice, so we have access to the Son through the Mother, who is a mediatrix of grace, and obtains for us, by her intercession, the graces which Jesus Christ has merited for us. Hence St. Bernard says, (serm. de aquæd.) that Mary has received a twofold fulness of grace: the first was the incarnation of the eternal Word made man in her womb: the second is the fulness of the graces which we receive from God through the intercession of the divine mother. Hence the holy doctor adds: "Totius boni plenitudinem (Deus) posuit in Maria, ut proinde si quid spei nobis est, si quid gratiæ, si quid salutis, ab ea novimus redundare, quæ ascendit deliciis affluens, hortus deliciarum, ut undique fluant et effluant

2 M

aromata ejus, charismata scilicet gratiarum." Thus whatever good we receive from God, we obtain it through the
intercession of Mary. But what is the reason of this?
The same St. Bernard answers, because such is the will of
God: " Sic est voluntas ejus qui totum nos habere voluit
per Mariam." But the strongest reason is taken from the
words of St. Augustine, who has said that Mary is justly
called our mother, because by her charity she has co-operated to the birth of the faithful—the members of our
head Christ Jesus, to the life of grace: " Sed plane mater
membrorum ejus (quæ nos sumus) quia co-operata est charitate ut fideles in Ecclesia nascerentur, qui illius capitis
membra sunt." (lib. 3, de symb. ad catec. c. 4.) Hence
as Mary has co-operated by her charity to the spiritual
birth of the faithful, so God wishes that she should co-
operate by her prayers, offered in the name, and through
the merits of Jesus Christ, to obtain for them the life of
grace in this world, and the life of glory in the next. It is
on this account that the holy Church makes us salute and
call Mary *our life, our sweetness, and our hope.*
Speaking of her, St. Bernard said: " Filioli, hæc peccatorum
scala, hæc maxima mea fiducia, hæc tota ratio spei meæ."
He calls her a ladder: because as we ascend the third step
by means of the second; and the second by means of the
first; so we ascend to God only through Jesus Christ,
and to Jesus Christ through Mary. He then calls her
his greatest confidence, and the entire ' reason of
his hope : because, (as the saint supposes) God wishes
that all the graces which he dispenses to men, for the
sake of Jesus Christ, should pass through the hands of
Mary. Finally, the holy doctor concludes in these words:
" Let us ask grace, and ask it through Mary, for what she
asks she obtains, and cannot be disappointed."

19. The heretics object first, that the saints in heaven
do not know that we ask their prayers. " Their ears,"
said the impious Calvin, " are not so long that they can

hear us." But the contrary appears from the Scripture: The angel Raphael said to Tobias: "When thou didst pray with tears......I offered thy prayer to the Lord." (Tob. xii. 12.) And in the Apocalypse we read that "the four and twenty ancients fell down before the lamb, having every one of them harps, and golden vials full of odours, which are the prayers of the saints." (v. 8.) They held in their hands golden vessels full of odours: these odours are our prayers, which, according to the words of David, "Let my prayer be directed as incense in thy sight, (Ps. cxl. 2,) ascend like the smoke of incense. But the adversaries rejoin, and say that God alone knows our thoughts and prayers; "Thou only knowest the heart of all the children of men." (3 Kings viii. 39.). We answer that God alone by his own nature knows our desires; but the saints know them by communication. Some say that the saints know our prayers by a divine revelation; but St. Gregory holds that they see our prayers in God, whom they behold unveiled: "Quia quæ intus omnipotentis Dei claritatem vident, nullo modo credendum est quod sit forte aliquid quod ignorent. Quid est quod ibi nesciant, ubi scientem omnia sciunt?" (lib. 12, c. 13. apud S. Thom. p. 1, q. 89, a. 8.) However, St. Augustine thinks that the saints know our prayers by the ministry of the angels: "Deus omnipotens, qui est ubique præsens, nec concretus nobis, exaudiens martyrum preces per angelica ministeria usquequaque diffusa, præbet hominibus ista solatia, quibus in hujus vitæ miseria judicat esse præbenda et suorum merita martyrum, ubi vult, quando vult, quomodo vult, maximeque per eorum memorias, quod hoc novit expedire nobis ad ædificandam fidem Christi, pro cujus illi confessione sunt passi, mirabili atque ineffabili potestate ac bonitate commendat." (lib. de cura pro mort. c. 15.)

20. Secondly, Calvin objects (lib. 3, c. 20, Inst.) that in the third Council of Carthage (c. 23.) it was forbidden

to direct the prayers on the altar to any one but the Eternal Father; and this is confirmed by St. Augustine (lib. 22. de civ. Dei c. 11.) who says that the saints are not invoked by the priest offering sacrifice.   I answer that, in the Council of Cathage there was nothing said about the invocation of saints, but only that the priest should direct the sacrifice, not to the Son, nor the Holy Ghost, but to the Father, as is done at present: in offering sacrifice we always offer it to the three persons of the Trinity.   But it does not follow that because in offering sacrifice, God alone is invoked, we cannot invoke the saints, that they may pray for us.   That it is lawful to ask the prayers of the saints is taught by St. Augustine, (tr. 84, in Jo., et serm. 17.); and by St. Cyril. (Catech.)   This doctrine may be inferred also from the liturgies of St. Chrysostom, and other ancient authors, in which the saints are invoked.

21. The heretics object, thirdly, that the Lord is most ready to hear us: " Ask, and you shall receive; seek, and you shall find."   Of what use then, they say, is it to ask the prayers of the saints ?   It only tends to diminish our confidence in God.   This, they say, is confirmed by the words of St. Chrysostom, (hom. de prof. evang.) who says: " Certum non opus tibi patronis apud Deum...sed licet solus sit, omnino tamen voti compos eris."   I answer that, although God is ready to hear us, and has no need of the saints in order to console us, still, on account of the greater merits of the saints, he is more ready to hear their prayers than ours.   Hence he said to the friends of Job: " Go to my servant Job......and my servant Job shall pray for you." (Job xlii. 8.)   In the place quoted from St. John Chrysostom, the holy doctor reproves the rich who give alms to the poor, that the poor may pray for them: and he tells them that it is more useful to pray in person than by means of the poor.

22. They object, fourthly, that Jesus Christ has said,

that we ought to direct our prayers only to the Eternal Father. Thus, you shall pray: "Our Father who art in heaven," &c. (Mat. vi. 9.) This argument proves too much, and therefore proves nothing: were it conclusive, it would prove that in our prayers we should not address either the Son or the Holy Ghost: but this the Centuriators themselves, who have proposed the objection, do not admit. (Cent. 1, l. 1, c. 4.)

23. Fifthly, they object that there is no precept obliging us to ask the prayers of the saints; nor any promise that, when we have recourse to them, God will hear us. I answer, that if there is no precept, there is no prohibition, to invoke the intercession of the saints, although the heretics forbid it. And although God has not expressly promised to hear us when we pray to the saints, still he has sometimes exhorted men to have recourse to the intercession of his servants. Hence he said to the friends of Job; "Go to my servant Job; and my servant Job shall pray for you; his face I will accept." (Job xlii. 8.)

24. They object sixthly, that the saints in heaven are incapable of merit, and by consequence can obtain no grace, either for themselves or for others. It is true that they are incapable of merit, because they are out of the way; but on account of their previous merits they can obtain for us the graces which we ask of God through their intercession. Nor can it be said that the Lord has already given them the reward of the merits which they acquired on earth; for among the rewards which God gives them is the power of obtaining for a client the graces which he asks through their intercession.

25. They object seventhly, that the invocation of saints is injurious to God. The Apostle asks: "How, then, shall they call on him in whom they have not believed?" (Rom. x. 14.) We then should invoke him alone in whom we believe. We believe only in God: therefore, say the inno-

vators, we should invoke God alone, or should consider the saints as Gods. I answer, that as a monarch is not injured, but is honoured, when a person asks others to intercede with him, so no injury is done to God by invoking the saints as intercessors with him. Otherwise St. Paul would have done an injury to God by recommending himself to his disciples, as he did several times in his Epistles. In the passage from which the objection is taken, the Apostle only means that they who do not believe in God cannot invoke him.

26. They object eighthly, from the words of St. Paul: "There is......one mediator of God and men, the man Christ Jesus." (1 Tim. ii. 5.) Hence, by taking the saints for our mediators, we do an injury to Christ, who is our only mediator. I answer, that we do not intend to invoke the saints that they may intercede for us in the place of Christ, or that they may assist Christ to enable him to obtain graces for us, but only as mediators with Christ, the principal and only mediator, who, through his infinite merits, procures for us the divine graces from God. We invoke the saints as intercessors with Christ, or with God, that we may be the more easily heard through the merits of the Saviour. A person may be a mediator for others in two ways: first, by paying the debt which they have to discharge; secondly, by entreating the creditor to remit the obligation of paying the debt. Jesus Christ is our mediator in the first sense; because by his sufferings he has paid our debts; and it is in this sense the Apostle calls him our only mediator, as appears from the words which follow the passage which has been quoted: "Who gave himself a redemption for all." (Ib. v. 6.) In the second sense, even the saints can be our mediators, but mediators only of grace, and not of justice, as Jesus Christ is: for, according to the compact which he has made with the Son, the Father is bound to hear him, and to grant all that he asks through his own merits. Hence St. Gregory

Nazianzen does not hesitate to call the holy martyrs mediators between us and God: neither did Moyses scruple to call himself a mediator between God and the Jews: "I was the mediator, and stood between the Lord and you at that time." (Deut. v. 5.) But it is always true, that all the graces which the saints obtain for us, they obtain through the mediation of Jesus Christ.

27. The innovators object ninthly, that on account of the words of St. Paul: "Let no man seduce you, willing in humility and religion of angels," &c., (Col. ii. 18.) the Council of Laodicea prohibited the invocation of the angels; and that this prohibition accords with the words of St. John Chrysostom: "Deus salutem nostram non tam aliis pro nobis rogantibus vult donare quam nobis." (Hom. 5, in Mat.) I answer, that in the passage quoted from St. Paul, the Apostle condemns the idolatry of Simon Magus, who taught that certain angels should be adored as minor Gods, because they had constructed the world: the words of the Apostle are thus explained by St. Jerome and other Fathers. In answer to the objection from the words of St. Chrysostom, I say that the saint speaks of persons who wish to be saved by the prayers of others, without praying for themselves; hence he adds: "Hæc dicimus non ut supplicandum esse sanctis negemus, sed ne dormientes ipsi aliis tantummodo nostra curanda mandemus."

28. They object tenthly, from the words of Jeremias, in which the Prophet says, that we should place our hopes in God alone, and not in men, and pronounces a malediction against those who trust in creatures: "Cursed be the man that trusteth in man." (xvii. 5.) I answer, that we trust in God alone as the author of all graces, and in Jesus Christ as our principal mediator: but in the saints we trust only as intercessors, or secondary mediators, who by praying for us through the merits of Christ can obtain for us the divine graces more easily than we can ourselves; because

their prayers are more efficacious and more acceptable to God than ours. A curse shall certainly fall on him who trusts in man independently of God; but not on the christian who knows that all graces depend on God, and recommends himself to the saints, that by their intercession they may obtain for him the graces which he stands in need of.

SECTION III.—ON THE VENERATION DUE TO THE RELICS OF THE SAINTS.

29. The Lutherans say that the bones of the saints should be treated with reverence, but not with religious veneration, by kissing them, carrying them in procession, kneeling before them, or paying respect to them by lighted candles. We say that there are two kinds of religious veneration: one which is *absolute*, and is paid to any thing on account of its own excellence; the other is *relative*, and is shown to one thing on account of its relation to another. The latter is the veneration which we pay to relics on account of the saints whom we respect in them. We know from the Acts of the Apostles that the handkerchiefs and cinctures of St. Paul were carried about to heal the sick. "So that even there were brought from his body to the sick handkerchiefs and aprons, *(that is, narrow cinctures,)* and the diseases departed from them, and the wicked spirits went out of them." (xix. 12.) Thus says Grotius, (Adnot. ad art. 20, consult. Cassand.) God himself has anticipated us in honouring the relics of the saints. Besides, we know from the Scripture, that the waters of the Jordan respected the mantle of Elias: "And he struck the waters with the mantle of Elias that had fallen from him, and they were not divided." (4 Kings ii. 14.) Now, if the Lord wished to honour by miracles the garments of his saints, how much more must he wish that we honour the bones of their bodies, which have co-operated to the divine glory? And be it here observed, that in

conformity with the examples which have been brought from the Scriptures, we justly venerate not only the bones of the saints, but also their clothes, staffs, and other things which had been sanctified by their use, or by contact with them, such as the instruments with which the martyrs were tortured.

30. That it is lawful to venerate the relics of the saints is proved from the tradition of the Fathers. In the Apostolical constitutions, (l. 6,) which have been attributed to St. Clement, we read: "Eorum qui in Deo vivunt nec reliquiæ sine honore manent." St. John Chrysostom writes: "Sæpe eos invisamus, capsulam attingamus, ut inde benedictionem aliquam assequamur." (Hom. 40 in SS. Juvent. et Maxim.) St. Augustine says: "Reliquias B. martyris Stephani, quas non ignorat sanctitas vestra, sicut et nos fecimus, quam convenienter honorare debeatis." (Ep. 103, vide l. xxii. c. 8, de civ. Dei.) In another place (l. 1, de civ. Dei. c. 13.) he says, that the relics of the saints should be venerated because they were the organs and vessels which the Holy Ghost employed in the works of his glory: "Quibus tanquam organis et vasis ad omnia bona opera usus est." St. Jerome writes: "Christianos solum Deum honorare, sed martyres, et reliquias eorum venerari, quorum honor ad Dominum redundat, qui dixit: Qui vos suscipit me suscipit. (Ep. 11, ad Rip.) In his work against Vigilantius, who called the Catholics idolaters because they venerated the relics of the saints as the Pagans adored the idols, the same holy Doctor says: "Idolatras appellat ejusmodi homines: illud fiebat idolis, et ideo destestandum est; hoc fit martyribus, et idcirco recipiendum est." This is also the doctrine of St. Athanasius, of St. Basil, St. Eusebius, and St. Gregory of Nyssa. See Bellarmine, (lib. de reliq. et imag. SS.) who, in confirmation of it, quotes the second council of Nice, the fifth council of Carthage, and the third Council of Bracare.

31. Through fear of the Pagans, the Christians, in the first ages of the Church, abstained from certain external demonstrations of religion, and, among the rest, from the veneration of relics. But in the fourth century, after the persecutions ceased, the bones of St. Stephen were the first that were disinterred, and were carried with great veneration in various places, in which, as St. Augustine attests (de civ. Dei c. 8), many miracles were wrought through these relics. The disciples of St. Polycarp also endeavoured with great care to procure his relics, and, after having obtained them, they preserved them in a decent place (*ubi decebat*), as we find in the letter from the Church of Smyrna, (apud Eus. hist. l. 4, c. 15.)

32. The heretic Amesius objects, that God concealed the body of Moses, that it might not be worshipped by the Jews. I answer that God acted in this manner, because at that time the Jews were very prone to idolatry; hence, to prevent them from paying divine honour to the bones of Moses, God wished that they should be concealed. But, after the Babylonian captivity, God himself rendered illustrious the graves of Isaias, Jeremias, and Ezechiel, and was pleased with the veneration paid to their remains.   And by stating that the Lord buried Moses, (sepelivit eum) the Holy Ghost himself has taught us that honour should be shown to the bodies of the saints.

33. The adversaries object, secondly, from the rebuke which Jesus Christ gave the Pharisees, for having adorned the sepulchres of the saints: " Wo to you that build the sepulchres of the prophets, and adorn the monuments of the just." (Matt. xxiii. 29.)   I answer, that our Lord rebuked the Pharisees for their hypocrisy, because, being satisfied with these external acts, they neglected the interior virtues, and sought to be esteemed holy on account of their external veneration of the prophets.

34. Thirdly, Amesius objects, that the greater number

of relics are supposititious and false, and that, instead of the bones of a saint, Catholics often venerate the bones of robbers, and even of dogs. I answer, first, that it is not true that false relics are frequently venerated, particularly when they are exposed to the veneration of the faithful by the authority of the bishops, who are very vigilant in this matter. Now, without their authority, it is forbidden by the decree passed by the Council in this Session, to expose relics to the veneration of the people. I answer, secondly, that though in some particular case, a false relic should be exposed, through the malice or ignorance of an individual, we should not on that account refuse to venerate all other relics which we have no reason to suspect to be false. And should it ever happen that any relic were not genuine, to render the veneration of it lawful, it is enough to have the intention of honouring the saint of whom it is supposed to be a relic; for we always venerate relics on the tacit condition that they are genuine.

SECTION IV.—ON THE VENERATION OF SACRED IMAGES.

35. In latter times, the first who persecuted sacred images was Andrew Carlostad, in 1522, as we find in the life of Luther, by Cocleus. He was followed by the Zuinglians, by the Centuriators of Magdeburgh, by Calvin, who, along with all his followers, reprobated the veneration of sacred images. But about the year 781, a fierce war was waged against sacred images by the emperors Leo, the Isaurian, and Constantine Copronimus, against whom the Seventh Synod, or Second Council of Nice, was held under Pope Adrian. At first this Council was not received in France because the doctrine which had been defined was not well understood. But when it was afterwards understood, the Council was received, and held to be, what it really was, a

truly Ecumenical Council. In the west, a Council was held in Rome, under Gregory the Second, in which there were about a thousand bishops; in that Council the heresy of the Iconoclasts was likewise condemned.

36. The heretics condemn us as idolaters, because we venerate sacred images, without distinguishing between an idol and an image: an *idol* or image-god is (according to the language of the scripture) an image which is adored as a false god; a sacred *image* is a representation of the original, which is directly venerated. Thus the image is a figure of a prototype which really exists; the idol is the figure of a prototype or of a god that does not exist. Hence the honour paid to an image is always referred to its prototype or original, which is venerated: hence Durandus unjustly says, that it is not lawful to venerate the image, but only the prototype in the image. This is contrary to the common opinion of Catholics, for although the veneration is always paid to the prototype, we also venerate the image.

37. Calvin asserts that in the first five centuries images were never venerated. But this assertion is refuted by Tertullian, who says (lib. de pudic), that on the sacred chalices used in the Catholic Churches there was an image of Jesus Christ, in the form of a pastor, carrying a sheep on his shoulders. The veneration of sacred images is proved conclusively from Apostolical tradition, and by the continual practice of the Church, as the Seventh Council attests, in the second and third action. In the seventh action the Council declared: "Nos SS. Patrum doctrinæ insistentes et catholicæ ecclesiæ, in qua Sanctus Spiritus inhabitat, traditionem observantes, definimus venerandas sanctorum imagines, et in templis Dei collocandas tum parietibus et tabulis, tum in ædibus privatis, in viis publicis &c., quo omnes illis honorariam adorationem exhibeant, non veram latriam, imaginis enim in prototypon redundat. Sic

disciplina vel traditio catholicæ ecclesiæ, quæ a finibus usque ad fines evangelium suscipit." In the sixth action of the same Synod, we find that St. Epiphanius, who lived in the fifth century, said: " Usque adeo venerandarum imaginum observatio in ecclesia obtinuerit ut ab eo hæc usque tempora recepta fuerit." And, according to the rule of St. Augustine, which has been already quoted, a usage, the authors of which are not known, must be supposed to descend by tradition from the Apostles; this may be justly said of the veneration of images. That the practice of venerating sacred images has come from the Apostles, has been attested in a work attributed to St. Basil (in Julian.): "Historias imaginum illorum (*apostolorum et martyrum*) et palam adoro. Hoc enim nobis traditum a SS. Apostolis non est prohibendum; sed in omnibus ecclesiis nostris horum historias eligimus." In a treatise, ascribed to St. Chrysostom, we read: " Sacerdos conversus ad Christi imaginem inter duo ostia inflexo capite cum exclamatione dicit hanc orationem, &c." (tr. 5 in liturg.) Nicephorus (l. 6. c. 16,) relates that St. Luke painted an image of the Blessed Virgin; and it is said that this image may be seen in the Church of St. Mary Major, in Rome. Besides, Anastasius, the Roman librarian, in the preface of the Seventh Synod, addressing John the Eighth, who succeeded Adrian II., writes: " Quæ super venerabilium imaginum adoratione præsens synodus docet, hæc et apostolica vestra sedes, sicut nonnulla scripta innuunt, antiquitus tenuit, et universalis ecclesia semper venerata est, et hactenus veneratur."

38. In confirmation of this doctrine, Sozomen (lib. 5, c. 20) and Nicephorus (lib. 10, c. 50) state, that at the time of Julian the apostate, the Christians introduced into the Church the statue of Jesus Christ, which was near Pemade; this happened before the year 400. In his life of Constantine (l. 3, c. 4), Eusebius also relates, that in the churches which that emperor built in Palestine, there

2 N

was a great number of sacred images of silver and gold.
St. Gregory Nazianzen laments that the city of Cesarea, in
the church of which he had venerated certain statues was
to be demolished, and adds: " Si statuæ dejiciantur, hoc
nos excruciat." In his life of St. Sylvester, St. Damasus
states that Constantine placed in the Lateran Church silver
statues of the Saviour, of the twelve Apostles, and of the
four Evangelists.   In the seventh synod (act. 6,) it is
related that the disciples of St. Epiphanius erected a temple
under his name, and placed his statue in it.   Nicephorus
also mentions (lib. 14, c. 2), that the empress Pulcheria
erected in the temple which she had built in Constantinople,
an image of the Divine Mother, which Eudoxia had sent
her from Jerusalem.   It is also related that our Saviour
impressed his image on a sheet, and sent it to king Aba-
garus.   This fact is denied by many moderns, but is asserted by St. John Damascene (lib. 1. de imag.) and, according to Evagrius, who holds it to be certain (lib. 4,
c. 26.), the fact was confirmed by a great miracle wrought
in Edessa.   In his history, and particularly in the life of
St. Simon Stilites, Theodoret relates that images of the
saint were suspended in all the shops in Rome.

39. The representation of God and the Most Holy Trinity, in a corporal form, gives displeasure to the heretics.
But we know that God appeared in a corporal form to Jacob
leaning on a ladder, on which the holy patriarch saw the
angels ascending and descending.   " And he saw in his
sleep a ladder......and the Lord leaning upon the ladder,
saying to him: I am the Lord God of Abraham, thy
father, &c." (Gen. xxviii. 13.)   And, in Exodus, the
Lord says: " I will take away my hand, and thou shalt
see my back parts; but my face thou canst not see."
(xxxiii. 23.)   Besides, in St. Matthew's account of the
baptism of Jesus Christ by the Baptist, we read that the
Holy Ghost appeared in the form of a dove : " And

Jesus being baptized......saw the Spirit of God descending as a dove." (Matt. iii. 16.). The seventh synod approved of the image of the Holy Ghost in the form of a dove. Besides, Daniel describes God as a hoary old man, seated on a throne: "The Ancient of days sat: his garment was white as snow, and the hair of his head like clean wool." (Dan. vii. 9.) We also find human members attributed to God in the sacred Scriptures. Now, if the Scriptures attribute human members to God, why may they not be represented in pictures? The Council of Trent, in this 25th Session, permits the images of God, particularly in historical pictures. However, the Fathers wish that the people be instructed not to believe that, on that account, the divinity can be represented as if God could be seen by human eyes: " Quod si aliquando historias et narrationes sacræ scripturæ, cum id indoctæ plebi expediret, exprimi et figurari contigerit, doceatur populus non propterea divinitatem figurari, quasi corporis oculis conspici vel coloribus aut figuris exprimi possit." Hence, we do not paint the likeness of the Most Holy Trinity, in order to represent the image of God such as he is, but only to instruct the people in the knowledge of God by these analogous similitudes.

40. Some think that we should pay to sacred images the same veneration with which we honour the original: thus, they say that to the images of God is due the worship of *latria*, to the images of the Blessed Virgin, the worship called *hyperdulia*, and to the images of the saints, that of *dulia*. But it is better to say with Bellarmine, that although images should be venerated differently, according to the prototype which they represent, still we should (as was observed in the seventh synod,) pay them not strictly, but in an improper sense, the veneration due to the originals; just as the ambassador of a king receives the same honour which is shown to the sovereign, but only in an improper sense. But St. Thomas solves this

difficulty better than any other author. (2. 2, q. 81, a. 3, ad 3.) He says, as the advocates of the first opinion hold, that the worship of latria or dulia, shown to God or the saints, may also be paid to their images; but with this difference, that the worship of the prototypes is absolute, and the veneration of the images relative: thus every difficulty is removed.

41. We shall now say a few words on the sign of the holy cross, in particular. Surely, on account of their contact with the sacred body of Jesus Christ, the relics or particles of the very wood on which he died, merit greater veneration than other relics ; we should also pay greater veneration to the sign of the cross than to the images of the saints. But on this point the heretics dissent from us, and say, that if honour is due to every image of the cross, because Christ died once on a cross, we should also pay respect to every cord, to every scourge, to every nail, to every tomb, since our Lord was tortured by the cords, the scourges and nails, and was laid in a sepulchre. I answer, that all cords, scourges, and nails have not been made to represent those from which Christ has suffered, whilst all crosses are made to represent the cross of Jesus Christ; and, therefore, crosses alone can be called sacred images, and deserve veneration. God himself wishes that the sign of the cross be venerated, as is clear from the words in St. Matthew: "And there shall appear the sign of the Son of Man in heaven." (xxiv. 30.) By the sign of the Son of Man all the ancients have, in opposition to Calvin, understood the sign of the cross; and the sixth, seventh, and eighth councils have framed special canons regarding the veneration of the cross.

42. But the adversaries say, that the cross of Christ merits detestation rather than reverence, since it was to him the cause of so much sorrow and ignominy. They say, that the son who should honour the gibbet on which

his father had been executed, would offer the father an insult rather than a tribute of respect. I answer, that although, according to the intention of the Jews, the cross was an occasion of ignominy to Jesus Christ, still it was to him a source of glory; because upon it he accomplished the redemption of the world. Hence we justly venerate the cross not as a cause of ignominy, but of glory, to our Saviour. Besides, the cross merits honour on account of its contact with Jesus Christ. Has the ass then, they say, on which Jesus Christ sat, become an object of honour? To this objection we find the answer in a work ascribed to St. Athanasius: "Christ has not conquered the devil and demons through the ass; neither has he wrought redemption on him, but on the cross." (L. qu. ad Ant. q. i, 5.) With regard to the relics of the cross, the adversaries object, that if all the particles of it which are scattered through the world, were united together, they would far surpass in magnitude the tree of the cross. But Cardinal Gotti says, that notwithstanding all the particles that have been taken from the cross, the holy wood has not been diminished; and for this assertion he adduces the authority of St. Cyril of Jerusalem, who attests that (like the multiplication of the loaves) the sacred wood of the cross, "ad hodiernum diem apud nos apparens et apud eos qui, secundum fidem ex eo capientes, hunc universum orbem repleverunt."

43. But of what use, they ask, are images, when we have the originals? They serve to keep alive in men, who are affected by sensible objects, the remembrance of Jesus Christ and his saints, who teach us the virtues we ought to practise, and at the same time remind us to invoke them in our necessities. St. Gregory of Nyssa says that even simple pictures suspended on the wall, though mute, speak to us and assist us greatly in the way of God: "Solet etiam pictura tacens in pariete loqui maximeque prodesse."

But the council of Trent describes better than all, the utility of sacred images: (decr. de invoc. sanct.) "Illud vero diligenter doceant episcopi per historias mysteriorum nostræ redemptionis, picturis vel aliis similitudinibus expressas, erudiri et confirmari populum in articulis fidei commemorandis et assidue recolendis: tum vero ex omnibus sacris imaginibus magnum fructum percipi, non solum quia admonetur populus beneficiorum et munerum quæ a Christo sibi collata sunt sed etiam quia Dei per sauctos miracula et salutaria exempla oculis fidelium subjiciuntur, ut pro iis Deo gratias agant, ad sanctorum imitationem vitam moresque suos componant, excitenturque ad adorandum ac diligendum Deum, ac pietatem colendam. Si quis autem his decretis contrarie docuerit aut senserit, anathema sit."

44. The adversaries object, first, that the Scripture prohibits all religious worship to images: "Thou shalt not adore them, and thou shalt not serve *them*." (Deut. v. 9.) The words, *thou shalt not adore*, forbid external worship, and the words, *thou shalt not serve*, prohibit internal veneration. I answer, that in the passage quoted, God forbade the idolatrous worship with which the pagans honoured their statues, believing that they really possessed some divine virtue, but not the religious veneration which is shown to sacred images on account of the originals which they represent. The Jews were forbidden to worship images, because they were prone to idolatry: however, they had figures of the Cherubim, which were really images of the angels. But, now that the danger of idolatry has ceased, the ceremonial precept imposed on the Jews has also ceased.

45. They object, secondly, that since images are venerated on account of their relation to the prototypes, we cannot venerate them as images. I answer, that images are capable of honour on account of their relation to the originals which they represent, and not otherwise. For as St.

Thomas says, (3 p. q. 25, a. 3.) on account of that relation we either venerate the prototype in the image, or the
image for the sake of the prototype; which is reduced to
the same relative honour.

46. They object, thirdly, that the Council of Illiberis
prohibited (can. 26.) the use of pictures on the walls of
the church. I answer, that this prohibition was made for
many reasons which do not exist at present. It was made
that the pagans might not think that we adore pictures and
images, or that they might not maltreat sacred images;
for at that time the christians were persecuted, as appears
from the 25th canon of the Council.

47. Fourthly, they object, that in one of his letters,
(lib. 11, epist. 13, alias. ix.) St. Gregory forbade the worship of images. In answer, I say that, in that letter, as
appears from the context, the saint spoke of certain images
to which a superstitious worship was paid to the great
scandal of the faithful. But we know that the same St.
Gregory, as we find in the 54th epistle (lib. 9,) sent
Secondinus a present of an image of the Saviour, and in
that letter said that he knew that Secondinus would not
adore the image as a God, " sed ob recordationem Filii
Dei, ut in ejus amore recalescas." Besides, he also sent to
the same Secondinus a cross, with two garments or shields on
which were painted the images of the Saviour, of the most
holy Virgin, and of the Apostles Peter and Paul.

48. Fifthly, they object that the Jews did not adore the
calf, and, (as Calvin says) that the pagans did not adore
their idols as if they believed them to be gods, but honoured the true God in them. I answer, that in these
image-gods the Pagans and Jews really adored false gods,
or at least acknowledged in them a certain divine virtue:
for in them they placed their hopes, and made them the ul-
timate object of their adoration, which is really idolatry.
Hence the prophet writes: "They drank wine and praised

their gods of gold." (v. 4): and of the Jews, David has said: "And they were mingled among the heathens,...... and served their idols." (Ps. cv. 35, 36.) Hence they said to Moses: "Make us gods that may go before us." (Exod. xxxii. 23.) And to turn them away from the true God, Jeroboam made two golden calves, and said to them: "Go ye up no more to Jerusalem: behold thy gods, O Israel, who brought thee out of the land of Egypt." (3 Kings xii. 28.) Hence, alluding to the golden calf, Aaron reproved the Jews, saying: "These are thy gods, O Israel, that have brought thee out of the land of Egypt." (Exod. xxxii. 4.) Catholics have no such belief with regard to sacred images: they never imagine that these images possess any hidden virtue; the honour which they pay them is all referred to their prototypes. Hence our veneration of sacred images is not forbidden, but is acceptable to God; as appears from numberless miracles which the Lord was pleased to perform by means of such images. To say that all such miracles are false would be great temerity.

49. Sixthly, Calvin objects and says: Since images possess no hidden virtue, why do Catholics flock to, and even make long pilgrimages to one image rather than to another? I answer, that the reason is not because that image has any particular virtue, but, because according to his divine judgments, the Lord is pleased frequently to bestow greater graces by means of one image than of another, and infuses into the souls of the faithful greater devotion to one image than to another.

ON INDULGENCES.

50. In the twenty-fifth session was also framed the decree on indulgences; in which it was said that, since the Church had received from Jesus Christ the power of conferring indulgences, which were in use from the most

ancient times, and were approved as very salutary by several synods, the Council teaches and commands that the use of them should be retained, and pronounces an anathema against all who assert that indulgences are useless, or that the church has not power to grant them. The council also commands that all abuses be abolished, &c. "Cum potestas conferendi indulgentias a Christo Ecclesiæ concessa sit, atque hujusmodi potestate, divinitus sibi tradita, antiquissimis etiam temporibus illa usa fuerit: sacrosancta synodus indulgentiarum usum, Christiano populo maxime salutarem, sacrorum conciliorum auctoritate probatum, in Ecclesia retinendum esse docet et præcipit; eosque anathemate damnat qui aut inutiles esse asserunt vel eas concedendi in Ecclesia potestatem esse negant. In his tamen concedendis moderationem juxta veterem et probatam in Ecclesia consuetudinem, adhiberi cupit; ne nimia facilitate ecclesiastica disciplina enervetur. Abusus vero qui in his irrepserunt et quorum occasione insigne hoc indulgentiarum nomen ab hæreticis blasphematum emendatos et correctos cupiens, præsenti decreto generaliter statuit pravos quæstus omnes pro his consequendis, unde plurima in Christiano populo abusuum causa fluxit, omnino abolendos esse. Cæteros vero quæ ex superstitione, ignorantia, irreverentia aut aliunde quomodocumque provenerunt, cum ob multiplices locorum et provinciarum apud quas hi committuntur corruptelas commode nequeant specialiter prohiberi, mandat omnibus episcopis ut diligenter quisque in prima synodo provinciali referat; ut aliorum quoque episcoporum scientia cognita statim ad summum romanum pontificem deferantur, cujus auctoritate et prudentia, quod universali Ecclesiæ expediet, statuetur; ut ita sanctarum indulgentiarum munus pie, sancte et incorrupte omnibus fidelibus dispensetur."

51. Behold the rock of scandal which was the beginning of Luther's perversion: hence he and all his followers have had a mortal hatred to the very name of indulgences which

they but little understood.   Gerard, a Lutheran, the second minister of the innovators, said that we teach that Jesus Christ has atoned for our sins, but has left on us the obligation of making satisfaction for the eternal and temporal pains due to our transgressions: and that to exempt ourselves from these penalties we have invented indulgences, which we purchase from the holy See, and through which we expect remission of the punishment due to our sins.   In answer, we say that although the satisfaction of our Redeemer was offered precisely for our sins, and for the eternal pains which we have merited, still he has also satisfied for the temporal punishment due to us.   But the satisfaction of Christ is applied to the discharge of temporal punishment only by satisfaction on our own part, or by means of indulgences granted to us by the vicar of Christ.   It is a gross falsehood to say that indulgences are mere inventions of Catholics; the use of them has been taught by Christ himself, and by the uninterrupted tradition of the Church. It is also false to say that we purchase indulgences; for, as every one knows, they are all granted gratuitously.

52. Moreover we say that, according to the true doctrine which the Church teaches, indulgences obtain for us the remission of the temporal punishment due to sins, the guilt of which has been forgiven. This remission of temporal punishment is obtained by the application of the merits of Jesus Christ, which are laid up in the treasure of the Church: for Christ himself has given to his vicar power to grant such indulgences to the faithful. The treasure of the Church contains also the merits of the saints, who have in this life made full satisfaction for their faults.   The merits of the saints are laid up in the treasure of the Church, not because the satisfaction of Christ, which was infinite, is not sufficient, but that their merits might not be useless; hence the Lord receives them in satisfaction for the debts of others.

53. Bellarmine says (tom. 2, l. de indulg.) that every good work is in itself meritorious and satisfactory. That every good work is meritorious is admitted as certain by catholics, and is clear from the gospel of St. Matthew, (xxv. 34, 35,) where our Lord extols the merits of the elect, and on account of these merits promises to make the saints partakers of his kingdom. "Possess you the kingdom prepared for you......For I was hungry and you gave me to eat." And St. Paul has written: "Who will render to every man according to his works." (Rom. ii. 6.) That every good work is satisfactory appears from the words of Tobias: "Alms deliver from all sin and from death." (iv. 11.) And in Ecclesiasticus we read: "Water quencheth a flaming fire, and alms resisteth sins." (iii. 33.) Hence St. Cyprian has written: "Eleemosynis atque operibus justis delictorum flamma sopitur." (Serm. de eleem.) St. Thomas teaches (p. 1, q. 21, art. 1.) that a reward is due to satisfactory works, according to commutative justice, and to meritorious works, according to distributive justice. A work cannot be applied to others inasmuch as it is meritorious; but may be applied to them inasmuch as it is satisfactory; for a prince can accept from one person the payment of a debt due by another.

54. It is certain, as Clement VI. declared in the constitution (Unigenitus, de pœnit et rem.) that the church possesses the infinite treasure of the satisfactions of Jesus Christ; the superabundant satisfactions of the Blessed Virgin, who, because, as the church holds, (Sess. 6, Can. 23,) she had been exempt from all actual sin, had not to make satisfaction for herself, and also the satisfactory works of the saints who, as has been already said, have, during life, made greater satisfaction than was due to their sins.

55. It is likewise certain that the Church has power to apply this treasure to the souls of the faithful. This is proved first from the article in the creed regarding the

communion of saints, which requires that the satisfactory works of one may be applied to another, on account of the communion of mutual charity which exists among the saints. That the pastors of the Church have power to apply to the faithful the satisfactory works which are in its treasure, we know from the power of the keys given to St. Peter and his successors, in these words: " Whatsoever thou shalt loose on earth, it shall be loosed also in heaven." (Mat. xvi. 19.) This power of the keys implies the power of loosing souls from every bond which impedes their entrance into the glory of the saints. To St. Peter was given the power of loosing even in heaven: his power, then, extends to the remission, not only of the guilt, but also of the punishment, which as long as full satisfaction is not made, deprives the soul of the possession of glory. And this is the fruit of the indulgences which are applied to souls. The guilt of sin cannot be remitted without the sacrament of penance, because the remission of sin requires the infusion of grace; but the debt of punishment may be remitted without the sacrament, since, for its remission, new grace is not wanted,

56. That the practice of granting indulgences always existed in the Church is evident from the fact of the incestuous Corinthian, in whose favour his friends, seeing him penitent, entreated St. Paul to remit the punishment which he had merited, *lest he should be swallowed up with sorrow.* The Apostle yielded to their entreaty, saying: " And to whom you have pardoned anything, I also. For what I have pardoned, if I have pardoned anything for your sakes I have done it in the person of Christ." (2 Cor. ii. 10.) What the Apostle calls pardon, we call an indulgence. In the seventh century, St. Gregory (see St. Thomas in 4 sent. dist. 20, q. 1, a. 3, q. 2), granted many indulgences for the stations. St. Leo III., as Surius relates in his life of St. Suibert, and as St. Thomas also

attests (loc. cit.) granted many other indulgences; and Urban II. (apud S. Antoninum) granted a plenary indulgence to those who engaged in the holy war. We should not be surprised if the Fathers do not speak in express terms of indulgences; for, in their time, the faithful submitted to the rigour of the penitential canons, for which, on account of human infirmity, more frequent indulgences were substituted.

57. Besides, in the eleventh (alias 12th) canon of the first Council of Nice, we read: " Licebit episcopo de his aliquid humanius cogitare." Hence this Council ordained that true penitents might obtain from the bishop an indulgence, on account of the satisfaction due to their sins. We find the same doctrine taught by the Councils of Ancyra and Laodicea. Pope Sergius, also, who sat in the chair of St. Peter, in the year 844, granted several indulgences. It surely cannot be supposed that these Pontiffs invented indulgences without having before them the examples of their predecessors. The general Council of Clermont, in 1096, granted a plenary indulgence to every one who would go to the holy war. In the year 1116, Paschal II., in the general Council of Lateran, granted an indulgence of forty days to all who assisted at the synod: and in the next Council of Lateran, in 1213, Innocent III. granted a plenary indulgence to those who contributed to the relief of the Holy Land. Martin V. in the Council of Constance, as we know from the second Clementine, granted a plenary indulgence. Tertullian makes mention of indulgences, in these words: " Quam pacem quidem in ecclesiâ non habentes, a martyribus in carcere exorare consueverunt." (lib. ad mart. c. 1.) And St. Cyprian says: " Pœnitenti, operanti, roganti potest clementer ignoscere; potest in acceptum referre quidquid pro talibus et petierint martyres, et fecerint sacerdotes." (lib. 3, ep. 15.) Hence the bishops were accustomed to apply the merits of the martyrs in satisfaction for the punishment due to penitent sinners.

2 o

58. The adversaries object, first, that the merits of Jesus Christ, as well as the merits of the saints, which are in the treasure of the Church, have received sufficient remuneration from God; therefore nothing remains for the treasure of indulgences. To this objection the answer has been already given, viz.: that the works of Christ and the saints are not only meritorious, but also satisfactory. Hence, although inasmuch as they are meritorious, they have received their reward, still, if, inasmuch as they are satisfactory works, they were not applied to sinners, they would remain useless as well in Christ, as in many of the saints who have made greater satisfaction than the debt of temporal punishment due to their sins required: therefore they are added to the treasure of the Church, and are applied to others by means of indulgences.

59. Secondly, they object that every mortal sin causes an infinite loss to the person who commits it: hence, to take away sin from a guilty soul requires the entire of the infinite satisfaction of Jesus Christ. Were this true, the passion of our Saviour would not be sufficient to atone for more than a single mortal sin, since a single mortal sin would absorb all the merits of Christ. Hence, I answer, that the merits of Christ, being of infinite value, are most abundantly sufficient to satisfy for all the sins of men, though they were infinite. Hence St. John has written: " And he is the propitiation for our sins; and not for ours only, but also for those of the whole world." (1 John ii. 2.) Besides, the most probable opinion is, that the malice of mortal sin, though immense on account of the infinite majesty of God, (malitiæ quasi infinitæ, says St. Thomas,) is not really infinite: otherwise all mortal sins would contain equal malice; for what is infinite can neither be increased nor diminished.

60. Thirdly, they object, that because the satisfaction of Christ is infinite, the satisfactory works of the saints are

useless in the treasure of the church for indulgences. I answer, that the satisfactory works of the saints are not added to the treasure of the church, because the satisfaction of Christ, which was of infinite value, is not sufficient: but, that they may not remain useless, the Lord, in order to honour his servants, wishes that their works also should contribute to the relief of the faithful. Besides, as Dominicus Soto says, (in 4 sent. d. 21, q. 1, a. 2,) the merits of Christ are applied only *in a finite manner:* and therefore the merits of the saints may contribute to the indulgences which the church dispenses.

61. Fourthly, the adversaries object, that the saints in performing their good works, have only done what was their duty; hence Jesus Christ says: "When you shall have done all these things which are commanded you, say: we are unprofitable servants; we have done that which we ought to do." (Luke xvii. 10.) Hence, they say, in the merits of the saints there is nothing which can be added to the treasure of the church to be afterwards applied to others. This objection we have already answered, in speaking of the merit of good works: (Sess. vi. n. 94.) but here we will briefly repeat the answer. Although we are bound to obey the divine commands, God rewards our obedience, and gives a special remuneration for works of supererogation which we were not obliged to perform. Hence, when the merits of these works are not necessary for the payment of our own debts, the Church applies them to others.

62. Fifthly, they object that, were the sufferings of the saints capable of satisfying for our sins, we could call them our redeemers: but this we cannot do, since Jesus Christ alone is our Redeemer: "Who of God is made unto us wisdom, and justice, and sanctification, and redemption." (1 Cor. i. 30.) Some answer this objection by saying, that the satisfactory works of the saints are not applied to

us by indulgences, but that, on account of these works, God shows us mercy. But this, among many other propositions of the Lovanians, was condemned by St. Pius V. Hence, in answer to the objection, we say, that our only absolute Redeemer is Jesus Christ alone, who has, by his merits, delivered us from the power of sin and of the devil: in this true redemption consists, and in this (I add) the satisfactory works of the saints have no part. Besides, there is no inconvenience in saying that the saints are in a certain manner our redeemers, inasmuch as by their superabundant satisfactions they deliver us from the penalties which we have not as yet paid. And, in a wide sense, we may call the saints our redeemers, as Daniel exhorted Nabuchodnosor to become a redeemer to himself, atoning for his sins by alms-deeds: " Redeem thou thy sins with alms." (Dan. iv. 24.)

63. It is asked whether an indulgence is a payment of the debt, or an absolution from it? On this point there is a variety of opinions: but Bellarmine justly says, that an indulgence is both a payment of the debt, and an absolution from it. The absolution is given by the power which Christ gave the apostles, of absolving the faithful: "Whatsoever you shall loose on earth, shall be loosed also in heaven." (Matt. xviii. 18.) This, Alexander III. declared in the chapter (Quod autem consuluisti, de pœnit. et rem.) where the Pontiff said, that a superior can grant indulgences only to his own subjects: because no one can absolve, as a judge, a person who is not subject to his authority. Martin V., in the Council of Constance, granting a plenary indulgence, calls it *a plenary absolution.* Thus, also, Gregory VII., in giving indulgences, generally used the word *absolution.* Besides, Bellarmine says, that although the Pope grants indulgences to the living by way of *absolution,* he could also give them by way of payment, as he does with regard to the souls in purgatory, who cannot be absolved

because they are no longer subject to the authority of the Church. Hence, the Pope applies to them only by way of payment or suffrage, as many indulgences from the treasure of the Church, as are necessary for the discharge of their debts. He could do this also with regard to the living: but indulgences are ordinarily applied to the dead by way of payment, and to the living by absolution.

64. Secondly, it is asked who can grant indulgences? The pope alone can, as we find in the chapter (Cum ex eo, de pœnit. et rem.) *by the plenitude* of his power, grants a plenary indulgence. Bishops can, as appears from the same chapter, and from the chapter (Nostro, eod. tit.) grant a partial indulgence of a year on the dedication of the church, and an indulgence of forty days on the anniversary of the dedication: they can also grant this indulgence of forty days in other cases. Behold the words of the chapter, (Cum ex eo) to which I have referred: "Hunc quoque dierum numerum (that is forty days) indulgentiarum litteris præcipimus moderari, quæ pro quibuslibet casibus aliquoties conceduntur cum romanus pontifex hoc in talibus moderamen consueverit observare." And in the chapter *(Nostro.)* it is said with regard to archbishops: "Nostro postulasti responso utrum per tuam provinciam possis concedere remissionis litteras generales. Nos igitur F. t. breviter respondemus quod per provinciam tuam libere potes hujusmodi concedere litteras, ita tamen quod statum generalis concilii non excedas.

65. The question whether bishops can, *de jure divino,* or by the concession of the pope, grant these indulgences, depends (as Bellarmine says) on the question whether their power comes immediately from God, or through the pope. Bellarmine mentions that it comes through the pope; but the opposite opinion is sufficiently probable, and perhaps the more probable. Some hold that Abbots, and even parish priests and confessors have this power: but this is

commonly denied; and in the chapter (Accedentibus de excess. prælat.) it is expressly said that bishops alone are permitted to grant indulgences. St. Thomas says (in 4 sent., dist. 20, q. 1., a. 3, q. 2,) that bishops alone are really prelates. But regulars, though exempt, may partake of the indulgences which the bishop grants to the faithful generally. And if they cannot perform the works enjoined without violating regular observance, they must, as St. Thomas says, obtain permission from their superior to perform these works.

66. To grant indulgences a just cause is necessary, even with regard to the Pope: since they depend on the divine law. However, in order to gain the indulgence, it is not necessary that the works enjoined be equal to the satisfaction due by each person: but there must always be a certain proportion. However, St. Thomas says, (in 4, sent. d. 20, q. 1, a. 3, q. 2,) and St. Antonine, Paludanus, Durandus, and Turrecromata, agree with him, that it is sufficient to enjoin any pious work, however small; others, along with St. Bonaventure, require a greater proportion: hence, Gerson, Richardus, Cajetan, &c., (apud Bellarmin.) hold, that the indulgence, if it be very great, and the work enjoined very light, is not gained. In the Council of Trent it is said, that the indulgences ought to be conformable to the usages of ancient times, in which they were very rare. Innocent III. (cap. cum ex eo de pœn. et rem.,) says, that ordinarily the Pope does not grant any of the greater indulgences more frequently than once a-year. Bellarmine adopts the second opinion: but says that the indulgence is gained when, by the work enjoined, the end of the indulgence is attained, as is the case with regard to the plenary indulgence granted to those who assist at the canonization of saints. By the attendance of the faithful, though the work be not proportioned, the end of the indulgence is gained, which is that, by being present, the people may be confirmed in the faith,

Moreover, when an indulgence is granted to a particular person, there must be a proportion between it and the work enjoined: but when it is granted to the people generally, it is not necessary that there be a proportion between the indulgence and the work performed by each individual: it is enough that the works of all, taken together, bear a proportion to the end of the indulgence. It does not belong to the faithful to pronounce on the justice of the cause, on account of which the indulgence is granted: each person should presume that the cause is a just one.

• 67. To gain an indulgence, it is necessary that the work enjoined be satisfactory, and that the person who receives the indulgence be in the state of grace. Some do not admit the second condition, because, they say, that the indulgence depends not on the satisfaction of the individual, but on that of Christ and the saints. But the opinion of Bellarmine is the more probable: for the works of his enemies cannot be pleasing to God. Bellarmine excepts the case in which the end of the indulgence is obtained by the work performed, as would happen if the indulgence were given to those who contribute to the building of a church, or of any other pious place. But in order to gain an indulgence actually, it is always necessary that the person be, at least afterwards, in the state of grace. When, in granting an indulgence, the Pope says, *pœnitentibus et confessis*," many hold that contrition is sufficient. But Bellarmine thinks it more probable that confession is necessary: this is the opinion also of Cajetan, Navarre, and others: and Benedict XIV. (in constit. Inter. præteritos. s. 3, Bull. tom. 3, p. 140.) remarks that, for the jubilee of the holy year, the words *vere pœnitentibus et confessis*, should be understood of actual confession.

SIXTEENTH AND LAST TREATISE.—APPENDIX.

ON THE OBEDIENCE DUE TO THE DEFINITIONS OF THE COUNCIL, AND CONSEQUENTLY OF THE ROMAN CATHOLIC CHURCH, OUT OF WHICH THERE IS NO SALVATION.

1. A church, which is not one in its doctrine and faith, can never be the true church. " One faith," says the apostle, " one baptism, one God." (Eph. iv. 5.) Hence, because truth must be one, of all the different churches which teach a variety of doctrines, only one can be the true church: and as Calvin himself has said, out of that church there is no salvation. Now, in order to determine which is this one true church, in the new law of the gospel, it is necessary to examine which is the church that had been first founded by Jesus Christ. For, when the first is ascertained, it must be confessed that this alone is the true church, which, having been once the true church, must have always been, and must for ever be, the true church. For to this first church has been made the promise of the Saviour, that, as he said to St. Peter, the gates of hell (that is, the heresies) should never be able to overturn it: " Thou art Peter, and upon this rock I will build my church, and the gates of hell shall not prevail against it." (Matt. xvi. 18.) Hence, in his first epistle to Timothy, St. Paul called the church founded by Christ the pillar and foundation of truth. " That thou mayest know how thou oughtest to behave thyself in the house of God, which is the church of the living God, the pillar and ground of truth." (1 Tim. iii. 15.)

2. Let us now see which is this true church which Jesus

Christ has founded. In the entire history of religion we find, that the Roman Catholic Church alone was the first church; and that the other false and heretical churches afterwards departed and separated from her. This is the Church described by St. Paul, which was propagated by the apostles, and afterwards governed by pastors whom the apostles themselves had appointed to rule over her. "He gave some apostles......and others some pastors......for the edifying of the body of Christ." (Eph. iv. 11, 12.) For, this character can be found only in the Roman Church, whose pastors certainly descend, by an uninterrupted and legitimate succession, from the apostles to whom Jesus Christ promised his assistance, to the end of the world. " And behold I am with you all days, even to the consummation of the world." (Matt. xxviii. 20.) Hence, St. Ireneus has written: " Per Romæ fundatam ecclesiam, quæ habet ab apostolis traditionem et fidem, per successionem episcoporum provenientem usque ad nos, confundimus omnes eos qui per cæcitatem et malam conscientiam aliter quam oportet, colligunt." (Lib. 3, c. 4.) It was this that assured St. Augustine that the Roman Church is the true church of Jesus Christ. "Tenet me," says the saint, " in ipsa Ecclesia ab ipsa sede Petri, usque ad præsentem episcopatum, successio sacerdotum." (ep. fundam. c. 4, n. 5.)

3. The innovators themselves do not deny that the Roman Church was the first which Jesus Christ had founded. Behold what Gerard, the great Lutheran minister, has said of the Church of Rome: "It is, indeed, certain, that it was the true church for the first five hundred years, and that it held the doctrine of the apostles." (De Eccl. c. 11, sect. 6.) However, they say what the heresiarch Donatus said in the time of St. Augustine, that the Roman Church was the true church till the fifth century, or, as some say, till the third or fourth century, but that it afterwards fell away, because it had been corrupted by the Catholics, in

the true dogmas of faith. Could the Lord, then, for nine centuries, have permitted men to live without a church till the coming of these new enlightened reformers of the faith, as Luther, Zuinglius, Calvin, and such innovators boastingly call themselves? But how could that church fail which, as has been already observed, St. Paul calls the pillar and ground of truth, and against which Jesus Christ has promised that errors and heresies should never prevail? No; the church has not failed, and according to the promise of Christ, it could not fail. The truth is, as St. Jerome says, that all the false churches which have separated from the Roman Church, have fallen away and have erred: " Ex hoc ipso, (says the holy Doctor, speaking of the heretics,) quod postea instituti sunt, eos se esse judicant quos Apostolus futuros prænunciavit," that is, false prophets. By the argument taken from the promises of Christ, to show the impossibility of the failure of the first church founded by Jesus Christ, St. Augustine confuted the Donatists. A learned author (Pichler theol. dogm. contr. 3 de Eccl., in præf.) wisely says, that to convince all heretical sects of their error, there is no way more certain and secure than to show that our Catholic Church has been the first founded by Jesus Christ. For, this being established, it is proved beyond all doubt that ours is the only true church, and that all the others that have left it and separated from it, are certainly in error. After the death of Charles II. of England, a paper was found which he had written with his own hand, and shut up in a little case; in that paper it is said: " Christ cannot have here on earth more than one church (which to me appears evident): and this one church can be no other than the Roman Catholic Church: hence, I think, the only question to be decided is, where is the church which we profess to believe? We should then believe all that this church proposes to us." Convinced by this reason, Charles finally embraced the Catholic faith.

4. But, pressed by this argument, the innovators have invented an answer: they say that the visible church has failed, but not the invisible church, which consists solely of the predestined, as the Calvinists say, or solely of the just, as the Lutheran confessionists hold. But these doctrines are diametrically opposed to the gospel, in which it is declared that the church militant is composed of saints and sinners, of the predestined and of those that are not predestined: and therefore it is likened at one time to a threshing floor in which there is wheat and chaff; at another to a net which contains good and bad fish; and again to a field in which there is wheat and cockle. John Baptist Groffio (apud Pichler), in the year 1695, stated, in a published document, that he had several times challenged the innovators to produce a text of the sacred Scripture, which would prove the existence of the *invisible* church which they had invented, and that he was unable to obtain any such text from them: but how could they adduce such a text when, addressing his apostles, whom he left to the world as the propagators of his church, Jesus Christ had said to them: "You are the light of the world. A city seated on a mountain cannot be hid." (Matt. v. 14.) A city on the summit of a mountain cannot be concealed from the eyes of men. Thus he has declared, that the Church cannot but be visible to all. He declared the same when he gave the power of the keys to St. Peter and his successors: "And I will give to thee the keys of the kingdom of heaven. And whatsoever thou shalt bind on earth, it shall be bound also in heaven; and whatsoever thou shalt loose on earth, it shall be loosed also in heaven." (Matt. xvi. 18.) Hence, in his conference with Claude, the Calvinist minister, which was afterwards published, Bossuet states, that it was admitted on both sides, that the true church is that which externally exercises the ministry of the keys.

5. The church has been at all times, and will for ever

be, necessarily visible, that each person may be always able
to learn from his pastor, the true doctrine regarding the
dogmas of faith, and the precepts of morality; to receive
the sacraments, to be directed in the way of salvation, and
to be enlightened and corrected, should he ever fall into
error. For, were the church at any time hidden and
invisible, to whom should men have recourse, in order to
learn what they are to believe and to do? "How (said
the apostle) shall they believe him of whom they have not
heard? And how shall they hear without a preacher?"
(Rom. x. 14.) If the teachers be hidden and unknown, how
can the people be instructed in the maxims of salvation?
Besides, St. Paul has written: "Obey your prelates, and
be subject to them: for they watch, as being to render an
account of your souls." (Heb. xiii. 7.) Now, how could
the faithful practise towards their prelates the obedience
commanded by the apostle, if the church, and by consequence its pastors, were invisible, and concealed from the
eyes of men? But no, says the same apostle: the Lord
has, for this end, appointed in his church visible apostles,
pastors, and doctors, to teach the true doctrine, and to
guide their sheep in the straight path of salvation, that
thus they may not be led astray by the teachers of error:
"And he gave some apostles......and other some pastors
and doctors, &c.;......that henceforth we be no more children tossed to and fro, and carried about with every wind
of doctrine by the wickedness of men, by cunning crafti-
ness by which they lie in wait to deceive." (Eph. iv. 11. &c.)

6. But it was necessary that the church and her pastors
should be obvious and visible, principally that there might
be an infallible judge, who would have power from God to
resolve all doubts which might arise from time to time, and
to whose decision all should necessarily submit. Otherwise
there would be no certain rule of faith by which Christians
could know the true dogmas of faith, and the true precepts

of morality: and among the faithful there would be endless disputes and controversies. For if there were not such a judge, or if he were fallible, no one would submit to his decision, unless it was in accordance with his own opinion. But were decisions on points of faith, or on the moral precepts, to be given according to the opinion of each individual, all men would certainly be for ever divided and discordant in belief, and thus faith would be ambiguous and doubtful.

7. The pretended reformers themselves have, as Monsignor Bossuet says, acknowledged the necessity of an infallible judge, to decide questions of faith. He states that, in a book composed by the Calvinists *on the discipline of the reformed religion*, there are two acts, or statutes, which they have adopted. The first is: " That questions on points of doctrine, should be ultimately decided (if possible) by the word of God, in the consistory: when it cannot be thus decided, the matter should be brought to the colloquy, then to the provincial, and last of all to the national synod, in which a final decision should be given, with the aid of the word of God: and that if any one should refuse to submit to this decision on all points, or should not expressly abjure his own errors, he would be cut off from the church." The second act, or statute, was a condemnation of the *Independents*, who held, "that each particular church should be governed by itself, independently of every other." This proposition was formally condemned in the synod of Charenton, by the Calvinists themselves, as one which was *prejudicial to the true church, and which gave liberty to form as many religions as there are parishes.* Hence, the celebrated Puffendorf himself, though a Protestant, has written: "The condition of those who obey the Pontiff, is better than that of the Protestants: they all acknowledge the Pontiff as head of the church: Protestants, on the contrary, being without a head, are tossed

to and fro, and shamefully torn and divided. Each repub-
lic governs and directs all things according to its own caprice."
(De mon. pont. p. 134.)

8. The Calvinist Jurieu, seeing that no one could deny
that the true Church of Jesus Christ cannot reside among the
societies, separated from the Roman Church, which was the
first of all churches, has invented a false system, which has been
embraced, especially by the Calvinistic sects. He says that
all, or nearly all, their societies, agree in the fundamental
points of faith, and that they have neither left nor have
been separated from the Roman Church; but that they are
the Church itself. As (he says), in the Church of Rome,
there are different opinions, according to the different
schools of Thomists, Scotists, Augustinians, &c., while all
profess the same faith: so among us the faith and the
Church are the same, although our canons and discipline
are different. To the advocates of this doctrine, we may
justly say what St. Augustine said to the heretics of his
own time. "You believe what you wish: you do not
believe what you do not wish: you believe yourselves
rather than the gospel." (Lib. 13, contr. Faust. c. 3.) But we
say, in answer to this new teacher of the faith, that
although among Catholics there are different schools and
different opinions, still the questions on which they are
divided, are certain points on which the Church has defined
nothing: but all agree on the articles which the Church has
declared to be of faith. For example, all the schools
acknowledge the necessity of faith and human liberty for
every good act: these we hold as dogmas of faith: but
with regard to the manner in which grace is efficacious,
whether it is efficacious of itself, or by the free concurrence
of the human will, &c., are controverted points on which
the Church has not as yet decided, and which are not at
present opposed to faith.

9. But let us examine the points which Jurieu holds to

be fundamental and non-fundamental. With regard to the fundamental points, he either does not explain them, or he explains them in a very confused manner. "A fundamental article," he says, "is that on which depends the ruin of the glory of God, and the destruction of the last end of man." But, as far as we can infer from his writings, there are four fundamental articles: the mystery of the Trinity, the mystery of the Incarnation, the eternal glory, and remuneration of the just, and the eternal punishment of sinners after the present life. But we say that, besides these articles, all the others proposed by the Church as points of faith, should be believed firmly, and with equal assent, and that all are fundamental articles. Hence the sects that have rejected these points have been pronounced heretical, and have been declared to be cut off from the Catholic Church, as well by the holy Fathers, as by the Councils; and particularly by the first Council of Nice, (can. 8,) by the first (can. 6), and second Council of Constantinople. (art. 3.). Hence, in the second century, in the time of St. Victor Pope, the Church of Rome separated from her communion the Asiatics, called *Quartodecimans,* who wished to celebrate Easter on the fourteenth day of the moon of March, and not on the following Sunday, on which the Catholic Church celebrates it, in order not to conform to the Jewish Pasch. The second Council of Carthage condemned the Novatians, who denied that the Church could remit the sin of those who had fallen in the persecutions. The second Council of Constantinople cut off from the Church, those who said that the soul was created before the formation of the body (can. 1): and also those who asserted that the heavens and stars were animated. (can. 6.). Moreover, we read in the gospel of St. Matthew: "If he will not hear the Church, let him be to thee as the heathen and the publican." (xviii. 17.) In order, then, to be out of the Church, which, according to St. Paul, (Eph.

iv. 4,) being but one body, can have but one soul, it is
sufficient to refuse assent to her dogmatic definitions.

10. But, says Jurieu: To distinguish between fundamen-
tals and non-fundamentals, is a knotty question, and one
that is difficult of solution.   He adds: It does not belong
to the Church to define what are the fundamental points:
they are fundamental of their own nature.   But who, I
ask, will define the points that are fundamental or not
fundamental?   Perhaps the private judgment of each
individual.   But, were this the case, there would be a
thousand contradictory definitions.   And then there would
be as many churches and religions, as there are definitions
of these points?   No (replies Jurieu): it does not belong
to any one to define what points of faith are fundamental:
for they are fundamental of their own nature.   But if they
are of their own nature fundamental, why does he say, that
to distinguish them from the non-fundamental points is a
knotty and difficult question?   Who will define the points
which are of their own nature fundamental?   These points
are either manifest or obscure: if they are manifest, the
determination of them ought not to be a knotty and
difficult question: and if they are obscure, they require to
be defined.   Hence, it appears, how confused and groundless is this new system of Jurieu: new to all the reformers
themselves, who never called themselves members of the
Roman Church, but boasted of having separated from it,
because (they say), after the third, fourth, or fifth century,
it became an adulterous church, and the seat of anti-Christ,
infected with errors and idolatry.

11. Besides, how can Jurieu say that all the reformed
churches are one and the same church, professing the same
faith, when the divines of Zurigo, in the apologetic preface
directed to the reformed churches in 1578, assert, that
among them there were several controversies regarding
fundamental points, such as the person of Christ, the union

and distinction between the two natures, the divine and human, and other similar articles? They afterwards add, that their discords had reached such a pitch, that they revived many heresies which had been before condemned. Behold their words: "The contention is carried on with such fury, that not a few of the old heresies, which had been formerly condemned, being as it were recalled from hell, raise their heads." Speaking of the controversies which prevailed among the Protestant Churches, John Sturmius, a Protestant writer, also says: "The principal articles are called in question, and many heresies are brought into the Church: a broad way is opened to Atheism." This author may be said to have been a prophet: for at the present day we find that a considerable number of the reformers have fallen into Atheism, as appears from the works which they constantly publish. For, in truth, length of time has exhibited matters in such a light, that the reformed sects themselves have seen the groundlessness of their pretended evangelical religion. Hence they have abandoned themselves to the extreme of Atheism, or materialism, denying every maxim of faith, saying that everything is material, and therefore that there is neither a God, nor a rational human soul, nor a future life. Thus, they have endeavoured to rid themselves of remorse for the brutal life which they lead. But all their thoughts and efforts will never be able to remove these remorses of conscience. The most they shall be able to effect is, to raise doubts in their own mind about the existence of God and eternal life: but to persuade themselves fully that there is not a God, or another life, will be for ever impossible: since natural reason itself dictates that there is a God, the creator of all things, and a just remunerator of good and evil, and that our souls are eternal and immortal. In a word, these miserable men seek to find peace by imagining that there is no God, in order to be freed from the fear of

2 P 2

a censor and avenger of their iniquities: but they shall
never find this peace: for the very fear of the existence of
God will continue to torment them with the terrors of
divine vengeance.

12. But let us return to the point.   According then to
the statements of the innovators themselves, the reformed
Churches doubt of the principal articles of faith; and in
reality, as Cardinal Gotti says in his learned work (*The
True Church*, c. 8, S. 1, n. 9.) the Lutherans admit one
person in Christ, while Calvin and Beza, adhering to the
doctrines of the impious Nestorius, hold that there are two
persons.   Luther and his followers say that in Christ the
divine nature suffered and died: but Beza justly reprobates
this execrable blasphemy.   Calvin makes God the author
of sin: the Lutherans on the other hand say, that this is a
blasphemy.   Luther says that Christ even according to his
human nature, is in all places, but Zuinglius condemns this
doctrine.   Luther admits only three sacraments, Baptism,
Eucharist, and Penance;   Calvin admits Baptism, and
Eucharist, but rejects Penance; he afterwards admitted
the sacrament of Order, which Luther rejected; Luther
confesses that we should adore Jesus Christ really present
in the Eucharist, but Calvin calls such adoration idolatry.
Melancthon (whom Luther afterwards followed) says that
good works are necessary for salvation; but the Calvinists
hold that good works are not necessary, but meet.   It
must then be said that all these new reformed Churches in
contradicting each other in these articles, have erred regarding the principal points of faith.   And in reality Calvin
calls the Lutherans falsifiers, and idolaters, because they
adore Jesus Christ in the Eucharist: and on the other hand,
Luther says that the Zuinglians are condemned, blaspheming
and heretical sects: "Hæreticos censemus omnes sacra-
mentarios, qui negant corpus Christi ore carnali sumi in
Eucharistia." (Apud. Ospin. par. 2, hist. sacram. p. 326.)

13. On the other, its constant uniformity of doctrine in the dogmas of faith, from its first foundation by Jesus Christ, demonstrates the truth of the Catholic Church. It has been the same in all ages; so that the truths which we believe at the present day, were believed in the first ages; such as human liberty, the efficacy of the sacraments, the real presence of Jesus Christ in the Eucharist, the invocation of saints, the veneration of their relics and images, the existence of purgatory, and the like. The innovators call these truths of faith, errors: but how could these errors in matters of faith exist in the first ages in our Church, which, the adversaries admit, was then the true Church of Christ. They say (as Bellarmine relates de notis Eccl. c. 5.) that these errors were certain little defects in the countenance of the infant Church. Was it then a mere little defect in the first ages, to adore the presence of Jesus Christ in the Eucharist, or to venerate the cross and sacred images? How then could these become impious idolatries, as the adversaries call them at present? And how could God have permitted such enormous errors to reign in his Church from its origin, till the new teachers, Luther, Zuinglius, and Calvin, came to dissipate them? No, this Church which was from the beginning the true Church, has been always the true Church.

14. But, your Catholic Church, say the innovators, has assumed authority to frame new dogmas of faith, and pretends to give authority to the sacred Scriptures. No, the Church does not, and cannot frame new dogmas of faith, but only declares what are the dogmas which God has taught us by means of Scripture and tradition, both of which are the word of God, the one written, and the other unwritten. Nor has our Church ever intended to give authority to the word of God, but only to declare, after being assured by tradition, and the assistance of the Holy Ghost, what are the dogmas which should be held as of

faith. This the famous Calvinist Basnage, admits in his annals: " Partes Ecclesiæ sunt in ea re, non auctoritatis quidem, quam canon ex se habet, adjunctio, sed declaratio." Thus the Catholic Church, in teaching what is the true sense of the Scripture, does not prefer herself to the Scripture, nor give authority to the Scripture, but prefers her own decisions to the judgment of private individuals, who should obey the Church on account of the authority which she has received from God.

15. But the innovators say: this is a vicious circle, since you believe the infallibility of the Scriptures, because such is the doctrine of the Church; and the infallibility of the Church, because the Scriptures say that she is infallible. But they err: for whatever force the objection might have if we were disputing with infidels, who deny the infallibility as well of the Church as of the Scripture: it has none when we argue with a Christian, who admits the infallibility of the Scripture; for in the Scripture itself it is clearly taught that the true Church cannot err, and therefore he is bound to all that the Church declares, and believing it, he cannot err. Hence, St. Augustine said: " I would not believe the Gospel unless the authority of the Church moved me to believe it." (lib. 1, controv. ep. manich. c, 5.) The innovators really fall into a real vicious circle: they say that the Scripture proves the doctrine of private judgment, and that private judgment establishes the infallibility of the Scriptures; both propositions are false. It is false to say that the doctrine of private judgment is proved from Scripture, and most false that the inspiration of the Scriptures is proved by private judgment. Thus the innovators receive no aid from the sacred Scriptures; for, explaining them not according to the judgment of the Church, but according to the private judgment of each person, they form as many different creeds as there are individuals. Hence, I know not how they can brand as

heretics the Socinians, Arians, and others, who deny the Trinity, and the divinity of Jesus Christ. They will say that, with regard to these two truths, the Scriptures are clear: but the Socinians will answer that on these two points the Scriptures should be understood not literally, but allegorically. Now who will decide this question, when these heretics will not submit to the decision of the true Church which alone can define it? Ah! when obedience to the church is taken away, there is no error on any point of faith, which can be proved to be an error.

16. But, they reply, the Roman Church has from time to time defined several things to be of faith which were not of faith before the definition of the Church: therefore, she has not been uniform in her dogmas of faith. I answer, that it does not follow that, because the Church has in the course of time defined several articles which were not defined before, she has not been uniform in matters of faith; for that proves not that the Church has changed her dogmas, but only that being enlightened by the Holy Ghost, she has from time to time, on the foundation of Scripture and tradition, declared several articles which though not previously declared, belonged to faith before they were defined.

17. But, oh God, how does it happen that these new masters of faith do not see that being separated from the Catholic Church, and having lost obedience to her, they have also lost the rule of faith, so that at present they have no certain rule by which they can ascertain what is of faith, or what is not; thus they walk in the dark, changing from day to day the articles of their belief? The entire rule of faith of the heretics consists in the sacred Scripture: but here is the delusion, for the Scripture alone cannot always render them certain of the dogmas which they ought to believe.

18. They then say that the Scripture is the sole rule of

faith. In the first place, I ask them how they know that there are any divine Scriptures, that is that books written by men have been inspired by God? How can they prove the existence of the true Scriptures? Is it by the prophecies and miracles which are therein contained? But who assures them that these prophecies were not written after the events had happened? And how do we know that the miracles have really taken place? In a word, how is it shown that the books of Scripture which we have at present, have been really inspired by God? Is it by the words of the Scripture itself? No: the words of Scripture cannot prove that the Scripture is divine, since the precise question is, whether these words are really inspired or not?

19. Secondly, though it were evident that there were divine Scriptures, how can we know what are the books that are really inspired, since it might happen that, among the Scriptures, the heretics had inserted a book which is not canonical, or which, though canonical, is not yet known to be canonical? The Catholic canon contains 72 books: 45 of the Old, and 27 of the New Testament, as we are assured by the Council of Trent (sess. iv.) which received this canon from the Council of Florence, and the Council of Florence received it from the council held in Rome, under Pope Gelasius. To these, I add the third council of Carthage (according to others the fifth or seventh) which was afterwards approved by the sixth Ecumenical Council, in which the Fathers declared that they received the same canon from Innocent I., who lived in 402, and declared that he had received it from the Apostles, by an uninterrupted tradition, which, on account of the persecution in the three preceding centuries, was not known in all places.

20. Luther rejected, without any grounds, several of the books contained in this canon: of the books of the Old Testament, he rejected those of Tobias, Judith, Wisdom, Ecclesiasticus, Baruch, and the book of Machabees; in the

New Testament, he rejected the Epistle of St. Paul to the Hebrews, the Epistle of St. James, of St. Jude, and, also, the Apocalypse of St. John. Now, I ask the Lutherans: How do they prove that these books are not inspired, and that the books which they admit are really inspired? They certainly cannot prove it from the other Scriptures; for they do not say what books are inspired or otherwise.

21. They say that the private spirit of the Holy Ghost, which internally enlightens them, makes known to them the true canonical books. But if, as they say, every Christian has this interior light, why is it not also given to the Arian, the Nestorian, and the Calvinist, who belongs to their own pretended reformed religion? The Calvinists acknowledge the divine inspiration of the epistles of St. Paul to the Hebrews, the epistles of St. James and St. Jude, and the Apocalypse of St. John. Your private spirit, then is very obscure and fallacious, since it does not manifest itself equally to all; hence if the truth of the Scriptures could be proved only by the private spirit, one uncertain thing should have to be known by another, which is still more uncertain.

22. Thirdly, though they knew the true canonical books, how could the heretics prove that their version of these books is correct and free from corruption? The Bible was originally written in three languages, the Hebrew, Greek, and Latin. The books of the Old Testament were written in Hebrew: those of the New were written in Greek, with the exception of the Gospel of St. Matthew, the Epistle o St. Paul to the Hebrews, which was written in Syriac, and of the Gospel of St. Mark, which was probably written in Rome, in the Latin tongue. Besides, many versions of the Scripture have been made, but only the Vulgate has been declared authentic by the Council of Trent, in the fourth session; for, as the learned say, the present Hebrew and Greek texts are defective. It is true that even the Vulgate,

as Pope Clement says, is not, even at present, perfectly free from errors; but it has been defined that such errors are only accidental and not substantial. This we must firmly believe, since Jesus Christ has promised that the Church, which speaks through the Council, cannot err in substantial points of faith. On the other hand, the heretics have published various Latin versions, but all corrupted and differing, not only from the Vulgate, but also from each other, and from their own versions in the vulgar tongue, which are more corrupt than their Latin versions; so that, in their different versions, they have added several sentences, and have omitted words, according as the additions or omissions were necessary to prove their own particular doctrines. How, then, can they say that their scriptures are legitimate or uncorrupted?

23. Fourthly, were it certain that some of their versions were the true Word of God, how could they determine the true sense of the Scripures? St. Jerome teaches that the law of the Gospel is contained, not in the words of Scripture, but in the meaning of the words: " Non putemus in verbis scripturarum esse evangelium sed in sensu...... Interpretatione enim perversa, de Evangelio Christi fit hominis evangelium, aut quod pejus est diaboli." Thus the words: *The Father is greater than I*, (John xiv. 28.) as understood by a Catholic, are the words of God; but, as understood by an Arian, they are heretical. Thus, also, the words: *He that believeth and is baptized, shall be saved*, (Mark xvi. 16.) in the Lutheran sense, are heresy; in the Catholic sense, they are a truth of faith.

24. It is necessary, as has been already said, (sess. iv. n. 53,) to distinguish the various senses of the Scriptures. The literal sense is one, and the mystical another: God may have intended both. In general, the literal sense is the true sense; however, in some passages, the mystical is the true sense; that is, when the words cannot be understood in

the literal sense. In some texts, the mystical as well as the literal sense is the true sense, as in the text of St. Paul: " Abraham had two sons, the one by a bondswoman, and the other by a freewoman......which things are said by an allegory. For these are two testaments." (Gal. iv. 22, 24.)

25. Now in such a diversity of senses, by what rule can the true sense be known? In the text from St. Matthew: " Take ye and eat, this is my body." (Matt. xxvi. 26.); by the word *is*, we Catholics understand the present time, so that when all these words are pronounced, the bread is no longer bread, but the true, real, and permanent body of Jesus Christ. And being made certain of this sense by the authority of the Church, we have a firm belief in the sacrament of the Eucharist. But by the word *is*, Zuinglius understands *signifies;* that is, *this signifies my body;* and for this he adduces an example from Exodus, where it is said; " For it is the phase (that is the passage) of the Lord." (xii. 11.) *It is the phase*, that is, *it signifies the passage*. On the other hand, Luther understands the word *is*, in the literal sense, but does not understand it as we do of the present time at which the words are pronounced, but of the future time when the sacrament will be administered, that is: this will be my body at the moment it will be received by the faithful. Now in the midst of so many expositions, how shall we able to ascertain the true sense of this text, unless the authority of the Church declares it to us? Perhaps it is by the private spirit, as the innovators say. But the words, *this is my body*, are understood by Luther of the real body of Jesus Christ, and by Calvin in a figurative sense; both these heads have, as their followers say, had the internal light of the Holy Ghost, and both have been sent by God to teach the true faith. But one says, that in the Host, Jesus Christ should be adored as God, while the other says, that to adore him in the Eucharist would be real idolatry. Which of them are we to believe?

2 Q

Is it Luther or Calvin? For they say there is no other rule of faith than the Scripture and private interpretation. But how shall we ascertain the truth when the Scripture may have different senses, and their private interpretation is fallacious and doubtful, since the interpretation of the one is opposed to that of the other?

26. But what faith can we learn from these false teachers, when, in consequence of separating from the Church, they have no rule of faith? Monsignor Bossuet justly remarks, that as these teachers have despised the authority of the Catholic Church, so their own disciples have disregarded their authority, and have separated from them, forming a variety of sects, creeds, and religions. In the space of fifty years, the Lutherans were divided into three sects: the Lutherans, the semi-Lutherans, and anti-Lutherans. The Lutherans, as Lindan relates, (ep. proem. in Luth.,) were sub-divided into eleven other sects, the semi-Lutherans into eleven, and the anti-Lutherans into fifty-six sects. The Calvinistic school was likewise soon divided into many different sects: of these we can count more than a hundred. In the ecclesiastical history of Natalis Alexander, you can see (s. xv. et xvi. c. 2, a. 7, s. 3.) into how many sects the Calvinists have been divided in England: the Puritans, who follow the pure doctrine of Calvin: the Piscatorians, who were declared heretics by the Calvinists of France: the Anglo-Calvinists, who consecrate bishops and ordain priests, which the other Calvinists reject: the Independents, who acknowledge neither ecclesiastical nor political superiors: the anti-Scripturians, who reject all the Scriptures: the Quakers, who boast of having continual revelations and ecstasies: the Ranters, who consider everything lawful to which corrupt nature feels itself inclined. In Holland there were two factions, the Arminians and the Gomarists; but afterwards, in a certain council held in the year 1618, Arminius, the head of one of the sects, was condemned as a schismatic:

and because Grotius and the chancellor Barnebeld refused to obey, the former was imprisoned and the latter beheaded. Behold the uniformity of faith among the societies of the innovators! This is the fruit of the spirit of pride; as the heads withdraw themselves from the obedience due to the Church, so their followers shake off the authority of these heads, and form new sects and new systems.

27. And in vain have their preachers sought to apply a remedy to this disorder, by monitions, decrees, threats, depositions, and excommunications, as they did in the synod Vallone, which was held in Amsterdam in the year 1690. The other innovators and their followers, laughed at the pretensions of the preachers, and said that decrees, depositions, and censures, belonged to popery, and not to the reformation, which enjoys the privilege of liberty of conscience. But do they not see, that from this accursed and exterminating liberty of conscience, have arisen the immense variety of heretical, deistical, and atheistical sects, that have filled England, Holland, and Germany? The minister Papin (who was afterwards converted by Monsignor Bossuet) was so terrified at the sight of the deplorable consequences to which he saw himself dragged by the force of liberty of conscience, that, with the divine aid, he retraced his steps, and returned to the bosom of his ancient mother, the Catholic Church, which laughs at all these new religions, that are discordant even among themselves, and but a group of errors which every unbeliever adapts to his own caprice, and changes as he pleases, so that in the end these unhappy men abandon themselves to all vices, and to a total disbelief of all religion. Edmund Gibson, Bishop of London, has wisely said in one of his pastorals: "Between relaxation of morals, and impiety, there is a very close connexion." And Monsignor Fenelon, Archbishop of Cambray, said, that "there is no middle way between Catholicism and Atheism."

28. It is no wonder that the disciples of Luther and

Calvin are discordant among themselves on points of faith,
when, as we have already seen their very teachers are so opposed to each other? Read the history of the variations of
the reformed churches, written by Monsignor Bossuet, Bishop
of Meaux, and mark the spoken and written contradictions
of Luther and Calvin. Luther was called by the reformed
churches, the first source of the pure faith, and was called an
apostle by Calvin, who did not hesitate to write: " Res ipsa
clamat non Lutherum initio locutum, sed Deum per os ejus."
Hence the sole contradictions which he uttered and wrote,
from time to time, on matters of faith, are sufficient to show
the falsehood of his creed. During his life he was constantly
contradicting himself: he was always in opposition to himself, impugning his own very doctrines, particularly on
justification, on the efficacy of faith, and the number of
sacraments: on the single article of the Eucharist, he fell
into thirty-three contradictions. Hence, the Catholic Prince
George of Saxony, was accustomed justly to say, that
" to-day the Lutherans know not what they shall have
to believe to-morrow." How often did Calvin also
change his opinions on the Eucharist! His variations may
be seen in the work of Monsignor Bossuet. But I have
been wrong in saying, that so many contradictions were
sufficient to demonstrate the falsehood of the creed of these
pretended reformers: for, according to the words of Luther:
" Qui semel mentitur ex Deo non est," a single contradiction
is sufficient to show that they had not the Spirit of God.
The Holy Ghost "cannot deny himself." (2 Tim. ii. 13.)
Most unjustly, then, did Luther boast of having the Spirit
of Jesus Christ, saying: " I am most certain that my
doctrine is not mine, but is the doctrine of Christ;" he
would have more truly said, that it was the doctrine of the
devil. But how could the Spirit of Jesus Christ dwell in
the man who (as Saunders relates) did not hesitate to say
of himself, "I did not love, nay, I hated the just God

chastising sinners; and if not with tacit blasphemy, at least with great murmuring, I was indignant, and therefore raged with a furious and disturbed conscience." (Apud Saunder. de visib. mon. l. 7.)

29. In a word, take away the authority of the Church, and neither divine revelation, nor natural reason itself is of any use: for each may be interpreted by every individual according to his own caprice: each person can at pleasure say that the dogmas of the Trinity of Persons, of the Incarnation of the Word, of the immortality of the soul, of hell, of heaven, and every other dogma are false. Ramsay said of Locke, that a philosopher who is not guided by the authority of the Church, cannot but err. Speaking of the synod of Dordrect, John Wytembogard (ep. ad Lud. colin. &c.) an Arminian, said against the reformed sects: "All the doctors of the reformation, among whom Calvin and Beza are considered the principal, agree in the general point that all the councils and synods however holy they may be, can err in matters of faith." Hence, he afterwards proceeds to say: "The foundation of the true reform......requires that no one ought to submit, or subscribe to any synod, except on this condition, that after having well examined its decrees by the test of the word of God, which alone is the law in what belongs to faith, he finds them in accordance with the divine word." On the other hand, the reformed sects hold that each person should submit absolutely to their synods: but how will the people submit *absolutely* to the synods, if each person should submit only when he finds that the decrees of the synod accord with the word of God? Hence, he concluded: "But if they change maxims and require the absolute submission to their synods they can no longer give a valid answer to the papists, and will be obliged to give up the victory as lost." I repeat, if you take away obedience to the Church there is no error which will not be embraced, or at least tolerated in others. This is the great

argument which (as Valsecchi states) converted a certain French minister; seeing that the Calvinistic system led him into the toleration of every error of heresy and infidelity he became a Catholic, and published a very useful work, entitled: *The two opposite ways in matters of religion,* And from such a system of toleration and of permitting every one to examine whether the decisions of the Church are conformable to the sacred Scriptures, has sprung that immense number of impious men who in the past and present century have published so many pestiferous books in the countries of the reformed sects.

30. A certain reformer says in reply: but among you Catholics notwithstanding the infallibility of the Roman Church which you preach, there are many Deists and Materialists even in Italy. I answer, that such indeed is the case: and would to God that it was not true, that among us certain libertines, in order to live in vice without remorse of conscience (a punishment by which sinners purchase the pleasure of sin at a very dear rate) have joined the unhappy number of the incredulous. But has not this evil resulted from the works of the reformers and their followers, which have been spread in every direction in order to infect the people? But these unbelievers, if discovered, are not tolerated among us, as they are among the innovators. But the infallibility of our Church is well calculated to extirpate every error against faith: and the impious are impious because they do not obey the Church: but the religion of the reformers is not calculated to restrain the liberty of conscience to believe what each individual wishes. By the false principle of the examen, which each person is permitted to make with regard to matters of faith, is opened to all the way to embrace every error, and to lose all lights of faith.

AN ACT OF THANKSGIVING TO GOD FOR HAVING GIVEN US THE GIFT OF THE HOLY FAITH, AND A PETITION FOR THE AUGMENTATION OF THIS FAITH.

O Saviour of the world, I thank thee in my own name, and for all the faithful my brethren, for having called and permitted us to live in the true faith which the holy Roman Catholic Church teaches. "Good God, (I will say to thee with St. Francis de Sales,) manifold and great are the benefits by which thou hast imposed on me infinite obligations, and for which I return thee most cordial thanks; but how shall I be able to thank thee sufficiently for having enlightened me with thy holy faith? I tremble, O Lord, in comparing my ingratitude with so great a benefit." I thank thee, O my Lord, as much as I a miserable creature am able to thank thee, and I pray thee to make known to all men the beauty of thy holy faith. "O God," exclaims the same saint, "the beauty of thy holy faith appears so beautiful, that I die of love for it: and it seems to me that I ought to enclose this precious gift which God has given me in a heart all perfumed with devotion." But alas, O my Jesus, my Redeemer, how small is the number of those who live in this holy faith! Oh God! the greater part of men lie buried in the darkness of infidelity and heresy. Thou hast humbled thyself to death, and to the death of the cross for the salvation of men; and these ungrateful men are unwilling even to know thee! Ah, I pray thee, O omnipotent God, O sovereign and infinite good, to make all men know and love thee.

O great mother of God, Mary, thou art the universal protectress of all: behold the havoc which hell makes and is making every day among souls, by scattering numberless errors against the faith by means of so many poisoned books, which are unfortunately spread even over these Catholic king-doms: Ah, for mercy's sake, pray to thy God, who loves thee so tenderly, pray to him to apply a remedy to this great evil: pray, pray, thy prayers are all-powerful with Jesus thy Son, who delights in granting all thy petitions.

THE END.

Other in Print Titles by St Athanasius Press

The Treatise on Prayer by St Alphonsus Liguori

The Dignity and Duties of the Priest or Selva
by St Alphonsus Liguori

The History of Heresies and Their Refutation
by St Alphonsus Liguori

The Practice of Christian and Religious Perfection
3 Volume Set by Fr Alphonsus Rodriguez, S.J.

The Triumph of the Cross by Savonarola

Vera Sapentia or True Wisdom by Thomas A Kempis

The Valley of Lilies & The Little Garden of Roses
by Thomas A Kempis

A Thought From Thomas A Kempis for Each Day of the
Year, Daily Devotional by Alexandra J. Waller

Devotion to the Nine Choirs of Holy Angels
and Especially the Angel Guardian by Henri Marie Boudon

The Eternal Happiness of the Saints
by St Robert Bellarmine

The 1957 Latin/English Edition of the Raccolta
Official Prayers of the Church

Indifferentism or Is One Religion as Good as Another?
by John MacLaughlin

CPSIA information can be obtained
at www.ICGtesting.com
Printed in the USA
FFHW020648250419
52018145-57417FF